Bird on Fire

BOOKS BY THE AUTHOR

Nice Work If You Can Get It: Life and Labor in Precarious Times

Fast Boat to China: Corporate Flight and the Consequences of Free Trade–Lessons from Shanghai

Low Pay, High Profile: The Global Push for Fair Labor

No-Collar: The Humane Workplace and Its Hidden Costs

The Celebration Chronicles: Life, Liberty, and the Pursuit of Property Value in Disney's New Town

Real Love: In Pursuit of Cultural Justice

The Chicago Gangster Theory of Life: Nature's Debt to Society

Strange Weather: Culture, Science, and Technology in the Age of Limits

No Respect: Intellectuals and Popular Culture

The Failure of Modernism: Symptoms of American Poetry

Co-Editor, *The University Against Itself: The NYU Strike and the Future of the Academic Workplace*

Co-Editor, *Anti-Americanism*

Editor, *No Sweat: Fashion, Free Trade, and the Rights of Garment Workers*

Editor, *Science Wars*

Co-Editor, *Microphone Fiends: Youth Music and Youth Culture*

Co-Editor, *Technoculture*

Editor, *Universal Abandon? The Politics of Postmodernism*

BIRD ON FIRE

Lessons from the World's Least Sustainable City

Andrew Ross

OXFORD
UNIVERSITY PRESS

OXFORD
UNIVERSITY PRESS

Oxford University Press is a department of the University of Oxford.
It furthers the University's objective of excellence in research, scholarship,
and education by publishing worldwide.

Oxford   New York
Auckland   Cape Town   Dar es Salaam   Hong Kong   Karachi
Kuala Lumpur   Madrid   Melbourne   Mexico City   Nairobi
New Delhi   Shanghai   Taipei   Toronto

With offices in
Argentina   Austria   Brazil   Chile   Czech Republic   France   Greece
Guatemala   Hungary   Italy   Japan   Poland   Portugal   Singapore
South Korea   Switzerland   Thailand   Turkey   Ukraine   Vietnam

Oxford is a registered trade mark of Oxford University Press
in the UK and certain other countries.

Published in the United States of America by
Oxford University Press
198 Madison Avenue, New York, NY 10016

Library of Congress Cataloging-in-Publication Data
Ross, Andrew, 1956–
Bird on fire : lessons from the world's least sustainable city / Andrew Ross.
    p.   cm.
Includes bibliographical references and index.
ISBN 978-0-19-982826-5 (hardcover); 978-0-19-997552-5 (paperback)
1. Sustainable urban development—Arizona—Phoenix.   2. Urban ecology (Sociology)—Arizona—
Phoenix.   3. City planning—Arizona—Phoenix.   I. Title.
HT168.P46R67 2012
307.1'4160979173—dc23   2011016417

9 8 7 6 5 4 3 2 1

Printed in the United States of America
on acid-free paper

ACKNOWLEDGMENTS

Thanks are due, first of all, to Marilu Knode and Bruce Ferguson, at Future Arts Research, who invited me to Phoenix in 2008 to conduct research of my own choosing. Their hospitality, and Marilu's assistance in locating some of my initial interviewees, was very generous indeed. The 200 Phoenicians who agreed, eventually, to be interviewed (several of them on more than one occasion) are too numerous to be named, but I am grateful for the time they gave and the open expression of their views. For those who suggested others to interview, I am also grateful for their contacts. Those who were particularly helpful to me include Lori Riddle, Salvador Reza, Kimber Lanning, Mike Pops, Steve Weiss, Carol Johnson, Dan Millis, and Nan Ellin.

In a very few instances, the names of interviewees have been changed to protect their identities.

Interview transcribing was done by Andrew Bauer (who also prepared the maps), Vedonia Ingram, Madlyn Moskowitz, and Leigh Dodson. I am grateful to Dana Polan and Maggie Gray, two stalwarts of my Dutchess County support team, for detailed comments on a first draft, and to Rob Nixon, Ellie Shermer, Andrew Needham, and Jon Talton for useful suggestions on the final draft. Thanks to Matthew Moore and Dawn O'Doul for permission to use their images.

I am happy to add to the high repute of Dave McBride's editorial eye. He tailored the manuscript to make it fit and, hopefully, to shine. Alexandra Dauler and Marc Schneider, also at Oxford, took great care to send the final version into production.

Zola, my older daughter, accompanied me on some of my interviews, and she, quite rightly, expects to be mentioned here. Stella, my younger daughter, was too young to tag along, but she knows Phoenix as the provenance of not a few gifts brought back from my sojourns.

A.R.
New York City
April 2011

CONTENTS

ACRONYMS

ACC	Arizona Corporation Commission
ADEQ	Arizona Department of Environmental Quality
AFP	Americans for Prosperity
AGRA	African-Led Green Revolution
ARRA	American Reinvestment & Recovery Act
ASU	Arizona State University
BLM	Bureau of Land Management
CAP	Central Arizona Project
CGC	Charter Government Committee
CIS	Center for Immigration Studies
CPLC	Chicanos Por La Causa
CRSP	Concerned Residents of South Phoenix
CSA	Community Supported Agriculture
CSP	concentrated solar power
DAI	Dangerous Anthropogenic Interference
DG	distributed generation
DHS	Arizona Department of Health Services
DOT	U.S. Department of Transportation
D-PAC	Downtown Phoenix Arts Coalition
DPP	Downtown Phoenix Partnership
DVC	Downtown Voices Coalition
EPA	U.S. Environmental Protection Agency
FAIR	Federation for American Immigration Reform
FDA	U.S. Food and Drug Administration
FHA	Federal Housing Administration

GIOS	Global Institute of Sustainability
GIS	Geographic Information System
GMA	Groundwater Management Act
GPEC	Greater Phoenix Economic Council
GRACE	Gila River Alliance for a Clean Environment
GRD	Groundwater Replenishment District
GRIC	Gila River Indian Community
HUD	U.S. Department of Housing and Urban Development
ICE	U.S. Immigration and Customs Enforcement
IPCC	Intergovernmental Panel on Climate Change
IRCA	Immigration Reform & Control Act of 1986
LDS	The Church of Jesus Christ of Latter-day Saints
LEED	Leadership in Energy and Environmental Design
LISC	Local Initiatives Support Corporation
LOHAS	Lifestyles of Health and Sustainability
LULU	Locally Unwanted Land Use
MARS	Movimiento Artistico del Rio Salado
MPAC	Maricopa Partnership for Arts and Culture
NEPA	National Environmental Policy Act
PCA	Phoenix Community Alliance
REDD	Reducing Emissions from Deforestation and Forest Degradation
RES	Renewable Energy Standards
RFC	Reconstruction Finance Corporation
RIFA	Reform Immigration For America
RPS	Renewable Portfolio Standards
SRP	Salt River Project
SST	Southwest Solar Technologies
SV	Superstition Vistas
TAG	EPA Technology Assistance Grant
TCE	trichloroethylene
ULI	Urban Land Institute
UNFCCC	United Nations Framework Convention on Climate Change
VOC	volatile organic compound
WQARF	Water Quality Assurance Revolving Fund

READER'S NOTE

Metro Phoenix is used to describe the "Phoenix, Arizona Metropolitan Statistical Area," a designation given by the U.S. Census Bureau. It covers the urbanized areas and municipalities of Maricopa and Pinal counties, amounting to 1,000 square miles. Greater Phoenix is the term used to describe the Central Arizona region, which encompasses thirty-three municipalities, and six Native American nations and communities, and covers 17,000 square miles.

I have used "Latino" as a default term to describe communities often, and officially, referred to as "Hispanic" in Arizona. I have preserved "Hispanic" in quotes from those who used that term in interviews.

Bird on Fire

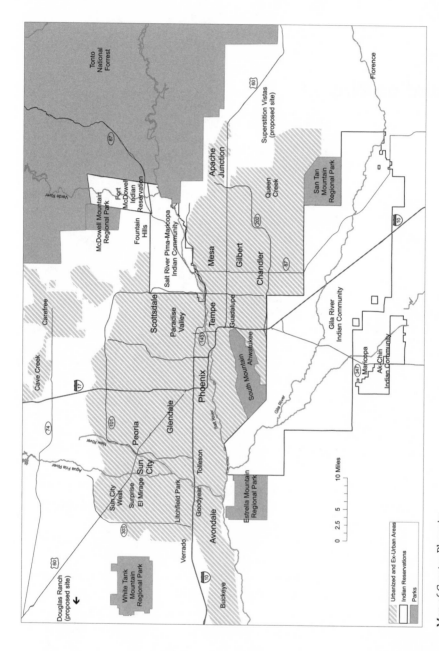

Map of Greater Phoenix
Sources: Arizona State Land Department, Arizona Land Resources Information System, ESRI

INTRODUCTION

By the Time I Got to Phoenix

The creature in the sky got sucked in a hole,
Now there's a hole in the sky, and the ground's not cold,
And if the ground's not cold, everything is gonna burn.
We'll all take turns, I'll get mine, too.
　　　The Pixies, "This Monkey's Gone to Heaven"

For those who prefer history chopped up into neat slices, John McCain's modest concession speech on the lawn of the Arizona Biltmore on November 5, 2008, seemed like a clean cut of the knife. With the economy in a nosedive, it was not just the end of a presidential campaign. The neoliberal era seemed to be over—its reigning troika of deregulation, marketization, and privatization cast into disgrace, along with its most recent fiscal vehicles such as debt leveraging and speculation in finance and land. Nowhere was the devastation more visible than in McCain's hometown. Phoenix had flown highest in the race to profit from the housing bubble, and it had fallen the furthest. Footage of the metro region's outer-ring subdivisions reclaimed by sage grass, tumbleweed, and geckos was as evocative of the bubble's savage aftermath as photographs of the Dust Bowl's windblown soil had been of the Great Depression.

Had Arizona's senior senator not owned a condo nearby, he would have stayed in the hotel's Goldwater presidential suite (every president since Hoover has slept at the Biltmore), stirring up associations with the Phoenix politician whose 1964 run for the White House pioneered the modern conservative temper of evangelizing against the power of government. Regarded locally as a carpetbagger when he first ran for Congress in 1982, McCain benefited from his wife Cindy's family connections to take over

Barry Goldwater's senate seat four years later, but his people-pleasing style found little favor over the years among the Goldwater faithful. On that night, at least, there was no dearth of commentators willing to see McCain's concession speech as heralding the end of the Sunbelt's long hold on national politics, an arc that originated in the postwar effort of Goldwater's circle at the Phoenix Chamber of Commerce to remake Arizona's decrepit GOP into an instrument of growth for growth's sake. Had the momentum behind the Sunbelt's mercurial rise—fueled by low taxes, light regulation, antiunion labor laws, cheap land, cheaper water, and big federal funding for defense industries and suburban infrastructure—finally run its course? Perhaps the future now lay elsewhere, a conviction that pulsed through the boisterous (and much more multicultured) crowd who greeted Barack Obama's victory speech in the public plenitude of Chicago's Grant Park.

For those whose sense of occasion was more international in scope, one of the comforts to take away from the 2008 election was the hope that the world's mounting environmental crises would finally be addressed by U.S. leaders. Global climate change had been flatly ignored by the previous occupant of the White House, even as the volume of atmospheric carbon nosed upward to levels that rang the experts' alarm bells. Although neither McCain nor Obama made any mention of the subject that night in their respective speeches, the election outcome promised the end of an epoch of denial about the costs of unsustainable growth and wanton use of the earth's resources. The incoming administration had every reason to cut a new energy path. Indeed, the postrecession recovery might well depend on the development of clean technologies and job creation tied to energy efficiencies. Going green was no longer simply a lifestyle choice for well-heeled consumers, it was being touted as the key to the next economy. There was even evidence of an investment bubble in clean energy—labeled the "Good Bubble" by some wags.

Again, the case for the prosecution lay just beyond the lush grounds on which McCain stood. The Biltmore—conceived as the deluxe antithesis of a railway hotel stop for westward travelers—had once stood in self-important isolation well to the north of the city. That desert perch, just below Piestewa Peak and west of Camelback Mountain, was now at the geographical center of a conurbation of more than four million people. The metropolis, whose six-lane arterial roads and canal networks spread out to connect single-family tract housing all across the Phoenix Basin, was a horizontal hymn to unsustainable development. With less than eight inches of rain a year, and the hottest summer temperatures of any city in the Northern Hemisphere, the 1,000-square-mile sprawl known as the Valley of the Sun appeared to subsist in a state of denial about its inhospitable location.

Although it benefits from the large mountain watersheds of the Gila and Salt rivers, the 17,000-square-mile region known as Greater Phoenix depends on a water supply pumped 300 miles uphill from the overallocated Colorado River, now in the second decade of a drought that has shrunk its volume to unprecedented lows. From 1990 to 2007, Arizona added fossil-fuel pollutants faster than any other state—the rate of increase was more than three times the national average.[1] The region is deluged with more than 330 days of bright sunshine, yet only a tiny percentage of its energy is drawn from solar sources. Once a haven for TB sufferers seeking respiratory relief, by 2005 the Valley's infamous Brown Cloud was drawing the lowest national grades from the American Lung Association for air quality in both ozone and particulates, and in 2010, reclaimed the number one slot for dust pollution after a few years of improvement in reducing ozone levels.[2] But the impact was far from even—there was ample respite for those who could afford the aromatic desert breeze of Maricopa County's northern reaches, while the lower-lying geography of South Phoenix hosted one of the dirtiest zip codes in the country, home to 40 percent of the city's hazardous industrial emissions.

To cap it all, climate change had targeted the state for special attention in the years to come. As Jonathan Overpeck, Arizona's leading climatologist (and one of the chief authors of the seminal 2007 assessment by the Intergovernmental Panel on Climate Change), warned the state's House Environment Committee in February 2009: "Whether it is drought frequency, the increase in temperature or the decrease in soil moisture, we are in the bull's-eye—the worst in the United States."[3] To many eyes, the fastest-growing U.S. city of the last half-century seemed more like a canary in the mine than a phoenix about to rise from the ashes of its latest speculator-induced crash.

SHARING THE SKY

Any mention of atmospheric or geological change tends to make a mockery of the decisive significance we attach to the dates of human events, but in the case of the 2008 election result, so did the political aftermath. After the drubbing that Goldwater took in the 1964 election, the pundits concluded that he had wrecked the fortunes of the Republican Party and the cause of conservatism for at least the next generation. They could not have been more wrong.[4] A similar consensus arose not long after the polls closed in 2008—the damage wrought by George W. Bush and Dick Cheney would surely consign the GOP to the status of a minority party composed of embittered white folks in the Deep South and a sprinkling of sparsely populated High Plains and Western states. That prediction soon proved unfounded too. The cold-shouldering of Sarah Palin on the Biltmore lawn that night—McCain's handlers would not allow her to speak—would become a potent symbol for the mobilization and resurgence of the hard right.

In the years that followed, the conservative movement reorganized around new citizen-based groups, derisively labeled by opponents as "astroturf" (i.e., not genuine grassroots initiatives) because they were in part conceived and funded from the top down by corporate magnates. The most prominent of these groups, Americans for Prosperity (bankrolled by the Koch family of oil speculators) and FreedomWorks, helped to launch the Tea Party movement, polish the stagecraft of populist protest in town hall meetings, and run firmly focused campaigns, like the Hot Air Tour, aimed at thwarting climate change legislation. These drives found ready recruits among Arizona's staunch libertarians and a loud echo chamber in the state's Republican-dominated legislature.

In the weeks leading up to the 2008 election, it looked as if Arizona might tilt to Obama. In the aftermath, the state's Republicans firmly reasserted their hold on policymaking, and distinguished themselves nationally by passing some far-reaching laws, including the notorious anti-immigrant bill, SB 1070, that pushed well beyond the nation's legal mainstream. Cheered on by the Hot Air foot soldiers, climate change denial became a point of honor among the state's GOP leadership. The same legislators who had listened to Overpeck's dire warnings voted to ban Arizona's Department of Environmental Quality from regulating greenhouse gases and withdrew Arizona from the Western Climate Initiative, an interstate effort to reduce carbon emissions that had drawn heavy fire from business interests. The state's political contribution to federal efforts was equally damaging. John McCain was the only Republican senator to push for climate change legislation during the Bush years, but he quickly reverted to the party line after his electoral defeat and played a prominent role in blocking any such legislation from reaching the senate floor, both before Copenhagen's UN Climate Change summit in December 2009 and in the months that followed.

The year that Obama took office saw a 6.9 percent decrease in carbon-dioxide emissions in the United States (and a 1.3 percent drop globally), but this welcome relief had little to do with policies in Washington, or any of the world's political capitals.[5] It was almost wholly a result of reduced industrial activity and energy demand brought about by the Great Recession. The International Energy Agency, which monitors global emissions, reported, in May 2011, that the return of GDP growth so fiercely urged by business and government elites had boosted 2010 carbon emissions to record levels (30.6 gigatonnes), far in excess of the rate at which renewable energy was currently being developed and consumed. In advance of the Copenhagen summit, climate scientists (traditionally a cautious community) turned in their alarming verdicts on the likely geographic impact of global warming—melted ice caps and thawed permafrost, mass species extinction, acidified oceans and salinized soil, loss of islands and low-lying land, prolonged drought, and rising temperatures in the next two or three decades that would outstrip any effort at stabilization.[6]

The abject failure of international leaders to reach binding emission-reductions targets in Copenhagen, and a year later in Cancun, at the next UN climate change meeting, compounded the despair that thoughtful people now felt about the future. Activists and officials who came home from these climate summits in a deep funk had to be persuaded that progress was being made somewhere. Where national and regional politicians were still in the pockets of the oil, coal, and gas lobbies, cities, we were reminded, had been putting green policies into action for some time now. The Large Cities Climate Leadership Group (C40), comprising forty of the world's largest cities collaborating on extensive decarbonization programs, issued its own Climate Communiqué at Copenhagen, in which mayors pleaded with the national representatives of the carbon powers to "recognize that the future of our globe will be won or lost in the cities of the world."[7] Aside from demonstrating that city governance was more progressive than policymaking at the state level, the mayors' statement reflected a growing consensus that only in dense urban environments could efficient, low-carbon living be achieved on a mass scale. Humans were fast becoming an urban species, and their survival would depend on how they lived in cities that already consumed 75 percent of the world's energy and emitted 80 percent of the greenhouse gases.[8] Even without a decisive shift in energy supply away from fossil fuel, more compact patterns of urban growth were delivering a sizable boost to efforts at decarbonization.

In the United States, looking to cities as sites of salvation was an old story, though the script for "city as redeemer" had changed several times since John Winthrop's 1630 exhortation to the Massachusetts Bay Colony pilgrims that they should build a "city upon a hill." For the best part of two centuries, American city-building was driven by the long-standing

Christian equation of godliness with city residence.[9] But the late nineteenth-century rise of the teeming industrial city—routinely depicted by reformers as a miasma of sin, filth, and corruption—turned urban living into a moral trap. The infernal Victorian city of industry was now seen as a threat to the physical and spiritual health of its inhabitants, raising their mortality rate and diluting their humanity. Urban improvers were inspired to redeem this fallen population, first through environmental uplift in the form of edifying contact with parks and other leafy spaces and then through planning aimed at decongestion by dispersing their numbers out to garden cities on the green and airy urban fringe.[10]

The shift to decentralization and mass suburbanization in the twentieth century had many overlapping causes (some of them clearly governed by racial prejudice), but it turned on the belief that low-density suburbia was a more salubrious environment than the congested center city. Yet, beginning in the early 1980s, the pattern of outward flight began to slowly reverse itself. Whereas before, moral homilies about ill-health had been directed at residents of overpopulated city cores, the new targets for scorn were increasingly the suburbanites whose auto-dependent and lawn-loving lifestyle was perceived as fundamentally selfish because it claimed a grossly unfair share of the world's energy budget.[11] Dense cities that used to be seen as parasitical organisms, dangerously out of synch with nature, were now would-be paragons of sustainability, carrying a much lower environmental load per capita than the pastoral suburbs that were created as antidotes to urban ills.

How did city officials respond to this sea change? From the early 1990s, urban managers began to set themselves sustainability goals, assessing their progress by performance indicators, and demanding that long-term planning be guided by "smart growth" principles. In Europe, where overall or whole city densities are 40–60 persons per hectare, more than 1,500 municipalities signed the 1994 Aalborg Charter and competed for awards as part of its European Sustainable Cities & Towns Campaign. In the United States, where densities are under 20 persons per hectare, the uptake was much slower, and confined, for many years, to a select group of cities (Portland, San Francisco, Seattle, Santa Monica, Austin, Chattanooga). Over time, however, a city's rise in national sustainability rankings became something for public officials to tout and for the local chamber of commerce to brandish as a competitive advantage in recruiting the kind of high-wage investment that major-league cities craved.

Jockeying for position as a "green city" has become the name of the metropolitan game. It has lately supplanted the race to be a "creative city," a development model that flourished in the early part of the decade. Mayors, especially, have found that green is a useful color to attach to their electoral profiles. More than one thousand signed the U.S. Conference of Mayors' Climate Protection Agreement, vowing to reduce carbon emissions in their cities below 1990 levels, in line with the Kyoto Protocol. ICLEI-Local Governments for Sustainability now comprises more than 1,200 municipalities from seventy different countries, each committed to meeting goals and sharing techniques for green governance. At the dawn of the Obama era, there was even more reason to become a contender in the green sweepstakes. Laid low by the recession, U.S. cities were desperate for a lifeline and were looking to land federal stimulus monies under the competitions sponsored by the American Reinvestment & Recovery Act (ARRA). Those with a portfolio of green projects to propose were well positioned to compete for the funds.

THE VIEW FROM CITY HALL

The Great Recession dropped the country's fifth largest city into the deepest of holes. Like its twenty-one sister cities in the Valley of the Sun, Phoenix relied heavily on sales tax for its revenue, and it was facing a dreadful budget shortfall. A high-pressure zone of antitax sentiment had settled over the state, and so, with no easy options for making up the deficit, the ARRA stimulus money beckoned. Phil Gordon, an affable and popular second-term mayor, became a frequent flyer to Washington, boosting his own carbon footprint by promising to reduce that of his city. "I've tried to spend a lot of time in D.C. emphasizing that Phoenix hasn't just jumped on the green bandwagon because of money," he told me after one of his visits. "Because Phoenix is a desert community and a new city," we have "an understanding that it has to be sustainable," he explained, adding that "we manage our resources very well while realizing this is a fragile environment." Reeling off a list of green achievements in areas as diverse as recycling, water conservation, LEED-certified buildings, smart growth planning, and a municipal fleet run on clean energy, he described bold plans for constructing jumbo solar farms, and for combating the steady rise in urban heat island temperatures. Nothing too blue-sky, but there was more than a touch of gee-whizzery in the way he imagined the city solving its problems.

Gordon had recently announced a novel aspiration for Phoenix—to become "the greenest city in America"—and the weekend before one of his Washington visits, his staff pulled together a 17-point plan to show how the city would reach the ambitious goal of becoming carbon-neutral. The plan drew heavily on expertise from Arizona State University's (ASU) new Global Institute for Sustainability, but, like any good politician, he distinguished pragmatic policymaking from the advice gleaned from the academics. What, for example, did carbon neutrality mean to him? "For some people," he averred, "if we only had one cow on the planet, we would not be carbon-neutral. For me, carbon neutrality means taking the existing baseline of carbon emissions we have today, and then, as we go forward, choosing not to add to that output." The plan's showpiece was a proposed green zone around the city's new light rail corridor, where an adjacent strip of retrofitted buildings would help stem the long-term rise in nighttime temperatures: parts of Phoenix had seen an alarming 11-degree Fahrenheit increase in nighttime temperatures over the last fifty years, and differences of as much as 15 degrees were routinely recorded between temperatures downtown and on the desert fringe.[12]

Like almost all of the city's mayors in recent decades, Gordon had a sometime career in real estate development—his previous job was chairman of Landiscor, an aerial mapping company that provided a direct service to land developers and homebuilders. Given his range of contacts in the industry, he ought to know if the region's developers were on the same green page. "I think that chapter is still being written," was the most he would venture. "Arizona has been built on a lot of unwise development," he acknowledged, and, recently, "we were building sixty thousand homes a year out in the middle of nowhere before they were needed." Gordon's cautious estimate was well warranted. Mayors could tinker with their little acre of city-owned land and buildings, but the destiny of land use in this growth-driven metropolis was well out of their hands. Developers and homebuilders were the most powerful players in the state of Arizona, and, as another public official put it to me, their lobbyists "inhabit the inner cavities of our elected representatives."

Nor was the mayor of Phoenix the most influential voice at City Hall. Like most Sunbelt cities, Phoenix has a council-manager government. A legacy of municipal reforms that swept away the corrupt political machines of the late nineteenth and early twentieth century, this type of government has left mayors with a largely ceremonial role beyond which they often functioned, as Gordon did, like publicists with a bully pulpit. In reality, the show was all but run by a professional city manager, and, in this case, it was the long-serving Frank Fairbanks, who had overseen twenty years of rampant growth and collected a raft of national awards for efficient government along the way. Did he share Gordon's euphoria for greening the city?

Fairbanks was known for his soothing presence, and so whatever passion he felt for the proposition was not on display when I met with him. It was his last official day before going into retirement, and he was more inclined to rest his case on documented evidence that Phoenix was doing relatively well when it came to resource management. San Francisco and New York, he noted, also piped in their water supplies, and, while Phoenix had been "a pioneer in energy conservation," it also had "fewer degree days than Chicago, Boston, and New York." Although renowned for sprawl, Phoenix's overall density compared favorably with other large metro areas. Handing me a 2001 Brookings Institution survey of metro regions, he noted, "You might be surprised that Honolulu has the highest density, LA is second, and Phoenix is number ten, ahead of Chicago, Boston, and Philadelphia." While "our reputation is for sprawl," he conceded, "Phoenix becomes more dense each year, and Atlanta becomes less dense."[13] Born at a time when Phoenix had only 80,000 residents, Fairbanks predicted that rising fuel costs and water scarcity would rein in the urban growth machine. "In the long run, I think that the old system is going to die. However, what brought people here will continue to bring them here in the future, but we will accommodate them in a different way from the past, and they will be attracted to a different, more fulfilling, more sophisticated and more dense lifestyle." "Phoenix's future," he emphasized repeatedly, "is in higher density."

For a manager without a political portfolio, he was blunt about the nature of the obstacles. "Phoenix is majority Democrat and fairly liberal for the West, but the state is overwhelmingly Republican and conservative and laissez-faire," and the fact that "the state contributes no funding for transportation" severely constrained the city's effort to reduce its carbon footprint. Hamstrung by a constitutional limit of 10 percent on the contribution of property taxes to the city budget, the campaign to win the newly established light rail line, for example, had been a bitter struggle: "There was huge opposition, because people think public transportation is a communist plot," but the city prevailed even though it was now only "where New York City was in the 1880s." Despite the constant pushback from the right, Fairbanks took some credit for supporting a denser, more sustainable downtown core with urban amenities that did not exist two decades before: "We have moved away from growing as fast we could to focusing on quality of life." As for the outlying suburban cities, he was even less charitable than Gordon in assessing their inefficiency and lack of demographic diversity: "They are building Omaha out there."

Facing down the swelling deficit in the city budget, with crippling reductions already ordered in payroll and services, and with no prospect of a quick recovery, Gordon and Fairbanks could hardly give vent to the full-throated voice of Western boosterism, but some muted version of it ran through the mayor's wonky cheerleading and the manager's gladsome assessment of his record. Outside of City Hall, the spectrum of opinion about the city and the region's prospects for becoming a center of green achievement was much broader, and I encountered the full spread in the two-year span of the interviews I conducted with the more active residents of the region.

PHOENIX MAN

Among them were downtown activists for whom a compact, vibrant core had become an evangelical cause, and business advocates who saw a profitable silver lining in this same vision. But I also interviewed affluent, quality-of-life suburbanites in North Phoenix, Scottsdale, and other East Valley cities, for whom green living meant a very private blend of solar roofs, open space conservation, and desert gardening (xeriscaping); low-income casualties of toxic pollution in South Phoenix, who fought dirty industry and government inaction as a matter of physical survival; big-dog developers who saw green features in their master-planned communities as a selling point to jump-start the growth machine on the urban fringe; GOP lawmakers and libertarians whose loyalty to the Tea Party ethos took the form of conservation based on private property rights; ASU administrators and academics for whom the public buzz about sustainability was an opportunity to make scientific research a basis for public policymaking; Anglo nativists whose fixation on chasing off immigrants was driven by the belief that border-crossers were threatening the region's ecosystem; and tribal activists trying to reconcile their quest for decent livelihoods with the roles allotted to them by others as traditional stewards of the land.

The most jaded among them saw a twentieth-first-century Detroit in the making, with the Valley's dominant industry—home construction—in a spiraling decline and little expectation of hatching or courting alternatives that might diversify the jobs economy. Even so, the likelihood that the metro population would not only stagnate but shrink appreciably was not a prospect they entertained for long, not even in their most despairing moments. Nor, for most of them, did their view of the future include the more alarming vision of urban eco-collapse from some extreme state of resource scarcity. Unlike in other Arizona municipalities, which impose water-use restrictions, Phoenicians have never had to dread being busted as water scofflaws, nor do they fear power blackouts during heat waves.

Those who leaned toward the more dismal scenarios were natural scientists or else environmentalists with a naturalist bent. Approaching unsustainable conduct from the standpoint of studying other life forms, they were bound to be frustrated by what appeared to be self-destructive decisions on the part of human populations. Jeff Williamson, longtime director of the Phoenix Zoo, and outspoken president of the Arizona Zoological Society, put this view well in describing the dysfunctionality of the city's dependence on land speculation: "I do not understand why the organism has not designed ways of existing where there is a secure pattern of life. It creates risks for itself, and it has decided that that boom and bust cycle is of greater value than sustainability. It could design more robust and diverse economic systems. But it has made a decision to invest substantial public resources in an industry that has one business cycle—boom and bust." His conclusion was that this kind of behavior "is irrational in living systems," but that it seemed to be typical of the organism that we could just as well call "Phoenix Man."

Williamson was no less critical of his own profession. "Zoos should go away," he declared, "they are part of the problem," because the concept of "wildlife as a form of recreational amusement comes from a European and Asian culturally elite model" that is outdated and ecologically damaging. In his view, if humans could not elect to help animals become resilient over time, there was little hope for their own species, especially in places like Phoenix, which "is almost a perfect example of how to incentivize and encourage lifestyles and business practices that cannot be sustained and will do damage over an extended period of time." Although he was a round-the-clock advocate of sustainable habits, he believed that a culture of "living on limited resources in an unlimited fashion" was "going to fail here sooner than most places, because the carrying capacity is just not here." What would be the best, immediate outcome? "I hope," he offered with a provocative twinkle in his eye, "that Phoenix goes down to about 40,000 people." That number, I reminded him, was the peak population of the Hohokam, the prehistoric inhabitants of the Phoenix Basin, just before the decline of their society set in.

For the most part, this kind of apocalyptic scenario was reserved for outsiders who tend to place Phoenix high in the ranks of American urban demonology, either because of the region's fierce brand of Sunbelt conservatism or its textbook profile of exurban sprawl. Indeed, some of the condescension toward this Sonoran desert metropolis crystallized in the belief that it should not have existed in the first place, and that it may not exist for much longer, succumbing, as it surely would, to the fate visited upon ancient desert civilizations that had also overshot their resources. In the 1960s, Edward Abbey, Tucson's most cantankerous environmentalist, wrote, "There is no lack of water here, unless you try to establish a city where no city should be."[14] Rebecca Solnit, today's most talented essayist of the West, tapped some of Abbey's spirit when she recently summoned up this vision of ruination: "Phoenix will be like Jericho or Ur of the Chaldees, with the shriveled relics of golf courses and the dusty hulls of swimming pools added on."[15]

Solnit was also adding a modern, environmental gloss to a tradition, dating from the Romantic movement's fascination with ruins, in which writers take a sharp, moralistic delight in depicting the wreckage of their own civilization.[16] Here, for example, is T. S. Eliot's version (from his 1934 pageant play, *The Rock*):

> And the wind shall say
> 'Here were decent godless people:
> Their only monument the asphalt road
> And a thousand lost golf balls.'

Although Eliot probably did not know how long golf balls actually take to decompose (up to 1,000 years), and was writing well before the era of public concern about the high ecological costs of highways and golf courses, these artifacts served him as convenient symbols of a culture whose misplaced priorities would surely lead to its downfall.

I live among New Yorkers who often imagine their city being decimated and depopulated by natural or man-made disasters, and there are many more outsiders than is the case with Phoenix who would dearly like to see Gotham in ruins. Indeed, there is an extensive library of films and novels that illustrate in acute graphic detail the near-future destruction of New York.[17] Given that sea levels may rise by several feet before 2100, those fictions may well cede to fact quicker than we think. Phoenix, by comparison, has rarely been the seat of catastrophe fantasies, despite its status as a natural target for destruction during the Cold War, when it served as the nation's premier location for Air Force pilot training and as a major manufacturing center for military hardware. The one exception I know of is Harlan Ellison's 1969 classic novella *A Boy and his Dog* (made into a film in 1976). It is set in the deserts of a postapocalyptic Phoenix Basin, underneath which a white-bread theme park of Midwestern Americana has been built for survivors.

WHY PHOENIX?

If Phoenix could become sustainable, then it could be done anywhere. That was the premise that drove my investigations from an early point. Even if it is not the world's least sustainable city (and some will quibble over this designation), it is a very close contender, and, in any event, the title is not worth arguing over. More than any other U.S. metropolis in the postwar period, Phoenix has channeled the national appetite for unrestrained growth, and American growth still consumes a vastly disproportionate share of the earth's resources, including its carbon allotment. The city's business model, in other words, is a clear threat to life and land in places even more vulnerable than the Valley of the Sun. If there is any hope of reversing the pattern of desertification, species loss, and ice-cap melt in more remote locations, then the culture that produced "Phoenix Man" will have to be transformed.

The nineteenth-century doctrine of Manifest Destiny made the settlement of the far West's semiarid lands a matter of federal resolve. Reclamation for homesteading was pursued through decade after decade of lavish government spending on public works and water infrastructure, while the region's economic backbone was built out of defense industry funding. Even with all of that federal assistance, the stark vulnerability of Phoenix's Sonoran habitat makes it stand out as a questionable location for more than 4 million people, let alone the 9 million that regional boosters have forecast for the megapolitan region—the Sun Corridor stretching from Prescott to Tucson—in the decades to come. Yet many of the world's fastest-growing cities are also in hot, semiarid regions, and so, as climate change intensifies, they will share much the same destiny as Phoenix. Solutions culled from Central Arizona may turn out to be applicable in the megacities of Asia, Africa, and the Middle East.

Sound lessons about the art of sustainable urban living have already been drawn from environmental showpieces like Portland, Curitiba, Reykjavik, Saarbrucken, Helsinki, Freiburg, Santa Monica, Kristianstad, or Singapore. More susceptible, or recalcitrant, places have other things to teach us—how we go about making green decisions or whether we even have the wherewithal to make the right ones. That is why I chose to write this book about the struggle to make Phoenix into a resilient metropolis. Faced with larger environmental challenges, and considerably more resistance from its elected officials than havens of green consciousness like Seattle or San Francisco, it is a more accurate bellwether of sustainability than these success stories. In any case, the sociology of climate change has made it quite clear that no one can opt out, or be left behind. The revolt of poorer nations at Copenhagen and their regrouping, six months earlier, at the World People's Conference on Climate Change and the Rights of Mother Earth in Bolivia's Cochabamba, showed that everyone has to be on board if climate action is to be both effective and just. Nor can the most profligate communities be written off as hopeless cases. They are simply the weakest links in a chain that has to be strengthened tenfold.

Anyone conversant with the scientific debate about global warming will know of Roger Revelle's 1956 testimony to Congress about the rise of CO_2 emissions. "From the standpoint of meteorologists and oceanographers," he submitted, "we are carrying out a tremendous geophysical experiment of a kind that could not have happened in the past or be reproduced in the future."[18] His tone and choice of words have long been criticized for suggesting that the impact of atmospheric CO_2 presented merely a rare opportunity for scientific study. Revelle made things worse in 1966 by remarking that our concern for the topic "should probably contain more curiosity than apprehension."[19] That clinical mentality no longer prevails. Natural scientists are now among the most apprehensive, to say the least. Today, it is the task of averting drastic climate change that might be described as an experiment—a vast social experiment in decision-making and democratic action.

Success in that endeavor will not be determined primarily by large technological fixes, though many will be needed along the way. Just as decisive to the outcome is whether our social relationships, cultural beliefs, and political customs will allow for the kind of changes that are necessary. That is why the climate crisis is as much a social as a biophysical challenge, and why the solutions will have to be driven by a fuller quest for global justice than has hitherto been tolerated or imagined. Moreover, if this social experiment is to avoid an authoritarian turn, then it cannot be strictly governed by the global math of carbon budgeting, nor can it be overridden by epic geo-engineering schemes (seeding the oceans with iron or reflecting sunlight though orbiting mirrors and brightened clouds).[20] These grand formulas probably have their appeal to the technocrat within all of us, but they are not democratic pathways, nor, if they become part of the language of government, are they going to sway individuals and groups who are conspiratorially inclined or who take pride in bucking any guide to conduct that issues from public officials. The growing habit of gauging the carbon footprint of every product and every personal act has already become a pseudopolitical obsession, reducing our actions and use of material things to a dull data set. We cannot afford to let this carbon calculus supplant the GDP as a new statistical tyranny with which officials assess our behavioral performance as citizens. Carbon should become an outlawed by-product of our civilization, not its loud scourge.

Readers of this book will find the same kind of caveat in the picture of Phoenix that I offer. In these pages, there is ample attention to the technical fixes and innovations that are typical of any focus on urban sustainability: water conservation policy; decentralization of energy production and distribution, the transformation of transit and transport, redesign of building and infrastructure, establishment of closed-loop waste systems, growth of a bioregional food supply, and the wholesale transition to carbon-neutral or renewable fuel.[21] But my conclusion is that if these initiatives do not take shape as remedies for social and geographic inequality, then they are likely to end up reinforcing existing patterns of eco-apartheid. If resources tighten rapidly, a more ominous future beckons in the form of triage crisis management, where populations are explicitly selected out for protection, in eco-enclaves, or for abandonment, outside the walls. The anti-immigrant mood that has sharpened during Arizona's recessionary years stands as a harbinger of the hoarding mentality that may well govern such a desperate future. Chasing off immigrants through legally mandated police intimidation flies in the face of the conviction that a community's resilience depends on its capacity to adopt the conditions of its most vulnerable populations as a baseline for green policymaking.

HOW TO DO PHOENIX

Most people view social progress through a local lens, and while their sources of information are usually institutional, their sources of influence are more often than not the doings and sayings of turf champions, community activists, and habit-formers in their own neighborhoods, towns, and cities. This can make for parochial behavior, but it is also what enables cities to improvise, both with the resources at hand and in their own regional orbits. It is no coincidence that the environmental slogan "Think Global, Act Local" was first employed by Patrick Geddes, the Scottish urbanist who pioneered the idea of regional planning. It was with this positive parochialism in mind that I opted to take the social and political temperature of Metro Phoenix by interviewing 200 of its more thoughtful, influential, and active citizens (some of them were interviewed several times) about the region's prospects for becoming sustainable. They were chosen primarily on the recommendation of prior interviewees, though many showed up on my own field radar, and a few through fortuitous encounters at meetings or events. Of course, there were differences in how my interviewees defined sustainability, and some had even abandoned that slippery term because its meaning has been hopelessly diluted by overuse. Nonetheless, I have retained it as a working term in these pages if only because it has become common currency, even among those who are allergic, as one GOP state senator was, to its use "as a buzzword within the area of community planning," or, as he put it more pointedly, "by bureaucrats who are paid either through the university system or who make their living off of government."

Aiming for broad coverage, I cast a wide net. Among my 200 were state legislators, government professionals in urban planning and economic development, real estate brokers and attorneys, policy analysts, land developers and homebuilders, nonprofit operatives, small business owners, civil rights champions, energy lobbyists, solar entrepreneurs, engineers, and technicians, utility regulators, industrial ecologists, banking economists, artists, curators, and gallerists, community activists, affordable housing providers, land trust officials, opinion journalists, urban farmers, archeologists, tribal activists and officials, green business advocates, environmental justice watchdogs, trade unionists, university administrators, and a variety of scholars engaged in sustainability research initiatives.

Although my interpretation of the interviews was that of an outsider, this book is based on the testimony of those insiders. I combined their experience and knowledge of the metropolis with my own assessment of the strength and quality of their appetite for change. While the book is broken down into chapter topics (on water management, urban growth, pollution distribution, downtown revitalization, solar industry, immigration policy, and urban farming), my goal is to offer a composite picture of Phoenix's potential for a greener future along with the many obstacles that lie in its path. Secondary research took me into the history books and through the record of environmental action in other cities. Prolonged sojourns in different parts of the metro region over the course of two years gave me a feel for its urban texture and desert milieu, and, for a while, Central Arizona became a kind of second home, both in the dozy warmth of the winter months, and in the parlous heat of the ever-longer summer season.

Phoenix boasts several organizations that take stock of the region's own performance. Self-analysis of this kind is conducted through the annual convocations of Arizona Town Hall—a "think tank" of regional leaders and experts called on to assess progress on topics such as transportation, housing, education, and land use—or the "do tank" of the Center for the Future of Arizona, which focuses on the same topics in a more applied fashion. The Morrison Institute, a busy center for public policy, issues regular reports on the social and economic health of the state, and a large share of ASU's research resources are now trained on diagnosing, and engineering solutions for, the region's problems.[22] In particular, the university's Global Institute of Sustainability aims at the kind of holistic study of regional sustainability (drawing on the research of interdisciplinary teams) that is echoed in this book. Lastly, the business community is well served by organizations devoted to assessing the climate for investment opportunities such as Greater Phoenix Leadership, Greater Phoenix Economic Council, Phoenix Community Alliance, or the East Valley Partnership.

Aside from all of this local self-scrutiny, my research unearthed a long record of commissioned studies from out-of-state organizations, catering mostly to the appetite for growth. Arguably, the most prominent example was a report, commissioned in 1976 from Herman Kahn's Hudson Institute by United for Arizona, a group of businessmen eager to take advantage of the new social science of "futurology" to pump up belief in the local religion of land development. The result was a landmark study, entitled *Arizona Tomorrow*, which envisioned a future scenario for 2012 that could not have been friendlier to the growth machine. In the report's paean to the Sunbelt way of life, the once forbidding desert environment was now, and for the foreseeable future, an "adult playground" to be enjoyed without consequences. Indeed, the Arizona lifestyle, the report insisted, was "largely responsible for redefining the very term 'desert.'"[23] More recent surveys commissioned from the likes of the Urban Land Institute or the Lincoln Institute of Land Policy have tended to emphasize "balanced growth" in their drafts of the future, largely in recognition of the ecological costs of development that were generally ignored by the authors of *Arizona Tomorrow*.

City newspapers have occasionally tapped outside consultants to produce assessments of the region's evolving reputation. Urbanist Neal Peirce was commissioned in 1987 by the *Arizona Republic* and the *Phoenix Gazette* to prepare one of his widely cited "Citistates Reports." In 2003, the alternative city newspaper, *Phoenix New Times,* brought in Richard Florida to address Phoenix's hopes of becoming the kind of "creative city" advocated by Catalyx, his consultancy group. Most recently, Florida's visit inspired Maricopa Partnership for Arts and Culture to contract Arthesia, a Swiss brand-building consultancy, to provide ideas for polishing and promoting the Valley's identity. "Opportunity Oasis" was the suggested brand moniker, though it proved to be a short-lived one.

My own study was not commissioned, but it was triggered by a no-strings-attached invitation, in the spring of 2008, from an ASU institute, Future Arts Research, to come and do research of my choosing in Phoenix. Consequently, my first interviews were conducted with members of the arts community involved in the "battle for downtown" that I describe in chapter 4. From there, the project grew into a more politically ambitious undertaking, with an eye on useful knowledge for readers to take away. It is not a book that presents a policy blueprint, but there are lessons in it for policymakers, and some of them have to do with the fate of blueprints. The last two decades have seen ample offerings of expert advice about how to plan for a more sustainable future for Phoenix, yet my interviewees uniformly complained that implementation had been thin on the ground. Such plans were all too easily ignored or subverted when powerful voices intervened from the world of land speculation and development. Deference to these voices is deeply ingrained in the political culture of a region so dependent for so long on unrestrained growth, and it may take a decade or two to uproot this subservient per mind-set.

Despite the vested power of the growth machine, I encountered people all over town working to dislodge business as usual. Although the odds were against them, sustainability advocates, practitioners, and activists were not difficult to find in the region. Many of them, and their efforts to change the game, are profiled in the pages of the book. Even those who were focused on their own twenty-block neighborhoods had reason to think that they were helping to make Phoenix a proving ground for ideas and practices that might be useful in far-flung cities faced with similar challenges. If urbanization is an open-ended process, as Jane Jacobs so firmly believed, then the greening of cities is a grand act of improvisation, maybe the last heroic effort in places where it can still make an appreciable difference. *Bird on Fire* is beguiled by that hope, even when there is little reason for it.

CHAPTER 1

Gambling at the Water Table

Out of the ash
I rise with my red hair
And I eat men like air
Sylvia Plath, "Lady Lazarus"

O
f all the livelihoods made possible by land development, Cory Breternitz's job was one of the more peculiar. He was paid to do archaeological excavations by people who hoped he would find nothing of interest. His Phoenix-based firm was one of many private archaeology firms that sprang up in response to legislation (the National Historic Preservation Act of 1966 and the National Environmental Policy Act of 1970) designed to protect cultural resources such as prehistoric artifacts or remains. These laws require government agencies and private developers to hire historians and archaeologists to survey sites and inventory the results before they start building. At the height of the Arizona housing boom, Breternitz, who had previously worked for the Navajo Nation for more than twenty years, spent much of his time on the urban fringe, sifting through desert soil, looking for evidence of Hohokam settlement before the bulldozers "scraped the desert clean" and the construction crews moved in with chipboard, two-by-fours, and stucco to throw up a brown-tiled subdivision.

If Breternitz uncovered a prehistoric structure, even a hamlet, it was still the developer's prerogative to plough it under. "The United States," he explained, "is different than most countries in the world in that private property is sacred, and the government cannot tell you what to do with it.

In places like England, historic properties on your land belong to the Crown, and whatever you find—like a hoard of medieval coins—belongs to the government. In the U.S. if you find a ruin on your land, it belongs to you and you can bulldoze it or sell the artifacts." Some of the developers he worked for might decide to preserve his discoveries and have them curated on-site by the state so that they could be promoted as an attractive sales feature to add value to the development. But ultimately, he reported, most of them simply "want their clearance, or their permits, to move forward with their projects and make money."

Human remains are the exception to this rule, since private ownership of these is prohibited by federal and Arizona law. Discovery of a burial site puts a costly stop to construction until the remains are properly excavated, removed, and eventually transferred for reburial to one of three of the state's tribal authorities—the Salt River Pima-Maricopa, the Gila River Indian Community, or the Hopi Nation. In accord with these protocols, Breternitz and his colleagues are permitted to do some tests for the scientific record. In addition, they have a short window of opportunity, before the hard hats take over, to extract data and artifacts, especially the ceramics that have proven so important to our knowledge of the Hohokam, whose irrigation-based society flourished in the Salt and Gila River basin for more than a thousand years before yielding, like the more fabled Mesopotamian and Egyptian river societies of antiquity, to mounting ecological challenges. The upshot has been a bittersweet irony. Much of what we know today about the Hohokam is a side effect of land development— the digs would not otherwise have been funded—but much of the evidence uncovered now lies underneath the carpet of subdivisions. This "double-edged sword" added an unsettling angle to the tragic outlook associated with Breternitz's line of work; "We look at civilizations," he mused, "that have come and gone."

In 2007, just after the housing bubble peaked, the activities of Breternitz and other archeologists were featured in an article by the wilderness writer, Craig Childs, that attracted a good deal of local commentary after it was reprinted in the *Arizona Republic*.[1] Entitled "For Phoenix, as for Hohokams, Rise Is Just Like the Fall," the moral of the article was that Phoenix's pell-mell growth might be tempting the fate of the Hohokam. This was an old commonplace, but the Valley's building frenzy had given it fresh legs. Annual population growth was pushing 115,000, and no one knew how far the region's water supplies—always the subject of anxious speculation—would stretch. So, too, the article echoed a growing public interest in the collapse of ancient societies, a topic fueled by chilling warnings about the coming impact of climate change.[2] Jared Diamond's book

Figure 1.1
Hohokam pithouse reconstructions, Pueblo Grande Archaeological Park. Photo by author.

Collapse, which analyzed the reasons why some civilizations were laid low while others survived, was a notable bestseller, and with the 2004 release of *The Day After Tomorrow*, Hollywood had begun to crank out disaster epics about climate change and ecological devastation.[3]

Catastrophe prediction had long been one of the favored house styles of the environmental movement. What better way to attract attention? Yet this brand of alarmism had diminishing returns, especially when the more baleful forecasts did not pan out, as happened with the overpopulation scare of the early 1970s, fomented by Paul and Anne Ehrlich in their book *The Population Bomb*. Today's well-funded industry of climate change denial seizes on these "false prophecies" to spread the view that global warming is just another fraud perpetrated by "apocalypse abusers."[4] Part of the problem is that our Hollywoodish imagination of disaster is dominated by the blockbuster spectacle of some future, definitive event that triggers a system collapse. In reality, the apocalypse has already begun and the ongoing evidence is all around us in the die-off of oceans, forests, reefs, and habitats, desertification or salinization of soil, species extinction, and bioaccumulation of carcinogenic toxins. Yet these slow-motion disasters are much more difficult to illustrate, let alone dramatize.[5] Global warming may be the slowest apocalypse of all; invisible and inaudible, its signal is garbled by the local fluctuation of temperatures from year to year.

Living with the knowledge of steady decline in human and environmental welfare is more soul-destroying than the prospect of being snuffed out by an abrupt collapse of civilization.[6] Yet this kind of knowledge does not lend itself to urgent, remedial action. Rebecca Solnit has argued that disastrous circumstances often give rise to our most noble moments of solidarity and civil society. Analyzing evidence of mutual aid and extraordinary altruism in the wake of catastrophes, she finds that affected communities resort more to social cooperation than to regressive, barbaric behavior. "Horrible in itself, disaster is sometimes a back door into paradise, the paradise at least in which we are who we hope to be, do the work we desire, and are each our sister's and brother's keeper."[7] Because they are slower-moving, the calamities of ecological collapse have much less chance of prompting the fraternal responses that Solnit holds dear, and yet those reciprocal sentiments may be the ones that are most needed to stave off the decline. Phoenix had already hosted the breakup of one civilization, and so perhaps there was less need to imagine another. But speculation about the fate of the Hohokam could not help but throw up some object lessons about the present-day capacity for social sustainability in the region.

SYSTEM CRASH

In ancient times, the demise of complex societies rarely had an impact beyond their own region of influence. In our globally connected era, local failures are more and more seen as potential tipping points for the whole system. The global financial network is an especially vulnerable example, and indeed was almost brought to its knees in 2008 by the parochial default of U.S. subprime lending markets. In recent years, climate scientists have stepped up their warnings that systemic collapses could be triggered by any one of several factors: ice-cap or permafrost melt, ocean warming, forest loss, or changes in the albedo temperature effect. In light of these alerts, it is a natural reflex to dwell on how so many ancient societies were vanquished by a pattern of unsustainable growth. The most well-known examples include the Akkadian empire of Sumerian city-states, the Old Kingdom of Egypt, the classic Mayans, Mycenae and Minoa in Greece, Tiwanaku of Lake Titicaca, Easter Island, Great Zimbabwe, Angkor Wat, the Harappan of the Indus Valley, and the Moche in Peru. In many of these cases, some temporary variation in climate, usually a prolonged drought, triggered the collapse, and, in civilizations that had flourished in deserts, the devastation was more rapid and cataclysmic.

The fifteenth-century demise of the Hohokam is the most evocative North American example and, since there are several theories about its causes, it serves as a multipurpose allegory for contemporary doomsayers. Hunters and gatherers were active in Central and Southern Arizona 6,000 years ago, but the Hohokam, from as early as 300 B.C., began to make the shift to irrigation farming. The canal network that sustained them was fully active by A.D. 600, and it flourished for the same reason that the irrigation systems of the Anglo farmer settlers in the late nineteenth and early twentieth centuries did: the combined watersheds (totaling 13,000 square miles) of the Salt, Gila, and Verde rivers drain into the Phoenix Basin. At their peak population of 40,000, the Hohokam were served by a thousand miles of canals, which watered 4,000 square miles of often densely settled villages. Their regional system comprised 30,000 square miles, and their trade routes extended westwards as far as California and eastwards almost to the High Plains. Signature edifices, such as ball courts (begun around A.D. 700), platform mounds (from the 1030s), and great houses (like Casa Grande, the first federally preserved archaeological site in the United States), marked them off from the Ancestral Pueblo peoples of the Southwest and distinguished their settlement as a northern pocket of the Mesoamerican cultures of the Toltecs, Aztecs, and Mayans.

Over time, the Hohokam developed a fairly advanced state-level society, with various levels of authority reaching down from the command centers at the all-important headgates of the canal system. For centuries, their water engineers and food arbitrators successfully managed the resources made available by the river flows, the Sonoran desert's edible plants (over 200 species of a 2,000 total), and the region's wildlife. But a combination of social and environmental changes undermined their ability to sustain the growing population. At its height, Hohokam agriculture extended to dispersed upland settlements that used dry farming techniques. As resources thinned, however, the population agglomerated in the dense villages of the riverine zones, long-distance trade fell off, and social isolation set in. Around 1100, a prolonged regional drought caused social disruption and widespread migration all over the Southwest. Snaketown, a great Hohokam pottery-making center in the Lower Gila valley, slightly southeast of Phoenix, was abandoned shortly thereafter.[8] Finally, between 1357 and 1384, as many as seven major floods, a calamity unseen in 500 years, took their toll on the canal system in the Salt–Gila complex.[9] The Hohokam never really recovered; they dispersed and became "archaeologically invisible" by the mid-1400s.

The fourteenth-century floods were a great trauma, but it appears that the Hohokam had being going downhill since at least the time of the great drought, 250 years earlier. In the early 1990s, in preparation for the realignment of Phoenix's new Hohokam Expressway, the Department of Transportation commissioned digs in and around Pueblo Grande, the headgate village site adjacent to the expanding Sky Harbor Airport. From the evidence they uncovered, the archaeological team built up a picture of a society in a state of precipitous decline during what scholars had called its Classic Period (1150–1350). With trees in the vicinity all felled, and with large and small game in the surrounding desert lands all but depleted, protein intake in the settlers' basic diet waned, and bone mass deteriorated. Nor were there any natural plant buffers to fall back on when crops failed, and so the default diet was more and more limited to maize. Infant morality skyrocketed, and the mean age fell to about 20 years. The team also cited field salinization and waterborne infectious disease as potential causes for the poor health of Pueblo Grande's residents.[10] Even though they were suffering from this extreme state of nutritional stress, their subsistence conditions must have been better than elsewhere in the Southwest because the Hohokam continued to see in-migration from the north all through the Classic Period.

In 2007, Tucson's Center for Desert Archaeology published an article that caused quite a stir among the community of regional archaeologists.[11] It focused squarely on immigrant overpopulation as the primary cause of Hohokam collapse. Drawing on a GIS survey of changing population densities for all known Southwestern settlements over the period from 1220 to 1700, the authors showed a marked southward migration from the Kayenta/Tusuyan communities in what is now the Four Corners region. These northern sites were permanently abandoned by the later 1200s just as the aggregate population in the Sonoran heartland of the Hohokam began to rise sharply. According to the Tucson study, the social tension and conflict between ethnically distinct groups sapped the ability of the Hohokam to absorb a swelling migrant population and sealed the fate of the river civilization.

Theories about the erosive pressure of in-migration on the Hohokam had been proposed before.[12] But the Tucson group's overriding emphasis on overpopulation by the newcomers was a novel perspective, and it was difficult to ignore how neatly this conclusion echoed the strong anti-immigration sentiment that had come to pervade Central Arizona over the course of the 2000s. Maricopa County outran the rest of the nation in its legal assault against Mexican migrants who had flocked to the region to staff the housing boom, and its sheriff, the shamelessly vindictive Joe

Arpaio, became a national poster boy for nativist backlash. For those who liked to draw on pop psychology for their views, the new research on the Hohokam was fresh support for their inclination to blame everything on the immigrants. Indeed, I would come across several Anglo nativists in my own research who believed that Mexican migrants contributed disproportionately to the "overpopulation problem" in Phoenix, and that the region's limited environmental resources could not support them.

Commentators looking to spice up their views with some evidence from the Hohokam often ended up calling Todd Bostwick, the city's own archaeologist. Only a handful of American cities fund such a position (the Phoenix office was established in 1927), and it meant that Bostwick was more fully exposed than his fellow professionals (in the academy or the private firms) to the anxieties and delusions of the public. "I get nervous," he explained, "because people who speak to me automatically look for confirmation of their own theories and beliefs that we are doomed because of our mismanagement of water and resources." Understandably, he was wary of those "who ask if there is a parallel with the modern times," but he himself believed that there were contemporary lessons about sustainability to be drawn from the pre-Columbian sites that he oversaw. "When we reconstruct human behavior, we do not simply say, 'This is what people did thousands of years ago.' We can say, 'Here is what people in Arizona were doing during a formative period when the adaptation may be very similar to our own.' They were different people and spoke different languages, but they were basically farmers, learning to adapt, as we have done here." Bostwick went on, "My own personal position is that I think the Hohokam exceeded the carrying capacity of the technology that they had. They were so good at living in the desert that they perhaps did not recognize there is a point where you cannot add more people into the valley if you want to have a sustainable lifestyle."

Unconvinced by the single-factor emphasis placed on in-migration by the Tucson study, Bostwick was even more skeptical about the nativist claims being made today around the harmful impact of immigrants from the South. As a primary investigator on the Pueblo Grande digs, he recalled that it was relatively easy to identify migrants in the site's burial mounds because "they received very little ritual and celebration." It is likely, he concluded, that the Hohokam's seasonal use of migrant labor was long-standing. With tens of thousands of acres of agriculture, and two growing seasons, it was natural that migrants would be drawn in to meet seasonal needs such as planting and harvesting. "There was always someone," Bostwick reasoned, "who was willing to come in and make a few extra monetary collections, barters, acquisitions of products, for having to work a short period of time and then be on their way again. That is a very attractive lifestyle to some people, and they were probably coming in at a certain time of year knowing there will be demands, just like the cow-pokes coming in for the cattle. It shows a dynamic, or flexible division of labor that is a highly adaptive strategy for desert living." Bostwick believed that the archaeological record did throw some light on "our heated debate today about migrant labor." His response was "to remove the emotional part of it and look instead at how people sustain themselves in the desert." In such an ecosystem, he concluded, "we might come to the realization that sustainability is not possible without migrant labor."

Certainly, Bostwick's observation was borne out by the history of Anglo settlement in the Phoenix Basin. Non-Anglo migrant labor was employed to farm the original Salt River hay camp that John Y. T. Smith established in 1867 to supply the U.S. Army at Fort McDowell, as well as the miners whom the soldiers protected from Apache raids. It was no different for the farms that prospered during the cotton boom of the 1910s (drawing in African Americans from the South) nor for the citrus, alfalfa, and grain operations that flourished when the cotton market crashed in 1920. The postwar land rush and the long housing boom that followed also relied heavily on migrant labor. Very little of that labor history has been well documented, either in Arizona or anywhere else for that matter. But if sustainability in the desert had always depended on the contributions of migrants, as Bostwick suggested, then the migrants were surely part of the solution, and not the source of problems that Arizona's nativists had become notorious for laying at their door. Nor was the value of these contributions limited to the undercounted cost of their labor. If there were any lessons to draw from the Hohokam, it was that a key to regional sustainability lay in how migrants were socially regarded and culturally absorbed. With an eye to that conclusion, Bostwick wound up our interview by emphasizing that environmental changes did not doom the Hohokam so much as the decisions they made in response. "When we talk about sustainability we talk about decision-making. Nothing just happens. The Hohokam were not a chiefdom with a pyramid structure of power, they were a federation, and the many autonomous decisions of individual farmers all added up to a collective decision-making system." Although it was by no means certain that a centralized chiefly authority would have made wiser decisions, his point about what could be learned from the rise and fall of the Hohokam was that the future of Phoenix would not be strictly determined by its limited resources but rather by whether its residents could cooperate and wisely interact with each other in order to stave off the most dire outcomes.

Bostwick's take on the Hohokam story echoed scholarship that focused on the resilience of societies in the face of long-term decline, or in their regeneration after a collapse. Unwise decisions are often made to stave off a system crash, when the costs, for example, of solving problems associated with unsustainable growth are deferred through temporary fixes such as more efficient technologies or stronger regulations. The expenses incurred in taking these actions mount up, however, and members eventually resist being taxed to fund the fixes.[13] In far Western states, the most recent wave of antitax sentiment, originating in the late 1970s, was tied to the belief, at the root of the Sagebrush Rebellion, that federal action on environmental regulation and preservation was an unjust restriction of citizens' rights to freely exploit land as private property. In turn, those not directly responsible for the exploitation resent having to pay taxes to clean up or mitigate its harmful impact. At the same time, all parties thrive on the artificially low price of scarce resources like water and nonrenewable energy that are heavily subsidized to hide their true environmental costs. The metropolis of Phoenix, an antitax stronghold, was a case in point. For several decades, its economy was largely based on deferring the costs of growth, if only because the rate of growth was so fast that no one had to verify if growth did indeed "pay for itself." A suitable pop analogy would be with the Road Runner cartoons (whose backdrop was the Sonoran Desert landscape) in which Wile E. Coyote has run off a cliff and is suspended in midair by sheer momentum, or by his unwillingness to look down.

The upside of resilience lies in the capacity of societies to alter behavior perceived to be destructive over the course of time. This is something Wile E. cannot do, but which Phoenix area residents were being asked to consider as they struggled to salvage lessons from the collapse of the metropolitan growth model. After all, populations that rebuild after a system crash have an opportunity to retain the most resilient pre-collapse features and jettison the harmful ones.[14] For example, the region's Pima Indians (Akimel O'odham), who claim descent from the Hohokam, adopted a more dispersed pattern of living. In due course, they made use of some of the irrigation canals, especially on the Gila River, to rebuild an agricultural base that brought them widespread repute in the nineteenth century. The Anglo settlers in the Salt Valley also took over parts of the Hohokam canal network, and today many of the Valley's vital canals follow the same prehistoric routes.[15]

The potential for recycling remnants of the past prompted Phillip (or "Lord" as he called himself) Darrell Duppa, an English adventurer who was among the original 1867 party of Anglo settlers in the Phoenix Basin, to bestow a new name on the community: "A great race once dwelt here, and another great race will dwell here in the future. I prophesy that a new city will spring Phoenix-like from the ruins and ashes of the old." More grandiose than Pumpkinville or Mill City, its original names, the choice of Phoenix was no doubt intended by Duppa as a tribute to the indomitable pioneer spirit. Over time, his symbol of rebirth would become a banal comment on the boom-and-bust cycles of land speculation that drove growth in the Valley. The instability that accompanied these cycles was a structural side effect of capitalist economics. In Phoenix, it was a way of life; the deeper the crash, the more dazzling the recovery. At least, this is how it was remembered. But the crash of 2008 provoked widespread fears that this one was different. The growth machine had broken down, and there was no real confidence that it would be fixed.

DEVELOPER'S TOWN

While periodic economic crises are a feature of all forms of capital accumulation, they are more severe when triggered by bouts of extreme speculation. Nowhere is this more visible than in the history of land fraud, which has driven every phase of Western settlement. It was runaway paper speculation on land sales in the West that led to the first epic money crash in the United States in 1837. When Andrew Jackson decided that land, which had been trading on the dubious paper of banks, had to be paid for in gold or silver, the speculators' house of cards collapsed. Yet these paper debt structures would rise and fall, again and again, over the next 170 years. After the panic of 1873, itself a product of railroad speculation, a succession of land rushes swept the West as Congress sold off public land. For the big speculators, the land grid was like one giant gaming table. For every 160-acre lot claimed by small farmers under the Homestead Act of 1862, nine others were snapped up by speculators.[16] Even more suscep- tible to land grabbers was the subsequent Desert Land Act of 1877, which offered 640 acres to settlers who agreed to water their land; as many as 95 percent of the claims were fraudulent.[17] Compared to the high rollers, the bona fide homesteaders who took advantage of these acts of federal lar- gesse were little more than bit players in the national lottery that drove the westward expansion of capital, population, and Anglo culture.

After the United States took possession of the river valleys of Central and Southern Arizona in 1848, many of the Mexican incumbents were fraudulently dispossessed of their Spanish land grants, and although the territory was too arid to attract a land rush of Oklahoma proportions, it still saw its share of swindlers selling pie in the sky to the folks back East and in Europe. One mining interest promoter circulated to overseas speculators resplendent images of ships steaming up the Colorado to Yuma, eastward along the Gila River, and then up the Santa Cruz.[18] Others, more restrained in their pitches, rubbed out any references to the harsh reality of existence in the parched lands, just as housing agents in the twentieth century were forbidden to mention Phoenix's scorching summers to their prospective Midwestern customers until the advent of air conditioning after the war.

It was an aspiration to gamble that carried the gold prospectors to California on the Arizona overland route through the Gila Valley. Humbled by the inhospitality of the desert, many of them were saved by the provisioning and guidance of Indian farmers in the oasis of Pima Villages. Gambling also drove the prospectors who came later to the territory to mine for minerals, and the region's myriad ghost towns are a record of when and where their luck ran out.[19] But farming in these semiarid regions was arguably the biggest gamble of all, and initially at least, it ruined the yeoman homesteaders who were sold on the fallacy that "rain follows the plough." John Wesley Powell, the great surveyor of desert lands, confirmed, in his 1879 *Report on the Lands of the Arid Region of the United States,* that their venture was an act of folly. If agriculture beyond the hundredth meridian had any chance of enduring, it would require a formula quite different from the Midwestern one of filling out a grid with 160- (or even 640-) acre homesteads. The planning of settlements, Powell reasoned, should instead be based around the region's watersheds and natural hydrological basins.[20]

But Powell's advice was already too late. Grady Gammage, Jr., Phoenix's semiofficial voice of conscience on matters of land development, pointed out that "most settlements had begun, like Phoenix, on the basis of immediate proximity to water. But when the local supply proved inadequate, existing investments in land made it preferable to search for new water sources rather than to move. . . . Instead of living where water made habitation sensible, water should move to wherever people settled."[21] This became the working principle behind the dams and the river diversions of the Reclamation era, and it inspired what historians came to call the "hydraulic West."[22] The result has been a society that depends on a vast federal plumbing system that moves water hither and thither, regardless of where it would naturally flow. Inevitably, the water was redirected toward profiteers, as exemplified by the gravity-defying feat of the Owens Valley Aqueduct, which gave rise to the Western maxim, "water flows uphill toward money." But the long-term ecological degradation caused by the plumbing has also given rise to the perception that many of the big cities in the region are mistakes, and that they should never have held large numbers of people in the first place.

For Powell, though even more for blithe boosters of Reclamation like William Ellsworth Smythe, desert farming was an opportunity to extend and restore the Jeffersonian idyll of agrarian self-sufficiency that was foundational to national identity—a strong cocktail made up of equal parts doctrine, folklore, and archaic remnant.[23] But American farming had itself long been an act of land speculation, and there was no reason to think that the West would be an exception. In his influential account of the "myth of the yeoman farmer," historian Richard Hofstadter argued that the American farmer, from a very early point, was "a country businessman who gambled with his land." By 1860, on the eve of far Western expansion, commercial agriculture was all but triumphant and independent freeholders in the Jeffersonian mold were increasingly thin on the ground.

As cheap land opened up to the west, the profits to be harvested from land appreciation far outweighed any sustenance that could be eked out of raising livestock and selling crops. Consequently, a speculator's psychology kicked in, and economic mobility from the proceeds of resales became a standard expectation. The self-reliant yeoman, in Hofstadter's view, was "condemned to live with the contradictions of being ennobled, on the one hand, while being driven by the dictates of market civilization to view land value as the richest source of profit and security."[24] One of the most ominous side effects was the careless cultivation of a one-crop system. Those who saw their farms primarily as a speculative asset had little incentive to look after the health of the soil. This attitude long predated the ill-conceived adventures in semiarid farming that generated the Dust Bowl in the 1930s, or indeed those in the same High Plains region today (southwestern South Dakota, western Nebraska, southeastern Wyoming, western Kansas, western Oklahoma, and northwestern Texas), which depend on groundwater pumping from the fast-depleting Ogallala Aquifer. There was even less incentive to do so for Salt Valley farmers as the twentieth century wore on. Most were counting the years until the urban fringe arrived, and developers handed over a check in return for their acreage.

The same speculator psychology would take hold in the mind of the late twentieth-century homeowner. A home became less a shelter than a tradable asset, and for those whose income reached a plateau in midlife, resale value of their houses had to be a dependable revenue source. Owning a home was like running a small business that had to be sold every so often, and timing the sale could be a risky matter.[25] By the end of the millennium, the average American homeowner sold that business every seven years. In real estate hot zones like Phoenix, the turnover was much more rapid, and so the population was in a constant churn. For sure, the professional speculators played for the biggest money, in a game where land banking and asset flipping were the ground rules. Indeed, for every Central Arizona land crash, there had been a high-profile huckster to pin the blame on: Ned Warren, "the godfather of land fraud" in the 1970s, Charles Keating, the developer and financier whose racketeering precipitated the savings and loans crisis of the late 1980s, and Scott Coles, the mortgage tycoon whose overextended lending practices epitomized the crash of 2007. But the high rollers only prospered because there was a critical mass of small players who shared the same mentality.

While they were in flight above Phoenix in the late 1940s, Barry Goldwater remarked to the journalist Stewart Alsop: "If you'd dropped a five-dollar bill down there before the war, it would be worth a couple of hundred now."[26] This was one way of looking at a city, and it was especially favored by developers who used aerial surveys to pick out and gamble on land that lay in the path of growth. But the mentality was also thick on the ground, among the little people. In Phoenix, land development has always been as natural as breathing. Any corner of the landscape is a "parcel," begging for a contract; each building is a renovation opportunity, every open space a "vacant lot," awaiting its improver, and, with a little backing, it could be you.

Among many of my interviewees, this was an ordinary, almost mundane, way of looking at the desertscape. People who had no hand or stake in land development still saw their surroundings through a surveyor's lens. For some of those who did development as a sideline, it had even taken on a philosophical cast. One example was the artist Sloane McFarland. His reputation around town as a creative entrepreneur rested on several small-scale development projects he had built or retrofitted—hip havens like Lux coffee bar and the Welcome Diner—but he had his eye on much bigger buildings too. "I consider developer to be my tertiary role," he told me. "My first role is that of a person, trying to answer my calling, and my second is that of an artist. This means I have a system of faith, understanding, citizenship, and expression to answer to, and so I view things through a concentric ring of obligations and perspectives." McFarland, a self-described "child of God," spoke at great length about how his involvement in land development "was inspired by the act of growing something" for future generations. He wanted "to create a place that didn't hurt, and wouldn't hurt the next group of kids growing up." So, too, this desire was bound up in his own personal quest for meaning—"to become more connected as a person to the ground, to heaven, and to here."

Over time, his photographic artwork had focused on what he called the "rich vernacular or idiom of development." "If I were in Paris 100 years ago," he explained, "I would probably want to paint people at the café or the ballet." But here, the business of constructing shelter—"the place where you and I go to sleep and eat and produce our life-force in"—was not only a topic of his art, it was also his local art form. In McFarland's case, as in so many others, he was carrying on a family tradition. "I didn't just put on my hat one day and decide to be a developer," he remarked. He recounted how his Italian immigrant grandparents had won a garbage pickup contract with the city. "As they saved money they bought and sold real estate like it was trading cards. It wasn't expensive and Phoenix wasn't even on the map. We went on drives all of the time and looked at property. In fact, my grandparents bought a piece of property way out west and went out to look at it almost every weekend for fifty years."

McFarland was by no means the only local artist whose work and livelihood was profoundly tied to land development. On his family farm, on the far side of the West Valley's 303 loop, Matt Moore, whose great-grandparents had arrived in the 1860s in a Mormon caravan, created one of Arizona's most iconic contemporary artworks. Since the family's property was directly in the growth path, and business was hurting, it seemed inevitable that some, if not all, of their acreage would be sold off to a housing developer. The potential loss of the farm was both a trauma and a creative catalyst for Moore, who was attending art school in San Francisco in the early 2000s. "I realized that the change in the status of the farm was the source of my art." In 2003, he returned to Phoenix to manage the farming operations, and he began his career in land art by sculpting the floor plan of a single-family residence from a field of barley. Shortly thereafter, he planted a one-third-scale replica of the layout of the first subdivision—Sycamore Estates—to be built on the 80-acre portion of the farm that had already been sold off. The homes were planted in sorghum and the roads in black-bearded wheat. Pictured from the air—the preferred perspective of the developer—the record of the sculpture was a stunning commentary on the destiny of farmland on the urban fringe.

A fast-growth region like Phoenix had little time for regret over the loss of farmland. Prior to the peak of the housing boom, a widely cited *Arizona Republic* article reported that the metropolis was gobbling land at the rate of one acre per hour (though its author, Kathleen Ingley, quipped to me that the main impact of the article was only to see the rate doubled over the next few years).[27] Indeed, in the twenty-five years before the crash,

Figure 1.2
Matthew Moore, "Moore Estates, 35 acres, sorghum and wheat," 2005. Courtesy of the artist.

half of the region's productive farmland was lost to urbanization.[28] Far from nostalgic for their vanishing bucolic life, ranchers and farmers eager for a buyout had been the most reliable allies of the Central Arizona Homebuilders Association in opposing any kind of legislative effort at growth management. After all, the footprint of an irrigated desert farm, with its basic infrastructure and graded land, lent itself to rapid conversion, and the region's old agricultural service roads, laid out on a square-mile grid, were its chief urban arteries today. But Moore's land art and his other multimedia efforts to document the fate of the family farm became a lightning rod for the mounting concerns about the sustainability of suburban growth. Now known as "the farmer artist," he was trying to parlay his fame and influence into advocating for responsible land stewardship and for local, or even organic food, provision.

Moore, who believed he would be the last of his lineage to run the farm, and also the last Anglo of his generation among all his neighbors with sufficient agricultural knowledge to farm, was consumed by the contradictions of his newfound identity. For one thing, he mused, "both environmentalists and developers want my work on their walls." Nor did he have the comfort of being a purist in his farming practices. "I'm a walking contradiction. I grow organic but I also run a conventional, huge farm. I'm an advocate of the desert, but I harvest water from hundreds of miles away and bring it in to feed people." On a day trip to visit the farm and its surroundings, I learned just how heavily his sense of familial responsibility weighed on him—the operation supported as many as thirty people, and many of them, especially the field workers from Mexico, had a long-standing relationship with the farm.

On the east side of the 303 loop (the West Valley's development "frontier"), land was priced at three dollars per square foot, and all the utility lines had been laid for subdivisions before the crash stopped in its tracks the march of brown-tiled roofs. On the west side of the road, where the price was only one dollar per square foot, citrus and rose farms stretched off in the direction of the White Tank Mountains. Passing up Cotton Lane in the direction of the homestead, Moore pointed to where his grandmother had planted the tall eucalyptus trees by the roadside. While his family had helped to shape the geography of settlement, their role as agents and beneficiaries of the Reclamation's megawater schemes had also brought into being a metropolis whose population he saw as heedless about water and energy conservation. "I feel partly responsible," he confessed, "for this metro oasis because we were the ones who figured out how to bring water in and build this whole la la land." This heady brew of guilt, commitment, and advocacy drove Moore's art and also his efforts to sustain the farm, especially the acreage that produced organic food for fifty families through a CSA cooperative. He accepted that it was the challenge of his generation to alter the prevailing mentality of "making the desert whatever we want it to be." To reflect on the folly of that attitude, he wanted us to visit a tumbleweed subdivision not far from the farm.

From the looks of the abandoned infrastructure, it was not a high-concept development, and had probably been designed to attract low-income residents with the kind of subprime loans—"drive till you qualify"—that fueled the boom on the urban edge. In any event, the roads and signposts with street names were all overrun with high sage grass. It was the latest version of the Western ghost town, and choice examples could be found all over the periphery of the West Valley. Perhaps they would never host houses or people, and, in Moore's view, the presence of the tumbleweed implied that the idea was flawed to begin with. Hollywood had made the vagrant plant into a symbol of nature's reclamation of failed human settlements in the far West, but tumbleweed is not native to the region, and it is a major cause of soil erosion when it sets itself in motion to spread its seeds.

Figure 1.3
Nature reclaims an abandoned subdivision. Photo by author.

Moore had a hard time straddling his commitment to the farm and the role he played, as an artist, in the city's creative renaissance, which included the rise of chefs and foodies devoted to local produce. As elsewhere, the local food movement had emerged as a health-conscious alternative to industrial food production but also as a way of saving farmland from the developers' D-9 bulldozers. In Metro Phoenix, the locavore food circuit was in its infancy, but there was already a sizable batch of small farmers, like Moore, willing to sponsor CSAs and farmers' markets, while retail giants like Walmart had begun to source locally. In some youthful circles, you could hear a lot of agrarian talk—hipster echoes of the republic of self-reliant yeoman idealized by the Reclamation boosters.

In the history of Phoenix, as in other far Western settlements, that freeholder vision had lasted only as long as the market in land speculation allowed. A worldwide cotton shortage during World War I created the first land bubble, when Salt River Valley farmers gave up their other crops to grow the "white gold." Land in the West Valley community of Peoria, for example, saw an increase of 833 percent in only three years. When foreign cotton growers reentered the market after the war, prices plummeted, and the wipeout was brutal.[29] In the wake of the crash, farmers diversified their crops, adding dairy and livestock, but there was no holding back the appetite for land profit. The Valley's irrigation farmers had been the instigators of the first federal Reclamation project—Roosevelt Dam, finished in 1911—but the large-scale water works approved after the cotton crash were increasingly designed to cater to urban growth, the real cash crop in the region.

Over time, and as a supplementary water supply from the Colorado River was tapped to guarantee new housing construction from the 1980s, an understanding took shape. The first priority of the state's water management was still to service agriculture (almost 70 percent of Arizona's water is currently used on agriculture). But since the most profitable use of land lay in housing development, water resources would switch over to urban use as and when the farmland was converted. In the event of shortages like an extreme drought, the farmers' water would summarily be reallocated for urban use. Since the growers used more water per acre than a housing subdivision would, the agricultural quotas were an insurance policy for the future growth of the metropolis, and farming was a temporary form of capital investment that would see its full dividend after the surveyors, bulldozers, and drywallers had pushed the urban fringe a few miles further out. The interests of farmers and developers were both well served by this understanding, and so small growers like Moore, with ulterior reasons for staying in the farming business, were few and far between. As long as the overall water supply was assured, and housing sales were healthy, there was no reason to question the formula. But by the time I got to Phoenix, there were more doubts than certainties about these matters.

THE NEXT BUCKET

Other than the platitude that "growth pays for itself," the most widely shared commonplace I found in the Valley's business community was that water management in Central Arizona had been a great success. Whenever the spreading metropolis needed more, its politicians had delivered, usually by extracting water pork from Washington. Until Jimmy Carter threatened to pull the plug on several new dam projects during his first months in office, no sitting president had seriously questioned the tradition of throwing slugs of money into the West's plumbing system. Carter's presidency never really recovered from the rancorous political backlash to his infamous hit list, but his bold stand turned out to be the beginning of the end for the Reclamation megawater projects that had so heavily subsidized Western settlement. Even if the habit was revived, its backers would have to contend with the proven record of damage to wildlife and riparian plant communities from the existing dam network.

By 2009, one of Phoenix's driest years on record, the Southwest was in the tenth year of a drought that Interior Secretary Gale Norton described as "perhaps the worst in 500 years." Climate modeling showed that even hotter and drier conditions lay ahead for a region that had hosted some of the Earth's longest documented "megadroughts" over the previous two millennia. A 2007 study from Columbia University's Earth Observatory forecast a more or less permanent drought for the next ninety years, and the federal government's Global Change Research Program warned of a "serious water supply challenge" in the coming decades.[30]

At the onset of the drought's second decade, the Colorado River was running at 66 percent of normal levels, while Lake Mead, the nation's largest reservoir, was at 39 percent of its storage capacity, and, according to a study by the Scripps Institution of Oceanography, had a 50 percent chance of running dry by 2021.[31] In March 2010, an official for the Central Arizona Project (CAP), the big canal that delivered Colorado water to the state, commented that "if current runoff trends continue, the CAP could run short of water by 2012 for the first time."[32] All over the world, freshwater supplies were plummeting, and the World Bank and OECD were calling for hikes in water prices in order to encourage conservation.[33] Yet, thanks to all of the subsidies its water managers had won, the residents of Metro Phoenix, with their hallowed Sunbelt lifestyle of swimming pools and golf courses, enjoyed one of the lowest consumer water rates of any city in the United States. The price of a gallon in the parched Valley was less than half the cost of its equivalent in rain-soaked Seattle, and the average daily per capita residential use was more than twice as much.[34] As other Arizona cities like Flagstaff and Tucson introduced water rationing, Tempe, which adjoins Phoenix, built itself a billion-gallon lake that needs a half-billion additional gallons of CAP water per year to compensate for evaporation in the desert heat. Outsiders could hardly be faulted for surmising that the Valley surely had a water problem, or else it had too much invested in denying that there might be one.

In Metro Phoenix, it was long forbidden to say such things too loudly, for fear of puncturing the protective cushion around the gospel of growth. Patricia Gober, who ran the Decision Theater for a Desert City, an ASU research center that uses climate change modeling to supply regional water information, described the perils of crossing the line: "One of our stakeholders who provided us with data told us that if we ever represented an anti-growth position we would not receive data from these agencies again." Gober explained that "we use existing data in our models," and "we try to represent ourselves as best we can as neutral purveyors of scientific information," but "there is always the risk of being associated with a particular point of review regarding your position on growth and climate." Up until recently, she reported, "we could not even talk about growth," but now she was seeing more interest in her unit's research from the planners and decision makers, and she hoped it would feed into rational, long-term water policies for the Valley.

Some of the interest in her center may well have been due to the parlous situation of strapped government agencies desperate for data input. In any event, the newfound regard for academic research had not penetrated the Arizona Legislature, whose majority GOP leadership regarded scientific expertise on climate change as little more than a source of communist propaganda. To operate in a policy arena so hostile to evidence, Gober and her ASU colleagues had adopted the strategic tack of acknowledging doubt and advocating action at one and the same time. "Our thesis is that there is profound uncertainty from a variety of sources about climate change, but we as a society need to learn to make decisions in the face of uncertainty. We make many decisions in the face of uncertainty: managing stock portfolios, choosing to purchase insurance or take drugs. As individuals or as a society, we seem to be able to function in the face of those kinds of uncertainties. So how much risk do we want to take with water shortage given what we know about the risks associated with climate change?"

Given the prevailing temper at the Capitol, this was probably a prudent strategy, though it removed environmental policy and planning from the daylight realm of rights, justice, and resource security, and put it back on the gambling table, along with stock picking, actuarial life tables, and risky drug regimes. Many environmentalists bristled when "risk assessment" was introduced by the EPA and FDA in the 1980s as a policy tool for regulating hazardous substances or dirty industry. Its adoption was seen as an acknowledgment that our society could not contain the damage caused by industrial civilization, and so government agencies would simply manage the outcomes by designating a certain level of exposure to radiation, toxics, or rising temperatures as an acceptable risk. In due course, the management of risk was handed over to market mechanisms. In this new phase of regulation, often labeled as neoliberal, polluting companies would be able to buy pollution rights on the emergent carbon markets in the same spirit as a speculator might stake a position on soybean futures.

My interviews with GOP legislators confirmed that, regardless of the care with which Gober and others chose their words, certainty still ruled at the state capitol; if the state had resource challenges, then it was assumed that technological innovation would solve them. This trust in technical fixes was a legacy of the blend of ideology and religious faith that drove the Bureau of Reclamation's water engineering in the first half of the twentieth century. The biblically inspired ingredient came from the Mormons who pioneered irrigation agriculture in the Great Basin desert around Salt Lake, the Little Colorado River basin in Northeastern Arizona, and in their Phoenix Basin outpost of Mesa. The Mormon blueprint of conquering nature at God's bidding shaped the water culture of the West, the mentality of the Bureau's administrators (many of whom were Mormon), and indeed the disposition of the Arizona Legislature itself, 45 percent of whose representatives were Mormon, though only 6 percent of the state's population were estimated to be LDS members. In other respects, the Bureau was the institutional vehicle of the Manifest Destiny doctrine that had spurred the westward expansion. Presumptions about the technical superiority of Anglo-Saxon ways provided the racialist ideology that inspired and steered the romance of Reclamation.

The Bureau's dam builders, who made the desert bloom, performed heroic engineering feats that made Reclamation a model to follow in other parts of the world. But arguably more influential in the long run were their critics, like the Sierra Club activists, led by David Brower, who cut their teeth on public campaigns to save several sites on the Colorado River from damming in the 1950s and 1960s. The publicity generated by these efforts led to a thorough reassessment of the dire environmental impacts of dam building, such as salinization, riverbed and bank erosion, and species extinction. Consequently, these destructive side effects became so widely acknowledged, and most persuasively documented in the World Commission on Dams 2000 report, that many countries, including the United States, stopped constructing them.[35] Today's Bureau, rebranded as a "water management agency," invests more time and research on repairing the damage, restoring riparian corridors, and anticipating climate change impacts than on adding to its legacy of redeeming the desert, though that is largely because every major river in the West has already been plugged or canalized, including the entire Salt–Verde–Gila complex whose waters are artificially distributed across the alluvial plains of the Phoenix Basin.[36] As Donald Worster has put it, the rivers of the West can best be described as "descending staircases of man-made tanks."[37]

The most expensive and audacious of the Reclamation projects remains the CAP aqueduct, a 335-mile-long diversion canal through which Colorado water from Lake Havasu City is pumped 1,250 feet uphill to Phoenix and Tucson. Conceived as the supply pipeline for the lion's share of Arizona's water allocation from the 1922 Colorado River Compact, the $4.4 billion CAP was not completed until 1993. Its annual capacity to deliver 1.5 million acre-feet of water quickly became the rationale, and the default water source, for further urbanization of desert lands. The dream of tapping the Colorado "ran like a drug through the veins of Arizonans" as Thomas Sheridan put it, "for most of the twentieth century."[38] The state's alpha politicians, Carl Hayden, Barry Goldwater, and Morris Udall, were responding to the needs of the postwar urban growth machine when, after decades of legal wrangling with California, they finally brokered federal approval for this Holy Grail in 1968.[39] In *Cadillac Desert,* his influential 1986 history of the Reclamation era, Marc Reisner described CAP as "a palpable mirage as incongruous a spectacle as any on earth: a man-made river flowing uphill in a place of almost no rain." Although Reisner was writing before hydrologists issued dire estimates about the impact of climate change on the river flow, he blithely predicted that CAP would become a "ruin before its time," on a "Sumerian scale." In that event, Phoenicians, he concluded, "from now until eternity will be forced to do what their Hohokam ancestors did: pray for rain."[40]

Whether or not it will come to resemble a Hohokam canal, silted over, and repossessed by chaparral and sagebrush, CAP only deferred a final reckoning with the state's water problem. Its lifeline was the reason why lawns, swimming pools, and golf courses in Chandler and North Scottsdale were well maintained during the drought, while water was rationed in other Arizonan and far Western cities. And, ever since CAP began taking the state's full quota in 1996, a considerable volume of surplus water had been "banked" by using it to recharge the region's depleted aquifers. Yet many of the water managers with whom I talked were already firmly focused on locating new water sources, or what is known in the industry as the "next bucket." The 1922 compact allocated 16.5 million acre-feet of Colorado water diversion rights, but since 1930, the average annual flow had been 20 percent less than that and under the CAP agreement, Arizona had the least priority if the river ran too low to serve all of its eight beneficiaries (the seven basin states plus Mexico). Indeed by 2009, drought runoff estimates showed Lake Mead might soon fall to the depth that would trigger restrictions. Under the terms of the CAP agreement, Arizona would be the first to incur cutbacks, and would, in fact, absorb 96 percent of the subsequent rationing. The state's farmers would be first in line to suffer, since the metropolitan communities of Phoenix and Tucson were relatively well cushioned from initial cutbacks, but it was only a matter of time before the urbanites' supplies were affected.[41] Most secure were the state's Indian tribes, entitled, ultimately, to nearly 46 percent of the state's

CAP's allocation, much of which holds a higher priority than that designated for municipal, industrial, and agricultural uses.[42]

Despite the efforts at recharging, groundwater in the region was heavily overdrafted in places, and, given the expense of CAP water, pumping from the aquifer was a matter of survival for many farmers. Climate change would almost certainly take its toll on all available surface water sources, and so additional supplies would be needed soon.[43] CAP's general manager, David Modeer, cited some of the sources of the next bucket that he and his peers were considering. "Is there untapped ground water in some parts of the state? Can you buy higher priority water by buying land along the [Colorado] river? Or enter into long-term leases with Native Americans who may not use all the water they're entitled to? Can you desalinate brackish water, or get involved with Mexico in desalinating ocean or sea water?" These solutions were being proposed to service future growth, but Modeer himself believed they may be "needed immediately for dealing with adaptation to changing weather patterns." The current cost of delivering CAP water was $135 per acre-foot, but he could see alternative modes of delivery boosting the state's water price up to $10,000 per acre-foot in the years to come.

Although Jimmy Carter eventually signed off on CAP, the condition for approval was an inspired piece of 1980 legislation called the Groundwater Management Act (GMA), aimed at limiting groundwater pumping from the aquifer that had accumulated in the Phoenix Basin over millions of years. Wells dug by farmers and developers had begun to make the desert floor subside in places, and the new law was designed to produce "safe yield" by 2025, balancing withdrawals against water recharged into the aquifer. While the GMA regulations potentially affected millions of Valley lives, their full ramifications were understood by few people, least of all the new suburban homeowners who were supposed to be the most affected. Not long after the ink dried on the CAP approval, agriculture and homebuilding lobbyists got to work weakening and dismantling the GMA's conservation requirements. Although legal challenges to the Act's constitutionality were rebuffed by the courts, noncompliance with its requirements became widespread as regulators took a hands-off attitude, while the legislature simply pardoned municipalities for missing their multiyear thresholds.[44] With a state legislature that put no regulatory teeth behind its water conservation policies, any effort at long-term water planning was almost certain to be ambushed by short-term interests.

The original GMA stipulated that all new housing developments had to show an assured water supply for at least one hundred years before permits were approved. While hydrologically sound, the requirement was a political nonstarter. Developers bent on building beyond the urban area would be especially hard pressed to meet this demand and so their lobbyists conspired to have it shredded. In response, legislators cooked up a new formula that would effectively green-light the march of the subdivisions to proceed unobstructed. Developers without an assured water supply would be allowed to rely on pumped groundwater if they paid into a Groundwater Replenishment District (GRD) agency to recharge the aquifer groundwater elsewhere with an equivalent volume of CAP water. Homeowners, who were not exactly encouraged to understand the process, were the ones left with the yearly assessment fees and depleting aquifers underneath their homes. Nor was the logic of the scheme immediately apparent to hydrologists. "I can't say that it completely makes sense to me," confessed Charlie Ester, the widely respected manager of Water Resource Operations for the Salt River Project. What does that say? I asked. "I think it says that politicians and lawmakers put the plan together," he quipped.

Critics of the arrangement argued that it was a "shell game," because the GRD itself was not required to have an assured 100-year water supply. CAP water was not a sustainable resource, and, if the drought on the Upper Colorado continued, CAP's current surpluses would evaporate quickly. Nor did the architects of the system envisage the explosive growth, at both ends of the Valley, which would take advantage of the GRD to expand far beyond urbanized areas onto desert lands that had no former agricultural use. None of the water experts I interviewed could say with certainty that the agency had enough supply to replenish the groundwater pumped for all the new subdivisions in Pinal, Pima, and Maricopa counties that were enrolled in the GRD. In addition, hundreds of thousands of undeveloped lots had been titled on the basis of the GRD's theoretical capacity to recharge, but there was a widespread fear that this capacity had already been exceeded, or would be soon, and that any developers of these "premature subdivisions" would have to look elsewhere for their water supply. Phrasing the optimistic view that was endemic to Western water culture, Jim Holway, water specialist at the Sonoran Institute, explained that even "if the GRD worked for twenty years and we had to create something new, if the demand is there and the money is there to pay for it, then we will figure it out."

Efforts at conservation on the demand side had shown mixed results. Other Arizona cities like Tucson and Flagstaff successfully reduced consumption by combining water-rate regulations with a slate of voluntary measures. Greater Phoenix, with its patchwork map of competing municipalities, was another matter. County authority was weak by design and there was little political will to regulate water consumption, either through land-use reform or water-rate hikes. As ASU's Patricia Gober pointed out, it was impractical to talk of a "regional" approach when there were as many as 120 water providers in the Valley, ranging from small companies set up to pump groundwater for a planned community to the mammoth Salt River Project (SRP), which owns or operates a vast network of canals, dams, hydroelectric plants, coal-fired electricity generating stations, as well as a large share of Palo Verde, the nation's largest nuclear power plant. The result was a very uneven map. Core urban communities within the SRP service area had a relatively stable water supply, but the water resources of fast-growth communities on the fringe were much more vulnerable, and that is where many low-income families, lured by subprime loans, had located in the last decade.

The most far-flung parts of the metropolis already functioned at what Gober called "the edge of habitality."[45]

> We will see spot shortages, as traditional sources are in short supply, and wells will begin to run dry. So what happens when they run out of water and we sit here [in Tempe] with water aplenty? How will these regional conflicts play out among the haves and the have nots? I've seen pictures of homeowners in Tempe hosing down driveways, wasting water at the same time as people in urban fringe communities are hauling in water in trucks to maintain their lifestyle while their housing values fall and while their water becomes increasingly expensive. How does that social, political, and economic dynamic play out when the first signs of shortage start to appear? That's the canary in the coal mine here.

Yet a similar question mark also hung over the future of supply distribution among the more water-secure, centrally located populations. Affluent Scottsdale, where per capita water consumption was among the highest of any city in the West,[46] depends on CAP water, while the low-income neighborhoods of South Phoenix rely on SRP water from the Salt–Verde watershed. If either of these delivery systems were in seriously short supply, would the communities cooperate with each other on a regional basis? Given how long and bitterly the basin states had fought over Colorado water, and continued to do so, no one expected California or Nevada to bail out Arizona if or when the cutbacks come. Would the same fractious distrust emerge between cities and communities in Maricopa County, and what would it look like?

The uneven geography of scarcity sketched out by Gober was a more telling scenario of the future than any that anticipated a disastrous net shortfall for the region. If or when the Valley's water supplies are no longer sustainable, the inequalities between populations will have more clear-cut consequences. Will communities act to protect their own hoard, turning their backs on the thirsty, or will a more cooperative culture develop to ensure that no one is cut off? Some theories suggest that the Hohokam faced this very challenge. In times of optimal river flow, there was more integration and communication between the populations in their two major canal systems, but, under drought conditions, water rights and group membership tightened, social balkanization set in, and territorial and family hoarding increased. Did the retreat from region-wide coopera-tive ties hasten the society's demise? Would the Hohokam have stemmed or reversed their decline if they had developed a stronger network of mutual aid, rather than turning their backs on one another? Such ques-tions not only apply to the past, they may also become relevant to the future of cities like Phoenix, just as surely as they are playing out in many semiarid regions of the world, where glacier loss from climate change is tightening the noose around populations already hard hit by the rapid decline in freshwater access.

COSTS OF NONCOOPERATION

Settlements in relatively rainless regions thrive best if they are truly coop-erative endeavors. Like the Mormons in Utah's Great Basin, Phoenix's nineteenth-century Anglo settlers quickly learned this lesson by banding together as the Salt River Valley Users Association (now a private corpora-tion that governs the quasi-public SRP monopoly) to knock out a deal with the government to build a dam, and eventually a vast water control system.[47] Reliance on collective provision for water, and then on several decades of federal investment in defense industry jobs and suburban infrastructure, had made government funding into a bedrock feature of the Valley's economy. Arizona is still a big net importer of taxpayer revenue. Yet this heavy dependence on federal largesse that supports the commonweal is not reflected in a political culture where strenuous local versions of libertarianism glorify an individualistic property rights mind-set that sanctions acts of predatory land speculation. Often cited in short-hand as the "frontier mentality," this outlook is associated with self-reliance, but it is the bane of the kind of cooperative sentiment that makes for resilient communities.

Most of my interviewees were skeptical about the ability of their fel-low citizens to think and act beyond their own interests. In a typical commentary, Jonathan Fink, a director of sustainability initiatives at ASU, observed that he could not "see responsibility towards the commons emerging as a major factor in Phoenix, given the kind of people who have chosen to move here over the last fifty years." Most often, this lack of trust in others was targeted at the region's large retiree communities (too self-absorbed to care and opposed to levies like school taxes), or at the heavily Mormon populations in East Valley cities like Mesa, Gilbert, and Chandler, whose uncompromising right-wing representatives held sway in the legislature. But the skepticism was just as likely to apply to those who had arrived too recently or who were unlikely to stay long enough to establish a sense of civic responsibility. These misgivings about the cooperative ability of others did not augur well for mutual action in the face of resource scarcity.

Weak community ties were to be expected in a relatively new and fast-growing city. In this regard, many of the Sunbelt's boomtowns were in the same boat, as were the megacities of Asia, the Middle East, and Africa, swelling with new migrants from the countryside and already facing down chronic freshwater shortages. For the more vulnerable, a combination of geography, wealth, and power already determined how the water was divided up. This informal and unequal method of allocating scarce resources would become more common as the aquifers below cities sank further, and the snowpacks and glaciers in the high country melted away. In the 1990s, in many countries, corporations like Suez Lyonnaise, Veolia Environnement, and RWE moved aggressively to privatize water management and supply. These schemes were viewed, and actively resisted, as efforts on the part of elites to monopolize resources by enclosing the commons.[48] As a result of the pushback, conscientious officials have begun to remunicipalize their cities' water supply, and, in July 2010, the United Nations General Assembly took a stand against marketization by declaring for the first time that access to clean water and sanitation is a fundamental human right.

Eastern states in the United States observed this public trust doctrine by adopting the riparian code of English common law, which grants usufructuary rights to landowners on a river's banks, allowing them to use water they cannot own. In the Western states, private water rights tend to prevail over public trust. Surface water in Arizona, as elsewhere, is governed by the doctrine of *prior appropriation* (or "first in time is first in right"), which grants absolute rights to the first, beneficial users.[49] Legal application of the doctrine all but transformed water into a direct commodity (since rights were transferable, through lease or sale) that could be transported to other locations. As a result whole rivers would come to be diverted in flagrant violation of their natural integrity. Since prior appropriation penalized efforts at conservation (and encouraged a "use it or lose it" mentality), the doctrine resulted in waste, hoarding, and overconsumption, not to mention the widespread collapse of riparian communities when river flows were dammed or deviated.[50]

As the West's water economy shifted from extractive and agricultural uses to urban consumption, the doctrine of prior appropriation has evolved over time. Its obituary has been written more than once, but it has survived, alongside emerging water markets, as the default mode of allocating water in the now highly urbanized West.[51] It has even been adapted to coexist, albeit uneasily, with federal environmental mandates that pre-empt state laws. The doctrine's endurance helps to explain why the infamous water wars of the West were not an inevitable outcome of water scarcity; they were determined by the competition that arose from regarding water as private property.

A less cutthroat alternative with deep, historical roots in the region did exist, both in the Hohokam record, and in the communal water ethos of *acequias* that prevailed in the Hispanic Southwest during the Spanish and Mexican periods. That system of water sharing, which was superseded by prior appropriation, was based on customary, usufructuary rights. Agroecologists agree that this system was an effective form of environmental management that served communities well, and with a high degree of equity, under conditions of periodic scarcity. Remnants of that cooperative culture can be found in the surviving *acequias* of New Mexico and Colorado. In effect, they are self-governing water districts (the oldest extant governmental units in North America) whose gravity-driven irrigation systems have done a remarkable job of preserving soil and water quality over the centuries.

The original SRP was a self-governing venture undertaken in a cooperative spirit that one of my interviewees likened to the *acequia*. If there was a plausible comparison to be made in those early years, it faded rapidly as the SRP ballooned into a complex political entity, with technologically intensive operations on a scale as large as any utility in the country. The present-day corporation had taken steps to reduce its water allotments (by as much as 33 percent) to the irrigation shareholders in its original reservoir district, championed a conservation drive among customers, and generally promoted its environmental stewardship, but no one would hold the SRP up as a exemplar of water democracy or of riparian integrity. The very existence of its vast plumbing network ran counter to the growing trend among water experts to "leave water in place." Yet its longevity and foundational role in the city's history had given the SRP plenty of bragging rights.

So, too, its service area—however artificial as a water ecosystem—was now a conveniently central territory around which to draw a growth limit. Journalist Jon Talton, who was the most tireless local critic of the Central Arizona growth machine, argued that all future migration should be channeled into the SRP's 250,000-acre system footprint. This would restore some semblance of a sustainable center to the sprawling metropolis, and it could be done by raising taxation and water pricing on exurban areas outside the core. The alternative, he pointed out, was that "the heat may do this anyway," referring to the likely impact of climate change on the watersheds of the rivers—Salt, Verde, Agua Fria, Gila, and Colorado—on which the region was so solicitously dependent.[52] There was zero chance of this proposal being taken up, as Talton well knew, but, as the Southwestern drought lengthened and the mercury steadily climbed, who would bet against the alternative?

As ever, Phoenix was a ripe target for writers willing to imagine that alternative in the form of the city's demise. The latest effort could be found in geologist James Lawrence Powell's 2010 book, *Dead Pool: Lake Powell, Global Warming, and the Future of Water in the West*, where, in the concluding pages of his analysis of the crisis facing the Colorado River supply, he offers a vignette of the eco-collapse of Phoenix in the 2020s:

> With both surface [water] and groundwater supplies severely limited and no relief in sight, Phoenix declares a stage-four water emergency, its highest level. The state legislature rescinds the Groundwater Management Act. Voluntary reductions having long since failed to conserve enough water, Phoenix enforces rationing.... Valves attached to water meters automatically shut off the flow when consumption exceeds the limit. Armed water police with the authority to shut off valves and make arrests patrol neighborhoods. Phoenix doubles the price of water to residences, raises it even more for the heaviest water users, and prohibits new water hook-ups. Home construction shuts down and the once-booming central Arizona real estate market collapses. As tax revenues decline, Phoenix runs short of funds and rating agencies reclassify its bonds as junk.
>
> Following Nevada's example, Phoenix begins to build a desalting plant on the Sea of Cortés. But as the border crisis intensifies, and with its own water supplies at dangerous lows, Mexico nationalizes all American-owned factories in the country, including the desalting plants and the maquiladoras. By the 2020s, with water, the stuff of life at stake, it is every nation for itself.
>
> Businesses and families begin to abandon Phoenix, creating a Grapes of Wrath-like exodus in reverse. Long lines of vehicles clog the freeways, heading east towards the Mississippi and north toward Oregon and Washington.

Burning hot, parched, and broke, the city that rose from the ashes achieves its apogee and falls back toward the fire.[53]

Phoenix is the most environmentally challenged of American cities, and so the likelihood of its succumbing so melodramatically to a Hohokam or Mesopotamian fate might depend, ultimately, on a failing water supply. But a small multitude of consequential decisions stood in the way, pointing the city toward or away from its fate as just another Southwestern ghost town. Prominent among them, as we shall see in the next chapter, was whether real estate market growth, currently in its most crumbled condition, would once again be permitted to dictate how people lived on these desert lands.

CHAPTER 2
The Road Runner's Appetite

"I meant no harm. I most truly did not. But I had to grow bigger. So bigger I got. I biggered my factory. I biggered my roads. I biggered my wagons. I biggered the loads.... And I biggered my money, which everyone needs."

Dr. Seuss, *The Lorax*

Political and business leaders know that their defects and blunders will be excused if they turn in a respectable growth performance. The quarterly or annual gains in corporate revenue or GDP are really all that matters. But when and why did these raw metrics come to surpass all other indicators of well-being? Although growth is often seen as integral to any capitalist system of accumulation, its recognition as a society's only relevant standard of worth is largely a postwar development.[1] For example, four-fifths of U.S. growth has occurred in the last fifty years, some part of it driven by Cold War competition to prove the superiority of a market economy. The consensus mood that developed after 1945—which historians have called "growth liberalism"—presided over an expansionist boom in the industrialized world that did not contract until the 1970s.[2] Subsequent doctrines—the supply-side gospel of the Reagan era, the high-tech evangelism of the 1990s, and the asset ownership creed of the 2000s—were all aimed at reviving and boosting the high growth rates that managers of a consumer society had come to expect.

Growthmanship spread abroad, along with the internationalization of production, and soon growth in GDP became the most important yardstick for nations, whether in the advanced or the developing world. Slowing growth rates were a cause for concern, while falling numbers were a sign that something was awry, and that close scrutiny, even intervention, from the World Bank or the International Monetary Fund was in the offing. Those who believed or behaved otherwise were not wrong; they were simply treated as dropouts from modernity. So entrenched was this orthodoxy that *The Limits to Growth,* the momentous 1972 Club of Rome report that concluded that current rates of industrial growth could not be sustained ecologically in the long term, was received among business and policy elites as a genuinely heretical document that had to be publicly pilloried.

Subsequent surveys, drawing upon a wider range of experts and a more comprehensive collection of scientific data, amplified the 1972 warning about the ruinous impact of unrestrained growth. In 2002, the *Limits to Growth* team reprised their original study, confirming the original predictions of economic and civilizational collapse in the course of the twenty-first century. That same year, 1,700 leading figures issued the World Scientist Warning to Humanity, calling on developed nations to drastically curb their overconsumption of resources. These estimates of eco-collapse were reinforced by the UN's Millennium Ecosystem Assessment, released in 2005, which had deployed more than 1,500 international scientists for four years to analyze the latest data. Last but not least, there came the influential testimony of the Nobel Prize–winning Intergovernmental Panel on Climate Change. Since its first report in 1990, which strongly supported the thesis of anthropogenic global warming, it has issued periodic assessments, each one more confident about the ability of the models used to calculate climate change and its calamitous impact.

Top-level resistance to absorbing and acting on this information has been profound, and is often compared, with some reason, to the force of religious dogma. Looking back on more than thirty years of widely publicized verification of all of these dire warnings, Dennis Meadows (one of the authors of *Limits to Growth*), reflected on why they "did not prompt any fundamental changes in the policies that govern growth in population or industrial activity and that are driving this planet to major ecological disruptions." Breaking with the gospel of growth, he concluded, has been the equivalent of overturning the most deeply rooted system of belief: "Think of the Catholic Church condemning Galileo to life imprisonment for his suggestion that the universe does not revolve around the earth."[3]

No doubt typical of this fundamentalist response were the views of Larry Summers (a leading economist in both the Obama and Clinton administrations), when he was a kingpin at the World Bank in 1991. "There are no limits on the planet's capacity for absorption likely to hold us back in the foreseeable future," he wrote in a notorious memo that also advocated outsourcing dirty industries to developing, or "underpolluted," countries. "The danger of an apocalypse due to global warming or anything else is non-existent," he continued and concluded that "the idea that the world is heading into the abyss is profoundly wrong. The idea that we should place limits on growth because of natural limitations is a serious error." It is possible that, in the intervening years, Summers had heeded Keynes's dictum—"When the facts change, I change my mind"—but there was no evidence of such a conversion. Nor, for all the improvements in environmental policymaking it introduced, did the Obama administration come close to pushing an alternative to carbon-based GDP growth as the lodestone of its economic policymaking. Larger federal investments in renewable sectors such as clean energy, mass transit, and smart grids were still dwarfed by the subsidies handed out to high-carbon industries, nor was climate change legislation accorded priority attention, not even during the long nightmare of BP's Gulf oil spill, the most optimal moment for any president to sue for divorce from fossil-fuel dependency. The time could not have been riper in general to reset industrial policy, but the will to do so was up against the much stronger (and easier) belief that a return to positive short-term growth figures would be the panacea for the recession's ills. Yet feeding the GDP beast meant turning away from the dictates of healthy living—good health, after all, actually equates with negative GDP because it does not lead to medical expenditures that show up as monetary exchanges.[4]

Those looking for insights into how to crack the seemingly unassailable dogma of growth had to look far beyond the ranks of alpha economists who cultivate and polish the national indicators of growth like the GDP or the Consumer Price Index. Cities, where a new generation of urban managers was now riding the sustainability bandwagon, were the obvious place to turn. Their predecessors had contracted a very bad case of the postwar growth bug, and it would take some powerful medicine to flush the effects out of the system. Harvey Molotch's classic 1976 study of the "urban growth machine" explained how easily all of a city's local institutions come to support the consensus that growth is good. On an individual basis, developers, newspapers, unions, utilities, universities, arts organizations, big retailers, small businesses, and sports franchises all stand to profit from expanding urban populations and markets. Because growth appears to "benefit everyone," it is cheered on by boosters, and enabled by politicians and planners. But honest fiscal analyses show that most forms of urban growth are not at all beneficial. Molotch argued that the costs of servicing the additional population with infrastructure and municipal resources can be exponentially expensive and that these services far

Figure 2.1
Money crash in the Great Recession. Photo by author.

exceed the public benefit that accrues from an increased tax base.[5] As for the corresponding rise in environmental degradation, the costs, if they were properly accounted for, would surely break apart every municipal budget.

One of the paradoxical results of this mismatch is that urban managers encourage faster growth simply to stay ahead of the cost curve. Growth A does not pay for itself, so it begets Growth B to cover the costs of A, and so on. This method of deferring a final reckoning (some would call it a Ponzi scheme) has no horizon other than the next crash—during the most recent credit bubble, the debts simply got restructured, repackaged, and sold as derivatives. Most American boomtowns match this profile of growth machines that go into overdrive when conditions are ripe, but none had accepted growth as its reason for being with such equanimity as the spreading metropolis of Phoenix. With building at a virtual standstill for the first time in more than sixty years, and almost half of the state's homeowners holding negative equity, and an alarming number of them out of work, there was a lot of talk around town about ditching the dependency on growth. What were the odds of legislating responses to hunger for change and what forces stood in the way?

BUILDING HOUSES FOR PEOPLE WHO ARE BUILDING HOUSES

Long before the emergence of the specter of climate change, no one would have faulted the managers of a desert city like Phoenix for deciding to set limits to the urban population that could be supported by available water resources. Yet that had not been a politically feasible option during the region's sixty-year growth spurt, not when so much local pride and municipal revenue were tied to the prize of being the nation's fastest-growing city (and one of the most populous overall—Phoenix nosed into fifth place in the course of the 2000s). Even in the trough of the Great Recession, and confronted with evidence of a stationary, or even shrinking population (the 2010 census saw Philadelphia regain the fifth slot), boosters stuck tenaciously to estimates of steady, long-term growth right up to the point when the region would be fully "built-out." No doubt, this blithe optimism was a resilient part of the Valley's culture, but it was a clear obstacle to what green advocates define as resilient cities.

Nationally, the 1980s and 1990s witnessed a rise in public concern about the environmental costs of runaway suburban growth, feeding into the anti-sprawl movement and its policy offshoot of "smart growth." These sentiments did not bypass the Valley, where urban liberals' burgeoning interest in their quality of life prompted calls for growth management legislation. In a 1998 study commissioned by the legislature, the Morrison Institute, which reliably mirrors the concerns of policy elites, noted that "the historic pro-growth posture is being seriously questioned." The study laid out all the reasons why growth does not pay for itself and issued a roster of recommendations, but none of them were seriously heeded by a legislature under the sway of the homebuilders lobby.[6] Yet after only one failed effort, Citizens for Growth Management, a coalition spearheaded by the Sierra Club, succeeded in placing a proposition on the 2000 ballot. It was the nation's first-ever proposal to impose strict growth controls over an entire state; Proposition 202 called for the adoption of urban growth boundaries by every Arizona county, city, and town with over 2,500 inhabitants. Early polls showed the initiative had around 70 percent voter support, but the growth lobby spent far and wide to reverse those numbers (70 percent ended up voting against), delivering a crystal-clear warning that no legislation would be permitted that spoiled the appetite for urban fringe expansion.

Grady Gammage, Jr., was among the prominent figures who opposed Proposition 202. A land-use attorney who doubled as a public policy advocate at the Morrison Institute, his shrewd reasoning and widely cited views had made him one of the Valley's most influential opinion makers.

(N.B.: To be taken seriously as a public voice in Phoenix, it was almost de rigueur to have one foot in the land-development industry.) His father had been president of ASU for three decades, but, like almost everyone else, had dabbled in land development as if it were a card-playing hobby; "He was always getting together with a bunch of other college professors and buying a little bit of land here or there. He always sold it too early. He never made very much money on it but he thought it was fun."[7]

Proposition 202 supporters had been hopeful about winning Gammage over, but he could hardly afford to be dispassionate in the matter. Throwing his support behind the initiative, as he explained, "would have been politically very dangerous for me." As someone who earned his living representing big developers down at City Hall, he explained that he "skated the thin edge of advocating for things my clients already don't like," and Proposition 202 would have been "over my edge." In addition, Gammage believed that the initiative was an "insufficiently thought-out solution" to the problems posed by the region's hypergrowth, one more suited to cities that were "at risk of running out of land," which clearly was not the case in Central Arizona. In retrospect, Gammage "wondered if Prop 202 would have worked better as a rate-of-growth proposal, allowing towns to regulate the speed at which they expanded. In high-growth periods," he ventured, "people get more upset about that around here than they do about the geography of growth."

The year before Proposition 202 was voted down, Gammage published a lively book, subtitled "Reflections on Developing the Desert," where he weighed in with his own proposal for growth regulation. Estimates of the region's water supply, he argued, should be used to project a sustainable population and that figure should serve as a growth cap by consensus. By Gammage's own calculation (he had once served as president of the CAP board), the assured water supply would comfortably support a "future city of seven million, built in a pattern much like our current metropolis—a community of detached single-family homes at a relatively uniform density of between 2,500 and 3,000 citizens per square mile."[8] On the face of it, there was not much in the proposal to offend even Gammage's most hard-nosed clients. His estimated population limit was double the size of Metro Phoenix at the time of the 2000 Census, and the projected density was a faithful reflection of what he described as "our current values," meaning a preference for the low-density suburban housing that the development industry held sacrosanct. Even so, the proposal set off alarm bells at a time when the notion that the region's water supply could support 10 to 12 million was widely accepted. "People thought that I had lost my mind," he recalled. "'You are going to have population police turning people away?' I had to explain that I was not talking about a hard limit, but rather, how do we think about a mature Phoenix that is no longer growing fast, and how do we adjust public policies accordingly, because all of our policies are built on fast growth—it is the goal of Phoenix as an enterprise. This concept was completely dismissed by practically everyone I talked to. 'If we don't grow fast we will die,' they said. Most American cities are not any longer hypergrowth cities," he pointed out, "but it is so embedded into the consciousness of this place that I couldn't even have a dialogue with people."

Gammage had earned a reputation as an articulate defender of Phoenix's historical patterns of development against its most clamorous anti-sprawl critics. Indeed, he has argued (and not wryly either) that "what others see as sprawl we see as our heritage" and has insisted that Phoenicians fully embrace this legacy: "mass-produced suburban ranch homes are to Phoenix what Victorians are to San Francisco, brownstones to Philadelphia or bungalows to Los Angeles—a signature of the lifestyle heritage upon which a city is built."[9] Like other urbanists who warn against judging twentieth-century Sunbelt cities by the standards of more compact nineteenth-century industrial ones in the Northeast and Midwest, Gammage believed that Phoenix stacked up well against its pro-sprawl peers. Contrary to the most common understanding of sprawl, the metro area, he argued, had a fairly "clean edge." Because water provision required some forethought, it had acted as "liquid glue," producing a settlement pattern with a much narrower range of density—between two and six units per acre—than other postwar boomtowns. Commuting times and per capita energy consumption were at or below the national average, and trends were running against extravagant outdoor use of water. For example, the fashion among the affluent for desert xeriscaping was beginning to dislodge the taste for ash and maple trees, thereby coaxing a more ecologically appropriate "brown city" out of the wasteful green patchwork of suburban lawns.

Despite these indicators of normalcy, the abrupt collapse of the region's economy after 2007 showed how much of Phoenix's buoyancy relied on the single factor of servicing population growth. By the end of 2009, the rate of job loss in Arizona outran all other states, and unemployment stood at well over 10 percent of the workforce. Central Arizona's mass assembly builders—Pulte, Centex, KB, Morrison—had gone silent, or were filing, like Fulton Homes, for Chapter 11 bankruptcy. Lenders had foreclosed on 70,000 homes, housing values had fallen 50 percent, half of the state's homeowners were "underwater," and realty brokers reported that more than 60 million square feet of commercial space was lying vacant.[10] A year later, the rate of home foreclosures was still rising; almost

66,000 Arizona homeowners lost their houses to the mortgage holder in 2010, 12 percent more than in 2009.[11]

Worst of all for the region's self-image, people had stopped moving in. When an Urban Land Institute survey in the fall of 2009 reported that population levels had been flat for the past two years, the news brought cheers from those who had expected worse, even though the estimate concealed the fact that many Valley residents were so deep in housing debt they could no longer afford to move. Nor did the numbers reflect the departure of undocumented immigrants who had taken flight when the construction jobs dried up, or when the anti-immigrant mood turned ugly. A Department of Homeland Security estimate showed a drop of 100,000 (18 percent of the state's total) in the undocumented population over the course of 2008 alone.[12] Of course, those figures were a comfort to nativists who were all too happy to see that targeted portion of the area population shrinking.

The crash took a heavy toll on the booster psychology that had so reliably drawn wave after wave of Midwestern in-migrants, "equity refugees" from California, and "Alzheimer's buyers," as one developer described his retiree clientele to me. Even so, government agencies continued to turn out rosy growth estimates. In a fall 2009 survey, planners at the Maricopa Association of Governments projected 400 miles of new highways (double the current number) and 320 miles of new rail by 2050 to support future population expansion into the East and West Valleys. But such estimates were based on long-term migration data, or on existing land-development rights, and they assumed that jobs aplenty would materialize. No one I interviewed could see a favorable climate in the near future for job creation, and most were quick to back the belief that Phoenix was a "one-industry town," overly dependent on land development for employment and revenue.

This was a long-running diagnosis. Two decades earlier, after the last big real estate crash, a much-cited 1988 article in *Barron's* magazine estimated that 20 percent of jobs, and one out of every three of the regional economy's dollars, were tied to land development.[13] In response to the article, business, government, and academic elites launched a public-private initiative (Arizona Strategic Planning for Economic Development) to diversify the region's economy with high-tech clusters. But the recovery of the housing sector proved too lucrative to ignore, and home building quickly reasserted its dominance over the workforce and the general economy. Shortly thereafter, when *Arizona Republic* editorial writer Katherine Ingley moved from California, she was told that the business of Phoenix was growth. "It struck me as weird," she told me. "You are building houses for people who are building houses? How is this possible?"

Developers I interviewed were not slow to acknowledge the excesses of the real estate industry over the course of the fifteen-year housing boom. "The party was so good for so long," conceded John Graham, CEO of SunBelt Holdings (developer of golf and residential master-planned communities) and president of the Urban Land Institute (ULI) chapter. "Then it was as if someone hit the light switch," he added, "and things deteriorated overnight." Graham, who had been through several boom-and-busts, saw the current recession as "structurally different" and fervently hoped "it would break the cycle of bad judgment and bad policy, and improve the pace and quality of development." A former board chair of the state's Nature Conservancy affiliate, Graham was on the "ethical" end of his industry, favoring land preservation and what the ULI called "balanced development." Regardless, he could not envisage anything other than a warm return to housing growth, albeit at a slower rate. Even if efforts to diversify economically were to succeed, he expected that metro Phoenix would "always be a growth-driven economy." What rate of growth would the development industry consider to be sustainable? In his view, that would be 25,000 units per year, rather than the 60,000 to 70,000 units that had been built annually at the peak of the credit bubble, many of them on a purely speculative basis.

Randolph Birrell, an executive for one of the city's largest merchant builders, was less repentant. "Growth will be always be the business of this town, and that makes sense, because we have some of the best people in that business right here." According to this view, it was the developer who "created" growth, rather than responded to demand. Previous growth estimates, he pointed out, "have always fallen short, and people obviously love to move out here for the lifestyle and freedom. There are no real limits to the land we can build on." Birrell's firm was currently looking into infill opportunities, but he had no doubt it would return to outlying tract development when the growth machine cranked up again. "It's a big speed bump right now," he acknowledged, "but it's still just a speed bump and our industry will lead Phoenix over it."

Not everyone saw home building as the primary driver of growth. Elliott Pollack, an economic consultant whose voice was frequently featured in the city's media, warned me: "Don't let anyone tell you that land development runs this place. It is an effect and not a cause. If jobs were not created, people would not move here, and there would be no reason to develop one stick in the ground. Land development is a domestic and not a base sector item, and people get confused about the difference." No doubt, he had reasons to be defensive. Like so many other legislators and public opinion makers, Pollack had a large professional stake in land development. Aside from his consultancy, which did economic feasibility forecasts for its clients, he ran a real estate business. "We are in areas all over metropolitan Phoenix," he explained. "We originally bought land and sat on it, waiting for value to grow," but, after the late 1980s crash, the realty firm moved more aggressively into "assembling properties, putting in infrastructure and selling them off to homebuilders."

Conflicts of interest aside, Pollack was in no two minds that something had to change: "Phoenix is at an economic crossroads. We've been living off the same economic base for about fifty years, and that base [electronics, semiconductors, and aerospace] has run its course." The "high road," he reasoned, would be tied "to some form of manufacturing, software, or export-related industry. If this creates high-wage jobs and a demand for higher quality housing, then the growth will continue, and there will be more pressure for infill and high-rise housing." As for the low road, "if we continue to become a population-based economy, then per capita income declines, and it becomes a relatively poor place, dependent on retirees and tourists, and most of the housing will be of moderate quality and on the periphery."

Pollack's forecasts had comfortably guided the developers who rode the boom, and so, when the 2010 session began, GOP legislators turned to him to devise tax incentives to attract these new, high-road employers to the state. He clearly believed that government had a role to play in fostering economic resilience. Indeed, his proposal to the legislature focused on cutting business taxes, even though Arizona's were already very low (forty-first among all states). As for sustainability, Pollack saw it as an issue that the market would take care of. "People will not do it because it is perceived as the right thing to do," he asserted, "but when they see an economic benefit from doing it, and that is the great thing about the capitalist system." As for global warming, he echoed the denialist view of climate change that was prevalent on the Republican side of the aisle. "These are the same scientists that said we were going to go into another ice age, over 40 years ago, and had ideas on how we could warm the planet." Even if anthropogenic global warming were a reality, he believed that "the jury is still out on whether or not we can do anything, because it may be too late." Indeed, as an economist, he was intrigued by the prospect that "it would be cheaper ultimately to deal with the fallout." He mentioned a Wharton study that "ran some models of what would happen if the seas rose two feet and if you had a major shift in the population" from climate change. "The conclusion," he recalled, "was that, however expensive, it would still be cheaper to deal with it than trying to prevent it." Economists, he concluded, could probably cost it all out, even though they had never made it their business to factor ecological impacts into their own forecasting models.

Later that week, at the state Capitol, I quizzed Chuck Gray, a top-ranking Republican senator from East Mesa, on how he and his colleagues approached the topic of climate change. "I don't think the American public is being properly educated about what CO_2 is," he told me. "When they say greenhouse emissions, it sounds evil, but it's not—'greenhouse' means flourishment of life. If you look at what a greenhouse is, it is a place where life can grow, and it's great for plants, and plants need humans, and humans need plants." Pressed to elaborate on the topic, he recalled being "taught that plants took the CO_2 we produce and turned it into oxygen," and that "in CO_2-enriched environments, plants do better, so, as the climate gets a little warmer you have more food for more people, which means that we can ship more food to the poor because of CO_2." Gray was no less dismissive of the "cap and trade" proposal for reducing emissions, even though it was a market-based mechanism. "It's based on the fallacy that CO_2 is somehow a bad gas. CO_2 is what you and I exhale every time we breathe and somehow now that is poisonous? I don't understand that." I can vouch that my second-grader, who tagged along on some of my interviews, had a more accurate understanding of greenhouse gases than that offered by the majority leader of the Arizona Senate. Nor was Gray a particularly extreme member of the "Kookocracy," a term habitually used by Jon Talton, former columnist for the *Arizona Republic,* to scold Arizona's political class.

Contenders for the kookiest of all would include state senator Sylvia Allen (R-Snowflake), who rewrote Geology 101 while arguing for a 2009 bill to allow more uranium mining. "This earth," she declared, "has been here for 6,000 years, long before anyone had any environmental laws, and somehow it hasn't been done away with. We need to get the uranium here in Arizona so that this state can get the revenue from it, which can be done safely, and you will never even know the mine was there when they are gone." Allen's safety assurances gave little comfort to the many Arizonans (and especially the Navajo miners themselves) living near abandoned uranium mines who had suffered cancers, organ damage, miscarriages, and birth defects. Leaving aside her creationist views (the population of Snowflake was heavily Mormon), her interest in uranium was part of the big Republican push to steer public monies away from renewable energy toward extending the state's nuclear portfolio. If successful—John McCain, Jon Kyl, and the GOP establishment were united behind this initiative—Arizona would be the first state in the United States to build a new nuclear plant since 1977.

Kookiness was not the only reason why many of my interviewees complained long and hard about the vacuum of political leadership in Arizona. As in California, the increasing role of voter propositions meant that more and more political decisions were made by ballot, and many of these propositions (which were often poorly drafted and generated unintended consequences as a result) had drastically limited the power of legislators to make good or effective policy. Consequently, in a budget crisis, there were few options available to the politicians, and especially since many in the majority party (38 of Arizona's 90 lawmakers—the largest percentage of any state legislature), including Governor Jan Brewer, had signed Grover Norquist's Taxpayer Protection Pledge to "oppose and vote against any and all efforts to increase taxes." First in line to remind legislators that their job was to reduce taxes was the home builders association, which won its members a controversial freeze on all development-impact fees in September 2009.

So severe was the state's fiscal shortfall (sales taxes accounted for more than 50 percent of Arizona's revenue) that Brewer approved a plan for the buildings of the state Capitol and both legislative chambers to be auctioned off in a sale-leaseback arrangement.[14] The sell-off was just another real estate deal in Phoenix, but you would be challenged to match it for high symbolism. As government, at every level, took a shrinking pill, and ranking politicians lined up behind the boisterous anti-government pledges of the Tea Party, it was hard not to be reminded of Barry Goldwater's plea, in his manifesto, *Conscience of a Conservative*, "to entrust the conduct of our affairs to men who understand that their first duty as public officials is to divest themselves of the power they have been given."

FEDERALLY INSURED LIBERTARIANS

There was a good deal of daylight between Goldwater's strict libertarianism and the kinds of social conservatism that energized the GOP of today. Yet on economic issues, at least, the Arizona conservatives I interviewed saw themselves in a clear line of descent from the postwar coup staged by Goldwater's circle to establish GOP rule over what had been a Democratic stronghold. But what exactly was the basis of Goldwater's legacy in Arizona? According to the standard GOP view, he and other select members of the business elite unshackled the state's urban economy from the harnesses of the New Deal, whose agencies had been particularly active in Phoenix during the 1930s. In doing so, the story goes, they liberated the region from a dependency that dated to pre-statehood days when the Arizona Territory was no more than a federal outpost for the army—the Goldwater family store, no less, got its start from contracts for army provisioning. This dependency had been revived during World War II by the heavy military presence in the region. In the interim, Washington had lavishly backed the railroads and the mining enterprises that dug gold, silver, and copper out of the badlands, and, of course, Reclamation dollars flowed into dams and other waterworks.

In the heroic GOP narrative, Goldwater and his close allies—Walter Bimson, Valley National Bank kingpin and president of the American Banking Association, Frank Snell, the city's most powerful lawyer, and Eugene Pulliam, the exemplary press baron—stood Phoenix on its own feet. They did so by breaking the back of labor (in 1946, Arizona became the first right-to-work state in the West), curtailed the reach of government regulation, and turned the metro region into a free enterprise champion that attracted several hundred top companies in the key industries—electronics, aerospace, finance—that would drive postwar growth throughout the Sunbelt. A region that had long been treated as a colony for East Coast financiers to quarry for their own advantage created a homegrown alternative to Wall Street in the form of Bimson's Valley National Bank. Pro-growth boosters nurtured a business climate that challenged and outbid the influence of the Yankee corporate establishment by unleashing entrepreneurs and offering opportunities for all comers.

In truth, and as all historians have noted, the free enterprise continued to rely heavily on federal funding.[15] The money just flowed in a less direct fashion, and, most importantly, it was channeled into and through large corporations that used Phoenix's secure federal ties to turn it into a profitable branch town. The major firms that relocated to Phoenix in the immediate postwar era—Motorola, Honeywell, Sperry Rand, General Electric, Kaiser, Unidynamics, and AiResearch—all subsisted on Cold War defense contracts, and their decisions to locate in the region were shaped by the Pentagon's policy of decentralizing military production facilities away from the more vulnerable East Coast population centers. In this respect, their arrival was simply an extension of the wartime production programs that had drawn Goodyear, Alcoa, and others to Phoenix's arsenals, ordnance plants, and flight training facilities in the 1940s. These firms were pillars of the military-industrial complex, and the Sunbelt, or "Gunbelt" as Ann Markusen labeled it, became its homeland.[16] At the height of the Cold War, federal income for Arizona amounted to between 16 percent and 24 percent of the state's economy, after which there were sizable upswings during the Vietnam War and the rearmament years of the Reagan era.[17]

Everyone remembers Eisenhower's famous warning about the growing power over government policy of the military-industrial complex, but few recall Harry Truman's more persistent caveats about the influence of the real estate lobby. At its height, this was a formidable coalition, consisting of the trade associations of petroleum producers, auto manufacturers, road builders, home builders, land developers, real estate brokers, tire makers, and several other industrial players.[18] The lobbying power of this coalition ensured that the conversion of cheap farmland into suburban subdivisions would prove a dependable engine of consumption, year in and year out. Nor was this engine any less subsidized by the federal state, which underwrote every aspect of it—FHA-backed mortgages, homeowners' tax credits, oil subsidies, roads, highways, bridges, and other costly infrastructure. Even more than the defense contracts, the federal momentum behind home building drove Phoenix's phenomenal growth. Bimson's Valley National Bank built its lending reputation, and its reserves, on the back of FHA and RFC (Reconstruction Finance Corporation) loans. By the end of the 1930s, Del Webb, the construction magnate and future builder of Sun City, saw the benefits to be reaped from all of this federal backing and declared that "construction is no longer a private enterprise, it is a subsidiary of the national government."[19]

Far from standing on its own feet, then, Phoenix (and other Sunbelt cities) was a prime beneficiary of federal tax and spending policies that redistributed wealth and industry away from the Frostbelt states. The Goldwaterites' welcoming business climate was certainly a pull factor, but government policy supplied a good deal of the push. The federal tax structure, for example, allowed corporations to write off plant closures, count relocation as business expenses, and win lavish investment credits for new technology products. In effect, the corporate flight to the South and West to escape unions and regulations was heavily subsidized and refinanced by the federal government.[20] Frostbelt deindustrialization and Sunbelt growth were two sides of the same government coin. Even Jimmy Carter, who did little to stem the flight, complained in July 1977 to a reporter that "there has been too much of a channeling of federal monies into the Sunbelt states."[21] Indeed, some of the resentment channeled at the Obama administration stemmed from the perception that its economic policies were efforts to redistribute resources away from the Sunbelt.

Thomas Sheridan, ethnographer and Arizona historian, once quipped that "behind every rugged individual is a government agency."[22] How did Goldwater's followers reconcile their godfather's claim of independence from big government with this long record of federal largesse? Byron Schlomach, director of the Center for Economic Prosperity at the Goldwater

Institute, agreed "that if it were not for the federal government, Phoenix would not and probably should not exist, certainly not at the size that it exists today." That said, he affirmed that the Goldwater Institute was against "compounding that record with even more government projects aimed at creating artificial wealth." "Individuals," he declared, "are in a better position to determine what's good for them than government." Tom Jenney, the de facto head of the state's Tea Party movement, who described his job as "like herding cats," compared the strict libertarian's use of federally built projects to the American League baseball rule that allows another ballplayer to bat in place of a pitcher. "Maybe you believe there should be no designated hitter, that there should be no federal highway system, or that government shouldn't be doing big water projects, but as long as they are, then you're not going to stop drinking tap water, or driving on public roads. You can't be a monk and live on a pillar and wean yourself completely off state support."

The GOP hold on the legislature was strong enough to override the contradiction between their members' fierce anti-government rhetoric and the reliance on the federal dollar. "That is something that they hate to talk about," reported House minority leader Chad Campbell. "Look at healthcare or the highway system or any major program in the state and you are getting massive money from the federal government. When the stimulus package was passed this year, the majority party was railing against it but, of course, when the check came they had no trouble cashing or using it." Kyrsten Sinema, one of the most liberal of the Democrat representatives, often made common cause with conservative libertarians. "We share a lot of common values," she said, "and they are some of my greatest allies." The Mormon representatives on the other side of the aisle were a different matter. As a lapsed Mormon herself, it was more difficult for her to reconcile the era of her childhood, when the "LDS was not involved at all in politics," with today, when the church "largely controls the legislative process," having "infiltrated government and policymaking over the last decade and a half." Indeed, Sinema went to war against the LDS in 2006 when the Mormon church spent $8 million to fund a proposition banning same-sex marriage in the state. Having led the campaign that defeated the proposition, she was well positioned to distinguish the true libertarian descendants of Goldwater (who had himself supported gay rights) from their less tolerant GOP brethren.

Yet it would be a mistake to take even the libertarian rhetoric at face value. After all, the original Goldwaterites needed a strong state to build their vision of free enterprise in Phoenix. Without full government backing, they would not have been able to maintain the business climate—an antiunion environment with low taxes, cheap land, and lax regulation—that was their hallmark. That is why they strove to create a state that would make these goals its chief priority. Elizabeth Shermer has recently argued that Goldwater's postwar Phoenix was the birthplace of the doctrine of deregulation and privatization that much later came to be called neoliberalism.[23] Most commentators see neoliberalism as originating in the response of financial elites to New York City's fiscal crisis in 1975 and then spreading to other parts of the nation and the globe over the next three decades.[24] Shermer shows how Goldwater and his allies stopped the advance of the liberal New Deal in its tracks by using the Chamber of Commerce to seize control of local and state government (while using their federal ties to consolidate the takeover). In the aftermath, the new political class, taking their orders from the Chamber, installed deregulation and regressive taxation at the heart of their policymaking.

This political coup was planned by a small elite known as the Charter Government Committee (CGC), who successfully ran a slate in 1949 to stamp out corruption in city governance and went on to rule City Hall, virtually unopposed, until the mid-1970s. The CGC, according to historian Philip Vandermeer, "preached a model of 'selfless' civic participation, and denied the legitimacy of interest group politics," but it was an "organized, self-perpetuating group that chose candidates, planned their campaigns, and financed them."[25] The CGC slate took advantage of the city's charter reforms to run as citywide, or at-large, candidates. This at-large electoral status was created to root out vestiges of the old ward-based machines, but it quickly became a new kind of machine for the middle-class Anglo interests entrenched in North Phoenix. Working-class and minority-dominated districts had no functional representation on the city council for the next thirty years. But the real, or shadow, government resided in the Chamber, which effectively took over responsibility for economic development.

The Goldwaterites' success at remaking government in this fashion was emulated in other Sunbelt cities, and the template of their pro-growth policies is clearly visible today in those parts of the world where governments promote a friendly business climate in hopes of attracting offshore investors. When local officials in coastal Chinese provinces lure foreign corporations today with lavish tax incentives, discount labor, and all kinds of legal exemptions, they are using a playbook that was largely written by the businessmen-politicians of Phoenix in their Cold War heyday.

Investors, then and now, are attracted by the promise of cheap labor and less regulation, but their executives and top employees are also looking for a healthy residential setting for themselves and their families. So a very particular kind of environmental promotion is required to reel them in. On the one hand, it is communicated that enforcement of industrial waste regulations will be weak, and so a certain degree of industrial befouling is both expected and tolerated in zones of production. On the other, officials are assured that air and water quality will not be compromised in the desirable precincts where their high-wage employees will be likely to live.

In their prime, the Chamber's protagonists, concentrated in a cozy circle known as the Thunderbirds, understood and preached this dual gospel. They boosted the glories of Arizona's sun, mountains, open spaces, and crystal-clear air to prospective investors, and made full use of the celebrated landscape photography in the iconic magazine *Arizona Highways* to do so. But they were also pushing urban industrialization and were well aware of its dirty side effects. The more polluting industrial plants were channeled, as they always had been, to areas south of the tracks in the poorer, non-Anglo sections of town, or to the newer working-class suburbs like Maryvale. In striking contrast, North Phoenix, as it sloped up toward the higher mountain elevations, developed as a pristine residential preserve for outdoors-minded elites, epitomized in Paradise Valley, the name of its most sought-after enclave.

Although the Valley's growth had exploded in all directions since then, its social geography was still shaped by this two-sided environmental mentality. No less attuned to it were officials and legislators. Initiatives to preserve aesthetically pleasing tracts of land or soaring mountain views were popular with politicians, as well as developers, and, since the state owned 11 percent of the land in Arizona, they could be enacted with little public pain and without unduly impinging on the sanctity of private property rights.[26] But citizens' complaints about dirty industry or LULUs (Locally Unwanted Land Uses) in their neighborhoods were more likely to go unheard. The state's Department of Environmental Quality had a record of shutting down polluting factories only after disastrous explosions or fires had taken lives and made media headlines.

Until recently, this Janus-faced response to environmental issues had been the norm. Open space in the desert or mountains was where people could breathe free and was part of the Arizonan birthright extolled by the nature-loving Goldwater, who once wrote: "[W]hile I am a great believer in the free enterprise system and all that it entails, I am an even stronger believer in the right of our people to live in a clean and pollution-free environment."[27] Goldwater may not have seen these twin beliefs as mutually exclusive, but the antiregulatory growth machine that he and his associates bequeathed proved otherwise. It more or less required government, as I will show in a later chapter, to turn a blind eye to the poisoning of its most vulnerable citizenry.

GREEN FOR ALL?

Open space preservation and pollution controls are two items on the spectrum of urban sustainability, and they tend to occupy the more extreme ends of it. Activating the whole spectrum across a metropolitan region is a tough nut to crack. In a location like the Valley of the Sun, which lacks regional oversight (the legislature has never allowed any home rule for counties) and is weak on intergovernmental relations, the challenge is even more formidable. But even in the presence of a strong planning authority, top-down efforts at regulation are asking for trouble if they do have not roots in a community-level movement. Given the prevailing mood in the Arizona Legislature, there was little chance, in any event, of green policy-making coming from the top. Sustainability initiatives were more likely to be dismissed as intrusions on private property rights, or as self-destructive caps on short-term growth, and indeed most of the environmental advocates I interviewed had concluded that lobbying at the Capitol was virtually a waste of time. Sandy Bahr, longtime president of the state's Sierra Club chapter and leading public voice for the environmental advocates in the corridors of power, lamented that she had to listen to a lot of "wacky talk" there. Citing a recent subcommittee session that "focused on how increased levels of carbon dioxide are good for us," she summed up her dim view of the legislature: "It is not a body that has a vision for sustainability in any way. If they do, it's an ugly vision, and it's not an Arizona I would want to live in."

In 2006, California's legislature passed a Global Warming Solutions Act, which mandated state entities to reduce their greenhouse gas emissions to 1990 levels, and, in 2007, Attorney General Jerry Brown sued Santa Bernardino County for failing to observe this mandate in its general plan update. By contrast, the terms "global warming" and "greenhouse gas" were all but *verboten* in the chambers of Arizona's Capitol. In the absence of any action at the state level, municipal leaders in the Valley's cities had forged ahead with their own green agendas over the last decade. Yet, so prevalent was the libertarian mentality among the general population, they were often hesitant about giving a full public airing to their sustainability programs. For example, when Mayor Phil Gordon's much-publicized 17-point plan to make Phoenix "the greenest city in America" was rolled out, it had not been citizen-tested through the usual channels of public hearings or neighborhood committee meetings.

The case of neighboring Scottsdale offered another kind of lesson. Its Green Building Program (which offered developers expedited permitting, tax exemptions, and utility rebates if they opted to go green) was one of the most respected in the country, and it had propelled the city onto the national stage for showcasing sustainable cities. The program was a voluntary option for building owners, and though it had attracted about 50 percent of new residential construction at the height of the boom, the numbers had dwindled to between 25 percent and 30 percent in the depths of the recession. In a period of fast growth, the expediting had been a clear financial incentive, but, with applications sharply down, program director Anthony Floyd reported that "now anyone can get their plans approved in a short time period." A leading figure in the movement to adopt national and international green building codes, Floyd acknowledged that a mandatory program would be not be politically feasible and recalled that when the program was launched in 1998, local home builders were not at all interested. It only took off as a result of pressure from "enlightened consumers who were the home owners moving here from other locations. They knew about green building and they complained that no one here was doing it."

In cities with the best track record on sustainability, grassroots initiatives had flourished before they were taken up by policymakers and adopted into general, long-range plans governing the operation of every government department. This had been the case, for example, with Sustainable Seattle, a model much emulated by other cities.[28] Scottsdale, which had placed high in national rankings since the 1990s, also had the reputation of being a city where lawmakers took their cue from local environmental groups. Dating to the 1970s, there was a long record of support for desert preservation efforts on the part of residents, especially the more affluent ones to the north, whose one-acre lots were the most spacious in the Valley.[29] The strength of this community sentiment resulted in voter approval for the funding of large signature projects like Indian Bend Wash and the McDowell Mountain Preserve, and the growth of a municipal culture that took seriously landscape appreciation and open-space protection.

In the course of the 1990s, Scottsdale saw the formation of advocacy groups of environmentalists and design professionals, such as the Great Sonoran, and Arizona Vision Weavers, with which the dreadlocked Floyd had been associated. Their dialogues with city officials led to the adoption of a set of "community design expectations" (Scottsdale Sensitive Design Principles) aimed at "protecting the character of the Sonoran desert." These principles sat well with the property values and recreational lifestyles of upscale Scottsdale homeowners, as did the green building program that Floyd instituted. By contrast, there was less interest in, and more instinctive opposition to, initiatives that seemed more urban in character. "What I discovered early on," Floyd recalled, "was that it was much easier to do green building than a sustainability program. Having attended the public meetings, I knew that, in the northern part of the city, people had bought into their own individual lifestyle vision, and that public input was against the adoption of planning principles like alternative transportation, mixed use, and higher densities. Once you cross that line, and start talking about sustainable urbanism, then the preservationists are more opposed to it." It was not just for tourist purposes that Scottsdale held on to its anachronistic brand identity as the "West's Most Western Town," with a cowboyish Old Town at its center.

Understandably, Floyd had run with the safer option, the path of least resistance, and had made the best of it, establishing Scottsdale as a national stronghold for green building codes and design. His story was an instructive account of how to operate within the limits of community opinion, sticking to terra firma and giving wide berth to the political quagmires. But it also illustrated very well the social psychology behind the checklist approach to sustainability favored by city managers nation-wide. According to this model, communities got to cherry-pick from a menu of policy choices: open-space preservation, mass transit, farmers markets, public composting, congestion fees, bike lanes, green building codes, mixed-use zoning, renewable energy, high-density overlays, local sourcing, clean fleets, mandatory recycling, and so on.[30] As with any menu of possible choices, the selection made by low-density suburban popula-tions will likely diverge from that of urbanites committed to denser, downtown living.

But to low-income populations whose basic needs have not been met, any such checklist may seem like an extravagance. Why should these kinds of green items take priority over the responsibility of city managers to provide good air and water quality, affordable housing, public safety, decent jobs, adequate education, and accessible healthcare? Are the latter any less integral to urban sustainability? Metro Phoenix was a good place to ask this question. It already sported features of the kind of eco-apart-heid that Van Jones, Obama's short-lived green jobs advisor, feared might grow out of the embryonic green economy: "On one side of town, there would be ecological 'haves,' enjoying access to healthy, morally upstanding green products and services. On the other side of town, ecological 'have-nots' would be languishing in the smoke, fumes, toxic chemicals, and ill-nesses of the old pollution-based economy."[31] In Jones's vision of "Green for All," where low-income populations have equal access to green jobs and services, no one can afford to be left behind; everyone has to be on board if the "eco-apocalypse" is to be averted. "If the green economy remains a niche market, even a large one, then the excluded 80 percent will inevitably and perhaps unknowingly undo all of the positive ecological impacts of the green 20 percent."[32]

Longtime critics of the growth pattern known as sprawl argue that some of the conditions for what Jones describes as "eco-apartheid" are rooted in the continued relocation to the urban fringe of investment, employment, commercial retail, and services. The reduced circumstances of central-city populations—less job opportunities, longer work commutes, diminished consumer options—are directly connected to the centrifugal push of the growth machine. No more equitable is the tax burden on those who foot the bill for the costly infrastructure of sprawl. Urban residents pay more than their share for the highways and surface roads, utility lines, and tax breaks for business relocation that disproportionately benefit suburban populations. In the face of these inequities, analysts are hard pressed to find evidence that "growth pays for itself." When the environmental impacts are factored in, the long-running public debate about the costs of sprawl looks more and more lopsided.

The first two waves of Phoenix's postwar suburban growth produced an extreme version of the classic sprawl pattern. By 1980, when its population had increased 1,100 percent since 1940, Phoenix was the nation's ninth largest city, but it had the lowest density, especially since its aggressive annexation policy resulted in ever more land being claimed.[33] At that time, a full 40 percent of its area was vacant land, exhibiting the tell-tale signs of speculative leapfrog development that leaves behind large acreages of bypassed land.[34] Since the 1980s, however, density across the metro region as a whole has steadily increased (notwithstanding the revival of leapfrogging made possible by the GRD water compact). Although urbanized Phoenix was dominated by low-rise, single-family dwellings, it now had an overall density higher than Washington, D.C., Philadelphia, Detroit, and Atlanta. Indeed, the semiarid West, which boasted by far the highest rates of urbanization in the country, hosted ten of the twelve densest metro regions—Las Vegas, Los Angeles, San Diego, San Francisco, Phoenix, Sacramento, Seattle, Portland, San Antonio, and Salt Lake City.[35] Carl Abbott, leading historian of the urban West, has concluded that "on the whole, there is no evidence that southwestern cities are spread more thinly over the landscape, depend more substantially on the automobile, or have extended the triumph of the suburbs over the central city."[36] Indeed, because they "have held close to the ground and spread evenly across it," he believes they are "our most comprehensible cities" on account of "their physical and visual openness."[37]

Most residents of Phoenix's supersuburbs, like Mesa, Gilbert, Chandler, Glendale, and Peoria, would be surprised to learn that the linear orderliness of their evenly spaced blocks and lots put them in the nation's high-density league. Indeed, their taste for low-density living is often cited as a point of pride. Responding to a survey of fast-growth suburban cities, Stephen Berman, the mayor of Gilbert, which grew faster than any other municipality in the nation between 1990 and 2003, reported that most residents were uncomfortable with any zoning above four units per acre—Gilbert had only ten multifamily apartment buildings. Despite the ballooning population, voters had resisted adopting a city charter. "I don't think there are ten people in Gilbert who want to have it called a 'city,'" declared Berman, adding that their aspiration was to remain "the only 300,000 person small town in America."[38]

Nor was Gilbert's growth an anomaly in the region. Based on precrash estimates, Jonathan Lang and Jennifer Lefursty predicted that several other area cities—Avondale, Goodyear, Buckeye, and Surprise in the West Valley, and Apache Junction, Queen Creek, and Casa Grande in the East Valley—would make it on to their list of top "boomburbs," which they defined as "accidental cities" with populations that had exploded beyond the 100,000 mark. Whether their residents were as antiurban as the mayor of Gilbert, none of these places had a downtown cluster of any significance and none of them had an urban feel. Indeed, for those who measure urbanity by some buzzworthy quotient of vitality, it was perhaps fitting that Gilbert and Chandler were named among the top ten most boring cities in the United States in 2007, according to a *Forbes* magazine survey, with neighboring Mesa taking the top spot. In response, the aforesaid Mayor Berman evinced pride in the recognition of his city as "a hotbed of celibacy."[39]

On the other hand, most of the municipalities that surrounded Phoenix had implemented a sustainability program for government services and were beginning to fill out the checklist for greening other parts of city life. Since the state required cities to adopt a General Plan and revise it periodically, most officials were taking advantage of the update process to introduce zoning changes that favored mixed use and higher densities, as well as form-based codes that favored adaptive reuse. These amendments were significant revisions of planning regulations that had been enacted to encourage suburban-style development, and so they marked the first real break with a sixty-year pattern of edge growth. In the course of these decades, the golden rule of Euclidean single-use zoning had more or less

decreed that residents enjoyed a relatively narrow range of lifestyle variation. Regional planning had been reliably tailored to the needs of land
development—to the ease with which desert and farmland could be converted into a standardized landscape of master-planned communities,
malls, and commercial complexes.

Some small municipalities on the fringe had used this old development
formula to project their growth, in size and population, far beyond the 76
square-mile spread of Gilbert. Surpassing the 517 square miles of Phoenix,
Buckeye, on the west side, boasted almost 600 square miles in its planning
area, and, in the southeastern path of growth of the Sun Corridor megare-
gion, Eloy could claim 545 square miles. Partially surveyed, platted, and
in many places fully titled, these yawning acres, currently featuring
saguaros, ocotillos, cholla cacti, yucca, and sporadic palo verde trees, were
just waiting to be filled in. As one prominent figure in the homebuilding
sector put it to me: "We can't afford not to be the first to market because
we've had infrastructure in the ground for years now that's costing us
money. We'll do what everyone else has always done to sell our interests—
come up with new ways of financing, and new ways of urging people to get
their stake on the land. That's the story of the West." Others, with no
assets or land claims to color their judgment, were hoping that the severity
of the recession would sap, if not extinguish, the swindler's appetite for
selling the Western dream of living free and large on the land. Everyone
who wanted a new order, whether they were pushing for zoning adjustments, urban code revisions, or extensions to the light rail system, was
doing their bit to turn the ship around, lest it run aground in the unforgiving desert soil.

Nineteenth-century agrarianists popularized the theory that making
cheap land available beyond the Mississippi would act as a safety valve to
ease employment pressure in the industrial East. Historians since then
have suggested that the expansion of Anglo-American capitalism
demanded the territorial conquest of the Southwest to resolve its need for
surplus space. In more recent decades, the dramatic shift of private and
public resources to the Sunbelt has been seen as a strategic move to boost
corporate profits. Whatever the explanation that fit best, the result has
been that, for more than a century, Western urbanization hosted not only
the most visible geographic spread of U.S. growth but also its most
intensive escalation. It was fitting that this long wave would break most
forcefully in Phoenix, which had been one of its most dependable
vehicles.

No one, to my knowledge, has estimated the ecological footprint of the
city or the region, but since virtually all of its goods, food, and energy were

imported from far afield, including all the construction materials that had filled out the Phoenix Basin, the desert metropolis depended on vast amounts of "ghost acreage" elsewhere to sustain the daily needs of its population.[40] In this regard, it had long ago surpassed its ecological limits. Those who viewed the region through a local lens were inclined to conclude that the growth machine had not yet reached its economic limits— surely there was time for one last housing boom!—but the severity of the crash bolstered the belief that the moment of reckoning was fast approaching, and that the message should be passed on to the Home Builders Association of Central Arizona.

CHAPTER 3

The Battle for Downtown

Part One: Artists Step Up

"We are the biggest city which has no city center."
Kimber Lanning, arts and small business advocate

Before the financial crash froze the motion of money, the plan to repopulate thinned-out downtowns had become an article of faith among advocates of low-carbon urbanism. Where else could the blueprint for truly sustainable living be realized? The technical difficulty and cost of retrofitting suburbs for higher density was prohibitive, even in the postwar inner-ring subdivisions that were more compact in their land use than today's sprawl counterparts on the urban fringe. It was in city centers that the biggest improvements in energy efficiencies and emissions could be achieved, and, since the carbon clock was ticking, there was a consensus that their repopulation by middle-class residents ought to be accomplished posthaste.[1]

Urbanists, guided unerringly by Jane Jacobs's prescriptions for vibrant street life, had long argued that the kind of society fostered by mixed-use and mixed-income downtown neighborhoods was more open-minded and mutually gratifying than the atomized lifestyle of the master-planned exurban community. After all, Jacobs's version of the city had been driven primarily by concerns about quality of life, or what could be called cultural health. In her view, those who had planned the urban renewal projects of the 1950s and 1960s and hastened the population flight outwards had bequeathed a soulless, antiurban city—"a Great Blight of Dullness," as she memorably put it.[2] Hence, her full-throated praise for the daily festival of street life in mixed-use neighborhoods, even those condemned by the improvers as examples of urban blight. Compared to the presumed conformity of the suburbs, the humming, cosmopolitan milieu of her downtown sidewalks surely boasted a superior civilization.

In the decades after Jacobs launched her downtown revolution, the argument for high-density core residence got a turbo boost from environmentalist quarters. Criticism of suburbia was no longer a matter of taste—how ugly and dull are these cookie-cutter houses and strip malls? Now it was backed up by estimates of the ecological costs of the unplanned, low-density tract development known as sprawl.[3] In recent years, climate change had lent an extra sense of urgency to the case for downtown resettlement. A hundred years ago, planners diagnosed "congestion" in the center city as a public health threat, and proposed, as the solution, the decanting of populations to the urban fringe. Raymond Unwin's slogan, "Nothing to Be Gained by Overcrowding," was the rallying cry of the Garden City movement whose heirs Jacobs lambasted. The new push back toward the center was no longer simply about middle-class quality of life, it was about reducing our carbon footprints, and this time, the health of the planet itself was a factor.

It would be naive to imagine that the real estate industry and its many beneficiaries were motivated by such noble considerations. As far as they were concerned, the fluctuation of land value was the all-important driving force, for wherever land and restorable building stock was devalued there lay opportunities for speculative profit.[4] The most recent asset bubble in housing was spread over all sectors, and its momentum was such that investors and developers entered into markets they might have shunned under other circumstances. As a result, the rate of gentrification in inner-city neighborhoods shot up, spurred as much by speculation as by real demand for residential property that could be upscaled through renovation.

City managers, desperate for new sources of revenue, saw the downtown revival primarily as a vehicle for economic development. After the flight of industry began in the late 1970s, and city tax receipts went into steady decline, they tried out a succession of turnaround strategies. The first, and most dismal, idea for luring people downtown and boost land value was to pump huge public subsidies into the building of sports stadiums. Much criticized for their failure to generate returns or to stimulate other forms of downtown investment, the stadiums nonetheless brought the patina of major league status to second-tier cities in grave need of a morale boost.[5] Other mega projects followed—convention centers mostly but also business-class hotels, courts, jails, and other government edifices. By the end of the 1990s, a new formula—"meds and eds"—emerged around the recognition that research universities and medical centers, already among the top employers in many cities, could be alpha drivers of the urban economy, spinning off a variety of jobs and commerce in the knowledge and life-science industries.[6]

At the same time, the dot-com boom gave birth to the first new urban industry in decades, and it was based on small-scale start-ups and the refurbishing of ex-industrial space in a manner similar to the renovation of old housing stock. In sharp contrast to the mega projects, this model was fine-grained, and it reflected the no-collar values of a new generation of young urban professionals who eschewed the work and consumption habits associated with corporate America.[7] The urban landscape that echoed and catered to these values was walkable or bikeable, human scale, "authentic" in appearance, and stocked with boho-boutique consumption outlets and art spaces.

After the dot-com bust, this neobohemian template morphed very smoothly into the formula of the Creative City. This new paradigm was adopted by urban managers around the globe who were persuaded by Richard Florida and others that the future of their cities depended on attracting a critical mass of "creative class" talents. Much cheaper than the giveaways devised to net large corporate investors, the effort to lure creatives turned on cultivating a certain quality of downtown life: one-of-a-kind clubs, galleries, coffee shops, and restaurants with hip credentials, a heterogeneous, unplanned mix of urban amenities, and a tolerance of liberal lifestyles, especially in matters of sexuality. The result was often risible. In tune with the hapless efforts of Midwestern mayors to attract gay college graduates, the government of Singapore tried to promote itself as a creative capital by relaxing (but not eliminating) the city-state's proscriptions against homosexuality.[8]

The Green City paradigm presented itself as a worthy successor. It dovetailed with efforts to attract clean energy industries as the next generation of high tech: it showcased the virtues of efficient government to prospective residents, it set a model for green conduct for its middle-class citizens, and it promoted green-collar job creation in a range of sectors, from brownfield restoration and waste management to urban landscaping and sustainable building. So, too, the neo-bohemian lifestyle championed by the "creative class" fit neatly into the low-carbon model of downtown habitation; friendly to pedestrians, transit pathways, 100-mile foodsheds, and locally owned business; and dense enough to deliver efficient forms of land use and public space. When mayors like Phoenix's Phil Gordon declared that their city would be the greenest in the country, they were pitching for their share of the attention economy and the rewards that come with such bold self-promotion. But if they also followed through and greened the many downtown city-owned assets, then they felt they were making the instruments of government itself into a vehicle of urban improvement rather than just using their bully pulpit to reform the wasteful behavior of the citizenry.

City improvers had been through an efficiency crusade before. The rise of urban planning in the early twentieth century was all about tapping the expertise of a new class of professionals to bring order and economy to the laissez-faire Victorian city. Zoning, building codes, land-use ordinances, and all the other regulatory tools of the new profession were designed to lend some rationality to an urban landscape that had evolved in a virtually unplanned and wasteful manner. With these new powers, planners now had the capacity not only to distribute population segments at will but also to effectively quarantine the more favored residents from contact with those considered undesirable. As a result, racial zoning flourished, and although it was legally struck down in the United States in 1917, local authorities, developers, banks, and homeowner associations continued to find legal and fiscal instruments with which to segregate the housing landscape along racialized lines.[9] By the time Jacobs penned her takedown of establishment planners, many of their efforts at urban renewal were being openly referred to as "Negro removal."

By the end of the century, the confidence, if not the reputation, of planners had been restored, and they found themselves actively seeking to change the rules, mainly by reversing the Euclidean separation of land uses that had been the birthright of the profession. Reforming codes and zoning provisions to allow mixed use was the key to New Urbanist initiatives in suburbia, and city-planning departments were soon following suit in their efforts to resuscitate hollowed-out downtowns. But, in many cases, these efforts led to a pattern of displacement of poor or minority populations not unlike that prompted by urban renewal. Critics of the new "urban revitalization" concluded that gentrification was a widespread, if not inevitable, outcome of the use of zoning regulations to raise land value and repopulate central city neighborhoods, primarily with high-income professionals. Efforts to protect the rent base of long-term, low-income residents, or to preserve a mixed-income homeownership were a losing proposition when set against the typical revitalization formula that sterilized city centers for tourism and upmarket shopping, or prepped streetscapes for affluent homebuyers.

Would the new regulatory direction of the Green City have the same exclusive outcome? In principle, there was nothing socially divisive about planning for technical improvements in areas like water and energy conservation, air quality, mass transit, emissions reduction, pollution prevention, renewable energy, and home weatherization. These initiatives could and should apply broadly and evenly. But the pursuit of these goals does not take place in a vacuum. Cities are places of acute inequality, and the deeds of policymakers and planners usually end up serving the needs and interests of the most powerful and affluent of their constituents. In this new paradigm, the capacity of activists and urban advocates to push back was still untested. On the face of it, the rhetoric of the Green City afforded more opportunities to promote environmental justice and prevent the new policymaking from turning into a recipe for eco-apartheid.

Greater Phoenix offered evidence on both sides. The existing inequalities were indisputable. The region actually boasted the nation's highest rate of income disparity among households, and there was already a "green gap" between populations living in a rarefied belt of upland health and others condemned to a brown zone of befouled air and water, and food deserts.[10] But the ferment about sustainability in Central Arizona had also prompted citizen groups, many of them artists, to petition City Hall in new ways, and the focus of their attention was firmly on downtown Phoenix.

DOUGHNUT CITY

Phoenix's Green City campaign was being pushed by a mayor who had been downtown's biggest advocate for two decades. That the city's downtown needed friends and allies went without saying. The hollowed-out core had long been an embarrassment, not only to boosters but also to those who believed that the feat of growing to become the fifth largest American city was worthless unless there was a distinctive downtown landscape to write home about. Since so many of the city's residents were relatively new arrivals, it could not be taken for granted that most Phoenicians would remember that things had once been quite different, before urban renewal and suburban flight took their cruel toll on the inner neighborhoods and central core.

The most effective public scold of the city's amnesia was Jon Talton, a fourth-generation Arizonan, who wrote for the *Arizona Republic* before his column was taken away and he moved on to the *Seattle Times* (from whence he pens longer Arizona-themed essays on his indispensable *Rogue*

Columnist blog). A scourge of the GOP wingnuts in the legislature and of the real estate-industrial complex that owned the political class, Talton's idyllic recall of his center-city childhood contrasted sharply with his serial indictments of the Metro Phoenix growth machine: "I carry a memory of old Phoenix—and feel its loss profoundly—in a way that's probably unusual even for natives of my generation. It's not nostalgia; I know too much about the place for that. It's a more complex reaction, to history thrown aside, opportunities lost and the destruction of a very flawed paradise, but a paradise nonetheless." The heart of this romance was the city's once thriving downtown of locally owned businesses and cultural institutions where rich and poor were equally accommodated. "Hotels," Talton pointed out, "ranged from the single-room-occupancy flophouses of the Deuce to the fancy Westward Ho, where presidents stayed and the local bigs held court and kept suites for their mistresses. The Legislature's informal caucus rooms were the coffee shop of the Hotel Adams and Tom's Tavern. Businessmen mingled with real cowboys.... The shops were almost all locally owned and usually shaded by large awnings proclaiming their names."[11] A busy railroad terminal, a sizable produce district, and one of the largest stockyards in the country added to the civic flurry—a bustle that was all but silenced not long after its postwar heyday.

Any city with this kind of lapsed history has to boast at least one good crime fiction writer. Phoenix had two, and one of them was Talton himself; his noir detective, David Mapstone, supplied the goods in a series of well-received novels like *Concrete Desert, Dry Heat, Camelback Falls, Cactus Heart,* and *South Phoenix Rules.*[12] A former history professor, who used his archival skills and professional memory to solve police cases, Mapstone was Phoenix's answer to the urban chivalry of Philip Marlowe: tough enough to take on the villainy of crooked politicians and businessmen, but marinated in a romantic longing for the city of his youth, with its endless citrus groves and guileless pleasures. Lena Jones, his female counterpart in the murky orbit of the private detective, was the fictional creation of Betty Webb, a former journalist at the *East Valley Tribune,* whose novels included *Desert Noir, Desert Shadows,* and *Desert Run.* Jones's unsparing exposé of the corrupt Scottsdale aristocracy was complicated, not by nostalgia for the way things were, but by the traumas of her orphanage past.[13] While Mapstone's success depended on his comprehensive knowledge of urban history, Jones was motivated by her urge to fill the yawning memory gaps in her personal history.

Even if the city's residents shared more of Jones's amnesia than Mapstone's total recall, few could dispute Talton's tagline of "opportunities lost" when it came to the history of downtown Phoenix. There was a long list of mishits, underpinned by venality and corruption so rife it would keep a team of investigative reporters in clover for a lifetime.[14] But how much of the lead story deviated from the pattern followed by so many other American cities in the same postwar period? Beginning with the flight of retail up the Central Avenue corridor in the late 1950s (including Goldwater's Department Store), downtown Phoenix suffered a sharp decline—the hemorrhaging of commerce and jobs, the decamping of affluent populations, and the acute neglect of those left behind—that differed from other cities only in its sheer rapidity. Just to take one example, downtown retail sales, from their peak in 1958, fell a remarkable 35 percent by 1963.[15] The descent may have been more precipitous, and the dispersal of resources to the urban fringe more far-reaching in scope than elsewhere, but the centrifugal flight pattern was in no way an aberration.

No less uncommon were the remedies wheeled out by policymakers in their efforts, from the mid-1980s, to revitalize the rundown downtown precincts. Indeed, Phoenix dutifully rolled out each of the models that I previously outlined. First, whole blocks of the city core were razed to build major-league stadiums for baseball (Diamondbacks) and basketball (Phoenix Suns); then a jumbo convention center and symphony hall were thrown up, along with several other commercial mega projects, like the Arizona Center, Civic Plaza, Renaissance Park, America West Arena, Heritage Square, Dodge Theater, Patriots Square Park, and the Mercado. Then, on another swath of bulldozed blocks, ASU began to construct a new branch campus, to work in "meds and eds" synergy with a bioscience research park. The downtown artist communities also had their moment in the sun when City Hall warmed to the Creative City model in the mid-2000s, while its successor, the Green City, was officially rolled out in 2009, shortly after the opening of the first phase of the metro light-rail system, its most visible achievement to date.

Phoenix was slow to accept federal funding for urban renewal projects in the 1960s. Money from the government that could not be readily spun into private profit was suspect. By contrast, the vast amounts of public money poured into downtown to fund the mega projects sat well with a powerful group of downtown investors, spearheaded by sports and real estate mogul Jerry Colangelo, who were longtime beneficiaries of this new suite of policymaking. An uneasy alliance shaped up between this clique and Terry Goddard, the mayor who was heralded for championing the turn toward the downtown revival. Goddard won four mayoral elections from 1984 onward, running on a reform platform that promised open government, and subsequently lost three gubernatorial bids. He disbanded the at-large electoral system (which had endured longer than in any other major city) and established ward district voting that gave minority populations an effective say in government for the first time. Declaring independence from the Phoenix 40, the business elite that had called the shots for so long, Goddard managed to push through a 1988 excise tax and bond initiative for major capital spending on downtown projects, many of them cultural in nature.

"It was the first time we had ever gone to the voters for anything that was cultural," recalled Goddard, "and there was a lot of opposition on the City Council. People were saying it was inappropriate, we shouldn't do that, and that it would never pass. And so we did a little bundling–the funding for parks, very frankly, was for political cover—but most of it was for downtown arts. The money was to make Phoenix into a community that had first-class venues." Despite the power struggle with the Phoenix 40, "the one common ground I had with them was the arts," he remarked. "For example, Richard Mallery [a prominent dealmaker] and I fought like cats and dogs over the development issues—he never saw a development that he didn't like—but we came together over the Herberger Theater. It was good business, and Richard Mallery is a hell of a businessman." Among Goddard's first acts as a reform mayor was to create an Arts Commission and a Historic Preservation Commission—"much of the popular belief at that time was that Phoenix had no art and really had no history"—but his later years in office saw a rapprochement with the developer elites that led to approval of the sports and other real estate mega projects that were pursued more zealously by his successors.

Politically speaking, Goddard's most enduring, but least tangible, legacy was to convene the Futures Forum, an extensive process of citizen participation in city planning that ran for more than a year and half in the late 1980s.[16] Ammunition for launching the Forum had been provided by a regional survey commissioned by the *Arizona Republic* from Neil Peirce, a national commentator on urban issues (and published in July 1987 as "Valley Destiny").[17] Highly critical of the development industry's growth machine, and firm in its recommendations for creating a genuinely civic nonelite culture, the Peirce Report fed directly into the Futures Forum workshops, and the community-oriented recommendations that came out of their deliberations.

The national recession of the early 1990s (in part triggered by Phoenix speculator Charles Keating's role in the savings and loans collapse) put paid to most of the plans for implementing the Forum outcomes. "Though he participated in the Forum," recalled Goddard, "I don't think my successor [Paul Johnson] really believed in it. Paul was a guy who liked to do deals and he did them well, but the idea of long-term planning was antithetical to him." When Goddard left office, Johnson asked, "Is there one piece of advice you would give?" Goddard responded, "The most important thing I learned was that every day you should try to do something in public life that would affect life twenty years from now. And it was as if I had insulted him. That wasn't the way he saw government. He thought it was about how to solve problems as they come up and smooth things over to keep people from fighting." But the principle of citizen participation in governance, like other Futures Forum ideas, became institutionalized over time, as it would nationally, in many cities where community boards were allocated powers of review over development projects. Phoenix was the first American city to institute an urban village model, in 1979, largely to combat the sense of placelessness generated by metro sprawl and also to reduce commuting (initially, there were nine semiautonomous village districts; now there are fifteen). Multicentric thinking became the norm in the planning department, with an emphasis, in the wake of the Forum, on devolving more and more governance overview to the village planning committees.

While the committee input was invaluable, the village concept ended up on the list of mishits. "The urban village model may work on paper but hasn't necessarily worked in reality," confessed Dean Brennan, a longtime head of the city-planning department. It was designed so that residents would work, shop, and recreate in each of the village cores, thereby reducing auto use, but the employment component never materialized. "There are jobs there," added Brennan, "but most are retail and commercial. There have been no efforts to bring in other types of employment opportunities." Initially, at least, the polynuclear concept was viewed as official acceptance of the city's centerlessness.[18] That changed with the campaign to revive the city center, which was driven initially by speculation in land value or in siphoning off the public funds into private profit. Revitalization advocates began to argue that downtown needed its own special development district, with zoning that departed from the standard regional template for suburban development.

The Phoenix Community Alliance (PCA), formed in 1983 to broker the large public–private downtown deals, and the Downtown Phoenix Partnership (DPP), founded in 1990 as the promotional front for property owners in the core business district, emerged as twin conduits for the big-dog developers to put their footprint on the "new territory" of downtown. The superblock building style of their mega projects echoed the scale of financing and urban ambition to which they aspired, long after this model had fallen out of favor with Jacobs-influenced planners. After a run of almost two decades, the mega-project formula finally lost momentum in 2002, when a full-on effort to build a third downtown stadium, this time for the Arizona Cardinals, encountered fierce resistance from an unlikely quarter—a group of artists who were tired of being evicted to make way for the hulking sports arenas.

WHEN ARTISTS UNITE

In typical 1980s fashion, Phoenix artists had sought out residence in abandoned pockets of the central city. The zone of vacated warehouses clustered above Union Station's rail tracks was an obvious nesting site for downtown veterans like painter Beatrice Moore and her partner Tony Zahn. "We were only down there for a couple of years," recalled Moore, "when we started hearing rumors that the city was planning on putting in a big arena. So we started lobbying, hoping they wouldn't put it right on top of the art spaces that were already down there. And sure enough, that's exactly where they decided to put it." In response to the outcry, the city "ended up relocating about fifteen of us—artists—that were down there and actually paid for renovation of new space for us in the warehouse district." Only a year or so later, Moore and Zahn realized "that they were going to be building a baseball stadium in the same vicinity. We just realized at that point in time that it was over for the warehouse district, that the rents were going to be too high, that the real estate was going to be too expensive to ever afford to buy." In 1992, Moore and Zahn relocated to a strip of Grand Street, zoned for light industry, where their subsequent acquisition of several properties would become the anchor for a more permanent artists community on downtown's west side. Among the few who stayed on in the warehouse district were David Therrien and Helen Hestenes, who ran the legendary Crash arts space, and then the Icehouse on Jackson Street. But they had to fight long battles with developers, city, and county authorities, each in turn bent on replacing the historic warehouses and other small businesses to make way for superblock buildings; stadiums, jails, morgues, parking garages, and most recently, a master-planned Entertainment District.

To the north of the business core, a cluster of artists' studios and residences had formed in the dilapidated quarter of city blocks around central Roosevelt Street, just below the I-10 freeway. Ominously, the Roosevelt cluster was adjacent to the site designated for the third stadium, and the area was zoned for high-rise in anticipation of development. The city had bought up and demolished several blocks to accommodate the stadium's footprint before running up against the ire of area artists. Kim Moody and Glen Johnson, whose art space, Alwun House, was the first on the Roosevelt strip of galleries and studios, were among those who formed an artists' coalition in opposition to the stadium plan. Moody recalled that "most people were saying, 'Oh, it's a done deal. Don't worry about it, Kim, you just have to accept it.' And looking around, I talked to Greg [Esser]— we're all partners and grew up together here—and we said, 'Jesus Christ, does this have to be accepted?'" As news spread about a coalition, "others joined in after they realized, 'Oh, it CAN be changed.'" The stadium site was eventually relocated to Glendale, largely because the city realized it did not have enough downtown land for fans' parking. But the loud resistance of the artists' coalition had made an impact, and their moment of unity would mark an important turning point in ideas about downtown development.

For the first time, artists had taken a strong stand against displacement and had been heard at City Hall. Previously, the city had ridden roughshod over residents' opposition to big projects, most conspicuously in the case of the Golden Gate barrio residents who were displaced by the Sky Harbor airport expansion in the 1970s.[19] Artists, predominantly Anglo, and with skills in public symbolism that were a match for bureaucrats, were not so easily ignored. Besides, some key figures had bought up buildings on the Roosevelt strip, and their privilege as property owners spoke just as loudly as their voices and connections. Greg Esser, who had inside knowledge of City Hall from his leadership of the city's Public Arts Commission, and his partner Cindy Dach owned multiple properties—the MADE art boutique, several gallery spaces, including the arts collectives, 515 and the Eye Lounge--and were the figurehead voices for this group of artists.

The saga of art studios displaced by stadiums "sent a very strong message," according to Esser, "that if artists wanted some stability they were going to have to purchase property. We've grown from five to twelve artist-owned and -occupied spaces, in the late 1990s, to probably over one hundred, just within this immediate neighborhood. So in terms of percentage of overall ownership of that particular business class, it would be very difficult to find an urban community this close to a city center that has as much artist ownership." Esser's perception—that property ownership by artists was a key factor in their influence—was echoed by all parties involved in downtown development. The relative stability of the artist communities in these zones was a warning sign to developers that they would not have an easy time building there, or even in the vicinity. But it was also an advertisement to those seeking to cash in on the

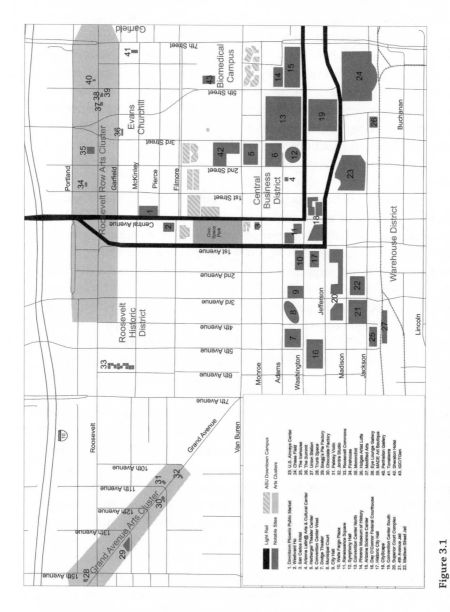

Figure 3.1

Map of Downtown Phoenix, with Roosevelt Row and Grand Avenue arts clusters

Sources: Downtown Phoenix Partnership, Arizona State Land Department, Arizona Land Resources Information System, ESRI

value-added component that artists' residence can bring to a neighborhood's position in the property market.

The artist-owners on the Grand Street and Roosevelt Street strips began to acquire artist-tenants, and not surprisingly, their more impecunious peers, accustomed to landlords who did not share their outlook on life, heavily criticized the rentier practices. When a private developer, in pursuit of artworld cachet, built the first live-work condos (the Artisan Village lofts) on Roosevelt, complaints about gentrification, inevitably, were directed against the artist-owners on the strip. A well-known local artist targeted several of their buildings with graffiti (RESIST!), and, in a further twist, some enterprising gallerists tagged their own Artisan Loft storefront, Retail Lab, as a publicity stunt.

Wayne Rainey, a photographer and native Phoenician, owned several of the buildings—rented out as artists' studios—which were tagged. "I think I get unfairly judged for playing both sides of the fence," he explained, "because I am also a developer. I have taken the most heat for the thing I worked the hardest on—to provide space for artists." When his fellow artist neighbors were uniting against the Cardinals stadium plan, Rainey was a prominent holdout, and was maligned for sitting down with the PCA and DPP to broker the standoff. "They reached out and I was more than happy to talk to them," he recalled. "Other people around here who are property owners, and who make their living from renting to artists, felt like I was sleeping with the enemy. Everyone was terrified of gentrification—that everything would be torn down and it would be all condos and there would be no artists left. I felt like this was a huge opportunity to work with the mayor's office and get the best of both worlds for artists."

Although Rainey was accused of seeking to profit personally from the stadium plan, he told me that his conversations with the city were about plans for the light rail, which he supported.[20] "I didn't think I had any leverage [as an artist] to speak of," he concluded. "I just offered my opinion as a property owner," and, in that capacity, his portfolio of assets got him a hearing. Esser, who had a more direct line of communication with City Hall, and who was not inclined to view his former colleagues there as the "enemy," further cemented this advantage by establishing Roosevelt Row as a community development corporation to represent the strip's small business owners and to maintain its distinctive character as an artists community. "As a business model, or as a redevelopment model," he expounded, "artists make an incredibly effective investment vehicle for positive redevelopment. They are unique in the toolkit of available businesses or individuals to support in terms of regrowing an urban core. I would liken them in a way to stem cells because they're very adaptable, unique, hard to classify, and, collectively almost always have the same impact if they congregate in an area for a good amount of time."

The role that artists' presence has played in urban gentrification is well documented and has been a formulaic part of the real-estate business cycle in many cities over the last two decades.[21] While the high ownership factor of the Phoenix artists may have marked them out as exceptional, that fact did not appear to have made much difference to the developers who built condos on downtown lots and exploited their proximity to the artist zones in marketing to prospective buyers. The ads of urban loft developers ("Urban Living Is an Art") kept close company with those for high-end furniture and home improvement stores in the pages of *Shade*, Wayne Rainey's virtuoso arts magazine and chronicle of the Phoenix urban renaissance that ran from 2002 to 2007.[22] Among the housing units sold before the crash, there was a high proportion of buyers seeking investment properties or second homes, as downtown became a land bonanza, with out-of-state speculators buying and flipping lots like breakfast pancakes. The price of lots on Roosevelt, in particular, skyrocketed as successive buyers won City Hall's approval for ever-taller building heights. Many of the buyers had no intention, nor any experience, of building anything. The overpriced,

Figure 3.2
Four zones of downtown ecology: vacant lot, artist space, condo lofts, business hotels and banks. Photo by Author.

vacant lots left over from the frenzy would give downtown an abandoned Detroit feel for decades to come.

None of the loft developers I interviewed could assure me that a solid portion of their buyers were bona fide "creative class" customers. In any event, the crash brought a premature end to all of the gambling on whether a critical mass of professionals would make the choice to live in downtown Phoenix. It also deferred the question of whether the ensconced artist communities could hold out in the face of developer pressure. The relief was palpable among their bohemian fellow travelers and other low-income renters in central neighborhoods like Evans-Churchill and Garfield. If the conditions for artist-driven gentrification had been ripe in these neighborhoods, the least we can conclude is that the outcome might have been complicated by a stronger-than-usual foothold on the part of artist-owners. But the jury was still out on whether the land economy of downtown Phoenix was even capable of hosting a classic gentrification cycle of that sort.

Much more significant than their role as property owners, precariously hemmed in by a tide of land speculation, was the career that many artists took up as urban activists. Their vision of a sustainable downtown turned out to be a game-changer, breaking the ground for policies conducive to transforming the central city into a livable, and potentially low-carbon environment.

LISTENING OR BRANDING?

The success of the Downtown Phoenix Arts Coalition (D-PAC) that came together to oppose the stadium plan convinced its leading lights that "the art community," as Dana Johnson put it, "can be cohesive and can fight social issues related to development. One of our big arguments," he pointed out, "was that we wanted a 24/7 facility, not something that was just going to be used for only 30 days out of the year, because the joke was that after five o'clock, there's no life in downtown." But it was the "social issues," as much as the utopian prospect of 24/7 street vitality, that spurred on the coalition's members to make common cause with other grassroots urban groups such as the Community Housing Partnership, Local Initiatives Support Corporation (LISC), Arizona Chain Reaction, and the Phoenix Historic Neighborhoods Coalition. According to Susan Copeland, a key figure behind this transition, "after the stadium, all of these other issues started appearing—affordable housing, historic preservation, diversity downtown—that were beyond the scope of just the arts community. So we started talking about bringing other people into the fold and that's what led to meeting at the Icehouse."

Downtown Voices, a convocation called by these groups on May 22, 2004, was held at the Icehouse, the last, and the grandest, of the raw art spaces left in the warehouse district. The organizers' goal was to host a summit on downtown development that would be much more inclusive than the tight circle of developers, well represented in the PCA and the DPP, who customarily made all the decisions. There were two outcomes of the well-attended summit: (a) an alternative blueprint for downtown redevelopment that was presented directly to City Hall, and (b) an activist pressure group, called the Downtown Voices Coalition, committed to pushing for the implementation of policies that respected the blueprint. Both would have a notable impact on the shape and tenor of the downtown renaissance.

Seven months earlier, in the fall of 2003, Richard Florida had come to town on a wave of euphoria about his own program for urban vitalization. His lecture, attended by thirteen hundred people in the downtown Orpheum Theater, was hosted by *Phoenix New Times*, the city's alternative weekly, whose business model was very much in synch with the lifestyle component of Florida's "creative class" ethos.[23] His visit helped crystallize the mood among opinion makers that the city had to get over the "edifice complex" that had placed so much faith in the stadiums, convention center, cultural centers, brand retail malls, and even the as-yet-unbuilt downtown campus that ASU had designed. Rather than trying to attract people downtown, Florida argued, Phoenix should be trying to attract downtown people, and the task of landing those creatives required the right mix of authentic street life and boutique amenities.[24] The recipe was easy to summarize: "Create the exceptional frying pan, then both the chicken and the egg will show up."[25]

As in countless other cities, desperate for a turnaround strategy, some key officials were persuaded that Florida's prescriptions amounted to an economic development policy. Phoenix, which was ranked 35 out of 49 on Florida's initial Creative City scale, soon joined the cohort of aspiring municipalities that signed the Memphis Manifesto, and the city manager commissioned a study from Catalyx, Florida's consultancy group.[26] The group's sketchy report—"Phoenix Downtown: Right Place Right Time!"—stitched together existing initiatives and blueprints, by urging a "paradigm-shift in planning" aimed at increasing density, mixed land-uses, shade, and pedestrian-friendly streets and scale (basically, Jane Jacobs plus the Southwest heat factor). It also threw in some new ideas, such as a "world-class urban skate park," and recommended the need for a "virtual developer" who could coordinate all the initiatives: "Can the Phoenix Downtown Partnership play this role and/or should the City of Phoenix secure the services of a free-lance entrepreneur who is familiar with the marketplace and knows the players?" The city, concluded the report, "should consider outsourcing this critical function in a uniquely creative way."[27]

Stopping short of implying that Catalyx itself might be contracted for the job, the latter recommendation delivered a vote of no confidence in Phoenix's own developer community. A more trusted, homegrown entity, the report implied, would be the new artist-led community coalition, whose draft of the Icehouse manifesto, *Listening to the People for a Change*, was in circulation by then, and who were likely to be a source of "valuable insight" and "design energy" if they could only "transcend" the "rhetoric and ranting" of their activist roots. It was a paternalistic tribute to Downtown Voices, but an endorsement nonetheless.

The Downtown Voices Coalition (DVC) issued the final version of its manifesto, *Downtown Voices: Creating a Sustainable Downtown*, at the same time as the Catalyx report, and only three months after the Icehouse meeting. In that short space of time, the drafting group, none of whom had any prior expertise in urban planning, produced a remarkably comprehensive document, described as a "catalyst for initiating a more inclusive planning process." In contrast to the fast-track fixes of the past, the report endorsed "long-term approaches" with sustainability in mind. A key part of the document was the call for a revolution in communication between City Hall and downtown communities: every downtown initiative, the authors insisted, should involve active dialogue with and representative participation from all stakeholders, "from the ground up." These and other guiding principles were fleshed out by a menu of detailed prescriptions for neighborhood protection, historic preservation, design guidelines, locally owned businesses, affordable housing, transportation, arts and culture, public spaces, and diversity and cultural inclusion.[28]

Over the last three decades, numerous plans and blueprints had been issued for downtown revitalization, beginning with an AIA regional design team report in the 1970s, and including DPP's Strategic Vision, the City Council's Growth Strategy and Downtown Redevelopment Area plans, the Maricopa Association of Government's Vision 2025, the PCA-backed Phoenix Futures (otherwise known as the Jerde project), PCA's own Strategic Plan, ASU's Catalysts for Revitalization, and the city's Downtown Strategic Vision and Blueprint for the Future, in addition to multifarious redevelopment plans and district overlays devised by the planning department.[29] As a noninstitutional effort with a firm community-minded tone, the DVC's draft stood out from this crowded field. It smacked of the kind of participatory process that Goddard's Futures Forum initiated, and the statement of its goals had a more populist, explanatory feel than these other blueprints, written by professionals for professionals. Nor did the document sit on a shelf, as had so many others. Determined follow-through on the DVC's part over the next few years ensured that many of its recommendations were incorporated into some of the city's official plans. Indeed, the public hearing draft for the Phoenix General Plan Update, presented for approval by village planning committees in January 2011, showed the clear imprint of the DVC approach. According to the preamble: "This General Plan is unique from previous plans in that it serves as a transition plan to a more sustainable future. It establishes a community vision, assesses the current state, presents scenarios for alternative futures if no action is taken, and establishes a structure for transition strategies."[30]

By contrast, consider the redundant advice offered by an expensive study from Arthesia, a Swiss branding consultancy that was commissioned by the Maricopa Partnership for Arts and Culture (MPAC) to come up with a new culture-based identity for the region. Acknowledging that "branding a region is not the same as branding a car or soft drink," the consultants concluded that the solution lay in finding a persuasive story line: "told correctly, this story can place Metro Phoenix on the world map." Unfortunately, their story turned out to be stunningly banal: "Metro Phoenix is the 'Opportunity Oasis.' In no other metro area in the United States will you find such a combination of unchartered ground, open space, meritocracy, and an unpainted canvas than in Metro Phoenix. Its DNA is based on providing new opportunities in an oasis surrounded by beauty and open space. People come to and live in Metro Phoenix for one thing: opportunity." According to the Arthesia team, even the Hohokam "came to Phoenix because they saw opportunity for themselves, their ideas, and their families."[31] En route to this vacuous conclusion, the report regurgitated a series of equally hollow commonplaces: Metro Phoenix was "a sleeping giant" that "needs to wake," or "an undefined canvas to paint your dream on," or is "reminiscent of the strange underdog from high school dismissed by everyone as commonplace and insignificant, but is revealed to be someone quite exceptional by those who understood him."[32]

MPAC itself was formed and funded in order to show how the arts could play a role in economic development. Director of research, Cyd West, who had previously used the regional arts scene to help recruit health professionals to Phoenix, explained that their goal was "to engage the business community in the work of arts and culture in a different way from usual—instead of seeing arts as a handout, to see them as a partner." Before the recession put an end to their efforts, West's team produced several studies (much more empirically grounded than Arthesia's rebranding document) of the economic value generated by the Valley's arts activities, each of which aimed at making the case that the arts provided a good return on investment, whether public or private.[33] These policy reports were a natural offshoot of the art-based development model that underpinned Florida's Creative City paradigm.[34] "Arts and culture are magnets which attract other creative people," West echoed, "in a variety of fields."

Compared to other large U.S. cities, she acknowledged that "we are perceived as pretty vanilla," and this is why Arthesia's skills were sought out to match the success of other cities in rebranding; for example, Zurich's own image shift from "a boring, bourgeois, chocolate city" to one based around its "incredible arts culture and prestigious university," or the blockbuster campaign that produced the slogan "What Happens in Vegas Stays in Vegas." Another promotional tool used by MPAC was a lavish, coffee-table book, *Phoenix: 21st Century City*, which showcased the city's burgeoning arts scene. The introduction, written by ASU's Nan Ellin, urbanist and tireless innovator of arts-driven development, breathlessly analyzed the swelling confidence of a city that was only just "coming of age" and finding its feet as a cultural center, "like Paris, New York, and Los Angeles at their critical junctures." Ellin, a relative newcomer herself, reported that, like other creatives flocking to Phoenix (or, more accurately, deciding not to leave), she felt that she was "finally in the right place at the right time."[35]

THE ART OF DIALOGUE

Half a century before, an elect group of Barry Goldwater's Chamber of Commerce colleagues (the Thunderbirds) took potential investors on tours of industrial facilities, country clubs, golf courses, and the area's desert attractions. One of MPAC's functions was to help recruit prospective newcomers through arts tours.[36] The number one stop—Phoenix's own carnivalesque artwalk, First Friday—was as remote in feel from the Goldwaterites' watering holes as a death metal band was from the slick crooners of the early Cold War era. Ellin described the tens of thousands who descended on the Roosevelt and Grand Street arts strips for the monthly event: "This human river winds through numerous galleries and studios open for the evening, partaking along the way in a great street party of plein aire fashion shows, performance and installation art, belly dancers, hip hop troupes, 'U-Haul galleries' rented for the evening and parked on vacant lots, and an itinerant band called the MadCaPs who play from the bed of a roving pickup truck."[37]

The downtown artwalk was pioneered by community veterans like Beatrice Moore in the mid-1990s, and its loose, DIY spirit flourished until the city realized its worth as a development asset. Aside from the scheduled sports stadium fixtures, it was downtown's only crowd-puller (up to 35,000 in attendance at its peak, many of them passengers on the new light rail system), and, for one evening a month, delivered the kind of organic street buzz that thrilled advocates of the Creative City. None of the mega projects the city had spent so much on had delivered the goods, and certainly not with anything like the spontaneity and low-cost snap of the artwalk. First Friday became an obligatory draw for suburban youth and, at least in the earlier part of the evening, for many of their parents, clearly stunned that the region's subcultures could deliver the range of human and artifactual exotica on display on the sidewalks and inside the art spaces. Among other things, it was a rare occasion for the city's "alternative" residents to advertise their presence to otherwise oblivious populations. En route, the entrepreneurially minded turned their own dwellings into arts spaces, echoing the developers who tried to exploit the proximity of their condo units to the scene.

Gallerists complained early on that the party vibe and the vendors of more commercial art (and street-fair paraphernalia) were drowning out the pull of their exhibitions and minimizing their sales. The vendorless Third Fridays, pitched to a more bone fide arts clientele, sprang up in response as a more sedate version of the walk. In addition, a related agreement with the city to license all the vendors, and close off the streets on and around the Roosevelt strip, drew fire from those who predicted that such regulations would eventually kill off the vitality of an event that thrived on its free-form spontaneity.

Among the wary were some of the artwalk founders, like Michael 23, who prized First Friday's spirit of improvisation and low-threshold access. He practiced that ethos as the figurehead of an arts collective of especially free spirits called Thought Crime (originally Little Guyana). Chased out of Tempe for practicing "ritual performance art" that involved body scarification and fire, they were branded as "satanists" by that city's police department. Their subsequent evolution as fire performers did not sit well with the authorities in Phoenix either. Reveling in their reputation as "the dirty artists from the other side of the tracks," their current location, just off Roosevelt, was a congeries of live-work studios and gallery space called the Firehouse. Every year, at the conclusion of the annual Art Detour weekend, they burned a large, elaborately handcrafted phoenix in an

Figure 3.3
Phoenix Burn: an annual artworld ritual. Courtesy of Dawn O'Doul.

undisclosed location at an event they called "Phoenix Burn." While city boosters were accustomed to use the image of the phoenix to suggest reinvention, Michael 23 and his fellow renegades focused on the element of fire itself, its ritual significance, and its performance potential. Needless to say, this was not an interest condoned by the regulators in City Hall.

Michael 23 had been president of Artlink, the committee that ran First Friday, during a crackdown known locally as Black Friday in the summer of 2005. On that evening, the police showed up en masse, and on horseback, interrogated gallery owners and underage drinkers, and made for an intimidating presence on the streets.[38] It was proof to many that the folks in City Hall did not understand the unrehearsed, social ecology of First Fridays, nor even the model of arts-driven development that might have governed their chief interest in the event. Other critics, more conspiratorially inclined, saw it as an aggressive move to assert the city's authority over the contiguous blocks, designated for the planned biomedical campus. Indeed, over the next few years, the police department effectively became the "arbiters," as Michael 23 pointedly put it, of the conflict within the artist communities about how First Fridays were run.

After Black Friday, an agreement about improving "dialogue" over the management of First Fridays authorized the city manager to set up two task forces; one to run interference over regulation of the monthly art-walk, the other to work with the planning department to expand the existing Artist Storefront Program by rezoning parts of the downtown core with an "Arts, Culture, and Small Business Overlay." This rezoning relaxed many of the regulations that stood in the way of storefront, street-level activity, including parking rules that were the bane of small- grain advocates. Among other things, the overlay showed how much in common the artist-occupied spaces had with other small businesses in the area. It was also one of the fruits of City Hall's decision to take a firmer hand over downtown planning. As Phil Jones, director of the city's Office of Art and Culture, and the chair of the task forces, recalled: "When the DPP and the PCA decided that they were going to do the downtown plan, they sponsored some public forums and, of course, the artist community came out in droves. The concern was that it was all driven by big business owners, and that there would not be a diverse downtown. There was such an outcry that the city actually took over the planning process by creating a separate downtown planning office, and they did develop a plan."

What was the fruit of this new engagement of the artists with City Hall? The first was the watchdog role over development adopted by the Downtown Voices Coalition (DVC), whose members harried City Hall over one contested site or another. "It was a boom time," recalled Steve Weiss, the DVC president, "and so it seemed many times we were playing Whack-A-Mole, that great carnival game where hitting one pop-up mole only made another rise." Using "the tactics of 'Agitate, Negotiate and, when all else fails, Litigate,'" their efforts were "both welcomed and disparaged," because they spoke up for "people who aren't moving towards the next buck or the next city, and to whom it's more important to raise living values than financial values." For Weiss, a photographer and film festival organizer, the abnormality of the DVC's value system was brought home to him at a City Council meeting "when the lawyer for a proposed out-of-scale development" responded to the DVC activists by declaring that he had "never before dealt with people who didn't want to raise their property values."[39]

The DVC's emphasis on inclusion in planning put it on a collision course with the elite downtown organizations like DPP and PCA. Don Keuth, PCA president, acknowledged that the dialogue "started out as a clash, because their position was that we were just going to create some artificial development, and that was never our intent, but it played well and it got some attention." Over time, there was more harmonization. "At the end of the day," Keuth reported, "we are pretty much in agreement with most of them—not all of them. There are still a couple of radicals out there who will never buy into anybody that wears a tie." Even so, it was clear that Keuth, whose organization included the big-shot developers, did not see a city block as an organic outcome of the chemistry between residents and business proprietors, but rather as an "unfinished canvas" upon which developers could make their mark, if they saw a profit in it. The Valley, he observed, "gets the big national awards for the master-planned community of the year and these are just gorgeous facilities and our development community is really, really good at those things: give them a thousand acres and they will create the Garden of Eden. But if you give them a city block, they have no idea what to do with it, because they have not wanted to venture into those waters."

Brian Kearney, president of DPP during the years of engagement, was more generous about the shift in thinking prompted by DVC: "I lived and breathed the mega projects, and was all for them, but I received an education myself on what the finer points of a downtown can mean" by listening to the "grassroots effort by the folks at Roosevelt Row." At first, he reported, "We had a polarization of views; their view was that mega projects were bad, and that we never paid enough attention to the small projects." Kearney acknowledged that he had to be "whacked over the head a few times" before he and others appreciated the importance of the urban fabric's small grain. "By 2005," he believed, "there was more of a true consensus about what needed to happen for downtown to move forward." If both sides were finally seeing eye to eye, much of the credit was due to the success of DVC's tactics, as summed up by Weiss, "We are trying to talk to and collaborate with you, but recognize that there is no collaboration if you are telling us what to do. Recognize that if you do not acknowledge us, we will remove ourselves and these guys back there, whom we support, will start to scream for attention, and put the city on the spot."

MODEL CITIZENS?

One of the fruits of this dialogue was reflected in the city's efforts to take firmer control over aspects of downtown development that had been driven in the past by the PCC and DPP. Above all, this was evident in the adoption of a unified "form-based code" for the entire downtown core, one mile wide and two miles long. Carol Johnson, the city planner responsible for overseeing the city's General Plan update, explained that the code was the first major revision since 1960s zoning ordinances, which had been geared to suburban development. The new code, which regulated according to the form rather than the use of buildings, was designed to foster mixed use, higher densities, and pedestrianism. Basically New Urbanist in character, it was also aimed at fostering newer green initiatives like community gardens and planting shade on downtown sidewalks.

A key part of this new planning ethos was adaptive reuse—the recycling of old buildings for new uses. Revisions to the downtown code made it easier to convert existing buildings and create the kind of refurbished street fronts that livability advocates cherished. The most prominent champion was Kimber Lanning, owner of the multimedia space, Modified Arts, one of the anchors of Roosevelt Row, and Stinkweeds, a record store and performance venue that was central to the city's indie music scene. The new rules about conversions notwithstanding, "the county," she pointed out, "still incentivizes people to tear buildings down by letting them pay 15 percent less on their property taxes. Over here you've got building codes pounding you into the ground, so that it's too expensive to renovate a building, and over there, you've got the county saying, 'Tear it down and we'll give you a 15 percent discount.'"

Lanning, whose name and Modified Arts building were synonymous with the grassroots beat of downtown culture, had developed a reformer's passion for grappling with the intricacies of zoning and coding details. At the same time, she had done more than any other individual to change the prevailing mind-set at City Hall: "It's difficult to get them to understand that no one comes back from Chicago and says it is an amazing city because of its convention center. It's the small grain stuff that makes Chicago what it is." Active in the original artists' coalition efforts, Lanning increasingly opted to fly solo: "Early on, a lot of the artists down here showed up with picket signs and wearing diapers to make a statement, and that's really not the way to get anything done at City Hall. You're closing as many doors as you are opening." Championing the interests of the artists-owners as small businesses was her point of entry into the political fray, and so it was a natural move for her to take over the Arizona chapter of Local First, the national organization that promotes locally owned businesses.

Buying and producing locally is becoming a fundamental rule of thumb for any community bent on achieving long-term sustainability. The upsurge of localist movements in the 1990s and 2000s was a widespread reaction to the concentration of wealth in multinational corporations with complex supply chains that snake all over the world. The dependence of cities on these firms and their far-flung resources has been an obstacle to the efforts of communities to build a resilient economy at home.[40] Phoenix was a top importer of food, energy, and materials, its urban metabolism relying on supplies from untold "ghost acreage" elsewhere. It was also a mecca for chain stores and corporate franchises, eagerly courted by the real-estate industry. "They think that nice new shiny shopping centers with Targets and Applebees and Walmarts are the way to go," snorted Lanning. "It's shocking to me that there's even a conversation" about the local alternatives that her organization promoted. Persuading the city to adopt a local procurement policy and building the Local First chapter membership to 1,700 members were the first steps in a campaign with obvious political potential. There were few opinion makers downtown or in city government who did not see Lanning running for office successfully in the near future.

Even if she did not become the next mayor of Phoenix, her high public profile represented a maturation of the downtown artist-activist movement. Inevitably, this involved a divergence of paths. Speaking frankly of her DVC allies, she expressed frustration with their oppositional mode: "You can't sue the city and then ask them for a favor six months later." DVC, from her standpoint, had narrowed its aims over the years to "picking the weeds off the leaf." Rather than saving old buildings one at a time, they should be "attacking the policy or the general culture" that allows the buildings to be demolished. To do that, Lanning argued, involved forming relationships with officials: "If you don't agree with a politician" on some issues, then "show up when you do agree with them."

In its defense, if DVC continued to focus on single projects or buildings, that was because the city had not kicked the habit of issuing variances for developers with outstretched hands and lots of clout. This had happened most recently in 2006, when the zoning overlay for the Warehouse District, established in 1993 to protect the historic character of the buildings, was substantially altered under pressure from big developers. On some occasions, city-owned or -subsidized projects such as ASU Downtown or the biomedical campus were beneficiaries of these exceptions. Nor were the variances for trifling technical details. Downtown advocates had imagined the new university branch would be fully integrated with the cityscape, and that its facilities and users would be dispersed all around the core. But the final outcome was a more tightly bounded campus, a "moated, gated community" in the eyes of critics who blamed the city and its ASU partners for reverting to the old rules for building mega projects as stand-alone superblocks. To add insult to urbanist injury, ASU had given campus storefront leases to national chains like Subway and Sbarro, making it less likely students would ever leave the castle to explore downtown. As Nancy Levinson, director of the university's Urban Research Lab, observed, "If you want to make downtown a destination you can't put in the same six stores that are in every strip mall every two miles."

No doubt, it was just as easy on the bureaucrat's territorial map to imagine the city's two artist communities, on Roosevelt Row and Grand Street, as bounded colonies, and the outlooks associated with them as equally distinct from those of other downtown stakeholders. From the outset, however, Phoenix's artist-activists refused to draw a line around their domains. Their downtown advocacy extended to the small businesses and long-term residents of the central neighborhoods where they had settled. The adaptive reuse reforms served interests beyond their own, as did their lobbying for affordable housing, community participation, and social inclusion. DVC's "bible" had nothing in common with the classic "artists' manifesto," nor did it mirror the policy model of arts-driven development pushed by MPAC, or the Creative City paradigm pitched by Florida and others.

Beatrice Moore, longtime DVC participant and doyenne of the Grand Street scene, explained why she was opposed to the idea of a bounded artists' district. "Would I rather look out there and see a bunch of yuppies sitting outside drinking coffee in a place all fixed up, or see those kids outside playing basketball? Other artists here think it's really cool to be surrounded by people just like them, and when I hear them say, 'People are finally starting to move over here,' I say, 'What do you mean? There are already people living here, and it is their neighborhood. Even the homeless have been here a lot longer than we have!'" Dead set against what she called "neighborhood cleansing" on the part of creatives, she agonized over the prettification of the buildings she had bought, aware of their attraction for developers. "Maybe our saving grace right now is the tow truck place across the street, or the used car lot." In her mind, these small businesses were "protective camouflage that we have to keep development from coming here too quickly."

Moore's observations spoke to the ambiguous position of the artists who gravitate toward cheap downtown real estate. Often cast as saviors of blighted neighborhoods—agents of a more organic, authentic makeover than any outside developer would achieve—they segue quickly into the victim role when the upscale gut rehabs arrive and they are threatened with displacement by rising realty prices. There was no shortage of blight in downtown Phoenix. Moore and Zahn (on Grand Street), Esser, Dach, Lanning, and Rainey (on Roosevelt), Moody and Johnson (in Garfield), and others who were "the first on their blocks" all spoke of their respective neighborhoods' share of crack houses, prostitution, assault weapon gunfire from warring gangs, and police helicopters overhead. They were well aware of their ability to stabilize, and bring some new local business, to neighborhoods that were safer and livelier a result.[41] But they could also see that their presence was an open invitation to purveyors of the upmarket culture that Moore excoriated, not to mention developers whose business depended explicitly on displacing their low-income neighbors.

The artist-owners responded to this predicament by becoming something close to model citizens, taking on many of the tutelary roles that are associated with the American civic ideal. Responding to these roles, they became advocates of small, locally owned businesses and affordable housing; preservers of public space and historic building stock; amateur-practitioners of urban design and urban planning; lobbyists for human-scale streetscapes; champions of inclusion and diversity; and arbiters of taste in decor, finish, and architectural proportion. It helped, of course, that almost all were Anglo and articulate, with varying amounts of capital—social, cultural, and economic—in their pockets. However much they advocated on behalf of their low-rent neighbors or fellow business owners, it was largely a paternalistic relationship, first among equals, if only because theirs were the voices that would get a hearing at City Hall. Indeed, as Cindy Dach acknowledged, one of the tactical successes of Roosevelt Row was "ask artists to think about themselves as small businesses rather than artists." The general public, she added, "may be willing to have a conversation with you about your small business, but they don't want to hear about you as an artist because they do think you are privileged."

This kind of civic idealism was rare in twenty-first-century America, and if it proved contagious, then the urban revival might take a healthier turn. Even so, it was remarkable that artists, of all people, had become the catalysts. Historically, artists had been marginal outcasts, instinctively hostile to the moral strictures built into the bourgeois idea of civic responsibility. To be thrust into the role of new model citizens was quite a reversal. Yet the part required skills and qualities with which they were familiar. Stewards of urban sustainability, after all, were nothing if not the conscience of the future—a profile to which artists had long aspired. In any event, the sober burghers (in Phoenix's case, merchant families like Barry Goldwater's) who invented civic responsibility forfeited their own custodial rights when they abandoned downtowns forty years ago. The new custodians saw no reason not to fashion rules that reflected their own values and their warm vision of the future.

A SPIN-OFF ON THE FRINGE

Phoenix was not the only area city where an arts-based formula was playing some role in downtown revitalization.[42] In 2009, the small city of El Mirage, sixteen miles to the northwest of the Phoenix core, announced an Artists Relocation Program, inviting artists from near and far to take up residence, under very favorable terms, in its dilapidated "old town" core. In the 1930s, migrant farmworkers had settled on the west bank of the Agua Fria River, and it was one of the few majority Latino towns (Tolleson was another) in the Valley. Encircled now, by Sun City's expansion to the northwest, and by the fast-growth boomburgs of Surprise to the west and Glendale to the south, El Mirage's landlocked status meant that it had little choice but to grow vertically. The blue-collar precincts of the old core were now surrounded by newer subdivisions with $300,000 homes, many of them hit hard by foreclosures. Only 12 square miles, with less than 40,000 residents, El Mirage was a mini version of a dual city, split down the middle by race and class, and, unless it found some creative spark to warm its economy, services were on a straight run downhill. Was the idea to attract a cluster of artists to such an unlikely corner of the Valley a sign of desperation or an act of managerial wizardry?

The architect of the program was the city's new economic development director, Scott Chesney. With decades of experience as a planning consultant for broken cities, he had been poached away from neighboring Surprise, where his team launched a program called "Sustainable Surprise" and invited the ASU experts to collaborate on planning an eco-friendly desert city on the Valley's fringe. The program was undone when city managers bowed down to the first home builder who frowned at the prospect of a departure from the low-density, single-family norm. Brought in to El Mirage to "fix the city," he had jump-started a number of planning initiatives that melded parts of the Creative City paradigm with the Green City model. For example, an effort was underway to rezone the entire city for mixed use and higher density. Organic field conversions were planned for the agricultural section to the south; a commuter rail line was being mooted for the Grand Street freight rail corridor; sections of the Agua Fria riverway were scheduled for restoration; a Women's Ecopreneur Project was networking green job opportunities; and a resort and theme park complex powered by renewable energy had been approved on a large brownfield site to the north of the rail tracks. Chesney had other plans for a solar farm, for developing pockets of infill, and for attracting rail-using professionals. "We are open to being a laboratory," he confessed.

The artists' program looked like a standard application of arts-based development. "It's taking an otherwise blighted part of town," he explained, "and trying to open it up to some form of revitalization by using arts and the creative sector." The artists—sixteen had earlier successfully applied— would receive city funds for down-payment assistance, and also for property renovation, which, under the new zoning, would allow for a residence, studio, and gallery under the same carbon-neutral roof. With downtown housing prices hovering around $50,000, Chesney acknowledged that the "gentrification risk" ordinarily associated with arts-based development was very low in this town. Besides, the arts, he vowed, "were not just a catalyst for development," they were to be "a permanent part of El Mirage."

Not all of the citizenry was ready for a downtown arts district. The more recent arrivals, many of them Anglo retirees, would no doubt rather have seen a bulldozer take care of the downtown blight. In this regard, El Mirage was a microcosm of Phoenix itself. It had seen some immigrant flight in recent years, but Chesney reported that the town's Latino identity meant that "families stay here for a long time," and he was hopeful about the prospects for what he himself called "social sustainability." The prospect of the artists in residence was clearly being viewed, and welcomed, by city improvers as a neighborhood stabilizer. It remained to be seen whether longtime downtown residents of El Mirage would see these heavily subsidized newcomers in quite the same light. I pointed out that artists often had "loose morals" that did not always sit well with working-class norms. "I hadn't thought of that," Chesney chuckled. "I guess we'll find out soon enough."[43]

Part Two: Who Can Afford the Green City?

"Families who lived here for generations are leaving."
Louisa Stark, downtown housing advocate

hoenix's artist-activists had persevered with their vision of a sustainable downtown and had even succeeded in winning over some of the big players involved in the urban revitalization business. But was there a place for their principles in the Green City program announced by Mayor Gordon in fall 2009? While the two visions were compatible in spirit, the mayor's new rollout was overwhelmingly technical in nature (improving the energy efficiency of city lights or green-retrofitting public housing) and DVC's was driven by humane values (quality-of-life urbanism enjoyed by resilient and diverse communities). The Green City, moreover, was presented as a physical challenge for experts and bureaucrats to implement, while Sustainable Downtown was conceived as an exercise in civic democracy.

Notably, there had been no community input in the process that led to the adoption of the Green City agenda, not even at the level of the village planning committees. Instead, the mayor's office looked to ASU for ideas, guidance, and blueprints. Cobbled together by the university's sustainability professors, the 17-point Green City program was primarily a pitch for Washington, hastily assembled over the course of one weekend, according to Rob Melnick, executive dean of ASU's Global Institute of Sustainability, who coordinated the effort. Devastated by budget cuts and cognizant of what Melnick described as the "perceived political opportunity associated with being green," the city was looking to snag some of the ARRA stimulus funding. "There was a big brass ring to grab that was called the recovery money," as he put it, "but if you forget the money grab, were these good things to do for the city, even if there was no money there?" The plan built on existing initiatives for water and energy conservation and air-quality improvement, while endorsing new schemes for solar applications, transit usage, and weatherization of buildings. Once the ARRA funds were secured, the goal was to create a 10-mile "green demonstration corridor" along the light rail line. Incentives for cooperation would be offered to property owners within half a mile of the tracks, and, if the outcome was an overall reduction in carbon emissions and "urban heat island" temperatures, it could be touted as a national model for green policymaking.

Because of the municipality's large footprint in the central core, most of the action proposals applied to public buildings and other kinds of city-owned property downtown. But that was not the only respect in which the Green City was an exercise in governance. Now that every corporation had its own sustainability officer, local governments and universities were following suit. Phoenix's city manager appointed a longtime insider, Tammy Perkins, to bring all his agencies into line with the new program: "I've run large and small departments," she reported, "and I have good professional relationships with people." Under her guidance, every department had to show results from its adoption of sustainability measures, whether on the balance sheet of cost avoidance or through the more effective delivery of services. Performance would be measured internally and against that of other Valley cities through a Sustainable Cities Network, run by ASU, with favorable regional impacts in mind.

It was by no means easy to change the customs of government departments, as Perkins attested, but wielding a green stick was a handy way of reforming the administration of government functions. In time, it would also become a whole new way of governing, by setting expectations of green conduct on the part of the citizenry and issuing rewards for compliance. The profile for conduct modification would be aimed primarily at upper-middle-class populations that were accustomed to look to City Hall for policies that would benefit them. Their responsiveness to the new norms of behavior would then be held up as a model for others who could afford to emulate it, as was typical of efforts to govern through the regulation of public conduct. Just as important, this mentality of governing was associated with a new template for development—there was money in it, for those who were quick off their marks, and there was surety from Washington, just as there had

THE BATTLE FOR DOWNTOWN [105]

been steady federal funding for the state's development models that had gone before: mineral extraction and ranching, irrigation farming, military provisioning, suburbanization, high-tech industry transfers, and absorption of retiree and other migrant populations.

But this was not the only direction for green governance to go. An alternative would involve delivering justice to those who had been side-lined and deprived by the models of growth the city had facilitated for the last sixty years. Addressing those justice claims would require government to approach sustainability more as a matter of civil rights than as a vehicle for redevelopment or cost avoidance. Green conduct, after all, was pri-marily a consumer proposition for those accustomed to enjoying choices about their lifestyles and the gizmos developed and marketed for them. Residents with adequate incomes could opt to live and work downtown, forgo a car, eat local at restaurants or farmers markets, and further reduce their carbon footprint by throwing up solar panels. Low-income popula-tions who could not afford cars, air conditioners, or mortgages had long been consigned to the food deserts of their central-city neighborhoods. Technically speaking, they had small eco footprints, but their low-carbon lifestyle had done little to improve their health, and many of them were in line to get pushed out of the way if and when downtown development ramped up. From their point of view, a green city ought to be an affordable proposition—one that was not delivered from above but won through the public will to make good on long-felt deficits in democracy.

The litmus test for this alternative was the provision of affordable housing, regarded internationally, though not in the United States, as a basic right.[1] During its long wave of expansion, the Phoenix region adver-tised itself as an oasis of affordability on the national housing landscape. Defenders of sprawl argued that cities with urban growth limits, like Portland, had become too highly priced as a result of land-use regulations, and that lightly regulated, fast-growth cities like Phoenix and Houston had done a better job of absorbing and housing newcomers with lower incomes.[2] Critics of this view pointed out that the costs of sprawl development were massively offset by state and federal government fund-ing for highways, infrastructure, and fossil fuel, and that none of these subsidies were factored into housing prices. Nor, for that matter, were the costs of environmental degradation, or the long-term risks built into bank loans. The "drive till you qualify" spirit of predatory lending during the last housing boom inflicted the greatest damage on those with the least resources. Stranded in remote and heavily foreclosed subdivisions, with underwater mortgages, dim employment prospects, and rising fuel costs, they were only the latest victims of speculative edge development. In any event, and despite the national advertising campaigns, the affordability of the region's housing had taken quite a hit over the last few decades; in 2000, the number of people that could afford a median value home was 21 percent less than it was in 1970, and in the boom that followed, the numbers dropped further.[3]

While many low-income buyers on the outer rings were flattened by the equity crash, the traditional losers were inner-city residents, who, from the 1960s onward, had watched public investment, commerce, and other resources being transferred out of their neighborhoods to the outer suburbs. Of the federal dollars that go to transportation departments, 80 percent nationally are allocated to highways that service suburban areas, and only 20 percent to public transit, which, in most cities, is overwhelmingly used by low-income inner-city residents.[4] The numbers for Maricopa County had been even more skewed—95 percent for freeways and only 5 percent for public transit—until the allocations were changed, under 2004's Proposition 400, to 55 percent for freeways, 35 percent for transit and light rail, and 10 percent for arterial streets. The flight of full-service supermarkets with fresh produce has also left the urban core with overpriced corner grocery stores and substandard convenience stores purveying junk food. Last but not least, the spatial mismatch between jobs and residence disproportionately penalized core communities; most entry-level jobs today are nowhere near public transit stops. Sunbelt cities like Phoenix led the pack of metropolitan areas experiencing rapid job sprawl toward the outer ring locations over the last two decades: nationally, only 21 percent of employees work within 3 miles of downtown, while twice that number (45 percent) work more than 10 miles away from the city centers.[5] In Phoenix itself, only 15 percent of centrally located jobs in 1998 were held by people who lived there, and much of the employment on the urban perimeter was located adjacent to freeways, necessitating auto commutes.[6] The evidence was clear. Land-use decisions favoring the health and livelihoods of suburbanites have had a direct negative impact on the life expectancy and access to opportunity of inner-city residents.

Environmental justice pioneer Robert Bullard has argued that the origins of smart growth can be traced to the civil rights movement and specifically to efforts to respond to criticisms of urban renewal and public disinvestment in the inner city.[7] The more recent initiatives to combat low-density sprawl have been driven by concerns about carbon reduction, but anti-sprawl advocates' efforts to draw the middle class back downtown have not been matched by an equivalent concern about how to sustain the low-carbon residence of existing downtowners while improving their health, quality of life, and economic stability. Arguably, this is most apparent in the failure of most downtown revitalization campaigns to prioritize or preserve affordable housing.

Compared to the urban fringe, the cost of building affordable housing in downtown Phoenix was prohibitive, but it was by no means impossible for private developers to take on. The planning codes were almost the same for the core as the edge and this was an obstacle, even to high-end builders. Allan Gutkin, whose development group had built condos near Roosevelt Row at the height of the boom, lamented, "We were trying to apply urban notions of space to codes which are designed for suburban development," and he confessed that "if we had known the downturn would be so severe, we would not have been so pioneering." Reid Butler, a downtown developer and a DVC member, confirmed that "true infill in Phoenix is not for the inexperienced. If you are a developer and all you are thinking about are your costs of development, then you are going to go to the edge of town." But if you think "about real estate from the perspective of its costs to the community," as he clearly did, "then you will be doing infill." Butler was one of a handful of developers who had got the numbers to work for affordable housing, albeit with a little help from government subsidies.

Most of the Phoenix business community preferred the term "attainable housing"—a local euphemism to evade the undesirable connotation of "affordable"—or even "workforce housing," but the definitions of each of these were quite hazy. Louisa Stark, a DVC founder who ran the Community Housing Partnership to house the homeless in the low-income Garfield neighborhood, reported that the mayor, "in his State of the City address, said he wanted to promote the building of a thousand units of affordable housing downtown," but that she had seen no follow-through. "To the mayor, a $250,000 condo or townhouse is affordable—but to whom? Maybe a police officer, or school teacher, or fireman, he says, but only if he or she is living with another adult that's also making money." Indeed, the DVC's 2011 update to its founding 2004 document recorded that virtually all the new downtown units built in the last decade were affordable only to families with incomes above $65,000, a figure starkly at odds with the area's median income of $20, 352.[8]

In defiance of these trends, the DVC's own Reid Butler had been building what he unabashedly called "affordable housing" downtown for the best part of a decade, beginning with the 200-apartment Legacy Bungalows (average household income in the $24,000 to $40,000 range) in the devastated area near the state Capitol. From watching the impact on that neighborhood, he "learned that affordable housing really can serve as an economic development revitalization tool." Subsequently, with the help of more city financing, he converted nine historic homes in the Roosevelt district into a connected complex called the Roosevelt Commons—with resident incomes below $27,000 for individuals and $38,500 for four-person households. In the initial planning stage, "there were many hard feelings in the neighborhood," he acknowledged, "but the community turned around and became a part of my advocacy group" to help raise the necessary funding. Now, he reported, "there are about twenty small businesses, restaurants, coffee houses, art galleries, and other small projects—but the project that spurred that growth was an affordable housing project." The outcome, he claimed, has been "one of the strongest mixed-income, mixed-use areas in the Phoenix region."

Tim Sprague, the only other developer who attended DVC meetings, was taking the lead on converting a 99-room motel on the Grand Street strip "with rent restrictions on 60 percent of the units" to keep them affordable. The project would be aimed at, though not limited to, artists' occupancy. Enterprises like that relied heavily on public money—especially from HUD—and Sprague, who was also a musician, was committed to cobbling together financing to make it viable. Even though public subsidies were readily available, most of his peers in the industry "would not spend the time," as he gently put it, to prepare the applications, let alone build an affordable project.

The other players in this field were community developers, like Chicanos Por La Causa and Native American Connections, and they were committed to doing more than providing affordable housing. Chicanos Por La Causa was founded by activists in the 1960s as a support organization for the South Central Phoenix barrio and had grown into a mammoth full-service organization, with statewide offices, seven hundred employees, and a $16 million operating budget. A direct service provider, with over thirty lines of business, it functioned as a kind of shadow government for many urban Latinos, trusted above all other community service organizations, including the Catholic Church, according to one local survey. The scale and range of the organization's services meant that clients' needs could be addressed in more than a piecemeal fashion: "When someone comes to see us about housing," explained David Adame, chief development officer, "we try to provide a net of other services they might need, whether it's substance abuse, a job, training, Head Start, or domestic violence." From charter schools to micro-lending programs, the organization's services to its clients went "far beyond the affordable housing component" to offer "comprehensive support—whatever they need to get through to self-sufficiency," because "it could be just one thing that knocks them off the edge." Even so, "it's a hand-up," Adame cautioned, "not a hand-out."

Figure 3.4
Edgy pitch for downtown condo lofts. Photo by author.

Native American Connections, a much smaller operation, used its housing as an anchor for a drug-and-alcohol recovery program for its homeless clients. Urban Indians make up a disproportionate number of Phoenix homeless, and those who fell prey to addiction and other behavioral health problems could find safe, transitional housing through the organization. Rising summertime temperatures posed especially serious problems. Joe Keeper, the organization's housing director, reported that "people are actually dying on the streets because they don't have water," at a time when homeless shelters were overflowing with the victims of "foreclosure or rent eviction, tied to losing their jobs or the restructuring of their home loans." Native American Connections, he explained, had four different levels of housing product, designed as stepping-stones to move clients "from homelessness to homeownership." The first was "for homeless people that are coming off the street, to wrap them with services from a behavioral health perspective that introduces them to job readiness, medical issues, and entitlement issues, whether it's social security or disability." The upper levels included "tax-credit housing that would target working families that are no longer considered homeless" and also "low-income, tax-credit, senior housing property to help some of our elders."

This capacity to wrap services around housing was considered a key factor by veteran advocates of affordable housing like Michael Pyatok, who had just given up his post as director of ASU's Stardust Center for Affordable Homes and the Family. He has argued that truly sustainable shelter for low-income residents depends on the existence of a robust network of social supports—a secure job base, a decent public school system, accessible public transit and health services, housing subsidies in the form of rent control or inclusionary zoning, and some palpable sense of community respect.[9] Without these, the greenest or best-designed affordable housing will not help low-income occupants make it, let alone enable them to adopt an environmentally sustainable lifestyle.

These kinds of social supports are beyond the reach of most community developers, even large outfits like Chicanos Por La Causa, and so the fallback for nonprofit organizations in this field is to tap into the social bonds and mutual aid networks of existing communities. Teresa Brice, director of the community development leader Local Initiatives Support Corporation (LISC), observed that Phoenix's high rate of population turnover and internal mobility distinguished it from older industrial cities in the East, where LISC's model of community development originated. "With all due respect to Jane Jacobs," she pointed out, "when you have a high-growth community like Phoenix you have to use a different playbook," one that does not "presuppose a neighborhood with longtime, committed residents who identify with their community and area." Her organization had launched a Sustainable Communities Initiative campaign "to tie housing affordability to energy and transportation issues" through working with partners like the Sierra Club. Citing LISC's alliance with the Sierra Club over energy policy, Brice noted that "while we understand the impact on climate change, we are coming at it from the perspective that older homes need to have energy retrofits to make them affordable for residents." Because these two organizations had quite different agendas, she admitted these were "issues which normally we would not have worked on together," but the new model of cooperation was encouraging housing advocates like her to address environmental concerns, while obliging smart growth advocates to confront class inequalities that had not been a high priority in the past.

ASU's own Stardust Center approached the problem Brice had cited by constructing demonstration green homes in tight-knit communities, like the small Yaqui reservation of Guadalupe, nestled between Phoenix and Tempe, or on the Navajo reservation in the northern tier of the state. In each case, the community itself was being encouraged to take on the role of housing developer by building off the prototype. As Sherry Ahrentzen, its research specialist, explained, the Center's role as a public educator was to try to "embed" affordable housing into the way people talked about sustainability and vice versa—to put "sustainable practices into the language of affordability." At root, she elaborated, "We are trying to say that having affordable housing in your community *is* a sustainable practice. If you do not have sustainable housing in your community you can become like a Paradise Valley," the affluent town between Scottsdale and Phoenix that was one of the most likely area models for the elite eco-enclave of the future.

In the poorer, underserviced neighborhoods where Brice, Adame, and Keeper did their community development work, the influence of monied elites was still being felt in unwanted ways. Residents there were especially prey to absentee landlords and, wherever housing prices fluctuated, to the impact of speculators looking for bargains. Brice and Adame both told me that postcrash speculation had stymied much of their efforts to use federal Neighborhood Stabilization Program funds, which were created to offset the impact of heavy foreclosures in select areas. The land crash may have frozen new development, but the deflated housing market had attracted a new wave of investors, determined to sit on their purchases for years before cashing in. These outside buyers were returning to buzz around a city that had lately been their honeypot. Or, as Local First's Kimber Lanning put it, "It's as if they have a secret dog whistle and all of a sudden you have speculators from all over the country."

THE NEWLY DISPLACED

A brand new factor in neighborhood destabilization was the flight of Latino immigrants in the wake of the economic crash. The evacuation, which was amplified by the repressive tactics of Sheriff Joe and by the impact of the Employer Sanctions Act of 2007, escalated rapidly in the months after the harsh anti-immigrant bill SB 1070 was passed in 2010. Neighborhoods struggling to stay above the line were hard hit by the flight. Many of the immigrants who stayed were living in a state of fear and were highly unlikely to be partaking of any government initiative aimed at sustainability. Vice-mayor Tom Simplot, whose electoral district included the heavily immigrant Maryvale, reported that his constituents "may qualify for a program," but if their "only access to the government is through their children," then "you won't get inside that home, they'd never let us in the door, out of fear." Ironically, many of these residents hailed from communities south of the border where self-building and energy efficiency were stable customs wrought out of necessity, but none of their skills or knowledge about local sustainability were being tapped as part of their new lives in Central Arizona. With conservation habits formed from long experience with meager resources, these immigrants carried know-how that was immediately relevant to their housing and livelihood needs, but it was never solicited, not even by the sustainability experts who were the architects of the Green City program.[10]

Advocates of sustainability from the bottom up often look to traditional indigenous practices for models of ecological stewardship, but almost always as applied to rural living and very rarely for urban environments. Yet, in cities like Los Angeles, immigrants have distinguished themselves as heroes of inner-city renovation, fixing up decaying neighborhoods with sweat equity and customizing them with the kind of colorful ethnic detail that would mortify the officials of most homeowners' associations.[11] These were plausible examples of what Jane Jacobs once called "unslumming," where residents of blighted areas, with or without block grants, did a better job of revitalization than any planning agency could hope to do. In some shrinking Midwestern and Rustbelt cities, the new arrivals had also been welcomed for stemming a steep population decline and salvaging near-abandoned neighborhoods. These renovations could also be seen in parts of Phoenix, where the swelling Latino population had long spilled out beyond its traditional barrio boundaries into the hastily built first-ring suburbs. Maryvale, Del Webb's 1950s master-planned community for first-time Anglo homeowners, was now predominantly Latino, its crumbling shopping malls brought back to life as vibrant marketplaces of small, family-run stores. But official recognition of this kind of urban homesteading, even among studious planners, was few and far between, and Anglo tolerance of it eroded as the anti-immigrant fervor mounted, and as ethnic customs like front-yard socializing and public street life (e.g. low-riding auto culture) were more and more surveilled and subject to police discipline.

Phoenix had a long history of neglecting, or erasing, the presence of its Latino population. The traditional adobe structures of the Southwest were quite common in the early years of the city's settlement, but were officially discouraged in favor of Anglo styles, built with brick and wood, toward the end of the nineteenth century (at the same time that Indian street names were replaced by Anglo ones).[12] Southwestern cities like Tucson and Albuquerque, which were built out around existing Mexican towns, could look to these traditional pueblos as early examples of what was now called New Urbanism: compact, mixed use, and with a good deal of overlap between private and public space.[13] Phoenix had no such pre-Anglo core, and the history and demographic power of its Latinos were not at all reflected in the self-image or promotional efforts of the city. Despite the Latino expansion into the West Valley, the legacy of the old color line—formerly, no Latinos were allowed to live north of Van Buren street—was still all too evident in demographic maps of the city.

Ruth Osuna, a former community organizer who was now deputy city manager, told me that the deed to her own house—above Van Buren—contained a "No Mexicans" clause. "The city of Phoenix," she observed, "was planned out with a Midwestern feel, and the communities of Native Americans and Mexicans got lost, because we were not the people in power. So you come here and you do not see their influence." Neither group felt they had a "place" in Phoenix, "but what," asked Osuna, "would that place be?" One example she gave was the new Latin@ Arts and Cultural Center, which opened downtown in December 2009. The central location (5,400 square feet on Adams Street in the business core) was chosen because the founders considered it symbolically important to have a kind of semiofficial Latino presence in the downtown area. Jim Covarrubias, a prominent local artist and one of the movers behind the center, explained that the existing high arts institutions in the core were perceived as Anglo spaces and that downtown in general was still not viewed as a "comfort zone" by the city's Latino population. "Many times, Mexicanos will only want to do things where they feel comfortable," he added, and the majority, "from Glendale or South Phoenix, may come downtown [for a ball game] and leave because they see no reason to hang out."

Latinos now had a downtown cultural location to match the George Washington Carver Museum and Cultural Center (housed in Arizona's first African American high school, Phoenix Union Colored High). But there had been very little Latino input or participation in the long battle over downtown redevelopment, according to Ruben Hernandez, a cultural journalist for *Latino Perspectives* magazine. Like Covarrubias, Hernandez recalled that "the community was at the heart of Chicano arts" in the era of the seminal arts grouping known as MARS (Movimiento Artistico del Rio Salado), because it was a time when the work of Chicano artists "reflected the struggle of our community for civil rights."[14] But the provisional spaces they had opened and operated since then left no permanent mark, until the Center's opening, on the downtown landscape, and nothing remotely like the impact of the artist zones on Roosevelt Row and Grand Street.

A critical mass of property ownership, as we have seen, helped to stabilize the Roosevelt and Grand Street clusters, and the artist-owners fashioned their own advocacy of downtown that extended to small businesses and to other kinds of low-income residents in proximity. Their voices got an especially attentive hearing at City Hall at a time when the "creative class" was being seen as a key vehicle for economic development. Indeed, the relationship ripened to the point at which some city officials relied on DVC to make a noise for them, from the outside. As Jim McPherson, a historic preservationist who was active in the coalition, recalled, "I can name six examples of times where we would get calls from people within the power structure— 'Help us, we can't do it, we can't raise the issue. You do it, Downtown Voices.'" The experience of being officially valued in this way, combined with the maturity that many in the DVC achieved as activists, guaranteed their inclusion, entitlement even, as citizen advocates. Susan Copeland, a veteran of the DVC, put it quite succinctly: "Really, how I got started was because I was tired of hearing myself complain and saying 'them' or 'they,' when the government is supposed to be 'us.' It's supposed to be 'we.'" The result was a leap forward, however uneven, for citizen involvement in downtown planning. In January 2010, the coalition convened another town-hall meeting to update its founding document. When the new report was issued, documenting where progress had been made in the last six years (a thin but appreciable record) and what still needed to be done (a much longer list), there was a much fuller expectation than there had been in 2004 that DVC's recommendations would bear fruit in policy changes at City Hall.

For others with no special pathway to entitlement, and for low-income Latinos especially (almost 40 percent of the downtown population), it was not so easy to make Copeland's transition from "them" to "we." In Arizona's escalating war of attrition against immigrants, some of Phoenix's central city neighborhoods were among those on the front line. The state of siege was directed at the undocumented, but it was being felt acutely by all Latinos, even by second- and third-generation residents. Whatever sense of place and membership they had attained in the Southwest's largest city was being rapidly eroded, if not shredded, in ways that would take at least a generation to repair.

Gentrification, and urban renewal before it, had produced its share of displaced residents, but the legions of those forced to leave by the anti-immigrant crusade may prove to be greater in volume. Well-heeled dwellers intent on residing in the "livable downtown" for which activists had fought were outnumbered by the population in flight, leaving instability and fear to rule over city-center and inner-ring neighborhoods that had been designated as potential beneficiaries of the plans for revitalization. As the housing bust neared its fifth anniversary, real estate commentators began to talk about some areas that had seen price declines of more than 80 percent as "beyond recovery."[15] For sure, the upshot had made those parts of the city more affordable, but not necessarily in a good way. This was less a market "correction" than a result of occupants being driven out of town. Any Green City plan that ignored the causes and consequences of that exodus would be a thin blueprint for moving ahead.

CHAPTER 4

Living Downstream

"Apartheid is complete. The two cities look at each other across a golf course."
Andrew Kopkind on Phoenix, in *The New Republic,* 1965

I n neighborhoods well to the north of the Salt River channel, Phoenix's artist communities and downtown advocates fought for mixed-use zoning that would allow places of residence to coexist with commercial storefronts. South of the river, where housing was placed in close proximity to dirty industrial facilities, mixed land use had an altogether different meaning. Residents in South Phoenix, long regarded as the city's human and natural sacrifice zone, were fighting for the right to enjoy clean air and water, unencumbered by the toxic hazards that government permitting had allowed to fester in their neighborhoods. The disparity between these two battles with City Hall spoke volumes about the environmental challenges facing Phoenix, and almost every other city divided by race and class.

Hydrologists talk about water "flow" in the West, but very few of the rivers flow naturally anymore, and many, like the mighty Colorado itself, rarely reach their destinations. Except for spasmodic floods, the Salt River has not really flowed through the Phoenix Basin since the early twentieth century, and it exists today primarily as an orderly system of canals. In its natural heyday, it was a wildly erratic river, and so its flood plain was several miles broad. Today's riverbed is a vast moonscape of sand and cobbles, though it is far from deserted. Cheap land and laissez-faire regulation have drawn in the region's worst polluters over the years. For decades, it was used as a dumping ground for all manner of waste, some of it exported from neighboring states, like California, with more oversight over disposal of hazardous materials than Arizona.

From a commercial standpoint, the riverbed was the mother of all brownfield sites, zealously eyed by developers hoping to cut a deal with government agencies with fast-track access to federal cleanup funds. Dreams of converting the urban portions of the Salt River into a waterside attraction dated back to the 1960s when ASU design students conceived a restoration project under the alluring name of Rio Salado. Although the project was aimed more at urban redevelopment than at riparian restoration, the vote on a countywide property tax to fund it was defeated in 1987, thwarting those who had begun to imagine San Antonio's Riverwalk in the middle of the Sonoran Desert. Undaunted, the city of Tempe forged ahead with its own stretches of the Salt channel, creating a mammoth lake (with almost a billion gallons of precious Arizona water) to anchor its downtown redevelopment plans.[1] Just off the lakefront, an anodyne mega-mall (Tempe Marketplace) sprang up on a complex Superfund site— the largest brownfield cleanup in the state's history.

Acting on a federal mandate to restore degraded ecosystems, the Army Corps of Engineers conducted feasibility studies on the Phoenix portions of the Rio Salado from 1994 onward. This time, the focus was not on condos and hotels but on restoring an "accurate desert riparian habitat" for wildlife, and primarily for the recreational use of those who might be drawn to a riverscape. The final plan called for the creation of wetland ponds, groves of mesquite, cottonwood, willow, saltbush, and palo verde, and, curiously, a golf course—thrown in, no doubt, to whet the appetite of developers.[2] A low-flow channel in the riverbed would be maintained by pumped groundwater. It was a dubious proposition to many of the city's environmentalists (one of whom described it to me as a "gigantic mosquito breeding ground"), but the city of Phoenix moved ahead with a 600-acre chunk of the restoration, funded mostly with federal dollars, and today it hosts an Audubon Society nature education center. Replanted trees and other greenery give the spot an oasis feel, but those tempted to take their dogs down for a walk are advised to make sure their pets do not drink the water that trickles through.

Aside from the toxic legacy of several hundred dumps, the riverbanks, during the time of my visits, still hosted a multitude of sand and gravel mining operations. Valley Forward, a green membership organization for businesses, had been pushing a plan for the extractors to dredge a canal through the riverbed in return for extensive mining permits along a 50-mile stretch of Rio Salado. Firms that cooperated would have the opportunity to flip their reputation as bottom-feeders, literally as well as metaphorically, into that of restoration saints. That would be a remarkable PR feat. "I'm sure they deserve some of the bad rep they get," acknowledged Diane Brossard, Valley Forward's director, "but this would allow for the balance of economic growth and environmental quality. If the city had to pay to build that channel, it would cost millions of dollars. So let them go in, mine it, and build the channel. It's a win–win situation, a wonderful landmark project that will create a recreation corridor that can connect cities and neighborhoods."

On the floodplain perimeter were dozens of asphalt plants supplied by the sand and gravel mines. At nighttime, when inspectors from the county's air quality agency were fast asleep, the plant furnaces and the mining machinery got cranked up, and the sky was an infernal cocktail of flares, dust, and smoke. The resulting pollution carried all over the metro area, but the most noxious impact was on those living nearby in South Phoenix. One of the asphalt plants I visited, operated by South Dakota–based Fisher Sand and Gravel Company, had been fingered by its neighbors as an outstanding health hazard. Arsenic, lime, and formaldehyde are only some of the many hazardous air pollutants associated with asphalt production, and the witch's brew that spewed out of the Fisher batch plant's 70-foot chimney had been linked to the deaths of several residents and the poor

Figure 4.1
Rare flow on the Salt River bed, ringed by sand and gravel operations. Photo by author.

respiratory condition of many others. Calls to shut down the plant from Concerned Residents of South Phoenix, a neighborhood coalition, and Don't Waste Arizona, an environmental justice watchdog, eventually found a response in the halls of power. Operating since 2006 without a valid city permit, next to a mine that had been an illegal dump, the company was issued literally thousands of violation notices and fines by city, county, state, and federal agencies from 2007 onward. Fisher's record of pollution violations elsewhere in Arizona and other Western states did not help its case, nor did the three-year prison sentence recently imposed on its owner for tax fraud. Facing criminal charges at the city and county level, the Fisher managers were ordered to close down the plant in February 2010, but continued to operate the neighboring mine, which had a grandfathered legal right to exist because it predated the area's annexation by the city of Phoenix.

The shutdown was hailed by the neighborhood groups who had been first to raise the alarm, research the site, and bring public awareness to the violations. Yet veterans of these groups knew that Fisher's conduct was not all that egregious, not when judged by Arizona's lax regulatory culture, and least of all by the standards to which polluters were held in South Phoenix. That the facility operated in a location that allows residential zoning (asphalt plants usually require zoning for heavy industrial use) was not unusual in an area where residential pockets are frequently interspersed with factories. Before South Phoenix was incorporated into the city in 1960, its traditional barrios and ghettos coexisted with the region's dirtiest industries, and the legacy of that public health nightmare is still alive and well in many neighborhoods.

Just as typical, according to the advocates, was the initial stonewalling from city and county agencies in the face of petitions from residents and activists. The sand and gravel industry (which had a $5.8 billion impact on the state's economy) supplied the raw materials for road building and construction, and so it was an essential part of the growth machine. Fisher, it turned out, had enjoyed several lucrative contracts with the city (worth over $10 million since 2005), and had recently won contracts totaling $45 million from the Arizona Department of Transportation to supply the widening of Interstate 10 to facilitate access to new developments in the West Valley.[3] More notably, the firm advertised itself as "the leading supplier of rubberized asphalt in the Phoenix metropolitan market." Rubberized, or "crumb," asphalt is a product of ground-up used tires and is associated with the sustainable wing of the industry. In addition to recycling tires, use of the product drastically reduces roadway noise. Arizona, and Phoenix in particular, pioneered rubberized asphalt overlay as a policy priority dating from the late 1960s, and Fisher, an industry leader in this process, operated mines and plants throughout the state. The company, which extracted and processed over 30 million tons of aggregate material annually, promoted itself nationally as an advocate of such "green" strategies.

Shutting down an essential player in the growth machine was not a step to be taken lightly, and so officials and lawmakers had to be lobbied hard on all sides before justice was served on the company. But the Fisher story also presented an illustrative paradox. The city's use of crumb asphalt was being promoted as a key item in its sustainability portfolio at the same time as the product's manufacture was sickening and killing nearby residents. This was only one of the many ironies that flowed from the long-standing use of minority-dominant South Phoenix as the preferred location for the region's dirtiest industry. Leah Landrum Taylor, the feisty state senator who represented one of its districts, summed up the yawning environmental gap between her constituents and the affluent Anglos who enjoyed cleaner air and mountain preserves in the city's northern suburbs: "Many of those people up there may own some of the companies that are polluting and doing this harmful danger to our community members, but they don't live here and that's where the difference lies." "In my district," she added, "we have one of the highest incidences of asthma in this nation."[4]

Landrum Taylor's most enduring legislative effort was to require companies to report to an electronic database any hazardous substances stored on their premises. In the event of a fire or a large spill, which, she pointed out, "was a regular occurrence" in South Phoenix, "first responders would now know what they had inside the buildings." Environmental justice was one of the top issues that had propelled her into state politics. "When I looked at a map and saw how many clusters of hazardous material companies are right here, as opposed to spread out throughout the state, it blew me away and just got me on fire." Nor, in her mind, did the situation appear to be changing. "Phoenix is not getting any smaller," she observed, "and yet the city is still issuing new permits for companies that are conveniently coming into my district. Why should we have a permitting process which allows that?"

OTHER SIDE OF THE TRACKS

The answer to Landrum Taylor's question was rooted in the history of segregation that had isolated her constituency from the more prosperous communities to the north of Phoenix's central business district. As in so many other cities, the establishment of an east–west rail corridor in the 1880s formed a racial and socioeconomic border that divided one population—Anglo, and well-serviced by urban amenities—from the other, primarily Mexican, with a growing, but still limited, African American presence, deprived of water services, sanitation, and paved roads, and living in shacks with noxious industry for neighbors.[5] Even without the rail tracks, the flood-prone Salt River would have been an effective boundary, since the low-lying ground was clearly not a desirable residential location. The land was cheap, however, and, decade after decade, this would prove a prime asset in the city's efforts to attract industry. The stockyards and warehouses along the railway line were joined, in due time, by food processing and meat packing factories, riverbed mining operations, auto junkyards, and a range of manufacturing facilities that supplied the postwar boom.

Minority residents eked out a living under conditions that bore comparison with the infamous tenement quarters of New York's Lower East Side. South Phoenix's legendary poverty advocate Father Emmett McLoughlin reported that federal officials in the 1930s described the area as the "worst slum area in the U.S." With poisonous runoff from industry in their midst, and no healthcare facilities to speak of, it was no surprise that South Phoenix, according to the man known as the "people's padre," had also achieved "the highest infant death rate in the nation."[6] Three decades later, in 1965, Andrew Kopkind wrote in *The New Republic*: "It looks like a cross between a Mississippi Black Belt Negro ghetto and a Mexican border town.... Many houses are no better than outhouses."[7]

Although Phoenix's African Americans were subject to the most rigid color line in residential location, education, and access to public space, the segregation of black, Latino, and Indian populations was also tightly enforced by redlining and zoning, and it was decisively marked by the treatment of the area as a dumping ground. It is no small irony that the city's first sewage processing plant was located in South Phoenix in 1921, at a time when neighborhoods there had no water or sewage infrastructure of their own.[8] As urban throughput increased, landfills were next to arrive, followed by facilities that processed industrial waste. None of these pestilential operations were sited in Anglo Phoenix, and, during the three postwar decades when at-large politicians controlled City Hall, there were no South Phoenix representatives to draw attention to the area's unfair burden of hazardous waste facilities.

In many respects, the racial geography of pollution and under privilege had changed little since the era of Anglo settlement in the late nineteenth century. The highest concentrations of bad air quality, toxic exposure, and poverty could be found in the same census tracts. In recent years, as concern has mounted about the city's urban heat island, the incidence of deaths from heatstroke in the summer months has also been highest in the low-lying tracts of South Phoenix.[9] While unshaded concrete and asphalt is a primary cause of the temperature increases, it is fair to postulate that the uneven social impact of global warming is already visible in these mortality statistics. Phoenix saw its share of population displacement during the era of urban renewal. Latino neighborhoods were bulldozed to make way for the expansion of Sky Harbor airport, resulting in the decimation of the Golden Gate barrio in the 1970s, and also for the construction of two urban freeways that ran parallel with the rail tracks and riverbed, in the 1980s.[10] So, too, central city neighborhoods immediately north and west of the central business district deteriorated in a pattern typical of population flight from urban downtowns during that era. While white flight was clearly evident in those neighborhoods, South Phoenix was relatively untouched, because Anglos had shunned it from the beginning, and, to this day, most regard it as a no-go area.[11] Only in the most recent property boom were there any significant changes in that pattern. The higher ground to the south, sloping up to the preserved South Mountain range, attracted a round of new, upmarket development, while the warehouse district, closest to the city center, was sought out for condo conversions for "urban pioneers" looking for a downtown lifestyle and proximity to their workplaces in the business district.

Because of its history and continuing toxic legacy, South Phoenix ranks among the most striking case studies of environmental injustice to be found among large American cities. Its predominantly minority population hosts a massively disproportionate number of hazardous sites, some clustered in industrial zones and along transportation corridors, but many still in close proximity to residences. Indeed, a 1999 analysis of Toxic Release Inventory Reports showed that one zip code in South Phoenix—85040—produced nearly 40 percent of all hazardous emissions in the city.[12] It was also the dirtiest zip code in the nation. Beginning in the 1990s, neighborhood groups formed to call attention to this pattern, and there has been a scattershot record of success, like the Fisher case, in closing down the worst polluters. Yet Phoenix does not really show up on the national map of the environmental justice movement, either as a top site of discrimination or as a city where activism has consistently flourished.[13] Bob Bolin, an ASU geographer and expert on environmental inequities in the region, had no doubt as to the reasons. "A big business and right-wing political culture driven with a pro-growth booster machine that is dominated by Anglos," he concluded, "has not been conducive to large-scale, collaborative minority movements for anything." The campaigns he had witnessed tended not to be "long, protracted battles, most are issue-oriented and short term, as opposed to correcting the pattern of industrial hazards."

In this last respect, at least, Phoenix was not anomalous. Residents of low-income neighborhoods rarely have the resources, or the time, to take on the task of correcting long-standing, or structural, patterns of land use that burden their communities. Campaigns against a highly visible, single-site polluter are the norm, especially when the health impacts of that site stand out against the backdrop of a history of contamination. Yet organizations with a longer life often develop out of citizen protest, and they are usually held together by one or two committed individuals, often with the help of national organizations. South Phoenix was no exception.

The president of Concerned Residents of South Phoenix (CRSP), the umbrella organization for a throng of neighborhood groups and causes, was the doughty Mike Pops, a sharecropper's son from Mississippi. An alumnus of the Watts riots in 1968, he came to Phoenix the following year, just as the civil rights movement in the city seemed to be winding down (school desegregation, notably, was won in Phoenix before the *Brown* decision). But the movement soon flared back into life over the long struggle to achieve a statewide holiday in honor of Martin Luther King, Jr. Initially proposed to the legislature in 1969 by Clovis Campbell, Sr., Arizona's first black state senator, the holiday was established by executive order by Governor Bruce Babbitt in 1986. When Governor Evan Mecham canceled the state's commitment to the holiday the following year (it was not finally approved by voters until 1992), Arizona became a national symbol of racist intransigence. Despite, or because of, the attention garnered by boycotts of the state over the next several years, Pops recalled that local support and turnout was more subdued than he expected. "Too many people were, and still are, on the sidelines. During the time that we fought for the holiday, there were too many who were afraid for their jobs to come out for marches and let their voice and body be counted." Job loss was not the only liability. "Am I afraid of being shot?" Pops was often asked. "If you are a disciple of a civil rights movement, then you are in it, just like Medgar Evers or Martin Luther King and others," he responded, "and one day you may die by a sniper's bullet or fire bomb, so you must be committed to the struggle." Pops particularly regretted that the silence often extended to his more recent efforts to remedy environmental injustices. "Our community is dying," he observed, "from advanced cancer, weakened immune systems, and respiratory illnesses. We are not in the best of shape. There are 272 churches in this area from Van Buren to South Mountain and they bury a lot of people. They receive a lot of burial money, but when it comes to fighting back, they are missing in action. I've said, 'Shame on you,' to our leaders who have been silent in our fight."

CRSP was formed in 1992 after fire gutted a circuit-board manufacturing facility (Quality Printed Circuits) in a South Phoenix neighborhood not far from the riverbed. In the aftermath of the 12-hour fire, which burned off several thousand pounds of sulfuric acid and hydrogen fluoride, residents complained of a wide range of illnesses. Other symptoms appeared over the years among those who continued to occupy houses contaminated by the fire's impact, and a pattern of deaths and cancer cases developed in homes closest to the site. Citizen meetings and protests initiated by CRSP brought an unsatisfactory response from city and state agencies. City Hall, it transpired, had granted the company a permit to rebuild in the same neighborhood after a smaller but similar kind of fire burned down its former facility in 1989, and the new permit actually included an exemption for installing overhead sprinklers. After the 1992 fire, tests of selected homes conducted by the Arizona Department of Environmental Quality (ADEQ) found evidence of elevated fluoride and zinc concentrations, but the agency concluded that no adverse health impacts would result. Several years later, more systematic EPA tests found statistically significant levels of these chemicals that were consistent with the symptoms. Residents had been living for several years with poisons and toxics circulating through the air ducts of homes that lay downwind from the fire. Many of the houses were subsequently demolished, but lax, or nonexistent, ADEQ inspections of other facilities in South Phoenix all but guaranteed that other fires would break out.

In August 2000, the area saw one of its worst airborne toxic catastrophes when the main warehouse of Central Garden, the Valley's largest supplier of pool and lawn chemicals, exploded and caught fire. "It was like the Fourth of July," recalled Pops. Firemen, motorists, and residents were captured vomiting in the streets on nightly news footage as the blackened fumes billowed far and wide. The fire burned for two days, hundreds ended up in the hospital, and many died or suffered debilitating ailments in the years following. Emergency responders had no idea what chemicals they were dealing with, and to this day, no adequate inventory of the warehouse contents has been compiled. ADEQ only tested air quality for standard hydrocarbon releases and, five days after the fire, announced that there was no "public health concern" to the residents of South Phoenix. Yet, a month later, the agency's water tests, not announced to the public, showed arsenic at more than 100 times the maximum level allowable for drinking water.[14]

In the fire's aftermath, community pressure stepped up to legislate electronic reporting of the hazardous contents of facilities.

Inspired by the high degree of citizen involvement after the 1992 fire, Pops's organization looked to other sites that needed preemptive action. The area's hazardous waste management facilities (five of the city's seven were located in South Phoenix) were an obvious target, and one in particular, operated by Innovative Waste Utilization, stood out as a threat to the entire neighborhood. The former owner of the site, which had several contaminated areas, including one from a significant arsenic spill, had operated for seventeen years without a permanent permit and had been allowed by the ADEQ to store hazardous waste (including DDT and lead) exported from California. When the new owner applied for an expansion of the facility in 1999, Pops and other activists responded with a civil rights complaint aimed at the ADEQ's long-term complicity in allowing toxic waste facilities to cluster in their neighborhoods. The expansion permit process was arrested, but the agency still approved a permit to store hazardous waste. The company subsequently contracted with the state of California to accept toxic waste collected in West Coast methamphetamine busts. Pops recalled that "the stench in that neighborhood was so vile that we accused the city and county of burning animals in incinerators." Over time, employees took to selling the seized chemicals to local meth labs, and the facility was raided in 2003. "The odor," Pops reported, "stopped immediately when the place was busted" and then shut down by the ADEQ. The state legislature, outraged that the agency had finally found some regulatory teeth, debated whether to abolish it.

A more formal victory was achieved at the Phoenix City Council, which, in the aftermath of the 2000 lawsuit, banned new or expanded commercial hazardous waste facilities from coming into South Phoenix. Yet I heard a more skeptical response from Steve Brittle, who ran Don't Waste Arizona, and who has had a hand in almost every fight for environmental justice in the state, and especially in South Phoenix.[15] "The problems we have with chemicals and hazards being sited in our neighborhood are the *fault* of the city council," he emphasized, "so putting these laws on the books is one thing, but if they never enforce them or respond to communities, then anything goes. In the years previously," he added, "they passed a law against incinerators, but that was routinely ignored." In an effort to take advantage of publicity over the Fisher shutdown, he was pushing for reform of city ordinances to establish time lines for enforcement.

Well versed, though not trained, in environmental law, Brittle had sued so many companies that the legislature voted to remove a citizen suit provision for enforcing the state's environmental laws because Brittle had personally "overused" it. The Chamber of Commerce and business institutions like the *Phoenix Business Journal* singled him out as a thorn in their side, smearing him as a profiteer from the lawsuits and communities he had helped to organize.[16] Over the years, polluters had developed a "fear of Steve," which he claimed was now partly responsible for the improved air quality in the area of South Phoenix where he lived. Brittle's personal tour of hazardous sites—he called them "bombs" that had been planted in the neighborhood—proved to be a harrowing experience. We did not have to drive far to pass a plant, or hollowed-out facility, that he had taken on, either through a lawsuit, or through community organizing. Even on a Sunday, there were areas we visited where the smell was sickening. Brittle rattled off an inventory of poisons he estimated were in the air: benzene, arsenic, lead, chloroform, cadmium, mercury, and hydrogen fluoride.

One plant that Brittle lingered over was a B. F. Goodrich aerospace facility, which was one of the biggest toxics emitters in the area, and the target of a high-profile 2007 campaign. Ever on the alert for new evidence against an old foe, he pointed to a hazardous waste container just inside the chain link fence. "That's a violation," he remarked. "By law it should be at least 50 feet from the perimeter." He recalled Goodrich employees going around to ask neighboring residents if "any projectiles had landed in their yards from recent explosions within the plant." Not surprisingly, the corporation's application for an expansion permit caused an uproar in the neighborhood. Brittle and others argued that the plant should be moved to a district zoned for heavy industry, rather than stay in close proximity to the César Chavez Elementary School. "The white members on the village planning committee voted to approve the permit," he reported, "and the people of color [with a slight majority] voted against," but the city overrode the decision on what Brittle considered to be spurious grounds.

Perspective was often hard to come by for veteran activists like Brittle. "In other parts of town," he mused, "residents fight over how tall a building can be in their neighborhood. We wish that were our only problem. Here our fight is about getting clean air to breathe." Beginning with the high-profile campaign against an ENSCO incinerator in 1990, his efforts had extended all over the state, especially to major-league polluters like the ASARCO copper-smelting complex in the predominantly Latino community of Hayden, a former company town to the southwest of Phoenix.[17] As a veteran of countless brush-offs from official regulators, his cynicism about government cover-ups and inaction ran very deep. "'We have to protect our polluters' is the unofficial mantra of government agencies," he remarked. "No matter what they say, they always look the other way." While he himself never tired of filing civil rights lawsuits against city, county, and state agencies, the pattern of nonresponses had not helped to inspire communities to action, and he well understood the "hopelessness and despair" of people whose everyday problems kept them from showing up for meetings and protests. Besides, he reported, "black folks are justified in saying that 'when white people protest, they get press, but when we protest, we get beat up, arrested, and go to jail.'"

On the difficulties of keeping together a coalition of watchdogs or organizers, he pointed to inter-racial fissures that ran deep in the city's history. "There is a lot of racial tension between blacks and Hispanics, who are always in a big power struggle in South Phoenix, and so they won't work with each other." Indeed, the partnership between Brittle and Pops—the latter called them "salt and pepper"—was resonant of white–black alliances during the era of the city's civil rights struggles. As Matthew Whitaker, a historian of civil rights in Phoenix, put it, "Few Mexican Americans participated in local sit-ins and marches...and even fewer spoke out in support of African Americans' calls for desegregation." The failure to form "a lasting coalition may be attributed, in part, to white subversion" ("divide and conquer" on the part of Anglo elites), but Whitaker concluded that, ultimately, the "two groups were responsible for their inability and unwillingness to collaborate."[18] Pops was more sanguine about the partnerships he had formed. "If we did not have multiethnic community involvement," he pointed out, "we would have had much less success." In the last decade, however, opposition to the nativist targeting of undocumented Mexicans had preoccupied the area's Latino activists. Fending off police harassment and upholding the actual right to live in the neighborhood took precedence over the fight to breathe clean air.

Sporadic, but insistent protest from activists like Pops, Brittle, and Greta Rogers (a salty octogenarian from Ahwatukee, who was a fixture at City Hall environmental hearings) helped to win an EPA grant in 2002 for a pilot study of toxic emissions in select South Phoenix neighborhoods. One of the official goals for the grant was to "restore public confidence and trust with the South Phoenix community." Fifty of the more active residents joined a community action council that ran the South Phoenix Multi-Media Toxics Reduction Project, and drew up an inventory of the area's worst offenders. Topping the list was the 85-year-old Phoenix Brickyard, which had no scrubbers of any kind on its smokestacks, and whose owners, as Rogers sardonically put it, "thought they had grandfathered rights dating to the birth of Christ." The community council's work had energized the participants, and there were hopes that the authorities would finally come down hard on the polluters by acting on their call for immediate action on "early reductions." Rogers, who was the council's chair during its final year, described the outcome. "At the conclusion, I said, 'I charge you Mr. Owens, as the director of ADEQ, to review these recommendations and to initiate Phase 2, or implementation.' After a year or more [of non-implementation]," she went on, "they sent the balance of the grant back to the EPA in San Francisco, who had never seen this happen before. The EPA wrote back to say they could not accept it because the recipient of a grant is obligated to use it to implement the recommendations. A year or two later," she added derisively, "the ADEQ turned the money over to the city of Phoenix to buy environmentally correct street sweepers."

Compounding the disregard of the state agency for citizen input, Maricopa County's Air Quality Department had initiated a rival process midway through the residents' deliberations. Its Industry Challenge/Good Neighbor Partnership was a voluntary program whereby charter companies could elect to reduce routine emissions and accidental releases of priority pollutants. The original partnership agreement was signed by twenty-one companies, though only nine ended up achieving their goals.[19] Notably, community members were not invited to the partnership's meetings. Shut out of a process which they saw largely as a PR effort, the activist residents concluded that it had been designed, in Rogers's words, to "subvert" their own efforts to bring some environmental justice to South Phoenix.

COLD WAR SUBURBAN CHEMISTRY

As part of his toxic nightmare tour, Brittle took me through working-class neighborhoods in the West Valley. Circling around a tank farm near Maryvale, the classic inner-ring suburb that had seen better days, he remarked that the facility may have contributed to a cancer cluster in the 1980s. The complex was part of a massive Superfund site, and its hulking storage tanks sat above multiple plumes of groundwater contaminated by the companies in the surrounding West Van Buren industrial zone. Benzene in the groundwater was first reported there by Chevron in 1985. Subsequent studies showed that gasoline products leaked into the aquifer beneath the tanks exceeded the health standard by a factor of 360,000, while trichloroethylene (TCE) levels were 350 times the federal standard for acceptable risk.[20] From 1965 onward, Maryvale children suffered an abnormally high rate of leukemia—indeed, the death rate was twice that of the national average. After twenty years of bitter confrontations with the ADEQ, the Department of Health and Safety, and the scientists hired by these agencies to conduct tests, residents had concluded that their families were likely poisoned by groundwater contaminated by industrial waste, and that government agencies colluded to keep this information from them.

Built in the late 1950s as a dream working-class suburb for ethnic whites, Maryvale was named for the wife of John Long, the construction magnate who developed much of the Valley's west side. The Levitt of the western U.S. building boom, Long pioneered many mass-production techniques, and Maryvale, where he was selling 125 homes a week by 1956, was one of the first "planned communities" in the nation. The FHA-backed ranch homes were eminently affordable, but, like most west-side developments, they were built on farmland that had seen heavy pesticide application in the period when DDT was in regular use. Maryvale also grew in tandem with an industrial zone, created for high-tech and aerospace companies arriving in the Valley with defense contract orders to fill. Located to the northeast of the tank farm, in Maryvale proper, this zone generated groundwater pollution from the likes of Corning, the United Industrial Corporation, and the Nuclear Corporation of America, and was eventually declared a state Superfund site—the West Central Phoenix WQARF (Water Quality Assurance Revolving Fund)—in 1987.

The dumping of chemicals at this site included huge quantities of TCE, which poisoned the Maryvale groundwater that residents drank for almost two decades. The carcinogenic solvent was first detected in the area's drinking water in early 1981, but the city did not test the wells until seventeen months later. At that time, two wells were shut down when TCE was found to be present at levels six times higher than the EPA standards. In subsequent testing, quantities as high as 350 times the federal health standard were found in the WQARF site's 2-mile plume. Two other wells were shut down in 1987, and, thanks to the arrival of CAP water around the same time, very little of the west-side drinking water has since been drawn from wells, but it is suspected that the contaminants have been spreading to aquifers to the west and southwest where wells still provide potable water.

There is evidence that state agencies knew about the Maryvale cancer cluster long before the results of the studies were announced. In the early 1980s, the Department of Health Services (DHS) brushed off a school principal's concerns about the high rate of cancer among her pupils, advising her not to speak publicly about her observations. The case did not go public until a 1987 investigative report in the *Phoenix New Times* alleged a cover-up. The following year, the DHS released statistics on the children's leukemia problems, and Long, representing the real estate interests in the West Valley, lobbied the governor to employ scientists who would put a boosterish spin on the results. Subsequent surveys conducted by the ADEQ concluded that the soil and water were safe, but fired-up residents, many of whom had lost their children to leukemia, persisted, year after year, with demands for more exacting studies and remediation efforts. Multiple neighborhood organizations formed and fell apart, as members tired of the slow pace of ADEQ and DHS action, and especially the lack of urgency on the part of public officials charged to go after the polluters themselves. Subsequent *Phoenix New Times* stories, by prize-winning investigator reporter Terry Greene (Sterling), kept up pressure on the agencies involved, and several residents turned into full-time activists.[21]

Prominent among them was Teri Johnson, co-founder of Mothers of Maryvale in 1988, whose daughter had died the year before from a heart defect associated with solvent-contaminated groundwater. Impatient with the lack of attention to the cancer cluster and dismissive of litigation ("it wouldn't bring my daughter back"), she sought out the national network of environmental justice through the Citizens Clearinghouse for Hazardous Waste (founded by Lois Gibbs, from Love Canal) and made contact with legendary activist Bradley Angel, who was Greenpeace's Southwest Toxics Campaign coordinator at the time. Learning that Arizona had plans to partner with ENSCO to build a massive waste incinerator in a low-income town to the southwest of Phoenix, Johnson saw an opportunity to score a clear victory against polluters. She invited Angel to wage a campaign out of her own home and joined forces with activists like Steve Brittle, and other Maryvale groups organized by Johnson's peers—Pam Swift (Toxic Waste Investigation Group), Debbie McQueen (Pesticide Watch Group), and Melody Baker (Mothers of Maryvale)—each of them outspoken neighborhood mothers who had personally sickened over the years.

Their combined actions against the ENSCO incinerator were the first large-scale environmental protests Phoenix had seen, and they drew in citizens who had never marched or picketed before. Two Greenpeace activists occupied a newsworthy bed (representing ENSCO and ADEQ, "in bed with dirty industry") that was chained to the gates of the Capitol. Media coverage of the bed and the cause provided an invaluable public education about the dangers of hazardous waste, and fueled the anger of those who resented Arizona's status as a dumping ground for the waste of other states. When Maricopa County sheriff's deputies infamously stun-gunned Angel and others at a public hearing overseen by the ADEQ, a wave of community sympathy turned the entire project, already at an advanced state of construction, into a political hot potato.

According to Johnson, one factor in newly elected Governor Fife Symington's 1991 decision to halt construction of the plant was the mobilization of children, including her daughter Kory. "When Symington signed off," she recalled, "he said, 'If I had not done that, my kids wouldn't have let me come home tonight.'" Kory Johnson had joined a Maryvale child bereavement group at the age of nine and founded Children for a Safe Environment after the public revelations about the cancer cluster that may have claimed her sister's life. The organization put her and other youth in the forefront of the ENSCO protests along with many other campaigns against chemical dumping, waste incineration, and dirty industry visited upon low-income communities all over Arizona. Kory was recognized internationally, with the Goldman Prize, for her efforts as a young environmental activist. After the ENSCO victory, the Johnsons were contacted by women all over the country who had decided to take on waste facilities in their own communities. They responded to the classic call of environmental justice, shifting the spirit of their involvement from NIMBY (not in my backyard) to NIABY (not in anybody's backyard). Every so often, mother and daughter would try to put aside their activism and take a vacation. "We would rent a car and try to go for a camping trip," Johnson recalled, "but Kory couldn't stop: 'Mom, what are they burning over there? What do you think is in that truck? Look at that stack, we gotta help those people.'"

"I've tried to get out of it, but I can't," she confessed, as if her activism was an addiction. In the two decades since her first daughter died, Johnson has had her own share of cancers (colon, breast, and uterine). Her mother and twin brothers died of other cancers, and she has seen many of her fellow Maryvale activists succumb. Working for a private investigator, she had learned some skills that came in useful for digging up dirt on polluters. More often, however, she found herself playing the sleuth to prize information out of the state's regulators, for whom she was a marked woman. Edged out of her Brownie troupe command and PTA presidency for being a "bad role model" on account of her activism, Johnson found another tactical tool during her part-time employment in a day-care center: "When I needed to extract information from the unhelpful staff at the ADEQ, I would take these kids and load them up with sugar and let them run and jump around in the agency offices, and mess with the computers. After a while, they learned that if Teri wants something, let her get it."

THE MOTOROLA LEGACY

Johnson and other residents of the west side were not the only environmental casualties of the electronics boom that drove the region's urban growth in the postwar years. They had many counterparts on the east side of town. When the new industries arrived, their "clean" workplaces were regarded as safer than the older generation of manufacturing plants. Consequently, residents felt more comfortable about living in close proximity to the facilities. In retrospect, it was this false sense of security that magnified the dangers posed by the new plants. The high-tech industry has left a trail of large toxic footprints all over the regions it has clustered: Silicon Valley (California), Silicon Desert (Arizona), Silicon Mesa (New Mexico), Silicon Hills (Austin), Silicon Glen (Scotland), Silicon Island (Taiwan), Silicon Plateau (Bangalore), and Silicon Paddy (China). Migration from one location to another was spurred by the promise of less regulation, and Arizona and New Mexico were the first stops on the flight route from Northern California. Both states offered sweet deals to semiconductor firms that were absconding from Silicon Valley for the friendlier business climates of the Southwest. Just as surely as they left behind Superfund sites, the jobs they brought to Arizona would carry high risks. Indeed, it has been estimated that the rate of illness in high-tech workplaces was three to four times higher than in the average manufacturing facility. The "clean rooms" of semiconductor fabs were designed to protect the products, not the workers, and Phoenix subsequently saw its share of birth defects among clean room workers. So too, their waste products were arguably more hazardous to land and life than those of the dark Satanic mills we associate with the first industrial revolution.[22]

The first big catch for the Chamber of Commerce rainmakers was Motorola, which agreed to locate its military electronics arm in Phoenix in 1948. One of the top corporate showpieces in the region's Silicon Desert, Motorola grew to become the Valley's largest employer, with a peak payroll of 21,000 in 1989. In the years since, however, the corporation found more profitable locations offshore, especially in China, where it was one of the first multinationals to take advantage of cheap labor and lax environmental regulation. By 2010, it had all but left the region—its one small, remaining division in Tempe was up for sale. Motorola had come to Phoenix because its defense research facilities would be relatively safe from a Soviet attack, but it left an impact on the region's environment that was more damaging in the long term than any conventional aerial bombardment.

From 1950 onward, routine dumping of chlorinated solvents and other volatile organic compounds (VOCs) at several of the firm's plants caused extensive groundwater contamination: in Scottsdale (North Indian Bend Wash), South Phoenix (Raymond Street), Mesa (Broadway and Dobson), and at three sites in East Phoenix (52nd Street, Mojave Street, and 56th Street). Three of these were listed as Superfund sites on the national priority list, the others were designated as state Superfund (WQARF) sites, not quite serious enough to qualify as federal priorities. The 52nd Street site was one of the nation's worst recorded cases of groundwater pollution. As in Maryvale, the chief culprit was TCE, widely used in the electronics industry for degreasing, but it was only one of many chemicals (including dichloroethene, dioxane, boron, and arsenic) that were dumped into unlined lagoons, wells, and drains by company employees for the best part of three decades. TCE was phased out in the plants from the late 1970s, but evidence acquired during a legal battle with the company revealed that Motorola was aware of the hazards long before.

The Scottsdale Superfund site—home to Motorola's Government Electronics Group among other defense contractors—sits above the North Indian Bend Wash aquifer, once considered a drinking water source for as many as 350,000 people. Extensive use of the ponds and drinking wells in the area probably exposed residents for more than a decade, until the wells were shut down in the early 1980s.[23] As in Maryvale, a variety of deaths and debilitating illnesses, including leukemia, cardiac birth defects, brain cancer, and lupus, were found to be clustered around the site. Scottsdale residents with resources took aim at the corporation's deep pockets by launching a barrage of lawsuits. The most high-profile personal injury case (*Loefgren v. Motorola*) was thrown out in 1998 in a judgment that had a chilling national impact on toxic-liability suits.[24] The remaining litigants were simply outspent by the company over the years. In the meantime, ace investigative journalist Terry Greene (Sterling) discovered that Motorola had back-billed the Department of Defense for cleanup costs at the Superfund site, which meant that taxpayers were footing the bill for the company's malfeasance.[25] When it became clear that the contamination affected more affluent areas of Scottsdale, and that the plume had spread to public drinking wells in tony Paradise Valley, residents there had ways of making their voices heard and getting responses from media editorials and high-ranking politicians. Most recently, when the site's TCE-treatment facility failed at the end of 2009, releasing contaminated water into the well-appointed homes and businesses of Paradise Valley and North Scottsdale, Congressman Harry Mitchell was all over the news.[26]

Above the contaminated Indian Bend Wash aquifer lies a 6-mile chain of parkland, lakes, golf courses, and ball fields straddling Scottsdale and Tempe. Planned in the 1960s as an innovative flood-control system, and hailed as a signal achievement by open-space advocates, today it is the pride of Scottsdale. But the residents and visitors who cycle, play, and jog in this generous greenbelt are mostly oblivious to the chemicals that cling to the bedrock below, poisoning the slow flow of ancient water with the second largest contamination plume in the Phoenix area.

The Central Phoenix Plume, which is by far the largest, flows from two former Motorola sites in East Phoenix all the way through downtown and far out to the urban fringe in the West Valley. In 1982, the company reported contamination from an underground storage tank at its 52nd Street semiconductor facility. TCE readings underneath this East Phoenix plant were among the highest recorded nationally—tests at a nearby private well exceeded by 1,554 times the federal standard.[27] The notoriously lax ADEQ was designated to oversee the cleanup of the 52nd Street site, and agency officials unaccountably allowed the company to collect and report its own data on impact of the spills. With the prerogative in Motorola's hands, a cover-up was assured, and so the public was not advised of any health risks until several years later.[28] In effect, the state's regulators left citizens in the dark as the contamination spread westward through the upper and middle layers of the aquifer. According to the ADEQ's final estimate, 200,000 gallons of chlorinated solvents were flushed down at 52nd Street between 1950 and 1983, 80 percent of which was TCE.[29]

Augmented by similar spills from the Raymond Street site, and from a Honeywell aerospace facility at 34th Street from the 1960s onward, the dragon-shaped superplume is now officially 7 miles wide, stretching below downtown Phoenix all the way over to 7th Avenue, where it commingles with the 8-mile-long West Van Buren plume. Some estimates put the combined reach of these plumes at 15.5 miles, since the contamination has compromised the drinking water supply of the west-side farming community of Tolleson. As with the Maryvale case, the ADEQ's scientific studies of the epidemiology surrounding the 52nd Street site were not well conducted or documented, and they relied on data reported by Motorola employees. Appalled by this inattention to their health, residents took to knocking on doors in selected blocks to gather their own data about illnesses and deaths. A cluster of reported cancers and TCE-related symptoms appeared on at least one block.[30] Convinced that the state had little interest in holding the company responsible, some residents, like real estate broker Velma Dunn, who formed the 52nd Street Oversight Committee, matured into neighborhood activists and litigants in their own right, at least until they succumbed to "Superfund fatigue."[31]

The 52nd Street site was added to the Superfund's national priorities list in 1989. Two decades later, the EPA and ADEQ had still to determine a final remedy for the contamination. As is typical of the "reverse gentrification" undergone by neighborhoods affected by contamination, the

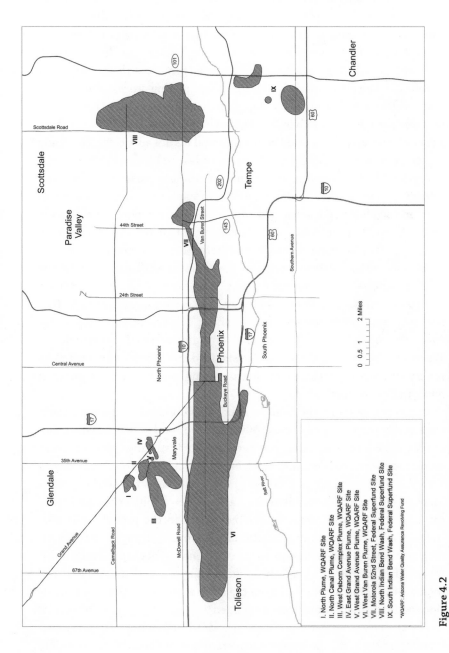

Figure 4.2
Major groundwater contamination plumes in Central Phoenix area
Sources: Arizona Department of Environmental Quality, Arizona State Land Department, Arizona Land Resources Information System, ESRI

I. North Plume, WQARF Site
II. North Canal Plume, WQARF Site
III. West Osborn Complex Plume, WQARF Site
IV. East Grand Avenue Plume, WQARF Site
V. West Grand Avenue Plume, WQARF Site
VI. West Van Buren Plume, WQARF Site
VII. Motorola 52nd Street, Federal Superfund Site
VIII. North Indian Bend Wash, Federal Superfund Site
IX. South Indian Bend Wash, Federal Superfund Site

*WQARF: Arizona Water Quality Assurance Revolving Fund

Lindon Park district adjacent to the site had undergone demographic changes over the years. It was now predominantly occupied by Latino and low-income residents, many of them renters and most of them with no knowledge of the Superfund site or its consequences. After Dunn's committee lost steam, the neighborhood association's vice-president, Mary Moore, took over the EPA Technology Assistance Grant (TAG), designed to educate residents about Superfund health hazards and encourage their participation in the decision-making process about remediation efforts. Soft-spoken but dogged in her efforts, she told me she had overcome much of her public shyness in the course of transitioning from a lay citizen into an informed environmental justice advocate. Like many of her peers across the Valley, Moore had learned to expect very little from the ADEQ. The state agency had repeatedly reassigned the site's project managers, thwarted her TAG team's ability to call public meetings, and sequestered its reports from them. "Environmental justice calls for early public participation and involvement in the process, and we don't feel that is being accomplished here," Moore reported. "Because ADEQ has the lead, often where we come in is at the tail end when they've made up their mind about something." According to the neighborhood association president, Rene Chase-Dufault, excluding residents in this way only confirmed their perceptions about "the executives and powers-that-be who live up on Camelback Mountain, or north Scottsdale, or Troon, or wherever the new hot place is, who don't have to deal with the reality of smelling weird stuff or wondering which family member is going to have cancer."

Inventory drills in the Lindon Park neighborhood had shown there were still concentrations of pure solvent in the aquifer at the eastern end of the plume. The results were clear grounds for justifying vapor intrusion studies to measure indoor air risks from the underground contamination, yet the ADEQ had dragged its heels in the face of repeated petitions from Moore's TAG team. Vapor intrusion had emerged as one of the topic concerns of the environmental justice movement in the preceding decade. Indeed, Moore's testimony at a national EPA forum on vapor intrusion in January 2009 drew attention to the Arizona agency's intransigence.[32] A year later, the EPA (its hands no longer tied by the Bush administration) took over the lead for the site from the state agency, and the vapor intrusion studies were promptly commissioned.

For the city's minority populations, Motorola's name was tarnished long before the toxic spills were uncovered. One of Phoenix's most visible civil rights struggles was against the company's employment policies that firmly excluded black recruits. The revelations about groundwater contamination in the 1980s sparked some new accusations about racial discrimination. It was alleged that the workplace safety standards at Motorola plants with a heavily Latino workforce were much lower than at the ones with better-paid Anglo employees. Tupac Enrique Acosta, a Chicano activist working at that time with Maricopa Organizing Project, claimed that a disproportionate number of Latinos were employed in the low-end jobs of the Valley's semiconductor industry. Their health was threatened by unsafe conditions like those in Motorola's Mojave Street plating plant in the Golden Gate barrio, while that community's drinking water and air quality was at risk from the plant's pollution. "One of the stories we heard," recalled Acosta, "was from a police rookie doing a street beat in the western barrio. He was given an order to evacuate from the neighborhood immediately because of a release from that plant, but none of the information was ever made public, not even to the cops." The backdrop, according to Acosta, was that "since 1848, Mexican labor has been treated as a disposable commodity, with the lowest levels of compensation, representation, unionization rights." "This had been the pattern," he added, "not only in the high-tech industry and in agriculture but also in the service industry today. Look at the construction industry right now. When they are done with the Mexicans, they just throw them out, they don't need them anymore."

After Motorola was handed its first fine in 1989 (a paltry $46,600) for multiple contaminations, it relocated its 52nd Street production line to Guadalajara.[33] Acosta and others traveled to the new plant in that Mexican city to request records relating to the company's use of TCE there, and they alerted residents to the pattern of hazards that the facility had brought to town. In the meantime, he found an ally in the Albuquerque-based Southwest Network for Environmental and Economic Justice, which was running an extensive campaign against the hiring and polluting practices of the region's high-tech employers in the Southwest. The organization's 1997 report on the industry's unsustainable practices imagined a state employee of the future ("your granddaughter") testing the chemical content of a Valley wellhead in 2026: "It's bad, real bad," she said to herself, shaking her head and wiping her brow. "We'll never be able to drink it." As it happens, this was her last day on the job: "Today's the end of the fiscal year—budget cuts."[34] In reality, Arizona's devastating budget cuts would come much sooner, in 2009–2011, though its environmental agency, federally funded in part, was not the hardest hit. As Brittle mused, the state "would never defund the DEQ, because then the EPA would have to come in and take over." The Arizona agency was too valuable, in his words, "as a pollution protection program."

Tens of thousands of people whose residence or workplace lies above the Central Phoenix plume have no idea the contaminated zone exists, less than 20 feet below the ground at its eastern end. At public meetings called by Moore's TAG team, which I attended in 2010, some of the residents of Lindon Park who showed up were still learning, for the first time, about the existence of the poisoned groundwater. To the team's knowledge, there were no active drinking wells along the plume, but water delivery authorities like the Salt River Project, which had several irrigation wells in the area, might have to resort to cleaning up the groundwater for use in the event of a prolonged drought. As in the West Central Phoenix and West Van Buren sites, the migration of contaminated water through the aquifer endangered neighborhoods that still rely on groundwater pumping. The same was true of several other Superfund sites that disfigured the aquifer maps of Phoenix, including those beneath the military airports–Williams, Luke, Goodyear—that had anchored the Valley's mid-century growth as a garrison facility.

For a region with limited water supplies, the courting of high-tech companies—especially those with semiconductor manufacturing facilities that can consume several millions gallons daily—was a highly questionable move. More unforgivable yet was the lax regulation that allowed systematic poisoning of the area's most productive aquifers by its most sought-after corporate employers. The shutting down of Phoenix's drinking water wells in the 1980s reduced overall groundwater supply by as much as 25 percent, and, by 1989, officials were projecting that an additional 20 percent would be lost to contamination over the next fifty years.[35] Since then, the piping in of CAP water from man-made desert lakes on the Colorado River has helped to ease this information out of the public memory—it is not readily available to most new residents. Yet the repressed knowledge would surely resurface in the event of a more serious drought, when someone might have to foot the bill, as water users in California's San Gabriel Valley now do, to try to make the groundwater drinkable again. In the case of TCE and other volatile organic compounds, however, it may be impossible, no matter how much public money is spent, to adequately clean the Phoenix aquifers.

In my interviews with citizen-activists who devoted their time and their lives to prioritizing public health over the profits of polluters, there was a clear consensus that the state's regulators had been under strong political pressure to look the other way. As Brittle put it, "The Chamber of Commerce or the industry lobbyists calls the Governor's office and the

ADEQ gets a call to back off." Except in the case of newly appointed officials who had not yet learned the rules, the phone calls were hardly needed—an institutional mentality prevailed "to protect the polluters and not the public," as Brittle put it. Some of this mentality was an offshoot of a political culture that equated pollution with profit. For example, as ASU's Bolin recalled, "After the Montreal protocols to ban CFCs, our legislators actually voted to make Arizona exempt so we could be the sole U.S. producer of CFCs." In environmental matters, responsible state agencies were carefully neutered. The legislature took care to limit the powers of both the Department of Water Resources (charged with preserving the groundwater) and the ADEQ (charged with policing the water's purity). Corporate managers in turn took their cue from the hands-off policies of government agencies and saw no reason to heed environmental laws, let alone take extra precautions. Having fouled the land and water, many of the high-tech firms followed Motorola's flight to better business climates offshore. Those who stayed learned to be better citizens only because citizen-activists like Pops, Brittle, Enrique, Swift, Baker, Angel, Dunn, Moore, the Johnsons, and others held them up to public scrutiny.

In the late 1990s, Brittle, for example, worked with residents of an affluent Desert Ridge community in North Phoenix to oppose zoning permits for a 13-acre semiconductor plant. By then, high-tech's reputation as a clean industry had been pierced, and well-heeled area citizens had voices that would be heard in City Hall. The controversial plant, operated by Sumco (now called Sumimoto), was finally approved and designed as one of the world's largest suppliers of silicon wafers. Brittle and the residents' coalition watched its first year of operations like hawks, however, and were quick to file a citizens' lawsuit when problems with emissions violations and wastewater treatment surfaced. After the imposition of a hefty fine (by Maricopa County standards at least), the plant has been violation-free.

Intel, the high-tech giant that succeeded Motorola as the Valley's largest private employer, came to the region with a bottom-drawer environmental reputation; it had left behind several Superfund sites in Silicon Valley. After some initial spills, the record has been quite different at their Chandler chip-manufacturing fabs, where workers, on average, earned four times the Arizona median salary. Invited to serve on a citizens' advisory board required for the company's enrollment in the EPA's (Project XL) environmental leadership program, Brittle inspected their operations very closely. "I asked them very hard questions, but they always answered them, and so I looked under every rock and questioned everything. They never lied, and when I found something I didn't like, they fixed it." Impressed with Intel's water recycling policies and its pledge to maintain an emissions cap—"only 1 percent of their toxic releases are emitted into the environment," Brittle held the company up as an example of how a "clean environment and good economy go hand in hand." "If you have a bunch of disciplinary problems," he concluded, "you usually don't spend much time on the better students." This sounded like faint praise, but it really was high kudos coming from a man whose fierce hounding of polluters had saved not a few lives in the Valley and elsewhere in the state.

ON NATIVE GROUND

The promise of clean industries and clean skies had been central to the corporate recruitment efforts of the Goldwater-era Chamber of Commerce. This picture of health was heavily advertised as the Sunbelt's antidote to the dying order of the Rust Belt's noxious northern domain. As one publication put it: "The emphasis with industry in metropolitan Phoenix is on cleanliness. Here no ugly smokestacks insult the Arizona sky, no growl of monotonous machines harshly stamp their audible imprint."[36] Yet the price for the clean air over Phoenix was being paid somewhere else. Three hundred miles to the north, on the Colorado Plateau, multiple coal-fired generating stations were built on Navajo and Hopi land to provide electric power to the city's expanding suburbs. Before the war, all of Phoenix's power had been generated within the Salt River Valley, but urban managers had to look father afield to fuel the appetite for growth. Just as Greater Phoenix would be dependent on water piped in from afar, so, too its energy needs were supplied by fossil resources on distant Native American land. Coal mined from the massive reserves at Black Mesa directly enabled the air-conditioned lives of utility customers in Mesa. The Mojave Generating Station, the Four Corners Power Plant, the Cholla Power Plant, and the Navajo Generating Station were quite literally the true engines of growth in the region, and their power output was matched by their prodigious emissions. Indeed, Mercury astronauts reported that the Four Corners Power Plant, distinguishable by its immense, smoky plume, was visible from space. But the toll of these emissions on the health of Navajo and Hopi lungs and soil was inestimable. Today, the state's six coal-fired plants account for 40 percent of the state's carbon emissions, and Four Corners (in New Mexico, but owned by Arizona Public Service) and the Navajo Generating Station are the nation's second- and third-largest emitter of nitrogen oxides.[37]

The EPA's recent call for emissions reductions at the Navajo station had generated a conflict between the revenue-conscious tribal government and Hopi and Navajo environmentalists bent on shutting down the plant. The Sierra Club, which had called attention to the related smog buildup over the Grand Canyon, got itself banned from the reservation by the Hopi Tribal Council for supporting local opposition to the plant. Responding to the EPA demand, Joe Shirley, the Navajo Nation's embattled president, came out as a climate change denier, though he was more vocal as a stalwart defender of tribal livelihoods. "They came onto our land," he declared. "They didn't tell me, 'Here, Mr. President. Here are other green jobs.' They just shut us down, put more people into impoverishment. You want me to accept that?"[38] Sandy Bahr, the Sierra Club's Arizona president, was more careful about laying out the context for her support of the EPA. "There is a long history of trying to make reservations into sacrifice zones," she observed. "The people on the reservation are the most affected by the pollution, and its reservation water that is being used for coal mining. The Hopi and Navajo are very dependent on coal royalties, so it's definitely a big issue for them. People in Phoenix don't have to breathe this stuff, and so the health implications here are limited." Accordingly, the press reports I read all treated the standoff as a local conflict in Indian Country, and of little consequence in the metropolis itself. Yet the Sierra Club had its own questionable history with the Navajo plant. Looking to save the canyon lands from more damming in the 1960s, its support for the building of the plant was critical to efforts to find an alternative source of power for pumping CAP water up to Phoenix and Tucson.

As historian Andrew Needham has shown, the postwar development of Greater Phoenix and that of the Navajo nation were inextricably linked.[39] Just as surely as Phoenix boosters chased growth by any means necessary, Navajo leaders hitched their hunger for self-determination to the mineral leases and tax revenues on mines operated by giant energy extractors like Peabody and Utah International. Both sets of boosters—the tribal authorities and Chamber of Commerce—touted inexpensive land, low taxes, cheap labor, and minimal regulation to interested corporations. The tribal leaders faced greater internal opposition over the years from members who alleged that they had sold off Indian birthrights, subordinated the tribe to outside interests, and poisoned reservation lands into the bargain. Environmental justice was fought internally, as well as with the corporate entities who took advantage of the tribe's limited options for economic development.

As Bahr indicated, the backdrop to the standoff over the Navajo power plant was the long-standing use of Indian land for the dirtiest offshoots of industrial civilization—landfills, waste dumps, and mineral extraction, including uranium mining. Cursed by their possession of underground natural resources and vast expanses of open land, tribal reservations with limited options shared the burden of inner-city minority neighborhoods in hosting a disproportionate share of hazardous facilities. Unable to avert the permitting of a medical waste incinerator on his reservation, one Dakota Sioux member reported, "Before they came to us, fifty-three other tribes had been approached by the same people. We seem to be easy targets."[40]

The Indian communities on the edge of metro Phoenix had their own version of this predicament. Before licenses were approved to run lucrative gaming facilities in the 1990s, the tribes built industrial parks, offering advantageous concessions to investors, including seventy-five-year leases.[41] In 1966, the Gila River Indian Community (GRIC), home of Akimel O'odham (Pima) and Pee Posh (Maricopa) tribes, established Lone Butte Industrial Park along Interstate 10 on its northern border with the city of Chandler. The largest of three such zones run by GRIC, Lone Butte would become the first, and one of the most successful, tribal industrial parks in the United States. Regulatory oversight of Lone Butte's dozens of tenants was known to be extra light, and so it became a choice location for the Valley's polluters. By the 1990s, five of the Valley's hazardous waste incinerators were in South Phoenix. The other two were on Indian land, in Lone Butte, and they were operated by Stericycle and Romic, two of the most notorious waste management operators in the West. The combined pollution from the industrial parks, six crop-dusting airstrips, and more than eighty illegal dumpsites, many of which had reportable quantities of toxic materials, prompted the federal Agency for Toxic Substances and Disease Registry to conclude that the community was hosting "more hazardous waste than any other Indian Reservation in the United States."[42]

Lone Butte was en route to the ENSCO protest site, and so Teri Johnson and her allies often stopped off to gather evidence on Stericycle and Romic. She and her daughter placed pennies around the Stericyle facility to see if they would oxidize. She also witnessed workers digging holes for the dumping of chemical barrels, and the use of rented U-Haul trucks for transporting waste openly. By the early 1990s, the environmental justice movement had arrived on reservations around the country. Indeed, Johnson (who is half Lakota Sioux) had helped Angel found the Indigenous Environmental Network in 1990, before he quit Greenpeace and moved to San Francisco to found Greenaction. Respectful of Gila River sovereignty, and conscious of how important Lone Butte was to the community's economy, they held off until they had a steadfast tribal ally. By the late 1990s, they had met Lori Riddle, a GRIC member with some personal experience of toxic harm, and, more importantly, someone who had the courage to lead the fight against the waste plants from within GRIC.

Riddle had some standing on the reservation as vice-chair of her district, and she had some well-known ancestors; Antonio Azul, the last Pima chief, was her great-grandfather, and Ira Hayes, her uncle, was among the five Marines immortalized in the flag-raising at Iwo Jima. Riddle received an early education in the trauma of harmful waste when her grandfather moved the family in 1977 to his allotment adjacent to a contaminated airstrip used for aerial pesticide spraying on West Valley farms. "As kids, we were sprayed on all the time," she recalled. "We cooked and bathed outdoors, and the mist would just descend on our clothes and our food." The soil, it turned out, was so badly contaminated by DDT, toxaphene, and illegally buried chemicals that the EPA's remediation of the site in 1984 had to be revisited twenty years later.[43] By then, the damage to the health of her family (Riddle and her relatives left in 1990) and other residents was done. The harm was magnified by cultural practices involving ingestion of soil and plants. "When we were building our sandwich [adobe] home," Riddle recalled, "the women and girls ate the mud from the walls as part of a ritual meal." Also growing in the vicinity "was the sugoi, a medicine plant which we boiled and drank for various ailments." It was no coincidence, then, that the women "were the ones with noticeably worse health problems, including eleven miscarriages among three women" in her own family. In addition, she reported, "There has been persistent arthritis of the lower spine, from which my daughter, mother, sister, and two aunts all suffered." She herself was no exception and was in some pain throughout our interviews. Her house had recently been burned to the ground, a suspected arson, and Riddle seemed to take it for granted that some of the enemies she had acquired over her years as an activist may have had a hand in it.

In the course of her own family's conflicts with the EPA, the Bureau of Indian Affairs, and tribal authorities themselves, Riddle accumulated a lot of knowledge about toxicology and environmental regulation. Working with Greenaction and Johnson (the two became firm friends) brought her another set of organizational skills. She founded the grassroots group GRACE (Gila River Alliance for a Clean Environment) just as rumors about the lax procedures at Stericycle's medical waste incinerator began to circulate on the reservation. "I heard stories about dogs running around with limbs in their mouths," she reported. "Non-natives abandon their dogs on our reservation so there are a lot of strays, and they went for the meat from amputations and the like." On top of the macabre stories, Stericycle's waste burning practices—associated with the release of dioxin, mercury, and other toxins—hardly endeared the company to tribal residents or to

Figure 4.3
Teri Johnson and Lori Riddle, environmental justice activists. Photo by author.

nearby Chandlerites. Such incinerators were under attack elsewhere as part of an international industrywide campaign led by Health Care Without Harm. When Riddle's GRACE and Angel's Greenaction finally succeeded in blocking an extension of Stericyle's Lone Butte lease in 2002, and shutting down a sister facility in Oakland, they effectively ended the life of two of the nation's largest medical waste incinerators. Today, largely as a result of these victories, medical waste is no longer commercially burned in the Western states but is now treated with a cleaner, steam-driven technology.

The campaign to shut down Romic's hazardous waste facility took much longer. For almost thirty years, the plant had stored and processed a range of highly toxic material, including ignitable waste used to produce fuel. Operating with an interim permit since it took over in 1998, Romic had accumulated a raft of EPA fines for emissions violations, improper storage, and deficiencies in logging and reporting. Fires were a frequent occurrence, and two more broke out just as tribal scrutiny of the facility peaked in 2007. Even so, there was considerable pressure to go easy on the facility. The tribal council feared a corporate lawsuit, and the Lone Butte board was protective of its tenants. GRIC's own Department of Environmental Quality, set up to enforce EPA standards in 2000, was cut from the same cloth as the state DEQ. Johnson recalled that the agency alerted Lone Butte's corporate tenants whenever an EPA visit was scheduled. As Riddle bluntly put it, "Their job is to keep the money flowing."

GRACE and Greenaction joined forces with an East Palo Alto group called Youth United for Community Action to target a Romic facility in their Northern California community. By then, Riddle and her daughter Laura, had founded Gila River Environment for Youth, loosely modeled on Kory Johnson's Children for a Safe Environment. The two groups of teen-agers shuttled back and forth between California and Arizona, plotting the downfall of their common polluter. When opposition to their protests mounted, the Riddles not only had support from their allies from GRIC and Phoenix; the battle-hardened California youth group was also there to stiffen their resolve.

In 2007, GRIC authorities finally denied a proposed expansion permit to Romic, and the firm closed its facility along with the one in California. At GRACE's prompting, the GRIC council enacted a moratorium against any permanent facility that accepts hazardous wastes on the reservation. Riddle said she had long been viewed as a "troublemaking housewife" (a typical slur on women who involve themselves in environmental jus-tice) and a grave threat to tribal revenue. Now she was a key figure in the tribe's own environmental protection efforts, representing her district on the relevant committees. By contrast, Laura, her daughter, wanted a dif-ferent life, and was moving further away from the reservation. Like Kory Johnson, she had been thrust into the draining world of environmental activism in her preteen years, but her insights into power, pollution, and land use had inspired a professional aspiration—she told me that she had her eye on a degree in land law.

In 2001, GRIC was the nation's first Indian community to receive EPA funding as a Brownfields Showcase Community. One of the abandoned sites to be cleaned up for reuse under the program was the new Diabetes Education and Research Center. The world's highest rate of adult-onset diabetes can be found among the O'odham people; more than 80 percent of GRIC members have diabetes by the age of 55, and Riddle was among them. As a result, the O'odham (comprising the Akimel O'odham in GRIC, the Onk Akimel O'odham to the north, and the Tohono O'odham to the south) have been one of the most closely studied communities in the world of medical research. Initiated in the 1960s, a National Institute of Health longitudinal study of their blood samples, tissue biopsies, and medical his-tories aimed to shed light on the diagnosis of diabetes. Even though diabetes disproportionately affects the indigenous poor all over the indus-trialized nations, researchers persisted in looking for genetic causes for the high rates in the O'odham's close-knit population.[44] There was ample evidence to make the case for dietary causation—the loss of the tribe's traditional lifestyle had been especially abrupt. But Riddle and her family were currently paying close scrutiny to more recent studies that have linked the diabetes to persistent organic pollutants like DDT.[45] As they well remembered, cotton farmers in the Gila River plains used the pesticide extensively against bollworms when it was still legal in the 1950s and 1960s, and then switched to toxaphene, until that substance was also banned in 1990.

Were those pesticides a factor in the high incidence of diabetes fatalities among the O'odham? If so, the sprayers were long gone, just like Motorola in East Phoenix, and the sunrise industries of Maryvale, and the past polluters of South Phoenix. Their lawyers and lobbyists had ghosted away their links to the suffering that lived on through poisons in the soil, water, and food chain. William Faulkner could have been describing the lifecycle of toxics when he wrote: "The past isn't dead. It isn't even past." When sustainability advocates talk of intergenerational commitment, most of them are pushing for planning with the next few generations in mind. That is the mentality of a forward-looking society, its eyes on the prize of a better future. Meanwhile, for most of the world's peoples, as Rob Nixon has pointed out, intergenerational includes those who have gone before us, and whose deaths are still full of meaning for the living.[46]

In the case of those who sickened from pollution or toxic contaminants, there was a pattern to their affliction, and that sociology of unequal suffering is not explained away, nor can it be ignored if we are to avoid reproducing it in other ways. One of the clichés of the nuclear age is that we are all downwinders. According to the National Cancer Institute, virtually the entire continental United States was exposed to radiation from 1951 to 1962 as a result of nuclear weapons testing. Yet most populations were not poisoned equally (Native Americans were subject to more than their share of what Winona La Duke and Ward Churchill call "radioactive colonialism,"), nor are they today.[47] The same is true of those living downstream, quite literally, as in some of the Phoenix case studies I have dwelled on in this chapter. Across the board, officials and government scientists declared the water and air (and nuclear technology) to be "safe" for human exposure and consumption. It took the testimony and tenacity of those most likely to be disregarded to expose the cover-ups and to reveal how and why some communities bore the brunt.

Because of the persistence of industrial chemicals, every place is a living repository of its past pollution, just as our warming climate is now the result of past emissions, as well as those currently being pumped into the atmosphere. There is nothing fatalistic about acknowledging this, though it offends the reassuring mentality of the booster who only wants to look ahead, or who sees all racial discrimination, for example, as a historical curse, vanquished now by a largely imagined, level playing field. As Arizonans readied themselves for a new generation of incoming industry—renewable technologies with light carbon footprints—there was much to be learned from the chemical legacy of the last generation. Microelectronics, after all, had been touted, in their own time, as clean, healthy, and life-affirming. Today's solar panels are heralded everywhere as the key to green salvation, and yet they are primarily silicon-based products of the same manufacturing processes as semiconductors. Non-biodegradable, and manufactured from advanced toxic materials with largely unknown health and environmental risks, many of them will be joining the e-waste stream in as little as twenty years.

CHAPTER 5

The Sun Always Rises

Consider Icarus, pasting those sticky wings on,
testing this strange little tug at his shoulder blade,
and think of that first flawless moment over the lawn
of the labyrinth. Think of the difference it made!
Anne Sexton, "To a Friend Whose Work Has Come to Triumph"

Nothing has driven the growth of metro Phoenix more than the sun's rays. For most of its residents and visitors, the chief reason for coming to the region was its 334 days of annual sunshine, yet precious little of this radiation showed up in the energy supply. Indeed, Arizona has often been held up as an object of shame for the cause of solar power. Despite the bounty of its sun cover, by 2009 the state generated only 7 watts of photovoltaic power (PV) per capita, while New Jersey, with only half the available sunlight, managed 14.6 watts per capita, and Germany, with even less, delivered 100 watts to each person.[1] If the solar industry was to have its long-deferred day in the United States, then the Valley of the Sun had to be at, or near the top, of the location list. Surely, it should be easier to generate "clean electrons" here than almost anywhere else. Yet the dismal historical record shows that the abundance of this natural resource mattered very little in the face of a political and economic environment that has prevented the sun's energy from being enjoyed by its liberty-loving residents, let alone developed on an industrial scale.

For a metropolis in the deepest trough of the Great Recession, the prospect of developing solar industry was just about the only source of boosterism I could find among the business community. Glenn Hamer, president of the Arizona Chamber of Commerce, bragged that, with the help of federal and state incentives currently available, "the cocktail is in place for Arizona to truly be a national and international leader in solar.... with our incredible natural advantage, we have just about the world's best solar resource." Someone in his position could reasonably be expected to be gung ho about any new local market for investment, but Hamer also happened to be former national director of the Solar Energy Industries Association. In that capacity, he recalled "being asked, as recently as 2001, by the energy czar for Governor Davis [of California] 'How much juice could you give us, if you were all going full steam?'" At that point, Hamer said that "the industry was deploying 20 to 25 megawatts a year," so he responded, "We can give you a couple of garden lights." Today, he reported, "It's real, the global explosion in renewables is off the charts," and, in Arizona, was "more and more in the bloodstream of people."

For his Chamber of Commerce members, the sun would no longer just be a magnet to attract retirees from the Frostbelt or to fill rooms in Scottsdale resort hotels, it was to be the lodestone of a new generation of industry and livelihoods. Back in the 1930s, Hamer's predecessors cooked up the "Valley of the Sun" brand name to serve the tourist and home-building industry, and the postwar Chamber embraced the moniker in its promotional efforts to draw investors, retirees, and snowbirds to the region. The new, smart name in town was the Sun Corridor, a future mega-region stretching from Prescott all the way down to Tucson. Unlike the Valley of the Sun, which was as much a therapeutic frame of mind as anything, the Sun Corridor concept evoked a landscape prepped for economic development. Brand managers are always looking for a story to associate with a place. What could be better than to fill this Sun Corridor with photovoltaic (PV) manufacturing and utility-scale solar farms, along with pollution-free skies and a multitude of green jobs?

This noble aspiration for the region's solar capability was entirely in sync with the national mood. There were very few silver linings to the Great Recession, but one of them was the prospect of launching a new industrial revolution powered by renewable energy. In the absence of any other candidates, green policies were prioritized by the incoming Obama administration as a recipe for economic recovery and the key to job creation, whether for building and operating the new energy infrastructure, or weatherizing existing homes and buildings. The urgency of responding to climate change raised the stakes. Shunning the call would not simply be a missed economic opportunity. It might be tantamount to a death sentence for large portions of the world's population. For politicians, the desperation of the unemployed was the initial trigger for moving toward alternatives to fossil fuel, but a humanitarian calamity of epic pro-portions would be the final verdict if the transition from dirty to clean was too slow, or too late.

A GOOD BUBBLE?

All previous attempts to jump-start a green economy in the United States were effectively shut down by the decisive lobbying of oil, gas, and coal giants. These efforts included the 1970s solar boomlet, which thrived amid rising oil prices (and hit a sweet spot in Arizona itself), and the so-called peace dividend after the collapse of the Soviet Union in the early 1990s. Both were nipped in the bud by federal policies long com-mitted to regarding the safe passage of cheap oil through the Straits of Hormuz as a matter of national security. Much to the chagrin of alternative energy boosters, the 1970s U.S. leadership in renewable tech-nologies, established through the innovations of the space program and postwar defense industry research, fell off rapidly after the Reagan administration abruptly ended federal support in the early 1980s. Companies and patents based on PV technology, fuel cells, and high-speed turbines were all sold for pennies on the dollar to German and Japanese industrialists.[2] In these and in other countries without large fossil fuel reserves of their own, national energy policies (like Japan's Sunshine Program or Germany's 100,000 solar roofs campaign) propelled the rapid growth and adoption of clean technologies. It is often argued that countries with homegrown supplies of oil, gas, and coal suffer from a "resource curse" that has taken a heavy toll on democracy and environ-mental well-being. Although the phrase is usually applied to authori-tarian nations like the Persian Gulf States or African countries like Libya and Nigeria, the United States has its own version of the affliction, with a sizable number of state legislatures and congressional representatives in the pockets of the large energy combines.

When the Obama administration came into office, all the ingredients for a fresh start were in place. The pressing threat of global warming had finally taken up residence in the public mind. The 2008 bailout of the financial industry established an appetite for federal Keynesianism that would include warm support for sunrise industries producing clean elec-trons. Swayed by forecasts about the long-term profitability of green capitalism, business and political leaders looked for ways to assuage the national shame at being left behind in the global competition for clean energy. Last, but not least, green jobs were held up as the solution to rebuilding a national workforce hollowed out by offshore outsourcing, destabilized by the rise of temping, and knocked to the ground by the recession.

By spring 2008, there was talk of a new speculative bubble in clean energy—it was even referred to as the Good Bubble.[3] Hot money, alienated from the collapsed real estate markets, poured into venture funds for backing alternative technology start-ups. In a highly touted move, Al Gore joined Kleiner Perkins Caufield & Byers, Silicon Valley's premier venture capital firm, to oversee its "climate change solutions group," charged with investing in solar technology, biofuels, eco-batteries, and other renewable power sources. It was even reported that Heidi Fleiss (the erstwhile Hollywood madam) had dropped her plans to open a bordello for female clients in Nevada because she had decided to invest instead in renewable energy. When asked why, she echoed the famous words of bank robber Willie Sutton: "Because that's where the money is."[4]

This upsurge in interest from entrepreneurs and speculators was driven by the plausible belief that Obama would be able to follow through on making clean energy a cornerstone of his economic recovery policies. Indeed he campaigned most solemnly on the promise to create five million green jobs, and, at every opportunity in the first eighteen months of his administration, he sounded the call for renewable energy. Beginning with the ARRA stimulus package in spring 2009, which allocated $60 billion to clean energy, his administration rolled out a series of federal subsidies and incentives to support a broad range of green initiatives. With federal funding came the requirement that the green jobs would have to be well paid. Wherever this precondition was implemented, it was a welcome upgrade from wage scales in the existing solar and wind sectors, which lagged far behind the average paycheck in the mature energy industries.

Naturally, most of the labor movement swung into line behind what looked like a progressive industrial policy, and commentators were not slow to conclude that the long-hoped-for alliance between labor and greens had finally seen the light of day. New coalitions between unions and environmental groups sprang into existence, most notably the Blue-Green Alliance, the Apollo Alliance, and Emerald Cities. The Sierra Club joined the campaign for labor's top electoral priority—the Employee Free Choice Act, aimed at making it easier to vote to join a union. On the other side, the AFL-CIO (which had stood apart from the international trade-union movement in its vigorous opposition to the Kyoto Treaty) threw its support behind climate change legislation, albeit for the most minimal levels of carbon reduction.

But the labor-green bandwagon was not the only one in town. Beginning in fall 2008, Americans for Prosperity (AFP), a significant player in the fledgling Tea Party movement, hoisted a balloon to draw media attention for its Hot Air tour around selected cities. The tour, publicizing opposition to climate change and clean-energy legislation, was the first of many AFP efforts to mobilize public opinion against Obama's policies. In fall 2009, the AFP achieved the ouster of Van Jones, just nine months after he took office as Obama's official green jobs advisor. Initially the mainstream media consensus reported that Jones was Glenn Beck's first scalp, and an African American one at that. But it soon became clear that the Fox News agitator's campaign against Jones had been masterminded by the AFP, an organization primarily funded by the Koch family, mega investors in oil and gas, and fixated on killing climate change legislation as its top goal.[5] Jones may have been red-baited by Beck for his past associations with radical organizations, but that was not the reason why he was deposed. In recent years, he had become a highly effective public advocate of the benefits to rich and poor alike of the clean-energy economy. Pushing green jobs as a solution to the plight of low-income communities, poisoned by pollution in their backyards, he brilliantly argued the need for environmental, labor, and social justice groups to find common cause in overturning the destructive order of fossil fuels. The coalition of forces imagined under Jones's banner "Green for All" was a clear threat to business as usual for the fossil-fuel lobby.

Obama's and Jones's sunny vision of a new generation of green jobs was intended in part as a lifeline to the jobless, but it was also a threat to those currently employed in the nonrenewable sectors. While many forward-looking unions initiated their own green policies, others fought hard to retain high-carbon jobs in industries that were plainly destructive to land and life. The Union of Mineworkers, for example, played its part in weakening the American Clean Energy Security Act, passed by the House in June 2009, even though the union's influence was dwarfed by the large corporate members (GE, Shell, ConocoPhillips, Dow, Rio Tinto) of the U.S. Climate Action Partnership who got to frame the final version of the legislation. Fierce lobbying and horse trading around this bill produced huge concessions to oil, gas, and coal industries—free carbon credits to the biggest polluters, reduced mandates for renewable energy production, and decreased targets for greenhouse gas emissions.[6] The House bill rewarded Big Coal with a cool $60 billion to fund research into commercial carbon capture and sequestration, even though there was little evidence to suggest the technology could ever feasibly be developed.[7]

In response to the voting power of coal-rich states, Obama had already made campaign promises about "clean coal"—a euphemism cooked up by industry lobbyists to rebrand the fossil fuel source as environmentally friendly. More circumspect were the signals he sent about restarting the nation's nuclear energy program. When Steven Chu was named as Energy Secretary, environmentalists expressed enthusiasm for a scientist who clearly understood the need to combat global warming. But Chu's confirmation hearings were marked by a barrage of questions about nuclear power from Republican senators, clearly designed to draw out the nominee's advocacy of federal support for building new plants. Seizing on the mood for decarbonization, the GOP quickly made a *cause célèbre* out of promoting nuclear power as a clean-energy source. With climate change legislation stalled in the Senate, the administration's need for Republican votes drove Obama's decision in February 2010 to extend loan guarantees for construction of two new reactors in Georgia. The GOP votes for a climate bill never materialized, but the nuclear door had been opened. After three decades in shameful exile, nuclear power was officially back in favor.

When Obama and Chu began to speak publicly about nuclear power as "safe and clean," it was because the industry and its advocates had succeeded in rebranding an energy source that had once filled the public mind with dread. There was nothing clean about uranium mining or fuel enrichment, both of which generate emissions and extremely hazardous waste. Indeed, the trail of cancer and groundwater contamination from tailings piles is a telltale mark of industrial extraction of uranium.[8] As there is no safe means of disposal for the radioactive waste produced by reactors, this deadly legacy runs entirely counter to the root principle of sustainability because the costs have to be passed on to future generations. Despite these and many other known hazards, the mere absence of direct CO_2 emissions during the reactor's operational life had proved enough to rehabilitate nuclear power as an environmentally friendly technology.

It was one thing to stretch the definition of "clean" to include nuclear energy, but "renewable" was another matter. The distinction between the two terms mattered a great deal, even though it often suffered from a lack of clarity in the public mind. Many states and large utilities, for example, considered hydroelectric power to be renewable, for accounting purposes. To classify nuclear power under that rubric, however, would be to risk ridicule, and few public officials, even the most ardently pro-nuclear, were prepared to go that far. A notable exception was the Arizona Legislature, where a GOP bill that proposed to include nuclear power in the state's renewable energy portfolio was speeding through the House of Representatives in

February 2010 before it was withdrawn amid a flurry of protest from the business community. How and why this came about is an instructive lesson, laid out in the pages that follow. Arizona, after all, had become a key battleground state in the new political wars over energy, and the outcome would have consequences far beyond its borders.

LAND BUST, SOLAR BOOM

Unlike dozens of other states whose political economies are constrained by their dependence on oil, gas, or coal for revenue, Arizona was not a hostage to its underground assets, at least not since its heyday as the Copper State. Notably, its most abundant natural resource had not been seriously exploited as an industrial energy source. Harvesting the sun for energy had a history in the region, but it was a troubled, if not entirely abortive, one. The Association for Applied Solar Energy, established in Phoenix in 1954, was an early center for solar advocacy, organizing the first international solar conference, and the first competition, in 1957, to design a solar house.[9] The Association mutated into the International Solar Energy Society, which was based at ASU until 1970. Shortly thereafter, Arizona was touted as a prime beneficiary of the 1970s solar boom. The rush to take advantage of new federal and state tax credits sparked a frenzy of business activity, but legislators failed to regulate the burgeoning industry. The absence of installation standards and product testing opened the door to widespread fraud, and Arizona quickly became known as the "solar rip-off state."[10] At one point, as many as 100,000 houses were equipped with solar heaters, but most of the gadgets were overpriced and many were badly installed (in shady areas or facing north).

Not long after President Reagan eliminated the federal solar subsidies, the Arizona Legislature cut off the state's own credits, pushing hundreds of firms out of business, and leaving homeowners with "orphan" technology. Despite solid research that showed the credits were worth twice their value in revenue, state lawmakers saw Reagan's move as a death knell for the industry and justified their own capitulation by arguing that industries had to prove they could stand on their own feet. Strategic rate pricing by the utilities commission continued to ensure that the cheapest energy sources would lie in coal-fired plants, hydro power, and the nuclear capacity of the Palo Verde plant's reactors, just 50 miles to the west of downtown Phoenix.

Central Arizona had the natural capacity to generate 70 percent more power from the same PV panels as in Germany, yet that country became the world's largest market for them in the decades that followed. First Solar, a pioneer of thin film modules, and one of the world's leading PV producers, was actually headquartered in the Valley of the Sun, but its operational facilities were almost all in offshore locations. Founded in Arizona in 1992, the company largely grew its business in Germany, where a friendly government climate for solar energy existed, and where the existence of a feed-in tariff, in particular, guaranteed both grid access and a long-term market for producers. According to CEO Mike Ahearn, "First Solar is to a large extent a German success story.... There was no American solar market, and no one in Washington or anywhere else was particularly interested in creating one, even though the jobs in the solar industry are pure manufacturing ones.... We purchase over half of the equipment used in our production lines from German manufacturers and we count suppliers in Eastern Germany as among our most important business partners.... Countries all over the world are now contacting us to build our next factory there, but so far no one in the U.S. has called."[11] Today the firm's offices are still in Tempe, but none of its manufacturing is currently in Arizona.

With a raft of clean-energy incentives issuing forth from Washington, this laggardly record was slated to change rapidly, and advocates began to dream that the state's solar potential would finally be realized. Once again, Arizona became a focus for investors drawn to the Southwest's solar abundance and eager to snag the subsidies from Obama's new energy policies. After several large solar projects went to other states, the legislature passed its own package of tax incentives in 2008 for manufacturers of renewable energy equipment. Arizona launched itself anew into the game of chasing after Spanish, German, Chinese, and Californian firms scouting around for the best deal. Much more important to the industry's future was the state's Renewable Energy Standards (RES), also known as Renewable Portfolio Standards (RPS), which required utility providers to generate a set percentage of renewable energy: wind, solar, biomass, or geothermal. Indeed it was the first state to introduce an RES target (0.2 percent initially), in the late 1990s. By 2007, the Arizona Corporation Commission (ACC), which regulates utilities, had raised the target to 15 percent by 2025. Unlike the feed-in tariffs favored in Germany and other European countries, which required governments to pay premium rates for renewable energy, the RES mechanism, adopted by twenty-six other states, obliged utilities to take the initiative and develop alternatives to fossil fuel. Lured by the RES commitments and the state tax incentives, investors were now keenly eyeing Phoenix area locations.

The first evidence that a solar boom was in the offing was something very familiar to Arizonans—a land rush. Utilities, investment banks, solar firms, and speculators moved to snap up land on the urban fringe that was unsalable in the wake of the real estate collapse. The land grab attracted buyers like Goldman Sachs, who were suspected of plans to simply flip the lots, but some were bona fide solar outfits, from Germany, Israel, and Spain. Another source of motivation was the congressional plan (under the Energy Policy Act of 2005) to generate 10,000 megawatts of renewable power on federal land by 2015. Robert Glennon reported that, as of mid-March 2009, "the Bureau of Land Management had received 158 applications for permits for solar power plants, covering more than one million acres of land—an area larger than Rhode Island," and thirty-two of these applications were for land in Arizona.[12] Matt Holm, a planner for unincorporated areas of Maricopa County, told me that virtually all of the zoning permit applications in his department in 2008–9 were for large solar developments. Just as the number of permits for new residential subdivisions had fallen to zero, he had seen a wave of applications from large, utility-scale providers for acreage out west, toward the Mojave Desert and closer to the rich California energy market where power transmission lines were accessible. "Everyone is trying to get in on the action," he reported, "and this is ground zero for solar development, so we've seen projects from 40 acres to three or four thousand acres." Many of the preferred locations were on land owned by the Bureau of Land Management, where even groundwater sources were scarce. Holm conceded that water drainage, "given the size or magnitude of these projects," was a challenge. "How can we develop something of this scale in relation to drainage patterns?" he mused. "Because we do not get much rain out there."

Holm was acknowledging a concern that the region's solar advocates did not always like to advertise. Concentrated solar power (CSP), the wet-cooled system used for large utility-scale projects, could use twice as much water as a conventional coal-fired power plant, and the parts of the state that developers were eying had the least rainfall, making the plants entirely dependent on precious groundwater. Air-cooled systems would reduce the water use, but the unforgiving desert heat made them less efficient and more expensive.[13] When APS, the state's largest utility, sited the first two large solar projects, Saguaro (built by ACCIONA Energy of Spain) and Solana (built and operated by another Spanish giant, Abengoa) on private farmland, it pioneered a compromise by buying the land and water rights from the farmers. However thirsty, these CSP facilities would still be using less water than the farmers had done.

Public lands were another matter. Since the Energy Policy Act did nothing to expedite the notoriously long permitting process, many of those who applied were still waiting for approval when the ARRA stimulus incentives, covering one-third of the construction costs on public land, ran out at the end of 2010. Siting large-scale solar farms on the BLM's fragile desert acreage was also a politically fraught proposition, and many California environmental groups called for a moratorium on the land rush. Unlike in California, however, where desert preservationists succeeded in keeping solar developers out of vast areas of the Mojave, there was only token opposition in Arizona. Indeed, Senator Dianne Feinstein's plan, introduced in Congress in December 2009, to protect a million acres of Mojave lands (prime solar real estate) threatened in plans for dozens of solar farms, but it was perceived as a boon to the neighboring Arizona industry.[14]

Responding to the Feinstein initiative, Kris Mayes, chair of the ACC, confessed that "frankly that kind of thing is precisely what we don't want to see happening in Arizona. California simply has too much regulation, and I say that as a regulator myself. You can't do what they do and expect to successfully build anything, so that is going to put more pressure on states like Arizona and Nevada to build projects for California." Mayes, who presided over what was effectively Arizona's fourth layer of government, was described to me by a Democratic senator as "our favorite Republican." A tireless proponent of renewable energy, she took some pride in reporting that "we have about 19,000 megawatts of highly developable solar in our state alone," and that 1,000 megawatts were already sited, "through a much faster permitting process" than in California. The Golden State had a stronger RES (33 percent by 2020), while the Arizona RES (15 percent by 2015) was one of the lowest of the 27 states that had adopted the regulatory mechanism. But Mayes pointed to her success in establishing a generous requirement for distributed generation of renewable energy: "Of the 15 percent renewable that we require by 2025, 30 percent must come from distributed generation sources, which is either solar rooftops, commercial or residential, or backyard wind." "On a per capita basis, our distributed generation requirement," she bragged justifiably, "is the most aggressive in the country."

This mandate for noncentralized production had special significance for critics of the utilities' monopoly on government-guaranteed profits. These profits were threatened by the most minimal energy conservation efforts, let alone alternative energy initiatives.[15] The critics regarded solar energy as a "commonwealth," and they looked forward, as Ralph Nader once put it, to "a consumer-sovereign future where people control and produce their own power."[16] Mayes's own Columbia University thesis on deregulation had been inspired by that vision: "There was a lot of excitement back then about neighborhoods and building cooperatives being able to buy their own power," she recalled, but confessed that, in light of the Enron debacle, "[her] findings would be different today."[17] Nevertheless, she was fond of predicting what she called "cascading natural deregulation," a process that would rapidly accelerate at the point (five years hence in her estimation) when the price of solar reached grid parity with traditional electricity. With the spread of solar rooftop systems and greater energy efficiency, more and more people could go off the grid, and utilities, in their current form, would become less and less necessary. "They'd better get used to it and, if they don't get on the train, they are going to get run over," she observed of the big companies, to whom she was fond of issuing tough warnings: "Your business model is about to be shredded." In her estimate, the utilities would soon be reduced to "providers of last resort," or, if their managers were smart, would evolve into "energy service companies that helped customers generate and save their own electricity."

The dispersed energy landscape Mayes harbored in her mind's eye appealed to the self-reliant values associated with Western libertarianism. If the utility monopolies lost their standing, then a republic of individuals or small cooperatives could thrive in their place. Sentiments like this had a long history in the West, where the long fight over public ownership of electricity provision was especially bitter. They were most recently activated in the 1970s when interest ran high in citizens' or municipal energy collectives with effective control over decisions about clean electricity.[18] Grassroots groups like the Solar Lobby, founded on Earth Day in 1970, were particularly active all through the Carter years, producing advocacy publications like *Blueprint for a Solar America* that were targeted at liberal policymakers.[19]

At least one local veteran of the solar cause, Renz Jennings, the ACC chair who had introduced the RES in the later 1990s, was less sanguine about this prospect today. Retired to his farm in South Phoenix, though still active on many public-interest boards, Jennings did not believe the "diffusion model would ever be able to provide bulk power as a public benefit," and, "unless big players like commercial home builders were to get into megawatt production and consumption," there would always be a public need for large providers. Even if the small producers reached critical mass, they would still need the "utilities to act as a giant battery. You don't have to buy it, just plug in and go, and your stuff stays on after the sun goes down." A former anti-nuclear activist, Jennings had sold solar appliances in the 1970s and was still an enthusiast. "Of all the alternative energy sources," he remarked, "solar is the most forgiving technology. It does not require you [as nuclear might] to leave town for five or six thousand years." But he had been knocking around Arizona politics for long enough to know that it took a lot of "economic imagination to make clean electrons flow and public benefit to accrue." As their former regulator, he concluded that it was still all "too easy for the utilities to greenwash by boasting about their sustainable achievements."

APS, the largest public service corporation that Mayes (and, formerly, Jennings) regulated, had fought increases to the RES for years, but now that the writing was on the wall, it had begun to promote its compliance as a PR asset. In exchange for a rate hike, the company even agreed to double its renewable energy target, and go to 30 percent by 2015. Partly in recognition, CEO Don Brandt received the 2009 "Utility CEO of the Year" award from the Solar Electric Power Association (Mayes had quipped to him: "It's kind of like President Obama getting the Nobel Peace Prize. Now you've got to earn it."). Ed Fox, APS's sustainability officer, acknowledged that the ACC's DG requirement was "a direct threat to our profitability" and that "the transition to a low-carbon future" would be a real challenge for a monopoly "incumbent" like APS "to remain viable." In a world of decentralized power, individual homeowners would be able to sell their surplus wind and solar energy back to the grid, or else share it with their neighbors.[20] Would utilities survive? Fox envisaged a future comparable to the breakup of the telecommunication monopolies, and the "entrance into the marketplace and proliferation of new technologies that allowed us not only to pick providers, but to pick the type of service we want." In this scenario, he thought that utility giants would survive by functioning like landline telecom providers. "There will be some people that stick with the landline utility because that is where they are comfortable and other people who will unplug." "Already," he reported, "we get a lot of customers asking, 'Can I store the energy so if I put on more panels then I don't need you at all?'" But until customers could bank the energy on their own, "storage would be the Achilles heel" of distributed energy, and utilities like APS would be needed, as Jennings had put it, to serve as giant batteries.

SRP, the region's other large utility, was nonprofit, and landowner-owned, so it was not subject to regulation by the utility commission, but it generally pegged its rates to those of APS and had agreed to meet the 15 percent RES target.[21] Jennings, who ran unsuccessfully as a reformer for the sclerotic SRP board (and again, in 2010, for a seat on the commission), remarked that "their only form of regulation is the worry that they won't look good to the community at large." He was also skeptical of SRP's RES accounting—methane recovery, energy-efficiency measures, and hydropower were all included in its portfolio. The utility had been heavily criticized for building a new coal-fired plant, in Springerville, at a time when the public mood and the political climate was firmly against adding to the biggest source of carbon emissions. By the time the plant came on line in December 2009, burning sixty rail cars' worth of Wyoming coal every day, there was a broad consensus that this had to be the state's last such plant.[22]

Dick Hayslip, an associate general manager and old SRP hand, confirmed that the company was investing heavily in carbon capture research to "get some extended life" out of its coal-fired plants, and that it had not closed its door on further nuclear plants. "I'm convinced," he declared, "that they can be operated economically and safely and compatibly with the environment" and added that his board was generally bullish on nuclear. As a nominally cooperative enterprise (accountable to those who owned portions of the original land area serviced by the Salt River–Roosevelt Dam) with a public utility profile, SRP had a vested interest in being perceived as more attentive to the rights and needs of all its customers. In this spirit, the company had plans to tap the growing interest in community solar farming—a share of a central solar facility would be sold to renters or apartment dwellers along the lines of a share in a community garden. "There's an opportunity to provide small solar farms," Hayslip reported, "where the ownership would simulate what they would have if they had rooftop solar."

This kind of arrangement, which resembled Community Supported Agriculture, excited solar enthusiasts like Geoff Sutton, a director-at-large of the Arizona Solar Energy Association, who ran advocacy workshops throughout the Valley. In his view, "it's probably a good thing to have a solar coop or a food coop where people do get the commonality of feeling" customarily associated with the democratic power that the sun sheds. "Energy to me," he added, "is something that should be owned by all the people, everybody should have the access and the right to be able to do that," and "utilities are the ones who are going to be fighting against them in this respect." When I asked Hayslip if the SRP's solar coops were a scalable model, he predicted that these pockets of renewable power would always be "small nodes on the grid," portending little change in the overall management and ownership of energy provision. That would be a far cry from the "solar commonwealth" utopia of the enthusiasts, in which everyone gets to harvest their own energy, with or without the say-so of the utilities.

"When I'm in front of Republican crowds," Kris Mayes acknowledged, "I often speak about solar in national security terms." In a business town like Phoenix, the best pitch for sustainable energy was to talk about its role in economic development. Not that there was much else on the horizon. As the dust from the housing collapse settled, the dream of becoming a solar capital looked like the only game in town. The Greater Phoenix Economic Council (GPEC), charged with bringing corporate investment into the region, had been set up after the last real estate crash in 1989 to revive the rainmaking role played by the Chamber of Commerce in the Goldwater era. GPEC pushed hard to get the solar tax credits through the legislature, and its first big recruitment coup came in November 2009, when Suntech, China's largest solar panel manufacturer, announced plans to build a facility in the Phoenix area. It was the first such plant to be built in the United States by a Chinese clean-tech company and, in this regard, was something of a national milestone. Media coverage drew comparisons with the U.S. entry of the first Japanese auto factories in the 1980s, touching off all the usual alarms about the loss of American competitiveness. But the analogy with Toyota and Honda was flawed—this time around, the potential losers were Germany and Spain, since the United States threw away its lead in renewable technologies many years earlier.

In Phoenix, the more resonant comparison was with the arrival of Motorola in 1948, sparking a wave of high-tech investors that turned the city into an important manufacturing center. "We just hit the reset button" was how a local politician put it to me just after the Suntech announcement was made. As with the defense-oriented industries of the 1940s and 1950s, federal incentives played a role in Suntech's location decision in the form of a 30 percent investment tax credit available to solar firms from ARRA stimulus funding. But that was about as far as the analogy went. The Motorola generation brought a wide range of jobs to the region—from high-wage positions in research engineering to low-skill production jobs. Beginning in the 1970s, these jobs were progressively sent offshore, many of them to China itself. The Suntech setup was a reverse cycle. Manufacturing (and design) of Suntech's solar cells would continue to be done in China. The jobs coming to Arizona were primarily for assembling panels that would be sold regionally and that were not cost-effective to ship from Asia. The panels would probably be stamped "Made in the USA," but only the least-skilled portion of the production process would occur on American soil. Fifteen years before, advanced U.S. manufacturers began to use China's coastal factories as an assembly platform for manufacturing. Now the tables were turned. With formidable state subsidies, central industrial planning, preferential treatment, and boundless cheap labor to draw on, China's clean-tech firms had sprinted ahead in the last years of the decade, establishing an unassailable lead in solar panel and wind-turbine manufacturing.

A week before the Suntech announcement, Senator Chuck Schumer (D-NY) opened a new front in the protectionist wars by assailing the use of ARRA funds to generate "Chinese jobs" for a 646-megawatt wind farm in West Texas. Notoriously, in an era of free trade, China had built up its clean-tech industries by requiring companies to use domestic materials and labor. Politicians, like Schumer, who cut a prominent profile for deploring the outsourcing of American manufacturing to China several years before, repackaged their appeals to economic nationalism by calling out the administration for not backing American-built products. In March 2010, Schumer and three other Democratic senators introduced legislation that would apply a "buy American" standard to all renewable energy projects that applied for stimulus funds, requiring them to rely on parts manufactured in the United States. Less than a year later, President Obama signed a military authorization law that contained a similar "buy American" provision for all Defense Department purchases of solar panels.

Still enjoying the plaudits from the Suntech announcement when I met with him, GPEC president Barry Broome was not at all concerned about the jobs imbalance, nor had he much patience for nationalist grandstanding. A Cleveland native, he did not want to see Arizona "make the mistake that Ohio and Michigan made with the Japanese and Koreans." "As an American," he felt "competitive toward China" but did not want "these patriotic instincts to interfere with the right economic decisions." In his opinion, "the Chinese should feel that Phoenix is the most welcome place in the U.S. for their industry and for their people." I asked him if Arizona was about to become an assembly platform for Chinese companies. "If we're lucky," he replied. "That's how tough things are right now." (Or, as Glenn Hamer at the Chamber of Commerce put it, "We're not going to sneeze at that"). While the Phoenix business community had dreams of re-living the glory days of its now attenuated high-tech sector, Broome was focused, more pragmatically, on the mass of livelihoods in a region where poverty levels had skyrocketed and joblessness was chronic. "In Arizona," he pointed out, "we have to put a million working-class Hispanics to work. Fifty percent of their children under the age of 18 speak English as a second language, and they are not all going to be at Google. Our preference has been to think of manufacturing in aerospace and semiconductor, but a big part of [the future] is going to be in simpler operations like solar panel assembly." Before the month was out, GPEC was reporting that a slew of out-of-state or overseas companies, including Yingli, another Chinese solar market leader, were eyeing Phoenix area locations with a view to taking advantage of the ARRA tax credits.

Broome's matter-of-fact acceptance of China's commanding lead in the new industries was at odds with the breast-beating of those lamenting how far behind the United States was in the race to dominate the clean-tech sector. Prominent among them was erstwhile champion of corporate globalization Thomas Friedman, who had become a zealous advocate for U.S. industry to rise up and challenge the Chinese lead. On more or less the same page were the Apollo Alliance, the green-labor group, and the Center for American Progress, the liberal think tank, who issued reports ("Winning the Race: How America Can Lead the Global Clean Energy Economy" and "Out of the Running? How Germany, Spain, and China Are Seizing the Energy Opportunity and Why the United States Risks Getting Left Behind") that sounded the same note of alarm about losing the race for global supremacy in clean energy. The United States already lagged on production and was on the brink of ceding its traditional R&D edge in innovation. Control over patents and other intellectual property, the oil of the twenty-first century, would move offshore, Friedman and others warned, unless a full-scale mobilization, akin to that of a war economy, occurred.

Behind all the nationalist bluster were real concerns about missing out on a new generation of manufacturing jobs. In the early 2000s, the storm over job loss from offshore outsourcing had been laced with anti-Chinese sentiment ("they are taking our jobs"). Never mind that it was U.S. corporations ordering the job transfers and reaping the profits. It was easier to blame the Chinese—one of the most reliable ethnic instincts of white America. Even at that time, corporate R&D centers were being steadily migrated to the People's Republic of China.[23] Now that the innovation was proceeding under Chinese auspices, in clean-tech sectors lavishly funded and groomed to command export markets, the fear of being dominated by the Asian behemoth was feeding into a new and arguably more ominous version of recessionary Sinophobia.

In September 2010, United Steel Workers filed a comprehensive trade case under section 301 of the U.S. trade laws against allegedly unfair policies and practices designed by the PRC to advance its domination of the clean-tech sector. China's government was being faulted for subsidizing renewable technologies for export to countries that needed them to meet mandates for greenhouse gas reductions. Yet under WTO rules, it was illegal to subsidize these technologies for export. How fair was the charge against the Chinese? In 2009, the PRC ploughed 0.31 percent of its GDP (or $34.6 billion) into clean energy—less than Spain at 0.74 percent, or the United Kingdom, at 0.51 percent, but far more than the United States, at 0.13 percent, or $18.6 billion.[24] Its government's keen nurturing of the clean-energy sector had helped push down the global prices of wind and solar energy, but these policies had also discouraged producers in high-wage countries from entering the market.

By 2010, the surge of speculative green investment in the United States was over, and, after the mid-term elections brought the GOP back into power in the House, the once bright prospects for long-term government support began to dim. The shift in congressional power made it less likely that any of the ARRA incentives for renewable energy would be extended beyond 2010. Start-ups either held back or dropped their plans to expand—an extension of the credits through 2011 was won, eventually, in the face of strong GOP opposition.[25] Inability to compete with the subsidized "China price" may have been one good reason for the slowdown of U.S. production, but why single out for blame a government that was doing whatever was needed to respond to the global demand for decarbonization? The labor movement and its allies should have been pressuring Washington to match China's subsidies on a long-term basis. After all, for the foreseeable future, renewable energy was going to be a "government industry." But as always, and especially in an election year, it was easier to blame the Chinese.

Yet even if U.S. companies were somehow to become leading players in the renewable energy field, what would guarantee their provision of American jobs? And what would ensure they were quality-pay jobs? Only long-term government subsidies or feed-in tariff guarantees would entice corporate America to reinvest in the domestic workforce. Tempe-based First Solar was a case in point. In November 2009, it reached an agreement with the Chinese government to build a massive 2-gigawatt solar plant in Mongolia, to be supplied by a new manufacturing facility built and operated by the company in the PRC. The deal went a long way to countering complaints that non-Chinese firms had been blocked from entering the PRC market. Furthermore, First Solar's interest was sparked by two conditions: Beijing's approval of a feed-in tariff, mandating utilities to pay a premium to renewable energy suppliers, and the enforcement of a national RES, setting targets of 20 percent by 2020.[26]

Only with the recent dangling of federal and state incentives did First Solar look stateside. In Fall 2009, it inked a deal with California's PG&E for a large 550-megawatt solar farm, in a state that was the first to institute a feed-in tariff, and in January 2010 the firm snagged $5 million in Advanced Energy Manufacturing Tax Credits to expand its token U.S. manufacturing plant, in Toledo. Finally, in January 2011, Barry Broome received news that GPEC had won the interstate competition to land the company's proposed new manufacturing facility, slated to provide 600 jobs. The $300 million factory, slated for a Mesa location, came at a steep price; First Solar was able to extract $51.5 million worth of incentives from state, county, and city coffers, in addition to substantial discounts on land purchase and on its utility bills. If the facility was expanded, the company would also receive $1 million for every 240 jobs created, up to a $20 million total.[27]

As welcome as these new green jobs were, it was by no means clear how long they would be kept in the United States. With the price of PV panels falling so rapidly, U.S. firms that entered the field with government help were already transitioning to Asia. Evergreen, a Massachusetts-based solar start-up, which opened its doors with more than $43 million of state backing in fall 2008, began to transfer operations to China only a year later, and, in January 2011, moved its entire production plant to a heavily subsidized joint venture with Jiawei Solarchina in Wuhan.[28] Indeed, a survey, conducted by the Apollo Alliance and Good Jobs First of the ninety recipients of ARRA's Advanced Energy Manufacturing Tax Credit, showed that twenty-three of them were also investing in manufacturing facilities in low-wage countries like Malaysia and China.[29]

As long as the government stuck by its commitment to renewables, employees and host communities could expect some degree of employer accountability when it came to the provision of decent pay and benefits. But in states like Arizona that were hostile to trade unions, the prospect of well-paid green jobs was especially precarious. Rebecca Friend, the AFL-CIO regional president, was happy to report to me that, at the very least, legislators were now obliged to set a place at the table for labor. "Before this administration came in, we were not even acknowledged. Now the state has to sit down with us, whether they want to or not. They need our signature on their federal grant proposals." But she did not expect the welcome carpet to lie around for too long after the grants and tax incentives were secured. Friend also envisaged well-paying union jobs at the utilities' power plant being displaced by substandard jobs in a new alternative energy sector dominated by exclusively private firms. "My concern is that international solar companies will come in with a completely different set of work ethics, and that they will go nonunion and also way below scale. Like other industries, such as the call centers, they might be coming here because we are a right-to-work state." The big utilities, she pointed out, were all unionized and locally owned, yet none of the new energy firms, including First Solar and Sterling Energy, the other sizable solar presence in town, had a union workforce. "Arizona is a service industry state and is already glutted with low-paying jobs," she observed. "We don't need any more."

Hers was a long-standing concern within the labor movement, and, in the past, it had often put unions in the dirty energy sector on the wrong side of the green equation. For Friend and other Arizona trade unionists, it would be unjust if the transition to clean energy were pursued on the backs of working people or at the expense of labor power. Even so, studies dating from the 1970s to the present day showed that investment, whether public or private, in decentralized and labor-intensive green enterprises would create many more jobs than in the highly automated, capital-intensive, centralized facilities of the old energy sector. These estimates punctured the employers' myth, recirculated by self-interested unions, that green industrial policy would only result in job losses.[30] At the international level, labor's efforts to gain some traction on this issue were focused on incorporating "just transition" language into climate policy agreements. The aim was to guarantee aid and retraining to workers displaced by any industrial conversions to clean energy. Thwarted in Copenhagen, the International Trade Union Confederation succeeded in pushing these provisions into the voluntary "shared vision" adopted at the Cancun summit in December 2010.

WINNERS AND LOSERS

Arizona had its share of "solar Republicans," but that did not prevent the GOP from decrying GPEC for pushing the clean-tech tax credits, and for its preferential courting of solar firms. "Government should not be picking winners and losers," was the mantra in libertarian circles. Even the utility commission's RES mandate was attacked as an unconstitutional intervention on the commission's part. From the left, the mechanism for fulfilling the RES quotas was also under fire. Under the rate-pricing schedule fixed with the utilities, all customers had to pay a monthly surcharge to fund the utility's program of rebates for those who wanted go solar. The result was basically a subsidy to middle-class homeowners, who, thanks to the incentives offered, could more easily afford to put PV panels on their roofs. In effect, the system of tax credits and surcharges amounted to a form of regressive taxation, since renters and poor homeowners were paying into a scheme that had very little benefit for them.[31]

The business argument for clean-energy subsidies rested on the claim that they were needed to build a market. Once prices came down, and a critical mass of consumers were on board, government, it was assumed, would reduce its pump-priming. Ecologically minded economists argued that clean energy already was quite competitive if all the environmental costs of nonrenewables were factored in. In addition, the subsidies enjoyed by the oil, coal, and nuclear industries were immense. Fossil fuel and nuclear power enjoyed as much as $21 billion annually of these "perverse subsidies" in the United States alone, according to a 2001 estimate.[32] These numbers included depletion allowances, tax-free construction bonds, R&D grants, income tax breaks, below-cost loans, sales tax breaks, highway construction and maintenance, and the funding of the U.S. Strategic Petroleum Reserve. They did not include the countless Pentagon billions required to safeguard the flow of cheap oil from overseas. Since the formulation of the Carter Doctrine in 1980, a large share of the U.S. military budget has gone to protecting these overseas energy assets.[33] As for nuclear power, its development has always been impossible without massive federal backing, both economically (no insurance company would ever underwrite a nuclear plant) and also in the critical matter of responsibility for radioactive waste storage and disposal, which the government assumes entirely.

The fossil industries have long used their formidable lobbying strength to protect these subsidies and to block any legislative efforts to make them pay the costs of pollution. It has always been much cheaper, for example, to employ an army of lobbyists than to install carbon-scrubbing technology in dirty power plants. As legislators came under pressure to adopt decarbonization measures, the volume and intensity of lobbying was stepped up. Legislative proposals that favored cap and trade, carbon taxes, or any statutory reduction in emissions were countered with extensive pressure and disinformation campaigns. In 2009 and 2010, the oil, coal, and gas industries spent vast sums to circulate the bromide that anthropogenic global warming was a falsehood generated by a conspiracy of scientists.[34] A similar campaign was directed at the economic viability of green job creation. Nationally, much GOP attention was focused on two studies, which estimated the taxpayer burden for clean-energy job creation in Germany and Spain, and concluded that the outcome of feed-in tariffs and other government incentives had not been cost-effective. These studies, which were rebutted by scholars and government officials, showed net job losses overall, a pattern of indirect subsidies (through imports of cheaper foreign products) to Chinese manufacturers, and, in the case of Spain, a ruinous speculative bubble in renewables.[35]

By the beginning of 2010, Republican opposition to alternative energy subsidies had congregated around the push for more nuclear power, and the Obama administration made its concessions accordingly. "Atoms for peace" had been a central component of Cold War industrial policy, both at home and in the export of nuclear technologies abroad. The success of the anti-nuclear movement in stopping plant construction in the late 1970s was a tremendous blow to hawks for whom the development of nuclear energy was a corollary of superior U.S. statecraft and military prowess. The new window for clean energy, combined with calls for energy independence stoked by the "war on terror," offered a rare opportunity to restart the program. Over its years of operating in other countries, especially France, the industry had recorded improvements in safety and in the technology of recycling fuel, but its basic shortcomings remained the same: soaring costs, lengthy construction time, unreliable operation, overcentralization of technical expertise, nonrenewable uranium resources, extreme environmental risk from meltdown and problems resulting from waste management, and, last but not least, widespread public distrust. The acute hazards leaped back into the public mind after the catastrophic meltdowns at the Fukushima Daiichi power plant in the wake of Japan's March 2011 earthquake. Yet pressure from the energy lobby and the GOP's congressional majority ensured that the Obama administration held firm, in principle at least, to its policy commitment of relaunching the U.S, nuclear program.

In Arizona, the pro-nuclear campaign fed into GOP plans to take on the authority of the utility commission (ACC).[36] Leading Republicans argued that the commission had overstepped its mandate by setting an RES with teeth, and many were gunning to have the standards legally overturned. The Goldwater Institute, a right-wing tank with a fierce appetite for litigating against government subsidies, filed suit against the ACC for "expanding its powers beyond its constitutional jurisdiction" by adopting "sweeping new rules requiring utilities to derive a specified share of their power from alternative sources." After the Arizona Supreme Court sided with the ACC, Republican senators threatened a bill to strip the ACC of its power to set the RES, with the goal of allowing the "free market" to determine the fortunes of the clean-energy industry. More controversial was House Bill 2701, aimed at creating an RES of the legislature's making, independent of the ACC. Under the proposed new standard, "renewable" would include nuclear power, making Arizona the first state to adopt such a definition. If passed, the bill would almost certainly have killed the renewable energy industry, since 27 percent of APS's power came from Palo Verde, the nation's largest nuclear plant, to the east of Phoenix. Under

HB 2701, the utility would technically already be in compliance with the RES mandate. The lawmakers' goal of decimating the fledgling solar initiatives was quite clear. Several big solar investors held off on their location decisions until the bill's fate was decided.

The bill was moving quickly through the legislature in February 2010 until it ran into a barrage of criticism from many sides. Opposition came not just from the solar industry and its advocates but also from the Arizona Chamber of Commerce, which had supported the clean-energy manufacturing incentives, and from Republican governor Jan Brewer, who was a pro-solar advocate, but who had also recently egged on the pro-nuclear forces with her declaration that "nuclear power is at the cornerstone of our clean-energy future."[37] According to Michael Neary, executive director of the Arizona Solar Energy Industries Association and coordinator of the opposition, the legislature's system for recording voter sentiment showed that "a record number of people registered opposition to the bill." The record number of supporters in favor of a bill, he added, was for the 2008 legislation offering solar manufacturing incentives. In any event, Neary expected the RES would be upheld at the ballot if the Goldwater Institute lawsuit ever prevailed in the courts. Most visibly, Suntech threatened to move out of Arizona if the measure passed—a hugely embarrassing prospect for the state. Facing down the business lobby and top Republicans, the bill's sponsor, a rookie from Glendale, adjacent to the Goodyear location of the Suntech facility, withdrew it from the floor. But considerable damage to the state's business prospects had already been done, and the impression of Arizona as a politically unstable environment scared off some prospective investors, especially in the solar field. By year's end, none of them had inked a deal in the wake of Suntech's announcement. First Solar's commitment to building a massively subsidized facility in Mesa came early in 2011 and was interpreted as a solid sign that the uncertainty had blown over.

HB 2701 may have been just another kooky play from lawmakers whose deliberations had already made the Arizona legislature into an object of national derision. It was also a cynical piece of politicking. A few days after the bill was withdrawn, I quizzed one of its would-be supporters, Andy Biggs (R-Gilbert), about whether he thought nuclear power really was renewable. "Let's just say they were stretching the definition of renewable," he replied, with a chuckle. "I believe it was Hayek," he added, "who said that the first battle is always over language." For him, as for others, the full intent of the measure was not to target the solar subsidies per se but to reduce business taxes across the board. "We are subsidizing this industry on the manufacturing end and the consumer end, which is not a good business model for the state or the solar industry," he asserted. "Instead we should just overhaul our entire tax code and make it less onerous." Biggs himself had little appetite for the massive government backing that would be required for any new nuclear plant. Given his druthers, he favored opening up Arctic National Wildlife Refuge to oil drilling. The local Tea Party operatives were on the same page. Tom Jenney, director of the state's AFP chapter, was gung ho "in favor of pre-growth tax cuts." And, he told me, "I was the only person to testify [on HB 2701] who mentioned climate change. No one who was advocating solar brought up global warming, it was all about creating jobs." In fact, he testified that "the only way you can justify this RES is if you believe that the externalities caused by man-made global warming are happening, and that we can do something productive with public policy that can affect it." Jenney himself insisted he was agnostic on the topic of climate change, but he was well aware that GOP legislators were not.

It was no surprise to learn that lobbyists like Jenney played to legislators whom they knew would take a dim view of scientific evidence about global warming. Amanda Osborne, a well-connected solar lobbyist who told me that she tried to avoid the legislature as much as possible, recounted her experience of committee hearings like the one she had recently attended on renewable energy: "It was really hard to sit in a room and listen to what was being said, because so much of the information that some of these legislators are believing and speaking is really just not based in fact or science." Even so, the breadth and power of the opposition to HB 2701 was more significant than the politicking around it. Shutting down a bill in progress was a rare occurrence, and it was widely seen as a turning point in the low-intensity conflict of the region's energy wars. Above all, it was evidence that there was a new pro-growth consensus in town, a perception supported by Glenn Hamer at the Arizona Chamber of Commerce, who spoke to me of a "massive coalition of stakeholders based on broad bipartisan support at all levels to advance solar, whether through deployment or manufacturing." Hamer acknowledged that "generally the Chamber would be aligned with the Goldwater Institute . . . but there were some areas such as renewable energy deployment where we do believe that tax incentives have an important role to play as do the major business lobbying groups, such as National Association of Manufacturing and the U.S. Chamber of Commerce." If solar energy was an unassailable part of Arizona's future, then to question its place in regional growth plans was a marginal, if not heretical, position.

While it was the shiny new technologies of the solar industry that attracted investors and polished the boosters' hopes for rebranding the region, green jobs were much more likely to open up in existing occupations or industries: mass transit, home insulating, salvage, HVAC (Heating, Ventilating, and Air Conditioning) contracting, waste management, organic and local agriculture, or low-carbon construction. Sizable energy efficiencies and employment opportunities could be gotten very quickly from weatherizing the homes that were thrown up to profit from the housing bubble. Such energy retrofits were a clear alternative to the practice of renovating homes to boost resale value—a popular custom that had generated mountains of waste material during the real estate boom. In the postwar era, merchant builders adopted nationwide construction templates with little regard for regional climate variation, and so their profit-driven models of mass production preempted the appropriate siting of houses to conserve energy in the desert. One very common design—with a garage and large-paned master bedroom facing south—made houses into suntraps, and, over the long summer, they were enormously expensive to cool. As a result, the typical suburban Arizona home was an energy pig. Plugging leaks, realigning ducts, repairing roofs, sealing gaps, and insulating furnaces could slice in half the utility bills in any of these buildings. As Van Jones put it, "The main piece of technology in the green economy is the caulking gun."[38]

In late summer 2009, Phoenix's new Green Chamber of Commerce organized an event on green jobs training. About a hundred attendees showed up, many of them jobless tradespeople or small employers trying to get back in business through the lifeline offered by ARRA funding. Chamber president Mara DeFillipis offered an analogy for the impact of the stimulus money. "It is like a giant holding a string up and moving it back and forth, and all of these people are following it, looking to see where it is going to stop." Among the Chamber's members were many self-employed individuals or small firms who had applied for funds for training, but they were proving slow to access. "The upfront cost of certification is a few thousand dollars," she noted, "and that is a lot of money for some people right now." Frustration at the slow pace of bureaucracy was more than evident at the meeting itself. Most of the speakers were from community colleges or government agencies charged with providing training certification or administering the rebates though competitive grants. The audience had its share of impatient souls. As the evening wore on, several stood up to voice their frustration at the red tape and application forms standing in the way of their direct access to grants and incentives. It was a very Arizonan spectacle. The government funds were plenty welcome—it was taxpayers' money after all—but the giant had to stop pulling the strings and get out of the way. "Show me the money," hollered one of the bolder attendees.

As with many of the stimulus programs, funds for weatherization were notoriously slow in working their way through states' bureaucracies. Yet, dollar for dollar, the program still promised to be the most effective way of creating jobs quickly. In addition, it entailed work that would be done in local communities through budgets that mostly went to hiring personnel rather than to equipment purchase. In other respects, the change in public consciousness prompted by weatherization promised to be as momentous as the mentality ushered in by recycling. For those who grew up in the throwaway consumer society, the novel task of separating waste on a daily basis amounted, over time, to a profound alteration of common sense. Recycling, for them, was the first step in considering the environmental consequences of their consumption. The crusade—if it turned into one—for homegrown energy efficiencies and carbon reduction would be the second phase of this long revolution in consciousness. Arguably, it would be more socially sustaining in the habits and social relationships it fostered than many of the top-down geo-engineering schemes and other macro technological fixes currently being proposed to reduce the planet's carbon stockpile.

Rooftop solar power was supposed to be an integral part of that domestic revolution, but its viability would depend ultimately on whether the current system of grid-tied, centralized generation could be altered. Truly local provision of renewable energy would require the complete reworking of networks built around power plant supply and high-voltage transmission lines. As Mike Pasqualetti, an energy expert at ASU, observed, "Solar would have to adapt to the existing infrastructure and the existing policies, laws, regulations, incentives, payment systems, everything. It is not just starting from scratch, you have to start from what you have, which means going back to readjust and re-jigger every-thing that you've already put in place over a period of almost a century now." However arduous, he believed it needed to be done, nor least for rea-sons of self-sufficiency, since he estimated that "less than 10 percent of our energy is provided from resources within the state, and the rest of it is brought in from elsewhere" (natural gas from Texas and New Mexico, uranium from overseas, and coal from neighboring states like Colorado and Utah).

Bud Annan, a solar consultant and former head of the U.S. Department of Energy's solar program, believed that a much larger, regional solution was required. "The Western Area Power Administration's 16,000 miles of transmission lines were created," he pointed out, "because the United States needed an energy infrastructure for dams built by Reclamation, but the authorities took that power and marketed it throughout the West. It seems like a small step to do that for renewables." Another model, with a similar historical antecedent, was the interstate highway system. "We ought to look at energy the way we look at roads, as if it were infrastructure," Annan insisted. "The Department of Transportation is a partner with the state in building federal highways through the state," he observed. "Why can't we have that same kind of partnership to develop an energy infrastructure?" But was it still possible to endow any government agency with that kind of grand ambition? The sense of destiny, for example, that pervaded the Reclamation project was either too immature for today's policymakers or too easily targeted by Tea Party ideologues. Besides, the monumental scale of the vision seemed at odds with the homesteader ethos of solar populism.

Rooftop power in particular made people feel they were self-fashioning engineers of their own destiny, even if most were not, technically speaking, off the grid. As Pasqualetti pointed out, generating sources like nuclear plants "concentrate power in a few hands while solar, which is a much more democratic resource because it is ubiquitous, tends to distribute power into everybody's hands." While Arizona sunshine fell everywhere in a relatively even-handed way, getting people equitable access to the clean electrons generated from its power was a formidable task. For energy libertarians, on the left and the right, the existing system of utility control over distributed rooftop generation was a recipe for solar sharecropping, especially since the utilities paid less for that portion of the "tenant's" energy crop than what they charged for their own product.[39] Retaining control over rooftop generation in this way also allowed the utilities to use solar and wind to supplement gaps in their baseload system rather than develop renewables as a real source of peak power.[40] This strategy of containment protected the utilities' monopoly and was quite at odds with the vision of local, citizen control over energy generation and decision making that had fired the solar movement in the 1970s.[41]

For those who saw the race to decarbonize as a life-or-death matter, the selection of vehicle made little difference. Since the window for climate action was closing fast, the quickest form of emissions reduction would surely be the best. But the choice of pathway is an all-important guarantor of justice and democracy. The UN-approved programs, for example, that allow corporate fossil-fuel burners to offset their emissions by "curating" a remote patch of rainforest might satisfy some global estimates of carbon accounting, but they do nothing to dissolve the concentrated power of big polluters. The transition to alternative energy was not just about decarbonization, it was also about bringing equity into the energy equation. Because renewable energy can be generated at or near the point of use, it lends itself to local control, and local control is quite the opposite of the Houston–New York–Riyadh axis of centralized power that stands in the way of a more democratic future.

In Arizona, as in other states, the utilities still held the reins, and could manage the growth of renewables at will. As a result, the pent-up demand for residential and small commercial solar installation was kept in check by the rebate programs offered by SRP and APS. In 2010, both utilities exhausted their respective program's annual budgets at an early point in the fiscal year, and promptly suspended the incentives that had been made available for their PV-minded customers to go solar.[42] The cutoffs were a stark reminder of how tightly these monopolies controlled the alternatives to their core business.

ACADEMIC ENTERPRISE

Even if the Arizona solar rush failed to yield any advance in citizen control over energy, or a critical mass of long-term quality jobs, it could still win the state a newfound reputation for innovation if its universities and start-ups came up with bright solutions to some of the challenges faced by the renewable energy industries. Phoenix had been late in adopting the "meds and eds" recipe for urban economic development, and the state's commitment to building out the much-vaunted bioscience campus in downtown Phoenix had faltered more than once. One reason was the recession, and the reluctance of the legislature to fund the Arizona Science Foundation, but the other was the perception that the region, so far behind, would be hard pressed to establish itself as a contender in biomedicine. But there was no such lag in the field of renewable energy. The universities, and the technology firms they were helping to incubate, had no reason not to be in the leading edge.

The University of Arizona in Tucson had a long-standing commitment to solar energy and currently hosted the Arizona Research Institute for Solar Energy. But ASU's more recent rise as a research center with an aggressive commitment to pushing technologies into the market made it the focus of attention for economic development in the region. Since the arrival of its go-go president, Michael Crow, in 2002, ASU's profile had been recrafted to make it responsive to the demands of the moment. In education, that meant a prompt expansion of multidisciplinary programs and overall student enrollment. At a time when college costs were ballooning out of middle-class range, "inclusion" was a key word in Crow's vision of the new ASU. As for research, the new mantra was "user-inspired," which implied a hands-on orientation toward public and industry needs. The fledgling School of Sustainability became a valuable training ground for recruits to the greening efforts of the region's municipalities and corporate organizations. Drawing on his background in applied science policy, Crow also installed a network of research centers aimed at developing clean technologies, mostly solar, but also algae-based biofuel and nanophotonics. All were encouraged to court industry partners and sponsors. The goal was to come up with the sustainability solutions that Greater Phoenix, and other metro regions like it, needed, and with a sense of urgency not normally associated with academic endeavors.

Crow's previous effort at a multidisciplinary initiative focused on sustainability was the Earth Institute at Columbia University, where, as Vice Provost, he had introduced a keen entrepreneurial edge to many of the university's research capabilities, generating a bounty of new revenue through technology transfer and other commercial ventures. At Columbia, he was also the primary champion of Biosphere 2, the quirky ecological project near Tucson that was his first high-profile engagement with Arizona. Biosphere 2 is remembered as a flawed experiment in simulating an artificial terrestrial environment, a technological ark for surviving mankind's destruction of its original ecosystem (Biosphere 1). Yet its chief purpose was to generate commercial spinoffs for the environmental management industry and for institutions like NASA. Media-friendly from the outset (Tim Luke described it as "technoscience soap opera"), its ultimate audience was investors in the future industry of planetary colonization and terraforming.[43] After his university team took over management for the project, Crow mused, "One hundred fifty years from now, there will be planetary engineering departments at major institutions like Columbia."[44]

Crow's departure from Columbia put paid to the plan to turn the Biosphere site into the university's "western campus." The "New American University" he rolled out at ASU was an ambitious upgrade of his plan to run a vast lab for policy and technological solutions. Biosphere 2 had been an eight-story steel and glass structure, sealed off from the Arizona desert ecosystem. ASU would take the whole metropolitan region as its laboratory, a badly damaged environment on which his researchers would be set loose to patch, heal, and relaunch as something more like an urban ark. As early as 1999, the Central Arizona–Phoenix Long-Term Ecological Research survey, initiated by environmental scientists Charles Redman and Nancy Grimm, had begun its systematic interdisciplinary mapping of the region's environmental features. Crow's arrival raised the ante with the creation of the Global Institute of Sustainability (GIOS), aimed at planetary-scale solutions for the ecological crisis. Academic initiatives like these that were so on-message gave a new sense of purpose to faculty veterans and attracted many stellar recruits from a variety of fields, persuaded to be part of such a timely enterprise. Whether or not these faculty members saw its mission as a practical call to arms, it was a rare effort to marshal a university's resources for a common cause, previously only seen in the mobilizing of teaching and research for wars. Jim Buizer, recruited from NOAA as one of Crow's top executives, mused about the outcomes of the experiment he saw his colleagues conducting. "If ASU is successful in reshaping the balance between the humans that live here and the natural system that supports us, and if we are successful in making the future of Phoenix as attractive as it is today, we will only be encouraging continued growth, and so it will become more difficult to remain sustainable. If we are unsuccessful, then people will stop moving here. That's the conundrum." The professors, if they were allowed to, would help build the ark, but it was by no means clear who would stay on board and who would be left behind.

A founder of the American College and University Presidents' Climate Commitment, Crow made sure that ASU came close to topping the sustainability rankings for campuses nationwide. Part of the profile was a large solar array that provided a sizable portion of the campus's energy supply. Full carbon neutrality was the watchword, though for almost 90,000 students, faculty, and staff, reaching that goal anytime soon was unlikely. More telling was the range of new research institutes and centers devoted to renewable energy applications, all primed for market development. Skysong, a high-tech industrial park, aimed at drawing in or incubating small clean-energy firms, was constructed on the working-class side of upscale Scottsdale. As the recession fell upon the region, economic managers looked to ASU's newfound potential as a magnet for solar firms. Lead researchers and administrators at ASU were instrumental in the effort to land Suntech, and GPEC's Barry Broome had no hesitation in pronouncing that "ASU is now the most important economic asset in our region."

To watch ASU's reputation morph so quickly from party school to that of an "innovation center," prized by the new wave of industrialists, was a giddy prospect for many old-timers. In some respects, however, the university was simply reprising a role it played in the postwar period when the creation of its engineering department was key to the relocation of the large defense corporations and electronics manufacturers. Indeed, the decision to transform what had been Arizona State Teacher's College into a research university in the mid-1950s was largely triggered by demand from the likes of Motorola, GE, Sperry Rand, AiResearch, and other firms for a stable, high-skilled workforce in Phoenix. Vocal in their complaints about having to import engineers and scientists from elsewhere, executives from these firms helped fund the lab space, equipment, and faculty hires for the new science and engineering programs.[45] The relationship between the university and local industry was an intimate one from the start, and it grew through the joint creation and co-management of various centers devoted to solid state electronics and semiconductors research. By the late 1980s, economic growth was driven more and more by construction, and so the development industry looked to ASU's Real Estate Center for market data, and to the aptly named Del Webb School of Construction for engineering needs.

As the fledgling solar economy struggled to find its feet, the business community would come to expect a similar range of services from the university. The most starry-eyed saw another Stanford/Silicon Valley in the making, with solar start-ups spinning out of the synergy between academic research, government stimulus funding, venture capital, and pent-up market demand. If this kind of industry cluster were to develop, no one was counting on the aid of the state legislature—ASU budgets were among the first to suffer deep cuts, and the dogma of climate change denial had instilled a general antipathy to science among the growing GOP majority in both houses. Like defunded public universities elsewhere, ASU was more and more forced to rely on sponsors and outside contracts to pay the bills. Administrators developed an entrepreneurial mentality that would have been alien to their counterparts in the postwar period, when ASU had largely functioned as a handmaiden to the private sector, plugging gaps in knowledge and delivering a skilled labor supply, trained in university labs that were co-managed by the corporations themselves.

That was not the only difference, however. The reorientation of so many different constituent colleges—as many as 27—around the commitment to sustainability teaching and research was aimed at a holistic overview, melding together many different approaches to ecosystem resilience, from the natural and social sciences, as well as the humanities. Whereas before, policymakers, city officials, or industry managers might rely on the university for pockets of expertise or graduates with specialized skills, now they were looking at what, in corporate terminology, would be called a full-service capability. Solar developers, for example, had long benefited from the proximity of the university's world-class Photovoltaic Testing Laboratory. By 2010, that facility had been joined by several other relevant sources of capability. These included physical components of the "solar supply chain," such as testing and synthesis of new materials, device fabrication, power systems modeling and design, and applications for integrating photovoltaic energy into a variety of building types. Environmental design was also part of the knowledge portfolio, along with green building know-how, and urban and community planning that integrated clean energy. So, too, ASU faculty could offer expertise about the impact of energy generation and delivery on climate change, land and water ecologies, social justice, behavioral psychology, livelihoods, legal reasoning, and cultural customs. The race to decarbonize, after all, would require a revolution in human conduct—every field of knowledge was affected.

ASU's transformation was a good example of the changes coursing through higher education as a whole. Whether you were primarily interested in profiting from green capitalism, or in staving off eco-collapse for higher ends, knowledge about sustainability was increasingly sought out, and no other institution in society was equipped to put all the pieces together with anything like the objectivity that academia tries to honor. In principle, this made academic research more valuable, and universities more influential voices in the sphere of policy. But policymakers who paid lip service to the "knowledge society" in their speeches were wary about ceding too much ground to professional expertise. The high-profile friction between right-wing politicians and climatologists was one symptom of this new balance of power. As for their relationship with industry, the two-way traffic between knowledge corporations and research universities was already a very busy superhighway. It was by no means easy to say where the rules and mentalities of these respective worlds began and ended. But however blurred the lines had become, it was a given that, as in the realm of politics, the balance of power would likely be decided by money.

With the university producing knowledge that was so tailor-made for the moment, some ASU faculty worried about their academic independence. More and more corporations had their names on campus contracts and were in a position to call the shots on the design of research projects. Nor were these new "partners" likely to tolerate research outcomes that conflicted with their interests. Faculty with backgrounds in environmental science, especially, were used to seeing their field on the receiving end of corporate attacks and were naturally suspicious to find it being courted by firms bent on rebranding themselves as green champions. "I am an old style academic who believes that corporations should stay off campus," confessed Bob Bolin, a geographer who had published widely on environmental injustice in metro Phoenix, and who was dismayed by the stepped-up corporate presence in the new ASU. Deeply concerned about the potential restrictions on academic freedom, he noted, "No corporation is going to invest in a campus if you have a researcher that's going to say, 'Look at how Motorola pollutes here and pollutes there.' It's only a short step to somebody saying, 'Maybe you shouldn't single out Motorola since we depend on their donations.'"

One case in point was the Sustainability Consortium, a Walmart-funded research project jointly run through ASU's GIOS and the University of Arkansas. Aimed at lifecycle assessment of consumer products, from provision of manufacturing materials to waste disposal, the Consortium's goal was to produce a sustainability index for thousands of retail items. Member corporations (early sign-ups included Cargill, Clorox, Dial, General Mills, Monsanto, Pepsico, Procter & Gamble, Tyson, Unilever, and Waste Management) were invited to contribute data and ideas about how to set the product ratings. Walmart renounced any proprietary claim on the results and promoted it as an open source project, but, as the world's largest retail corporation, in command of manufacturing supply lines that snake all over the globe, it had everything to gain from this kind of phil-anthropic consumer service. On the face of it, the outcome ought to reduce waste and improve the carbon footprint of major consumer sectors. Surely this was a laudable goal in its own right.

But the Consortium's methodology of lifecycle modeling was far from holistic. Its reliance only on easily quantifiable data excluded many of the factors that contributed to the destructive social and economic impact of so many of its corporate members' policies and practices. A truly compre-hensive assessment of Walmart's sustainability record, for example, would have to look at the consequences of the company's poverty-wage policy on its workforce's ability to make ends meet. As the world's largest employer, Walmart's labor practices, including its antiunion activities, had depressed wages in countless industries and communities. The company depended on sweatshop labor in the very same low-cost supply chain that ASU researchers were helping to decarbonize. A thorough analysis would also consider the geographic impact of its supercenters on sprawl and consumer traffic, and the economic effect of their displacement of small, local busi-nesses in countless retail locations. Last but not least, Walmart's pioneer-ing of a low-cost, low-wage retail model had given a new lease of life to the wasteful ethos of consumerism. These are not easy things to quantify, but who could ignore that the firm's outsized contribution to these ills were obstacles in the path of sustainability? Jonathan Fink, the former director of GIOS, acknowledged that "any company that's based on people buying more and more stuff is a dangerous paradigm." But to him, "the good that a Walmart can do if they're willing to use their size in a positive way offsets the negatives associated with their labor practices and some of these other issues." Indeed, he continued, "for all their social flaws, I think Walmart is doing more to promote sustainability than any company in the world right now because of their willingness to tell every part of their supply chain, 'You have to follow the guidelines set up by these NGOs.'"

When the Sustainability Consortium was announced in July 2009, Walmart made good on the publicity it sought from being proactive on green initiatives (courtesy of 2005 advice from McKinsey). In doing so, it joined the list of firms that had espoused the corporate social responsibility (CSR) doctrine of the triple bottom line—people, planet, and profits. Academic expertise of the sort provided by the Consortium would be a big boost to Walmart's CSR profile, but only if there were agreed-upon limits to what was included in its accounting model. Some of the academic researchers might need to be reminded that corporate cooperation and sponsorship depended on the observance of this mutual understanding. No doubt, one thing that would help was the presence of Walmart's own Rob Walton on the GIOS board.

SAVING THE WORLD, GODDAMMIT

ASU may have been the only university in the region with a research capability, but it was not the only higher education institution with a hand to play in the solar game. John Sperling, the 90-year-old founder and CEO of the for-profit University of Phoenix, had put some of his own fortune into a new company seeking to solve one of the biggest challenges faced by the industry—how to store energy for use after the sun went down, or when the wind stopped blowing. Until this *intermittency* problem was solved, neither solar nor wind would be taken seriously as a comprehensive energy source, capable of providing on-demand power with hundreds or thousands of megawatts. Storage was customarily referred to as the "Holy Grail" of renewable energy research, and scientists from far and wide, including several at ASU, were pursuing it—private investment, on the other hand, was mostly directed at developing batteries for the hybrid auto sector. With some of the proceeds from the global operations of his own university (valued at $10 billion), Sperling and his team had pieced together a system involving biofuel, wind, and solar technologies that seemed to offer one version of a solution to the storage problem. At a Sierra Club symposium in May 2009, he introduced the system with an incredulity redolent of the era of *Amazing Science* magazines: "It has not been experience, but rather a series of lucky events that has brought me the opportunity to present to you, and to the public, a utility-scale renewable energy technology that could be a solution to our climate crisis." Describing how he, as an amateur in the field, came to this solution, he concluded his presentation with a flourish: "Such then is an outline of the doable, affordable, and secure Practical Path to Renewable Energy Independence."[46]

Sperling had recently bankrolled California ballot initiatives for legalizing marijuana and for boosting the state's renewable energy standards. He had also, more notoriously, funded pet-cloning research. Active with his wallet in supporting Arizona's Democratic politicians, he made light of his motivation when I asked him why he had launched a solar business. "I want to save the goddamn earth," he growled, in his best imitation of a no-nonsense tycoon. Missy 2, his cloned Siberian husky, sat nearby as Sperling castigated the Republican-controlled legislature for its backward thinking, and questioned the zeal of environmentalists to have their cake and eat it too. "They knocked out a wind turbine plant [in West Virginia] because it endangered the bats. I would like to save all living creatures," he added, "but if we don't sacrifice some, the one creature we will lose is mankind. It's a trade-off." Acknowledging that his learning curve about clean technology had been a steep one, Sperling insisted that his new company, Southwest Solar Technologies (SST), would generate "manufacturing, construction, maintenance, and research jobs, all in the U.S. and as much as possible in Arizona." Leaning forward to interrupt him, Herb Hayden, Southwest Solar's president, corrected the excited nonagenarian: "We will also use the global supply chain."

Hayden, who had previously overseen APS's solar power program, was the person who persuaded Sperling to throw his hat into the ring. The two men had been introduced by Steve Brittle, the environmental justice activist, through their mutual ties in the Democratic Party. Hayden was looking for an investor to build a scalable prototype for a renewable process (he named it SolarCAT) for driving turbines devised by Brayton, a New Hampshire–based research firm. At night, cheap, off-peak wind energy would be used to compress air into vast underground salt caverns, and then the air, superheated to 1,700 degrees Fahrenheit by solar reflectors, would drive the turbines to deliver daytime energy when demand is highest. Sperling's burgeoning interest in the project was boosted by the realization that he could contribute to the system through his ownership of an agriculture biotech company called Arcadia Bioscience. His researchers there were put to work on genetically modifying sweet sorghum for a salt-tolerant biofuel that would drive the SolarCAT's turbo-alternators when the sun was not available. With the eventual addition of the fuel as a backup, the entire cycle could be run on renewables. Just as appealing, it would use virtually no water, no toxic materials of the sort that are critical to PV production, and its toll on the land (at average densities of three dishes an acre) was light enough to facilitate coexistence with wildlife.

This ambitious, multi-technology system, which included the largest commercial solar dish in North America, was in Hayden's words, "theoretically proven," and he and his team were clearly thrilled at being given the chance to make it technically viable. Given the deep pockets of his backer, Hayden had no need for venture capital to take on the risks of his start-up, and so SST quickly got in line with the other small independents hoping to seal deals with one of the two big utilities. A chunk of land with subterranean salt caverns was acquired in the West Valley, with bulk storage potential for one gigawatt of power (100 megawatts for 10 hours), enough to supply much of the metro region. In the meantime, a demonstration site was prepared in South Phoenix, coincidentally right next to the rogue polluter Fisher Sand and Gravel. Indeed, the two companies (a greater environmental contrast could hardly be found) shared more than a street corner. For several months, Fisher illegally got its water supply from an unmetered fire hydrant that had been allocated to SST to suppress dust during its site construction phase.

When I visited the site in April 2010, there was a still a veil of secrecy over the project, but Hayden reported that banks and other investors were showing interest, and would be approached if and when the firm had a power purchasing agreement with a utility. Josh Rosen, the firm's financial officer, was charged with making the operation cost-effective, and he acknowledged that the commercial side was a "significant engineering challenge" in its own right. Unlike the PV industry, the core of SST's system—bulk energy storage—did not rely on government incentives. Indeed, there were no such policy incentives for storage. "Policies come from lobbying," Rosen pointed out, "and lobbies come from a product-driven industry. We leverage large geological structures, we are not talking about widgets." Storage batteries fell into the widget category, but "pumped hydro and compressed air," which were currently "the only viable bulk storage technologies," did not.

Ultimately, Rosen argued, "the economically rational way to approach this is to put a proper price on pollution and externalities of fossil fuels and let the market figure out how to deliver the alternatives that fit, and then you end up with a market-based solution . . . people would pay more for storage in that kind of world." Until economic reason prevailed, the SST team would have to prove they could compete in cost, as wind and PV firms had done. In principle, their system could offer 24/7 power—if it

Figure 5.1
Prototype model of the SolarCAT dish, Southwest Solar Technologies research park.
Photo by author.

used natural gas as a proxy fuel, and conventional surface storage during
those periods when the salt caverns were being recharged. But Hayden
had more limited goals for the near future, and insisted that the firm
should not be held to the "holistic systems challenge" of that magnitude
from day one.

Beyond their passion for executing the technical and financial challenge
of their system, Hayden and Rosen had no shortage of environmentalist
zeal. They really did not want to do evil, to paraphrase the Google motto.
But Hayden had few illusions about the culture of the business world, even
in the renewable field. "What I have found is that the companies that create themselves for environmental motives don't stay that way for very
long. They very soon became companies that are interested in the financial
aspects and not environmental consequences. The cost issues take over,"
he observed, which is "how the PV business has had to run itself." Sperling,
however, was not interested in making money out of the enterprise. His
goal was to see the technology proliferate, as quickly as possible and by
any means necessary, whether through subsidiaries or licensing.

One of the many options made available to Barack Obama on taking
office was to launch a new Apollo Project, this time to win the race to

develop clean energy on a decisive scale. He was by no means the first president to do so; Nixon had used the Apollo analogy in his call for energy self-sufficiency (Project Independence) weeks after the 1973 oil embargo, as did Carter after him. Like his forebears, Obama would find that the government had neither the money nor the political wherewithal to prevail over the fierce opposition mustered by the fossil-fuel industries. Phoenix was the headquarters of the Apollo Group (Sperling's global educational company) and it was indirectly financing a smaller version of that elusive federal vision. In the eyes of its critics, Sperling's for-profit University of Phoenix had done more since its founding in 1976 than any other institution to erode the standards and fiscal structure of public education. That it would be underwriting an enterprise with such grand public ambitions was perhaps, too much of an irony to dwell upon. But, as yet another White House campaign to fund the post-petroleum future began to run out of patronage, attention was inevitably turning to what a new generation of billionaire philanthropists could do to save the world, goddamnit.

CHAPTER 6

Viva Los Suns

"There's no towel to throw in. We were never given a towel."
Sandra Castro, community activist, El Puente Arizona

I n other Southwestern cities, like Tucson, El Paso, and Albuquerque, with Mexican urban cores that preexisted Anglo settlement, a cultural, if not political, condominium of power sharing had evolved over time. Phoenix was a more straightforward product of Anglo America. Notwithstanding that Trinidad Mejia Escalante, the wife of the founding father, Jack Swilling, was Mexican, the city's origin myth was one of Anglos re-creating a city on top of Hohokam remnants, and it was reinforced by a strong presence of Mormon settlers in the East Valley, with their own version of white pioneerism. Anglo dominance was unquestioned for at least a century. As an early twentieth-century promoter put it, Phoenix was "a modern town of 40,000 people, and the best kind of people too. A very small percentage of Mexicans, negroes, or foreigners."[1] For sure, the public drama and energy of the civil rights era ushered some nonwhite politicians into high office—Raul Castro became governor, and Alfredo Gutierrez senate majority leader in the late 1970s. But it was only in recent years that Anglo ascendancy had been challenged by the mercurial growth of the Latino population (according to the 2010 U.S. census, 30.8 percent of the state, 31.8 percent of Maricopa County, and 34.1 percent of Phoenix itself, all numbers that had more than doubled since 1990), spreading well beyond the traditional barrio districts where its political representatives had been contained.

Anxiety about the decline of demographic and political dominance was a new wrinkle in the ongoing debate about population growth that Phoenix had long hosted. Historically, most of the anxiety about growth was founded, with good reason, on fears that water supplies would not be adequate for the rapidly expanding urban needs. Concerns about the deterioration of air quality, wilderness loss, and the overall environmental impact of urban sprawl had sharpened the anxiety over time. But the influx of Mexican immigrants from the south after the passage of NAFTA changed its tenor. Metro Phoenix had only 86,593 foreign-born residents in 1980, and by 2005, 612,850 were foreign-born, most of them from Mexico. One out of three Arizona children now had at least one immigrant parent.[2] Well before the jobs dried up and the "white flight migrants" from the Midwest and California stopped flocking to Central Arizona, an overtly racialized version of the arguments about population limits sprang up among those with nativist views. Phoenix was becoming overpopulated—with the wrong kind of people. Haranguing them as "illegals" was a polite substitute for racial slurs that had once been more pointed. With the future uncertain, resources already constrained, and government budgets shriveling, loud voices declared that it was time to get serious about trimming the alleged population surplus, starting with the most vulnerable.

The anti-immigrant mood had been swelling for more than a decade before it boiled over in Spring 2010, when the Arizona Legislature, backed by Governor Jan Brewer, passed the Support Our Law Enforcement and Safe Neighborhoods Act (SB 1070), one of the most restrictive anti-immigrant bill in modern U.S. history. The bill brought international attention to Arizona, most of it unwelcome, especially when it took the form of boycotts by city councils and by prominent individuals and organizations that took a cumulative half billion-dollar toll on the state's economy. Although parts of the bill were later struck down by a federal judge, its underlying spirit proved popular elsewhere, even in states that did not share a border with Mexico. Shrinking public resources should be reserved, it was widely argued, for bona fide citizens. Was this simply the kind of self-interested mentality one would expect in a deep recession, or was it the test run for a foreshortened future where resource decisions guided by triage might dictate which populations were to be preserved and which would be shown the door?

CLIMATE REFUGEES

The decade and a half after the 1994 implementation of NAFTA saw a rapid rise in migration to the United States from rural areas all over Central America. Although it took a while to register in the public mind, this mother of all free trade agreements, which forced small farmers and peasants into an unequal competition with massively subsidized American agribusiness combines, was responsible for the movement of as many as six million *campesinos* out of the fields and into swelling cities or, to the North, over the U.S. border. But trade liberalization was also amplifying an existing stream of climate refugees, set in motion by drought, desertification, and the proliferation of extreme weather events. These "environmental migrants" numbered in the tens of millions globally by 2000, and estimates from the Intergovernmental Panel on Climate Change (IPCC) and the influential 2006 Stern Report predicted that climate change would generate as many as 150 to 200 million by 2050.[3] To date, no international convention has recognized the needs and rights of climate migrants, even though, by 2010 according to a Red Cross estimate, they outnumbered the population of refugees from war and violence.[4] Climate justice advocates increasingly see them as casualties of the high-carbon policies pursued by industrialized nations, and therefore entitled not only to sanctuary and legal protection but also to reparations.

Mexico drew special attention because of out-migration to the United States. Land degradation resulted from the NAFTA-driven abandonment of traditional sustainable agriculture in pursuit of higher industrial yields alone, but the resulting soil erosion was also accelerated by an overall decline in precipitation from climate change. A 2009 United Nations University study predicted a decrease in runoff "by at least 5 percent and possibly more than 70 percent," by the century's end, with the greatest rainfall reductions expected in northern, semiarid parts of the country. According to research published in the *Proceedings of the National Academy of Sciences*, the impact of climate change on crop yields may force as many as seven million Mexicans to emigrate to the United States over the next seventy years.[5]

As early as 1994, a report for the U.S. Commission on Immigration Reform estimated that environmental migrants accounted for a substantial portion of the 900,000 annually who moved away from arid or semiarid regions of Mexico, and that the aridity was clearly on the increase.[6] The legacy of hardship back in their rural homes, combined with extreme deprivation and danger en route, rendered the refugees particularly vulnerable. In some of the more daunting U.S. border crossings, especially in the deserts of Southern Arizona, they faced down abandonment, kidnapping, and rape by *coyotes* (six of ten female border-crossers are raped or sexually harassed), painful death under the sun, and the cruelty of the U.S. Border Patrol to enter a culture increasingly hostile to their existence.

In fall 2009, the Pentagon published a report that isolated climate migration as a national security problem, and, for the first time, its 2010 Quadrennial Defense Review included climate change in its assessment of strategic threats.[7] In 2003, a study commissioned by the Department of Defense warned that "climate change could become such a challenge that mass emigration results as the desperate peoples seek better lives in regions such as the United States that have the resources to adaptation."[8] Military interest in climate change was by no means a recent development. In the mid-1970s, when predictions about "global cooling" were prevalent, the Pentagon, already sold on the use of climate modification for military advantage, suspected a vast Soviet plot. CIA reports noted that the agricultural yield of the United States would benefit from a cooling climate and warned that the hungry of other nations would try "to get grain any way they could. Massive migrations, sometimes backed by force, would become a live issue and political and economic instability would be widespread."[9]

The CIA reports were fueled by concerns about out-of-control population growth, inspired by Paul and Anne Ehrlich's alarmist 1968 book, *The Population Bomb*. Indeed, by the early 1970s, the argument for population stabilization had become a staple part of the environmentalist toolkit of remedies to protect against "overshoot" of the world's carrying capacity.[10] These concerns fed into worldwide efforts, by NGOs and governments of developing countries, at population control, often by coercive measures.[11] It proved difficult in many cases to distinguish these control policies and programs from the government-sanctioned measures of the eugenics movement in the early twentieth century. In both eras, those who were forcibly sterilized were poor populations designated as a threat to the resource consumption of others in a more advantageous social position.

Beginning in the 1980s, the rate of world population growth began to decline, whether or not the result of coercive control techniques. The call for population limits gradually became a taboo topic among progressive greens, though the Sierra Club's restrictionist policy on immigration was not fully abandoned until 1996. That was because much of the anxiety about world overpopulation had been simply displaced on to the threat of mass migration from poor countries to rich ones. Global warming, with its train of climate migrants, only exacerbated these fears. For those who remained fixated on overpopulation in spite of the taboo, climate change offered a ready-made argument for stopping emigrants from low-carbon countries from coming to adopt the high-carbon lifestyles of rich countries. Not surprisingly, the opportunity to utilize this environmental spin was fully seized by anti-immigration advocates.

Some of them were nativists in a direct line of descent from the overt white nationalists of the Citizens' Councils of America. Increasingly, they treated pro-environment arguments as a way of laundering their image, and the organizations they founded helped them win respectability as legitimate media and policy sources. The Federation for American Immigration Reform (FAIR), founded in 1979 by John Tanton, a former Sierra Club activist, was the parent organization, and in its early years was bankrolled by the Pioneer Fund, a foundation with a history of promoting research (including The Bell Curve, the notorious study of alleged racial differences in IQ) that argued for the genetic superiority of Euro-Americans. FAIR spawned a host of satellite groups, which the Southern Poverty Law Center, its most persistent watchdog, has called "the Tanton network." The list includes the Center for Immigration Studies, NumbersUSA, American Immigration Control Foundation, the American Patrol/Voice of Citizens Together, Californians for Population Stabilization, Pro English, Social Contract Press, Negative Population Growth, 21st Century Fund, Progressives for Immigration Reform, and Population-Environment Balance.[12] The Southern Poverty Law Center has been central in efforts to document the activities of the "Tanton network" and to combat their claims, especially those that involved greenwashing. When climate change finally became a pressing public issue, it gave fresh impetus to what population specialist Betsy Hartmann has called the "greening of hate."[13] Communiqués put out by FAIR and its spin-offs increasingly featured the language of decarbonization, all of them aimed at achieving the goal of immigration reduction. Virtually every progressive eco cause—biodiversity, water conservation, deforestation, wilderness protection, and even environmental justice—has been grist for the greenwashing mill of these groups.

To commemorate the fortieth anniversary of Earth Day in April 2010, FAIR, for example, updated and reissued its 58-page report, The Environmentalist's Guide to a Sensible Immigration Policy. Fingering "immigration-related population growth" as the "principal cause" of urban sprawl, the report insisted that "so-called environmentalists pretend as if this connection does not exist." And what was the organization's response to the land speculation, overdevelopment, and three-car mentality that drives sprawl? As on most every other issue, FAIR's solution, set forth as a pro-environment position, was to cut immigration to the bone. Yet the equation of immigration with sprawl was altogether specious. Undocumented immigrants are much more likely to live lightly in central-city neighborhoods than the U.S.-born population who, when they migrate to metropolitan areas, are more likely to settle in suburban subdivisions with high-carbon footprints. Nor is there any necessary correlation between population size or density and exploitation of resources. How we produce and consume energy are much more important determinants of hydrocarbon emissions than our net numbers. But FAIR's shady reasoning was typical of how it has pushed xenophobia as green wisdom in order to win mainstream acceptance and divide its critics.

Some of these FAIR arguments have gotten a surprisingly good hearing from prominent ecologists.[14] Carrying Capacity Network, a fellow-traveling organization, boasts on its advisory board the names of Herman Daly (theorist of the "steady-state economy"), William Rees (pioneer of the "ecological footprint,"), and Thomas Lovejoy (who introduced the concept of "biological diversity"), while Robert Costanza (a founder of the field of ecological economics) served on the board during the 1990s. Other heavyweights like James Lovelock, David Attenborough, Paul Ehrlich, and Jane Goodall have greased the wheels of the resurgent population control bandwagon through their patronage of the Optimum Population Trust, a U.K. organization that rehabs eugenics for the era of climate change. It holds that drastic population reduction is the most efficient way of averting global warming, and among its programs is a carbon offset project for the affluent in the global North to subsidize "family planning" in poor countries. So, too, several prominent public figures and academics who were Sierra Club members (Richard Lamm, Alan Kuper, Frank Morris, David Pimentel, and Paul Watson) played a leading role in efforts by anti-immigrant factions to take over the organization in 1998 and 2005.

BINGO!

The week before its Earth Day publication, FAIR celebrated its biggest legislative coup to date, when Governor Brewer signed Arizona's landmark anti-immigrant bill, SB 1070. Inviting analogies with Jim Crow and apartheid-era laws, the bill criminalized all undocumented persons in the state, and mandated police to determine their immigration status if a "reasonable suspicion" existed for doing so. Russell Pearce, the nativist GOP state senator from Mesa who sponsored the bill, outsourced its drafting to Kris Kobach, affiliated with FAIR's legal arm—the Immigration Reform Law Institute. Kobach had also been retained by Maricopa County's Sheriff Joe Arpaio to train his police force in the niceties of immigration law. Ever since he assisted U.S. Attorney-General John Ashcroft on draconian post-9/11 measures for profiling Muslim males, Kobach had become the go-to drafter of anti-immigrant legislation in various states and municipalities. The Ashcroft laws and several of the others were struck down as unconstitutional, and large sections of SB 1070 were headed the same way, but each of these efforts moved public opinion, and the legal envelope that contained it, further to the right. No sooner had the ink dried on SB 1070 than Kobach and Pearce were working on outlawing the granting of birth certificates to U.S.-born children with an undocumented parent—a legal quest that put them on a direct collision course with the citizenship clause of the Fourteenth Amendment.

Thanks to Kobach and Pearce, Arizona already had the most anti-immigrant laws of any state, including the most rigid employer sanctions legislation, enacted in 2007. Its increasingly hard-right legislature (which elected Pearce as Senate president after the 2010 elections) was more than receptive to the attention of the FAIR network.[15] Tanton himself was a founder of the U.S. English movement and had pushed hard in Arizona for the adoption of Official English legislation in 1988. In the course of that campaign, one of his more infamous memos to staff members was leaked to the *Arizona Republic*. In it, Tanton warned about the loss of demographic supremacy to the coming "Latin onslaught":

> *Gobernar es poblar* translates 'to govern is to populate.' In this society where the majority rules, does this hold? Will the present majority peaceably hand over its political power to a group that is simply more fertile?... Can *homo contraceptivus* compete with *homo progenitiva* [sic] if borders aren't controlled? Or is advice to limit one's family simply advice to move over and let someone else with greater reproductive powers occupy the space? As Whites see their power and control over their lives declining, will they simply go quietly into the night? Or will there be an explosion?[16]

The state's adoption of Official English that year had many repercussions, not least the requirement, more sharply debated in the aftermath of SB 1070, that school teachers speak English without a noticeable accent. In 2004, Arizona voters approved Proposition 200, which denied all public benefits to those with no proof of citizenship. Once again, FAIR and its coterie were heavily involved, funding and supporting the signature gathering of Protect Arizona Now, the group that was pushing the proposition. Indeed, FAIR had to issue a disclaimer when a public row broke out over the "white separatist" sympathies of Virginia Abernethy, a prominent adviser to the campaign, who was also a lead figure at Carrying Capacity Network and Population-Environment Balance. Nonetheless, the successful campaign relied heavily on FAIR money and on FAIR's sham estimate that Arizona taxpayers spent as much as $1.3 billion for the health, education, and incarceration costs of undocumented immigrants. By 2010,

FAIR had upped the figure to \$2.7 billion, and this figure was widely circulated on Fox News after the passage of SB 1070.[17] Less biased sources showed a large net benefit to the state from immigrants' buying power and other expenditures like banking fees for remittances.[18]

In recent years, FAIR's greenwashing has been primarily aimed at policymakers and environmentalists. Liberal publications, such as *The Nation*, *Harper's*, and the *New York Times*, were targeted with full-page ads in 2008, and Progressives for Immigration Reform was formed the year after to reach out to potential recruits on the left with publications like "From Big to Bigger: How Mass Immigration and Population Growth Have Exacerbated America's Ecological Footprint."[19] But wider public attention was garnered when tangible evidence of environmental spoilage could be provided. In the months leading up the passage of SB 1070, the Center for Immigration Studies (CIS), widely regarded as FAIR's research arm, focused on the physical damage done by the traffic of *coyotes* and their border-crossing clients to Organ Pipe Cactus National Monument, the Huachuca Mountains, and Coronado National Forest in Southeastern Arizona. "How long will these beautiful lands remain unspoiled if the border is not secured?" a CIS press release asked.[20] The Sierra Club and Defenders of Wildlife pointed out that most of the ecological mayhem in these protected lands and wildlife refuges was being caused by the construction and maintenance of the border fence's "tactical infrastructure." As part of the Real ID Act of 2005, the Department of Homeland Security was given the authority to waive all environmental and historic preservation laws in order to build the wall and the "virtual fence" operations just to the north of it.[21] Trash left by migrants was easily picked up, but the wall's bisection of wildlife corridors and the damage to ecosystems by border enforcement activities in the fifty-mile apprehension zone to the north delivered a long-term blow to the rich and diverse biology of the borderlands. But the intended impact of the CIS investigation did not turn on evidence; it was aimed at tapping a deep vein of public anxiety that connects the defense of pristine resources to the defense of racial purity.

A grotesque but telling offshoot of CIS's focus on ecosystem damage were the citations served on humanitarians who left plastic containers of water on migrant trails in the Sonoran desert. The charges, for "littering," were brought against volunteers with No More Deaths, one of the Tucson groups (along with Humane Border, Tucson Samaritans, *Derechos Humanos*) that offered samaritan assistance to migrants suffering from the hardships of the brutal desert crossing, just as the Pima Indians came to the aid of stranded gold-rush emigrants on the nineteenth-century Gila

Trail.[22] Minutemen vigilantes and Border Patrol agents took to slashing the water canisters left on the trails, and some of the samaritans were arrested, en route to emergency rooms, on charges of transporting aliens illegally.[23] The convictions for littering invited ridicule when placed alongside the nobility of the volunteers' strong belief that it was their "right and responsibility" to "protect and directly assist victims of human rights violations when the government is the violator."[24]

After a good deal of adverse publicity, a federal judge upheld the littering charges, but the conviction of Dan Millis, one of the volunteers, was finally overturned by the Court of Appeals of the Ninth Circuit in September 2010. Millis's contention that "humanitarian aid is never a crime" was not allowed to be debated as part of the legal process, and the final decision rested on whether or not water could be defined as "garbage." Earlier in the year, the U.S. Fish and Wildlife Service, whose officers patrol the Buenos Aires National Wildlife Refuge, agreed to allow the samaritans to operate a few more water stations on the 180,000-acre refuge, but the nature of the court's decision left the simple act of offering water to the needy in legal limbo.

In January 2011, Millis took me down to visit the trails on the refuge, which had been one of the main pathways used by border-crossers. Traffic, by all estimates, had fallen off in the previous year, but the overall death rate of those crossing into Arizona had risen dramatically (275 recorded deaths in 2010 alone). Millis explained that this was because the Border Patrol buildup on the plains of the refuge had diverted migrants further west through the Baboquivari Mountains or onto the Tohono O'odham reservation, where the terrain was more inhospitable and volunteer aid was sparse. This "trial by geography" is an explicit part of federal border policy, designed to channel migration, in a funnel effect, into the most desolate and foreboding terrain of the Southwest. The policy strategy is called "prevention through deterrence," and it utilizes the threat of dying in the Arizona desert or mountains as a psychological barrier. Even by its own criteria, the strategy has clearly failed, and more than five thousand migrants, by any estimates, have died as a result. No one died in the desert before the militarization of the border began in the mid-1990s.[25]

Reaching the Sasabe border checkpoint in the Altar valley, we took a dirt road along a section of the wall that ended just short of the foothills. Millis blithely scaled the wall to show how easily it could be done. Within two minutes, Border Patrol vehicles surrounded us, and a chopper buzzed overhead. The agents were belligerent and threatened us with citations—"You can be charged with aiding and betting aliens to cross this border." Other agents sped by to apprehend a group of migrants they had been surveilling, and their radio voices reported: "We are transporting the bodies now." Millis gri-

Figure 6.1
Border-crossing: Dan Millis shows how easy it is. Photo by author.

maced and muttered to me, "This is how they refer to border-crossers, as if they are already dead." His old nemesis, the agent who had ticketed him, arrived on the scene, and, for a while, it looked as if we might be spending the rest of the day in the detention center we had passed en route. Millis assured me and the agents that we had broken no laws, but the Border Patrol operated as a law unto itself in this domain. Finally sent on our way, the experience was just one more hostile encounter to wear down his will. In 2008, he had taken a staff position with the Sierra Club to run the organization's Arizona borderland campaign, with the goal of strengthening the coalition between the local human rights activists and environmental groups. After all, the border wall was what he called an "an unmitigated environmental disaster" and also a direct cause of the gruesome fatalities he and other volunteers routinely discovered on their desert patrols. "The only thing it does not stop are people" was the verdict of those, like him, who tried to reach migrants in desperate need of food, water, and medical assistance.

The activities of the samaritans were well received and supported in the relatively liberal enclaves of their Tucson home base. Indeed, one of the founders of No More Deaths, Rev. John Fife, former pastor of Southside Presbyterian, also co-founded the Sanctuary movement to shelter Central

American refugees of Washington's wars in the 1980s and 1990s. Robin Hoover, pastor of First Christian Church and founder of Humane Borders, was also a veteran of the movement. Not to be outdone by Tucson's religious leaders, the city council was the first in Arizona (to be followed by Flagstaff and others) to vote to sue the state over SB 1070, and Rep. Raul Grijalva, whose congressional district covers half of metro Tucson, was the first legislator to call for a boycott. All the more shocking that it was Tucson, and not Phoenix, that hosted the shooting of Grijalva's fellow congressional Democrat, Gabby Giffords, and several others on the very morning I arrived for my first visit to the Old Pueblo. Yet the open targeting of Giffords and other liberal figures (including shooting victim Judge John Roll) who took a public stand against the immigrant crackdown had been ongoing for several years, and it was only a matter of time before Southern Arizona triggers were pulled in their direction.

"We predicted that this was going to happen, but it is so sad that we could not stop it from happening," lamented Isabel Garcia, co-chair of *Coalición de Derechos Humanos,* who reported that she herself had received several death threats over the years. As with Giffords, her image had been publicly circulated, superimposed by the crosshairs of a rifle. A Pima County public defender and veteran of the immigrant rights movement, Garcia had no doubt in her mind about how to interpret the shootings. "These victims should be added to the list of casualties of our border policy," she asserted. "Death by policy," she added, had been a convenient way of absolving the general populace of guilt, so that nobody felt culpable when fatalities in the desert occur. After thirty-five years of hands-on engagement with borderland politics in Texas and Arizona, Garcia had quite a different standpoint from that of the Washington reform organizations. RIFA (Reform Immigration for America) and others, she argued, were too willing to accept the view that "migration is an enforcement issue, rather than an economic issue." "None of these groups," she explained, "are willing to talk about American foreign policy," which was the root cause of the suffering. It was she and other women in the Manzo Area Council who brought Central American political asylum cases to the white churches, like Fife's, in the 1980s and inspired the Sanctuary movement. They regrouped in 1986 as La Mesilla Organizing Project and then formed *Derechos Humanos* in 1993 to focus on the human rights of the NAFTA generation of migrants. In 2000, they again asked the churches to respond, this time to the mounting toll of deaths in the desert, and No More Deaths was founded as a result.

At the time she became an activist in the late 1970s, Garcia recalled that

John Tanton was trying poison the environmental movement with the idea that immigrants were responsible for degradation, and so we knew early on

that if we were going to be effective we would have to make the environmentalists into our allies. We started a purposeful effort to work together and it
bore fruit when the anti-immigrant fervor really hit. Our environmental partners said no, it is not immigrants who are degrading the environment, it is the
U.S. government that is responsible for what we are seeing at the border. That
was a result of our massive joint work here in Tucson.

In 2002, Garcia helped form the Coalition to Bring Down the Wall,
which firmly allied *Derechos Humanos* with Sky Island Alliance,
Defenders of Wildlife, Sierra Club, the Center for Biological Diversity,
and the Tohono O'odham Nation—each putting aside the silo mentality
of single-issue politics in order to combat the greenwashing of nativism.
In Tucson, this need to make common cause was deeply understood
among activists who increasingly catered daily to the needs of the most
powerless and vulnerable. Among the political class on Capitol Hill,
which catered to the needs of the most powerful, it was all but impossible to make real connections between climate policy and immigration
reform. Indeed, these were the two bullets that Congress was doing its
best to dodge separately.

ATTRITION THROUGH ENFORCEMENT

In a press conference that immediately followed the Giffords shooting,
Clarence Dupnick, the Pima County sheriff, famously lamented that
Arizona had "become the mecca for prejudice and bigotry." This was not
out of character for a sheriff who had earlier denounced SB 1070 as a
"stupid and racist" law, and while his comments drew fire from the likes of
Rush Limbaugh and Glenn Beck, and from Arizona Republicans, including
U.S. Senator John Kyl, they fell on relatively sympathetic ears in his Tucson
jurisdiction. Maricopa County was a different political beast.[26] Even the
Democrat-dominated city council of Phoenix was too divided to support
Mayor Gordon's call for launching a lawsuit against SB 1070. This was a
county that had earned national notoriety for its anti-immigrant fervor,
and where popular support for Arpaio had guaranteed the self-styled
"America's Toughest Sheriff" five terms in office. The record of his brutal
enforcement and detention techniques earned him widespread oppro-
brium from Amnesty International, the ACLU, and many other human
and civil rights organizations. His abuse of power had attracted thousands
of lawsuits from inmates; his jails, including the notorious Tent City, had
lost their accreditation on many occasions; and, in 2009, the Department

of Justice finally began to investigate him for extensive civil rights violations for his targeting of Latinos in Maricopa County.[27]

Sheriff Joe's political survival in the face of such infamy, combined with his willingness to bully the brown-skinned population and intimidate his own critics, made him a figurehead for the most virulent nativist sentiment in the county. Technically speaking, his office was the primary executor of a policy called "attrition through enforcement" that had been devised by Kobach and others within the FAIR network. It was designed to make life so miserable for the undocumented that they would simply leave town. Conceived as an alternative to mass deportation or to beefing up border security, the policy was aimed at shrinking the population already in the country who might be eligible for amnesty if the political winds blew in that reformist direction.[28] Existentially, the goal was to harass and wear down immigrants to the point of "voluntary compliance," where they would lose the will to live and work in the United States and leave of their own accord. As Kobach himself described SB 1070, "This law represents turning it up one more click. Increase the level a notch at a time, and people will deport themselves."[29]

Just as Arpaio's reign of fear seemed in danger of collapsing under the legal weight of a grand jury investigation, SB 1070 cemented the policy and his own policing tactics into state law: "The legislature declares that the intent of this act is to make 'attrition through enforcement' the public policy." The bill obliged local police to take on federal responsibilities, and it criminalized anyone who was in the state without legal papers. It also created a private right of action for any person to sue a city, town, or county if the governmental authority in any way limited the right of an officer to question or arrest suspects. To the degree that verification rested on the vigilance of citizens, this part of the bill extended the culture of deputizing created by Arpaio, who was notorious for deploying armed citizen posses in his pursuit of immigrants. Policies and practices like these were not simply aimed at enforcement powers, they were designed to reach far into civil society. Laws like the 2007 Employer Sanctions Act had effectively criminalized citizens who knowingly abetted the undocumented through employing them. The sharp escalation in surveillance ushered in by SB 1070 favored the kind of public mentality that some critics compared to the informer culture of totalitarian regimes. Arpaio's infamous immigrant sweeps were largely triggered by citizen tip-offs, and the measures included in the new law looked forward to a much sharper climate of distrust and intimidation.

Second- and third-generation Latinos, who had not felt personally threatened by the preceding legislation, were now more attentive to the

Figure 6.2
Public communications on a Maricopa County sheriff's bus. Photo by author.

net of suspicion that SB 1070 cast over all brown-skinned residents. When Jim Crow and apartheid were cited as appropriate frames of legal reference, African Americans, who had also dragged their feet, began to show up at churches for meetings called by organizers for immigrants' rights. The Catholic bishop of Los Angeles used the term "Nazism," and it was echoed far and wide. Alfredo Gutierrez, former state Senate majority leader and publisher of *La Frontera Times,* called it "the most oppressive piece of legislation since the Japanese internment camp act."

Gutierrez, who took a prominent role in the offensive against the bill, recognized that, as with the wartime Japanese and Jews, the criminalization of an entire population effectively required the public first to accept that it was subhuman. Because attrition though enforcement was "causing human misery of a great magnitude" for the targets of the policy, "creating those conditions could only be justified if the victims were seen as depraved." In his estimate, the policies of FAIR and Arpaio had been aimed at exactly that kind of dehumanization. Paraphrasing Hannah Arendt's famous analysis of "banality of evil" in *Eichman in Jerusalem,* Gutierrez noted, "Once it becomes public and commonplace and often practiced as part of the daily bread of life, evil loses its impact . . . and this is how it is accepted by a civilized people." He believed that FAIR and its allies in the Arizona Legislature were trying to recreate the kind of society that Arendt had described. "If you break up families daily," he went on, "and if the health care worker, instead of taking you to an emergency room, calls ICE to begin deportation procedures, and if you do raids into the schools, then it will become normalized. But to do these things, you have to first define the victims as depraved, and as evil themselves." In his estimate, FAIR had largely succeeded in cementing in the public mind the equation: "worker in a strange land = criminal in your house." Nonetheless, he was buoyed by the widespread moral outrage that SB 1070 had unleashed: "It is the first glimmer of hope I have seen in a decade."

"The international response has given me hope," agreed Mary Rose Wilcox, another longtime Latino political leader and currently a county superintendent. A recent legal victim of Sheriff Joe's harassment of his public critics, she was in no two minds about the reason for the recent uptick in overt racism among the GOP right. "They just cannot stand having a black man as president," she pronounced, "and a smart one at that." From the standpoint of her twenty-two years in public office, she saw the regional rise in xenophobia as a particularly desperate response: "They are grabbing at their last straws in power," she said of the state's Republicans. "The writing is on the wall for them, because the Hispanic vote is no longer restricted to traditional districts," she added, and the "voting clout of the children of the IRCA generation" (Immigration Reform and Control Act of 1986, which granted amnesty and citizenship to many immigrants) was about to come into its own. As ugly as the hate was, she believed it was like the sting in the rattlesnake's tail—an act of political suicide in the face of demographic destiny.

SOCIAL SUSTAINABILITY

Aside from its geographic location as the primary destination for migrants from Mexico, what made Central Arizona ground zero for anti-immigrant sentiment? And what did this outcome have to say about the prospects for urban sustainability that this book has been assessing? Sustainability, as I have argued, is a social challenge as much as it is a biophysical goal, and, in this case, the challenge would be to transform the trauma inflicted by harsh anti-immigrant policies and racial profiling into a climate of respect and cooperation. But what kind of community or polity flourishes when the stigma and sense of injury is allowed to linger on for generations? The resilience of communities is sorely tested when toxic social relationships become the norm at exactly the time when resources are constrained. Democracy gets tighter and thinner, and when decency is in short supply, green goals that are tied to equity and social inclusion get pushed lower and lower on the scale of priorities. Worst of all, in places where anxiety about population growth already runs high, ethnic conflict can become a straight contest over demographic supremacy, with the odds stacked against the least powerful constituencies. After the passage of SB 1070, *The Daily* Show's Jon Stewart described Arizona as the "meth lab of democracy," while his counterpart Stephen Colbert referred to the bill as the "Juan Crow law." By 2010, a significant portion of the U.S. electorate regarded these politically attuned jesters, rightly or wrongly, as the most accurate public barometers of the highs and lows of democratic process.

Most of my interviewees reported that anti-immigrant sentiment had been on a steady rise since the mid-1980s when Mexican migrants first flocked to find work staffing the growth machine, and when programs like U.S. English and Americanization classes were introduced as a cultural filter. By 2000, FAIR and their local advocates had succeeded in persuading the public that the undocumented were a dangerous drain on public resources, thereby preparing the way for harsher legislation. Efforts to pass these laws were launched on the wave of anti-foreigner revanchism that followed 9/11, emboldening the state's Republican majority to pass more and more punitive bills. High unemployment from the recession only reinforced the appetite for scapegoating and hounding the region's most vulnerable labor pool.

A similar pattern of victimage had occurred in many northern U.S. cities in the aftermath of deindustrialization. Southern blacks, lured to northern factories in the first half of the twentieth century, were abandoned to joblessness and deprivation when their workplaces were transferred to nonunion locations (in the South and then offshore) in the 1970s. Subsequently, their neighborhoods were demonized as the "inner city"— the product of a nasty cocktail of public policy (the "benign neglect" of the Nixon era), disinvestment, and social stigma—and they were soon hosting declining life expectancies for a population whose labor was no longer required.

But evicting a dispensable workforce was not the only, or even the primary, goal of Arizona's anti-immigration right. Migrant workers, after all, tend to move on when work dries up, and evidence suggests that immigration peaked even before the passage of the Employer Sanctions Act and the onset of the Great Recession.[30] The driving force had just as much to do with the racial demographics of electoral power. When the growth rate of the state's Latino population, with or without papers, began to outpace the white flight retirees from the Midwest and California, the state's GOP was put on notice that the "Latin onslaught" described so menacingly by Tanton was in full flow. By 2010, the IRCA generation had children (and grandchildren) who were nearing voting age and were about to register as Democrats. In an investigative report for *Rolling Stone* about the 2008 election, Greg Palast described how Jan Brewer, then Secretary of State, purged 100,000 registrants, mainly with Hispanic names, from the voter rolls. "Voting or registering to vote if you're not a citizen is a felony, a big-time jail-time crime," wrote Palast. "And arresting such criminal voters is easy: after all, they give their names and addresses. So I asked Brewer's office, had she busted a single one of these thousands of allegedly illegal voters? Did she turn over even one name to the feds for prosecution? No, not one." For Palast, SB 1070 was just one more effort to disenfranchise "the exploding number of legal Hispanics, U.S. citizens all, who are daring to vote," by scaring them out of the state.[31] Palast's conclusion was echoed by more than one Democrat operative whom I found registering voters in the Phoenix streets following the passage of the bill. In their eyes, it was all a form of population control designed to keep the Republican Party in power.

But was this the only motivation behind the faux-green reasoning of the FAIR groups? Was it all just a ploy to shore up right-wing political support? And, if so, exactly how did the greenwashing contribute to the crackdown on a vulnerable, surplus population? The outrage over migrants trashing the desert was fueled by images, and so it had a clear, discernible hold on the public mind. Messages directed at people's fear of population pressure were just as powerful but less conspicuous in their impact. That is because, in affluent societies, the ingrained, neo-Malthusian belief that there is never enough to go around invites a punitive attitude toward those who are perceived to have the least resources, but whose population is growing the most. In a community always on the lookout for the next bucket of water, this mentality is especially acute. Indeed, it almost goes without saying, because it appeals to such deep-seated fears of scarcity. Combining those fears with the misanthropic wilderness fundamentalism advocated by many proponents of the far West environmental tradition could produce a toxic result. It was telling, for example, that the desert solitude prized by Edward Abbey, one of Tucson's most famous sons, would segue into a virulent strain of anti-immigrant sentiment that marred the reputation of this most influential of environmentalists.[32]

Turning these sentiments into a serviceable, public xenophobia usually required some estimate, if not verifiable evidence, of harmful impact. In the world of FAIR's propagandists, that could come in a variety of forms, but the most recent played directly to newly aired concerns about hydro-carbon emissions. The public habit of forming opinions on the basis of carbon calculations was still in its infancy, but CIS jumped into the game with its estimate that, compared to life in the home country, the average immigrant emits four times more CO_2 in the United States. "That must be because we eat more beans over here," cracked Salvador Reza, a grassroots activist with El Puente Arizona. And perhaps Reza's quip was the only worthy response at that moment. Oversized carbon footprints were cer-tainly not the reason why Sheriff Joe's deputies were asking brown-skinned people for their papers. Nor had I or Reza seen any evidence of the sheriff's vocal supporters calling for immigrants to "go back to their lower-polluting countries."

The CIS factoid, like others trotted out in FAIR's greenwashing, was clearly aimed at influencing left-leaning minds, even though per capita figures of this kind tell us nothing about the source of national carbon outputs, or global emissions for that matter. As Ian Angus and Simon Butler remind us, "Most emissions are caused by industrial and other processes over which individuals have no control."[33] Even so, the CIS calculus was a harbinger of things to come in the fickle world of climate politics. Indeed, this kind of spin on greenhouse gas emissions was indic-ative of how the resource wars of the twenty-first century might be played out at home. As cities like Phoenix focused on their ecological footprints, vying to become more and more sustainable, inevitably other kinds of cal-culation would be made about who was entitled to go on polluting and who was not. As resources tighten, triage decision making was likely to put the most vulnerable citizens and migrants at risk of being cut loose.

Whether applied on a global scale, or even across a single city, the carbon calculus revealed an uneven distribution of resource consumption. Those at the fatter end of the curve were currently on the hunt for swap schemes, usually involving carbon offsets in developing countries, so that they could earn guilt-free enjoyment of their disproportionate share. In a modern version of papal indulgences, UN programs like REDD (Reducing Emissions from Deforestation and Forest Degradation) and the Clean Development Mechanism allowed major polluters to fund a forest set-aside in developing countries like Brazil, Indonesia, Cambodia, or Kenya in return for certified emission credits. The arrangement enabled them to go on with fossil business as usual in industrialized countries. The UN's Cancun climate summit in December 2010 further institutionalized this market-based mitigation scheme, drawing fierce criticism from interna-tional peasant and indigenous groups like La Via Campesina and Indigenous Environmental Network, who reject outright the principle of putting a price on the carbon-absorbing lands that traditional communities have preserved for millennia.

But will the kind of arm's-length arrangement typified by REDD stand for long when the flow of environmental migrants starts to swell? The Arizona example suggests it may not. For one thing, those displaced by climate change surely have a right to expect recompense from the high hydrocarbon emitters. At the very least, they are entitled to a sanctuary if their path of flight takes them to the North. That is the most minimal of the debts incurred. Indeed, climate refugees may have their own carbon-conscious version of the retort offered by postcolonials when they settled in cities like London and Paris: "We are here because you were there." But in order to flourish, a sanctuary requires a thick humanitarian culture to support it. Anti-immigrant sentiment with a strong policing backbone is a breeding ground for its exact opposite—the making of a heavily fortified resource island. Just before its implementation in July 2010, a federal district judge struck down those portions of SB 1070 that encroached on federal prerogatives to regulate immigration (and her judgment was upheld by the 9th U.S. Circuit Court of Appeals in April 2011). Among the provisions of the law that remained on the books was a ban on sanctuary cities, which prompted Russell Pearce to declare triumphantly, that this prohibition had "always been the number one priority of SB 1070."

FIGHTING BACK

The same week that Governor Brewer signed SB 1070, Bolivia's president Evo Morales addressed the People's World Conference on Climate Change and the Rights of Mother Earth, which he had convened in the city of Cochabamba, site of a famous popular movement in 2000 to resist privatization of the city's water supply.[34] Climate migration was high on the agenda, in a country that had itself seen mass population displacement as a result of ecological depletion.[35] One of the remarkable achievements of the assembly overall was to present a more democratic, bottom-up alternative to the Copenhagen climate summit, where a small group of nations—China, India, Brazil, South Africa, and the United States—had commandeered the decision-making process through backroom deals. Although the United Nations Framework Convention on Climate Change (UNFCCC) is supposed to abide by transparency in protocol drafting and consensus in decision making, the framework for the meetings at Copenhagen and Cancun was entirely driven by the major carbon powers. As many as 10,000 delegates participated in public sessions at the

Cochabamba conference, and they laid the groundwork for an accord on climate action that was justice-based rather than market-based.

The meeting in Bolivia also brought climate justice and its lead cause—the debt owed to poor countries and communities already affected by global warming—to a new level of public prominence. In this regard, Cochabamba was high-profile evidence that environmentalism had decisively outgrown its reputation as a feel-good cause for the affluent—making their pious choice to buy a Prius, eat organic, or support wilderness preservation. It was now part of the survival toolkit for the people who had borne the brunt of industrial pollution and who would pay the ultimate price if action were not taken soon. While the debates about climate justice revolved primarily around the rights of the indigenous or rural poor of the global South, they were hardly unfamiliar in North America. In many ways, climate justice was a global version of the environmental justice movement that emerged from the inner cities of the United States in the 1990s.[36]

There was at least one representative from Phoenix at Cochabamba—Tupac Enrique Acosta, the longtime cultural activist who came up in the Maricopa Organizing Project's campaign against Motorola in the 1980s and who had played a key role most recently in community opposition to the anti-immigrant right. Acosta's home base was an unassuming 2,000-square-foot building on the edge of the Garfield barrio that functioned as an Embassy of the Indigenous Peoples (Nahuacalli). This quasi-official status was recognized by the UN, City Hall, and neighborhood associations, and the site was also registered with the county as the equivalent of a temple, mosque, or synagogue. The building lay directly in the path of downtown development and fell within the overlay of the city's expanding biomedical campus, but it was unlikely to be pushed aside. "We represent a liberated territory," declared Acosta, "and we are in a domain without eminence."

In addition to its strategic location, Tonatierra, his organization, occupied a unique spot on the region's map of ethnic politics. A busy community development center where Azteca ritual and English language classes were both taught to indigenous Latino youth, Tonatierra hosted activities that cut across the most common local terms for labeling ethnic identities: Anglos, Indians, Hispanics, and "illegals." Regarded by some of the more mainstream Latino organizations in town as a throwback to more separatist 1960s-style politics, Tonatierra's transnational, or continental, viewpoint appealed to those who were looking beyond the logjam created by the debates about immigrant policymaking. From the indigenist perspective of Acosta and his coworkers, the administrative containers of federal law, such as the Indian tribal councils, the U.S. border protocols, and the legal/illegal immigrant categories, were all rogue products of colonization. For Acosta, Conquest was a more important time marker than 1848 (the Treaty of Guadalupe) or 1994 (NAFTA), and so references to the Doctrine of Discovery and its later offshoot, Manifest Destiny, peppered his flow. "I believe that white America will one day rejoin humanity," he mused with deep conviction. "I believe we will all become extinct in the process. I believe that both might happen at the same time." He recalled that "in the past it was the stated policy for mainstream environmental organizations that we can't have so many Mexicans coming into North America because it is going to be unsustainable," and after his trip to Cochabamba, he was inclined to see the lawmaking of Pearce and his FAIR allies as the scaffolding for "a fortress America" to keep out climate migrants.

Running a community food bank and a worker center for day laborers had drawn Tonatierra more and more into the fray of community organizing and immigration politics. Acosta's close partnership with Salvador Reza, an organizer at the helm of El Puente Arizona, further cemented Tonatierra's anchor role in the city's burgeoning immigration rights movement. The initiator of several large protest marches and numerous picket actions, Reza had become Sheriff Joe's primary street antagonist. "My tactics are confrontational," he warned. "If you do not confront the Sheriff, he will not respect you. If you kneel before him, he will destroy you. He is a tough character with a Wild West mentality." For all his militancy, he conceded that "Tonatierra has taught me that you cannot fight the Sheriff out of anger or hate," because his tactics are aimed at dividing "the big circle of the people." Reza also acknowledged that Arpaio's "neo-Nazi" policies were largely an outcome of his political opportunism. In his mind, the sheriff's extremist turn was a result of several factors: the election, in 2004, of key right-wing legislators, including county attorney Andrew Thomas; the gradual assumption of control over the legislature by Pearce; and the active intervention of groups like FAIR. Notwithstanding his savvy understanding of the contemporary political scene, Reza shared Acosta's long-term view. "This repression is the closing chapter of Manifest Destiny, and we are the wake-up call," he declared, predicting that "the people who will suffer the most are the populations who elected the Sheriff."

Reza, whose family was from Chihuahua, by way of El Paso, noted that "Arizonans do not have long-term relationships with Mexican laborers the way that Texans do," and so "they react emotionally in fear." Puente seized national attention after Arpaio marched 220 immigrant detainees in shackles along the streets toward his Tent City jail in January 2009. The media-hungry sheriff misjudged with this show of public humiliation. "People were very upset," Reza recalled, "and they called us from all over the country asking what we were going to do." The response—a massively successful, multi-sector protest march—pierced the sheriff's climate of fear, brought the energy of the immigration movement directly to Phoenix, and was followed by a series of actions that won some support from fractions of the city's elite.

Republican-dominated Chamber of Commerce constituencies had no appetite for the business-busting immigrant crackdown but had held their tongues when they saw even the most vocal Democrat critics in the press and government were being threatened and sometimes jailed by Arpaio's deputies. Indeed, business could not help but be a big loser when, according to Department of Homeland Security's statistics, 100,000 undocumented Mexicans took their cheap labor out of the state from 2008 to 2009. Government revenue also took a big hit. Since the wages paid to the remaining migrants were now increasingly off the books, there was no tax benefit to the state. One business consultancy calculated that Arizona would lose $26.4 billion in economic activity, $11.7 billion in gross state product, and as many as 140,000 jobs if SB 1070 succeeded in driving all of the undocumented from the state.[37] The boycott of Arizona, which had already taken a high toll on tourism and convention bookings, threatened to further stymie any hopes of jump-starting the growth machine. In March 2011, prominent business leaders weighed in on Pearce's efforts to push through a package of birthright citizenship bills by signing a collective letter advising against legislation that would further damage the state's reputation and economy. In response, the GOP's business wing voted down the bills.

As international support for the boycott poured in after the passage of SB 1070, Reza's Puente was the key group for coordinating protests on the ground. The organizers' meetings, held at Tonatierra, drew in more and more volunteers, both from the Valley and further afield. Two weeks before a massive march on May 29, 2010 (the largest popular protest in the city's history), a meeting that I attended there opened with a brief but effective history lesson. The assembled activists, mostly on the youthful side, learned that the history of the organization was rooted in the 1960s Arizona farmworker struggles of Cesar Chavez and also that Tonatierra's indigenist outlook involved a much broader approach to immigration politics than other reform organizations. Leading the sessions was the modest but confident Carlos Garcia, who had emerged as the group's ace organizer. Afterward, he told me that he was attracted to Tonatierra because it "complicates Hispanics to think about their identity." In Mexico, he points out, "We are told to forget that we are indigenous." Many Indians in the United States, he pointed out, "have the same mentality: Where are your papers? What tribe are you from? Are you federally recognized?" While the organization "challenges all of these comfort zones," he acknowledged that this approach was "not so beneficial for organizing *because* it complicates matters, and sometimes confuses people."

Sandra Castro, a younger member of the Puente team, said she felt "at home" at Tonatierra because she had been exposed to Azteca ritual in her Los Angeles childhood. "A grassroots organization which was close to the community and listened to what it had to say" was appealing to her. "We have a more comprehensive take on things that is based on human rights," she affirmed, and added that "we are often seen as radicals, because we say things that others won't." Coming from a city she regarded as more truly multicultural, her family quickly learned, on moving to Phoenix, that many areas and cities in the Valley were off-limits to Latinos. Even on the ASU campus, where she was a student, many of her peers were quite vocal about their prejudice.

While other groups were focused on the single-issue politics of immigration reform, the activism of the Tonatierra crew revolved around more holistic beliefs, which included embracing the ecological rights of Mother Earth, as set forth at Cochabamba. They saw the current flap over SB 1070 as part of a longer history in which indigenous land rights had consistently been denied, especially for small farmers and agricultural workers. Gustavo Gutierrez, the founding elder of Tonatierra, was living testimony of the continuity with the *campesino* movement of the 1960s. Too infirm now to attend rallies, he had grown up on local farms, at a time when Mexican workers labored alongside the remnants of the Okie generation. "When the Okies went on strike," he recalled, "the growers would bring in mostly undocumented Chicano workers to break the strike. When the Chicanos went on strike, they would bring in the Dust Bowl migrants. The one was played off against the other." In those days, he remembered, prejudice against Latino farmworkers, even from union mineworkers, was not directed at their race, or their legal status, but rather at their lowly social status as field hands. Gutierrez used his alliance with Cesar Chavez to organize Arizona farmworkers to win the first union contracts for undocumented migrants. They turned out to be the only contracts, however, since the GOP Governor Jack Williams went on to pass one of the most punitive antiunion laws in the land in 1972. In reference to the farmworkers, Williams once declared, "As far as I'm concerned, those people don't exist." As part of the campaign to recall the governor, Chavez undertook one of his famous fasts in South Phoenix in 1972, and it was there that the inspirational slogan *Si Se Puede!* was born.

"When we got the first contract," Gutierrez recalled, "the workers said they wanted 10 cents of every hour they worked to be put into an economic development fund in their home states." This was because they were worried about the social impact of their union wage: "What happens if we lift the wages up in the field and then local people want the jobs and they deny us work?" As a result, the union became a transnational operation, setting up at least one collective farm south of the border so that workers could come and go on a seasonal basis. Gutierrez retained the spirit of this transnational covenant in each organization he went on to help found: the Maricopa County Organizing Project, Chicanos Por La Causa, Tonatierra, and the Peace and Dignity spiritual journeys, a tradition of long-distance runs undertaken in every corner of the Americas ("our people have been traversing this continent since time immemorial, from Alaska to Tierra del Fuego").

What difference did this continental viewpoint make? For one thing, it gave substance to what had become a movement slogan about the history of longtime dwellers on the Southwest lands: "We never crossed the border, the border crossed us." It also challenged the contention, favored by many reform advocates, that immigration was the civil rights struggle of the twenty-first century. This latter commonplace was particularly evident in the effort to enlist black leaders in the fight against SB 1070. In an April sermon at Phoenix's First Institutional Baptist Church, the Rev. Warren Stewart, Sr. warned that "some of us may have to go to jail before it's all over." Stewart was the preacher who had spearheaded protests over Arizona's blocking of the Martin Luther King, Jr., holiday, and his goal was to drive home the continuity with that earlier struggle. Shortly thereafter, Al Sharpton came to Phoenix to call up "the spirit of the freedom riders" for the state's African Americans. "To my black brothers and sisters that think this is not your fight," he declared, "let me tell you something. After dark, we all look Mexican right now." In some circles, a new movement slogan emerged: "From Selma to Phoenix." Even so, there did not seem to be any real wave of enthusiasm in Phoenix's black community for joining the fray; for one thing, it was recalled that there had been scant Latino participation in the marches for the MLK holiday, and, in any case, "civil rights," for many African Americans, was still a proprietary affair.

It was obvious why immigrant advocates would gain traction from citing parallels with the storied history of the civil rights movement. In the United States, the concept of civil rights was instantly recognizable, indelibly and righteously associated with rectifying a long record of injustice against black citizens. Human rights violations, by contrast, were perceived to happen elsewhere, in poor, undemocratic countries. In truth, the black freedom movement of the 1950s and 1960s had aspirations far beyond formal civic goals such as the right to vote or enjoy educational equality, and it had crested a wave of worldwide, anticolonial struggles for human rights. In a similar fashion, the struggle over U.S. immigration was also being played out in most industrialized countries, and it revolved around a series of internationally recognized rights that could not, in many cases, be adequately covered by the existing civil statutes of nation states. Indeed, civil rights protections were more likely to be regarded as a bulwark against the immigrants they pointedly excluded. Nativists promoted these protections as a set of citizen entitlements whose worth would be devalued and demeaned if they were extended to noncitizen residents. According to this view, civil rights was one of the benefits of legal residence, and the whole package had to be "defended" from those with no formal claim on them. In this way, unauthorized immigrants could be cast as an active threat to the enjoyment of citizens' rights.

This siege mentality was further reinforced in a time of economic scarcity, and, in border states like Arizona, the label "illegal" had widespread currency, strengthening the public perception that the undocumented were not entitled to any rights at all. Under this logic, all kinds of inhumane acts were deemed acceptable. For example, Alma Minerva Chacon, who went into labor on the night after she was detained by Sheriff Joe's agents, was not only forced to remain in the shackles at the hospital while she gave birth but was refused any contact with the newborn. She was not able to hold her baby for 72 days until she was finally released.[38] In response to a wave of incidents like this, Puente took up the rallying cry, "Somos Seres Humanos" (We Are Humans), to appeal to the lowest common denominator of public empathy but also to communicate that Sheriff Joe's deputies were routinely engaged in the violation of basic human rights.

The protests and solidarity actions that Phoenix witnessed in the wake of SB 1070's passage sparked a new level of community organizing. Taking a page from the Salvadoran social movements, Puente formed Barrio Defense Communities in neighborhoods all across the city to circulate legal information and coordinate resistance to Arpaio's police sweeps. Responding to Puente's call for a Freedom Summer, activists flocked to Phoenix to register voters and help build a support structure for pro-immigrant actions. By the end of the summer, the "glimmer of hope" that Gutierrez had seen in May was on the verge of becoming a regional movement, quite distinct in its aims and methods from the mainstream Washington reform organizations like RIFA. The template for the barrio

Figure 6.3
Mothers March against SB 1070, Arizona State Capitol. Photo by author.

committees was being exported to other frontline U.S. cities in anticipation of states passing copycat SB 1070 legislation.

The international attention garnered by SB 1070 also put a spotlight on
the maltreatment of migrants in other countries. To date, there was more
understanding of the impact on migration of neoliberal economic policies
than of climate change, but that would likely change in the years to come.
In both cases, migrants' decisions to travel were largely the result of policies and actions in the global North that had adverse impacts on their
land and livelihoods at home. However indirectly, the emissions pumped
into the desert air above Central Arizona were already responsible for the
presence of some of the 500,000 undocumented Mexicans in the state.
That causal link would only intensify as the carbon buildup took its climatological toll on their parched lands to the south. Any assessment of the
ecological footprint of metro Phoenix, or any other immigrant gateway
city, had to take the cause of this human traffic into account. It could no
longer be ignored as an externality.

By 2010, the Southwestern metropolis had outpaced all others in its
zeal to police entry and residence. This had been the fastest-growing
postwar city in the United States, welcoming all and sundry if they would

only make a down payment on a new suburban home. Naturally, the Mexicans building the homes, and in many cases buying them too, felt that their contributions to the regional economy, based on great personal sacrifices, would somehow be recognized. Instead, they were living in abject fear; their families were being broken apart from deportations and imprisonment, the stakes they had laid for a new life were shattered, and their children (taunted now as "1070s" by classmates in the schoolyard) would live with the trauma of criminalization for a long time to come.[39] More than any of the other sustainability challenges Metro Phoenix faced, the ill treatment of its most vulnerable populations was a test of its ability to respond with its humanity intact to the fast-approaching era of resource scarcity. In the meantime, it was difficult to avoid concluding that the bitter fight over immigration—racially divisive to the core—was the first skirmish in the climate wars of the future.

CHAPTER 7

Land for the Free

And if you are ever southeast of Superstition Mountain, look to the top! You will see people up there, turned into stone. Those are the people who were drowned in the flood. How long ago did this happen? I cannot say, but the story was handed down to me by very old people.

George Webb, *A Pima Remembers*

In November 2006, just as the real estate bubble was running out of hot air, Arizona voters approved a proposition with drastic consequences for land-use regulation. Proposition 207 was promoted as a property-rights initiative that barred municipalities from taking private property through eminent domain for some other private development. In this respect, it was a direct response to the Supreme Court's 2005 *Kelo* ruling, which had partially legalized such powers. But a more far-reaching, and less publicized, provision of the Arizona proposition required local governments to compensate property owners if a government action, such as a zoning change or enactment of an environmental or other land-use law, led to a drop in the property's value. Bankrolled by Howard Rich, a libertarian developer tycoon from New York, the initiative was pushed onto the ballot in several states, but Arizona voters were the only ones to bite. Passage of the proposition put a large question mark over all plans to alter land use in the state. Fear of lawsuits that could drain their coffers prompted city officials to think twice about making any changes to zoning ordinances, the bread and butter of municipal planning. More comprehensive efforts at regulating fringe growth or re-urbanizing downtown areas were beset by uncertainty about the newly hostile legal landscape.

Prop 207 was the latest, and most urban, challenge to the exercise of government power over land use in the West. The Sagebrush rebellion of the 1970s and 1980s, which pushed for more local control over public land holdings, was a rural assault on federal regulatory efforts such as the protection of environmentally sensitive land as wilderness. The ensuing rise of the anti-takings movement, launched by Richard Epstein's 1985 book, *Takings: Private Property and the Power of Eminent Domain* was also directed against government support for environmentally minded initiatives like smart growth. Fallout from these backlashes turned the West into a prime zone of conflict over land use. In retrospect, it is fair to say that the region that cradled the rise of the environmental movement (in the epic struggles over Hetch Hetchy, Echo Park, Glen Canyon, and Marble Canyon) has also hosted the strongest reactions to the notion that land might be something other than a commodity or a resource to exploit for private gain.

The historical lineage of this face-off was molded by the era of federal land giveaways during the 1800s to jump-start westward expansion. Aside from the handover of millions of acres to railway companies, the 1862 Homestead Act (160 acre stakes for $10) and the 1877 Desert Land Act (640 acres for $1.25 an acre) were championed as efforts to appease discontented Eastern wage laborers who had become hirelings of the new industrialists. The settlement program was supposed to be their chance to live out the self-reliant ideal of the yeoman farmer and to establish that noble occupation as the anchor of American democracy in the far West. Speculators took advantage of the cheap land offers, however, and the Bureau of Reclamation's subsequent crusade to foster irrigation farming was launched, in part to put a stop to the corrupt seizure of these Western lands by big ranching and mining interests. By creating a water delivery system that serviced selected locations, the federal government would decide not only where people were to live in the West but also that irrigation farming, rather than waged labor, should be their chief livelihood. The effort came too late, however; waged labor was already the foundation of the West's mining and ranching economy, and the template for settlement was already in place. Nonetheless, the national government's active hand, combined with its ownership of vast public land holdings, established it as the prime regulator of land use in the far West, a role reinforced by subsequent federal decisions about wilderness parks and military reservations in the course of the twentieth century.

Libertarians and property-rights activists organized counterattacks when those regulatory decisions favored environmental protection, though there was much less outcry when Western lands were commandeered for military purposes. After all, nuclear testing, gunnery ranges, weapons centers, and other military proving grounds had turned large parts of the West into sacrifice zones (and much of its population into downwinders).[1] So, too, urban growth in the West (it quickly became the most urbanized region in the United States) was a direct result of Cold War defense budgets. Up until 1940, the region was still regarded as an Eastern colony from which raw materials were plundered. As the defense facilities and contracts proliferated, much of the West became a military colony, its cities more and more dependent on the Pentagon's dollar.

With American power extending across the Pacific, full mobilization in Vietnam during the 1960s and 1970s, and the escalation of Star Wars funding under Reagan, the militarization of the region was steadily stepped up. Until the end of the Cold War, the federal government was the biggest customer for goods and services produced in the Sunbelt, and its defense contracts generated jobs, profits, and rising property values.[2] Economic benefits like these did not flow directly from the actions of the other, conservationist hand of federal power. For sure, tourist dollars were generated by wilderness preservation, but when these lands were taken off the commodity market, their potential value for developers evaporated. Confrontation with this side of government power was guaranteed to escalate when the defense economy began to scale down in the early 1990s, and real estate development became the mainstay of the region's economy.

Even though Reclamation's core agricultural vision had long been superseded by urban subdivisions as the region's primary settlement pattern, its remnants still played an integral role in the real estate economy. Irrigation farms were regarded as a holding zone for land until housing came along to claim its rightful title of "highest and best use," and farmers understood that they were caretakers of water rights for future developers. Yet when the dust from the Phoenix housing crash settled, there were signs that the Reclamation romance of agrarianism was undergoing some kind of a revival in a metropolis once known as the "Garden City." A new generation of farmers was learning to look at their land and produce in a different cultural light. Urban farming had acquired an unforeseen cachet, and local food provision was beginning to drive the trends among consumer pioneers. In impoverished neighborhoods and on Indian reservations, the act of food cultivation began to emerge as a catalyst for rebuilding communities that had been in decline for so long.

Ninety years after the heyday of the irrigationists, farming was on the verge of being restored as one building block of the sustainable future.

It no longer resonated with the colonizing vision of Reclamation, which promoted cultivation as the vehicle of Manifest Destiny in the region. Nor did it echo the back-to-the land ethos that inspired the New Deal efforts to plant subsistence homesteading in Phoenix at the height of the Great Depression.[3] The agrarian revival had a date with a different kind of destiny, driven by the need for food security and resilience in a carbon-conscious age. The average American food item now traveled over 1,500 miles, and the challenge was on to shrink that mileage down to the scale of local distances. As land stewardship expert Gary Nabhan pointed out, "One out of every twenty-five calories of fossil fuel used in Arizona is used to package, refrigerate and transport food grown in other regions for our own consumption."[4] Local food was not the only version of sustainable land use in the region's future, as this chapter will show, but it was a visible alternative to the kind of land speculation that had wreaked havoc with the stability of households and communities. Needless to say, however, a lot of money had already been invested in the future turning out exactly the way it had been in the recent past.

SUPERSTITIONVILLE

One of the most graphic illustrations of the consequences of Proposition 207 could be found on the regional maps that adorned the walls of real estate developers' offices. These maps recorded not just current land development but also all of the future lots, on subdivided land, that were already entitled. In some quarters, these entitlements were known as "premature subdivisions," and their ghostly outlines could be found on maps all over the fast-growth areas of the West, especially those with a reputation for sprawl. In Arizona counties like Maricopa and Pinal, it was customary to set entitlements far in advance of development. As a result, high-carbon patterns of growth and settlement were already locked in, far into the future. In the Sun Corridor, the much-discussed mega-regional linkage of Phoenix and Tucson, more than a million lots were entitled (650,000 in Pinal County alone), many of them made ready for development plans that were frozen by the crash. Any efforts to change these entitlements in order to implement more sustainable development patterns might run up against Prop 207's requirement of compensation for adverse impacts on property values.

Premature subdivisions were hardly a new phenomenon. Urban growth in the Mid West and far West had been driven by subdividing land decades in advance of settlement. In the early twentieth century, gridiron plans were projected far out into the newly annexed territory of cities, and so when suburban developers after the war began to favor curvilinear street patterns, the change in preference was a major headache for regional planners. Arizona's Prop 207 would make it even more difficult to revise the initial plans and so its passage sent a chill throughout the sustainable planning community.

One of the potential casualties of the proposition was the hope that the Sun Corridor could be built out in a more compact, low-carbon way. The full extent of this desert empire reached from the middle of Yavapai County around Prescott to western Cochise County not far north of the Mexican border, and prerecession forecasts had projected an 82.5 percent increase in population from 2000 to 2030. The juiciest of real estate estimates saw two trillion dollars worth of public and private investment pouring into the corridor over the same period.[5] Of course, the prolonged recession knocked the stuffing out of all these growth estimates, and temporarily eased Tucson residents' fear that Phoenix was slouching its way through 100 miles of desert toward them.[6] Yet even with the more likely scenario of slower growth, Prop 207's impact was such that sustainable development of the Sun Corridor, according to one study, "may now be left largely to the marketplace."[7]

Still alive were hopes for a 275-square-mile chunk of state-owned land that abutted the fringes of Apache Junction, on the edge of the East Valley's path of growth. The sheer cliff faces of the jagged Superstition Mountains thrust up from the area's eastern border, and, aside from a portion of the slopes below the range that preservationists had long eyed, the scrub plains were flat and relatively featureless—in other words, a home builder's wet dream. Of the 9.2 million acres of state land still held in trust, this parcel, an area as large as the San Fernando Valley, was the one with the most potential impact on the shape of urban growth in the state. For most of its history, Arizona had leased out its trust land for ranching and mining, but in 1981, the legislature opened up the areas that lay athwart metro growth paths for retail sales to developers. Some of the initial auctions involved piecemeal sales of tract parcels for the kind of fringe development that enraged anti-sprawl critics. But in recent years, as Jamie Hogue, deputy commissioner at the State Land department pointed out, "the growth has just jumped all around us, and we are far behind the market in a lot of areas." As a result, most of the parcels remaining in the metro area were infill, "where infrastructure has already reached or surpassed us, because in many cases it is very complicated to try to finance the infrastructure upfront on a piece of state trust land." But these complications were nothing compared to the challenges involved in financing the expanse that had come to be branded as Superstition Vistas (SV). Implementing a sustainable vision for developing the vast site would require a quantum leap in trust land sales policy.

In 2005, the East Valley Partnership, a regional business coalition, made an ambitious proposal to treat these trust lands as a single unit for the purposes of an infrastructure master plan governing all the development across SV's 275 square miles. Corridors for freeways, surface streets, mass transit, and utilities would be established and set aside in advance, along with provisions for recreational and open space, and groundwater recharge facilities. Smaller parcels could then be sold, but only if the buyer followed the regulations set out in the master plan, including prescriptions for residential density. The State Land department possessed super-zoning powers, but Hogue did not believe they had ever been exercised: "We normally work with the cities and counties to obtain zoning and land uses." Trust land sales that placed strict conditions on development were unheard of. To make SV happen, this policy would have to be reformed, and high-profile public support would be needed to push the reforms. The first part was the most onerous. Before the citizenry even got to have its say, an agreement had to be thrashed out among the thirteen defined beneficiaries of the trust land, along with a fistful of other stakeholders that included cattle ranchers, hunters, developers, and environmentalists. Given the diverse range of these constituencies, this process would drag on for many years.

Raising the public visibility of the plan through opinion makers was much easier. A development study, *The Treasure of the Superstitions*, was commissioned from the policy intellectuals at the Morrison Institute, led by the ubiquitous Grady Gammage, Jr. The authors of the report wasted no space in touting upfront the site's commercial bounty, referencing the legend of Jacob Waltz, the Lost Dutchman who searched in vain for gold in the Superstitions: "Today, however, we know the treasure of the Superstitions lies not in mythical gold, but in a more tangible commodity—land.... The land now called Superstition Vistas is worth billions of dollars... Seldom in the history of the U.S. has there been a chance to envision the future of one piece of property this large, this strategic, and this close to a major metropolitan region."[8] Since the bulk of the proceeds of trust land sales were channeled directly into the public education budget, developers would not be the only beneficiaries of this bonanza. But the most valuable outcome of the SV venture, as the report saw it, would be the practical example it provided of sustainable development—a model, in other words, for spinning profits while orienting growth in the region away from the discredited model of unplanned sprawl.

The Morrison report, which estimated a future SV population of almost a million by 2060, laid out three options for how to design and enforce the planning regulations: (a) a master plan commissioned and implemented by the Land Department, (b) a set of performance standards aimed at minimizing heat island temperatures and water and energy use, (c) the pre-incorporation of a city government, Superstitionville, to shape and apply the plans. This latter proposal, for a government that would actually precede residents, provoked its share of rancorous responses; one ranking Republican legislator described it to me as the "ultimate socialist dream." Undaunted, the project's champions collected even more funds to hire Robert Grow, a consultant who pioneered "regional visioning" in Utah's Greater Wasatch area. Commissioned to undertake a more focused form of scenario planning, his team fleshed out four detailed options for development on the project's "blank slate." The most conservative scenario had no overall master plan and was composed of dispersed, single-family home communities with only 40 percent of the open land preserved and overall projected densities at 20 percent above the metro Phoenix average. The most radical scenario, with the smallest development footprint, preserved 73 percent of the land, and hosted townhomes and eight- to twelve-story condo and office buildings in four pedestrian and rail-oriented urban centers with density levels somewhere between Miami and Chicago, almost 80 percent higher than the Phoenix average.

Grow and his team rolled out the four scenarios at a September 2009 public meeting in Gold Canyon, a sequestered, exurban community at the foot of the Superstitions. Although fully one hour east of Phoenix, in the heart of cholla cactus country, the town's Bermuda grass lawns and golf courses were plush and confident. During the meeting, instant polling was conducted on a range of quality-of-life issues, and, ultimately, on the four scenarios being presented. John Fregonese, introduced as the nation's "number one scenario planner," was present to gauge the results. Grow, the master mediator, was practiced at avoiding hot button terms: "Let's not use the 'density' word," he cautioned to his audience. "It often equates with gridlock, so let's just talk about *walkable*." But the advice seemed to be lost on the vocal portion of the audience that was composed of locals; most of the other attendees were real estate or government professionals. Cries of "Go back to LA!" emanated from the back of the hall, along with complaints that a low-density option had been deemed off the table. An up or down vote on that option was spontaneously called for and adopted, and the results showed that the revolt was well supported: 31 percent of those present preferred densities lower than the Phoenix average. As for the options that were officially on the table, the concluding vote produced most support for scenario B: a master plan, with mixed-use town centers clustered around transit stops and major roadways, and with densities somewhere between Pasadena and Denver, or 20 percent above the Phoenix average. Only 12 percent voted for the high-density option. The following day, press reports described the outcome as an encouraging advance for the project's backers, but made no mention of the local insurgents, or their cause.

The growth plans for SV augured a shift in business as usual for a region that was hostile to strong land-use controls. Jim Holway, from the Sonoran Institute (one of its environmentally minded backers), described the project as an expedient vehicle for changing the law: "If we can come up with a great vision of what Superstition Vistas might be, and if we can sell it to the public...that will help us sell state trust land reform." As for the ideas themselves, "they might not actually get built there," he speculated, but since they were applicable throughout the region, "they might get built in Buckeye or Utah." Holway was under no illusion that anything would "change the strong bias private property rights in the West," and he subscribed to the view that growth in the corridor to the east and south was unstoppable. In fact, he was still holding on to fairly high population projections: "We should assume that we will get another 5 to 10 million people over the next 50 to 100 years," and, he added, "in the past we have usually exceeded population projections." With that kind of population influx, scattered sprawl-type development in that area was a dead certainty, and so it was responsible, in his view, to ask: "What would be the most efficient pattern that would preserve quality of life and preserve water and energy use, what would that pattern look like, and how could we drive investment to make it happen?"

At the other end of the environmental spectrum from Holway was the Sierra Club's Sandy Bahr, for whom the project was a wasted opportunity to use the recession to push for more fundamental changes to business as usual. From her perspective, the ideas behind SV were just a way "to facilitate the massive development involved in creating a new city." Why, she asked, "do we need to have a blank slate to build? Why can't we do New Urbanism planning right here in Mesa, Phoenix, or Chandler," or any of the other cities in the metro area? "It feels like giving up on the existing communities," she added, "and saying that we can't do it in Phoenix, and that we need to go out where there isn't anything and plan a do-over." Bahr believed that there was more than enough vacant, buildable land within the core to accommodate newcomers, but acknowledged that "developers like going out there because there are fewer neighbors to fight with you." She refused outright Holway's fatalistic view that growth was going to happen at the urban edge, like it or not, and so we should make it as green as possible.

While the project's partners were focused on how dense they could build, the highest priority of those polled in the visioning scenarios was for economic development. Without an adequate provision of quality jobs, SV would be a remote bedroom community, inevitably boosting the carbon footprint of its residents. Grow's team had included in its report an estimate of the area's "economic engine" broken down into three tiers of industry, arriving in waves as the region matured: the "key foundational industries" included clean energy, motion picture production, building and construction, warehouse distribution, advanced manufacturing, resorts, research parks, and higher education (self-evidently considered to be an "industry").[9] Mike Hutchinson, the SV project director, was optimistic about the task of "convincing the public that they can live differently," but acknowledged that the employment piece of the project was "a real challenge." The problem of "job creation is really vexing," he explained. "We are not creating jobs in this state or this country, and the people of Colorado and New Mexico are competing with Arizona for the same jobs. It is a real issue that I do not have an answer for."

In his former position as Mesa's city manager, Hutchinson worked closely on preliminary plans for another massive development on the urban fringe. This one revolved around Mesa's Gateway Airport, formerly Williams Air Force Base. If the residents of SV ended up commuting to work, then it was assumed most of the employment would be in the Gateway urban complex to the northwest where city officials dreamed of accommodating as many as 100,000 jobs in technology, aerospace, and higher education. In 2006, the East Valley Partnership commissioned an Urban Land Institute (ULI) report on the potential for overall development of the 52-square-mile area, dutifully described as "one of the most promising expanses of underdeveloped land in the Phoenix metropolitan area and in the western United States." Like the Morrison study for Superstition Vistas, the ULI report recommended "master planning the area for high-density, mixed-use development," and cautioned against "the checkerboard development pattern" and other "hallmarks of unbridled sprawl" that were typical of "a free-market environment where speculation has been active."[10]

Several interviewees familiar with the plan told me that one of the guiding concepts was what University of North Carolina urbanist John Kasarda called the "aerotropolis," where the airport is not only an economic engine for a region but is also closely integrated into the fabric of the city. Bestowing a charisma never before associated with the East Valley, *The*

Economist magazine boldly dubbed the Williams Gateway project as "the city of the future." By contrast, a housing activist who was critical of the project described it to me as "the new cash cow on the fringe" and a "death sentence" for the largely abandoned historic downtown of Mesa (a city larger than Minneapolis or Pittsburgh).

The key to realizing the Gateway plan lay in development of GM's former Desert Proving Grounds, adjacent to the airport. DMB, the Valley's most respected master-planned community developer, had purchased 3,200 of GM's 5,000 acres, and partnered with the city on plans for a mixed-use and mixed-income buildout that sharply contrasted with Mesa's traditional pattern of development. It was also a departure for DMB, more accustomed to working with a large landowner to deliver a high-concept product for the affluent ex-urbanite, like its nationally acclaimed DC Ranch, in Scottsdale's western foothills of the McDowell Mountains. Jill Kusy, the DMB planner who negotiated the entitlements and a higher-density zoning ordinance with the city, reported that DMB's involvement triggered "a paradigm shift" in favor of "an intense and dynamic mixed-use development" with much taller buildings than had previously been envisaged for the site. The company was calling it "21st Century Desert Urbanism," though none of the design principles appeared to diverge from the palette of New Urbanism, with the exception perhaps of the 22-degree rotation of the urban grid to maximize solar orientation (and the views). When First Solar announced acquisition of a chunk of the DMB land for constructing a solar module fabrication plant in March 2011, its project snagged its first big provider of green jobs, in keeping with the overall ethos of sustainability.

CEO Drew Brown confirmed that the plans for Mesa Proving Grounds (now on hold because of the recession) showed DMB moving away from its traditional focus on open space preservation for the enjoyment of well-heeled residents toward carbon reduction from altered commuting patterns or home energy use. In designing the prize-winning DC Ranch in the early 1990s, he acknowledged, "We were really good at 'pretty.' We were sensitive to the land and to the people, but as for carbon emissions, I cannot honestly tell you they were heavily discussed when we were doing that planning ten years ago." He was equally frank in his about-turn on the question of regulating development beyond the urban edge. "If I had to do it again I would have come down the other way on Proposition 202 [which called for urban growth boundaries]. I think it would have been a better thing."

Among the developers I interviewed, Brown was the one who could be expected to display that kind of honesty, and DMB was the company most likely to lead the transition to low-carbon development as a matter of principle. Yet, until very recently, few could contend that the Mesa Proving Grounds fell within any agreed-upon urban growth boundary. Indeed its remote location—to keep prying eyes away from GM's test models—was intrinsic to its function as a proving ground. But leapfrog development in the last few years of the housing boom had bypassed the site, along with vast areas of vacant land around the airport. Even so, it was risible for the *Arizona Republic* to describe it as "the biggest urban infill project on Earth."[11] This was stretching the definition of infill beyond any credible understanding of the term. In 1980, after decades of classic leapfrogging, a full 40 percent of the city of Phoenix has been made up of vacant land.[12] In the thirty years since, despite the city's infill programs and more recent efforts to build in a more compact fashion, that ratio had barely budged at all.[13] There were still hundreds of sizable bare lots in every area of town, especially closer to the core, and Mesa had its share of these too.

No doubt, the takings requirements of Proposition 207 made infill that much more difficult to pull off, but building on neglected land closer to the urban cores was still the most sustainable response to current and future housing needs. Yet while lots lay vacant all over the Valley's cities, many of them in the poorest neighborhoods, jumbo initiatives were still being built or planned in remote locations. In addition to its involvement in the Mesa Proving Grounds project, DMB was completing Verrado, a large New Urbanist leapfrog community out in Buckeye below the White Tank Mountains. Arup, the global engineering firm, had been contracted to draw up plans for a 33,800-acre "sustainable city" for 300,000 residents on the Douglas Ranch, the largest of more than twenty master-planned communities already platted along the Sun Valley Parkway, the old "road to nowhere" that stretches into the desert for thirty miles beyond the White Tanks. Loaded, like Superstition Vistas, with sustainability features, these projects looked less like game-changers than sexy rationales for continuing to do edge development. That they were being planned by the more conscientious and publicly minded members of the land development sector brought renewed credibility to the idea of extending the path of growth at a time when the region's reliance on its growth machine was in question.

PLANTS AND PLOTS

Not all bare land in urbanized areas had to be filled with housing, of course, and until the market improved, other uses could be proposed. As it happens, the land crash coincided with the upsurge of interest in urban gardening and local food provision. Growing your own food achieved a new kind of charisma, even nobility, for a generation that wanted to see its green commitments bear fruit, literally, through acts of personal labor. In fact, urban gardening was rapidly transitioning to hipster status as a pastime for younger people in cities all across the United States. In North Phoenix, Greg Peterson had turned his modest house and one-third-acre yard into a showpiece cornucopia of produce that he called the Urban Farm; figs, quince, almonds, dates, peppers, chard, yams, stone fruits, artichokes, asparagus, and all manner of fruit trees grew in profusion, while chickens scratched away in the backyard. Like a model home in a subdivision, its regular stream of visitors took away a fully formed vision of how to transform their own backyards into a bounty of green choices, while slicing domestic energy costs (his annual electricity bill was only $300 by his estimate).[14]

Down in Tucson, Brad Lancaster, doyen of dryland gardening techniques, had even more rigorous requirements for maintaining his much-visited residential lot.[15] Unlike Peterson, whose land was flooded every two weeks under an old SRP commitment, Lancaster used only natural rainfall to tend his gardens and run the house (disconnected from the grid) where he and his brother's family lived. Harvesting every drop of the 100,000 gallons that fell annually on his one-eighth of an acre, plus the street wastewater that he captured through cuts in the curb, his setup was a marvel of efficiency. With the aid of passive, gravity-fed earthworks in the gardens, he was able to cultivate up to 25 percent of the household food supply. It was all governed by the principle that he called "planting rain before you plant vegetables or trees." Lancaster had been effective in pushing rainwater and graywater ordinances through the city council, and in October 2008, Tucson became the nation's first municipality to require developers of commercial properties to harvest rainwater for landscaping. He showed me where neighbors were adopting his techniques, and how the results had translated into a steady improvement in the community's self-image and livability profile. Indeed, Dunbar Spring had become one of the city's most active and desirable downtown neighborhoods. Lancaster acknowledged, regretfully, that some degree of "green gentrification" had occurred—the elevated property values "only rewards those who leave"—and reported that the neighborhood association was considering some kind of land trust to stem the impact of their green reputation on the market

For those without work or ready income, choices about planting and harvesting could also be a matter of survival. As a symptom of the hard times, Peterson told me that he knew of "several nurseries and seed companies that have trouble keeping seeds in stock right now because people are so interested." One of the most striking aspects of the uptake was the flourishing of gardens as a tool of community development in low-income neighborhoods. The best examples I found were in South Phoenix, where land was empty due to lack of developer interest, as opposed to the downtown core where vacant lots were flipped every six months by high roller speculators at the height of the boom. Owners of these spaces could win some tax savings if they let them out as community gardens, and so allotments were sprouting, none more boisterously than the gardens managed by Darren Chapman, which functioned as a point of re-entry for ex-cons who shared his own gangbanging background. In a neighborhood with an 80 percent recidivism rate, his gardens were a gateway, for those on parole or release, to steady employment in the landscaping, security, or doorman businesses that Chapman's nonprofit foundation supported. "I have young men with ankle bracelets who are under house arrest or parole," he reported, "who are allowed by their probation officers to come into the garden because it is a safe zone." They had to volunteer and prove their reliability in the field before being offered paid jobs in the other operations. Like Chapman's other businesses, the garden initiative began as an effort to make peace between warring youth; "a Crip met a Blood in one of my gardens, and found out they were cousins," he recalled, "and then the next week, I saw them riding in a car together." Within a few years, the gardens bloomed as a symbol of community revitalization; they were meeting places for young and old, and nutritious produce was grown and distributed in neighborhoods otherwise fated to be "food deserts." Four of his gardens, Chapman pointed out, were on a mile-and-a half-stretch of East Broadway, which otherwise boasted a prostitute strip, three liquor stores, and two fast-food joints. "This is where I grew up," he pointed out. "It's the mothership, and if I can't clean up my own backyard, then I can't come to yours."

In his showcase Garden of Tomorrow, a collection of enthusiasts—locals and others who bused in to tend the rows of melons, peanuts, and peppers—worked the soil on Saturday mornings to the beat of DJ music. Youth, who were paid small stipends to cultivate, mingled with barbecuing seniors from the adjacent nursing home. Chapman, a magnetic evangelist for the cause, circulated tirelessly, joshing with some of the toilers, task-mastering others, always ready to explain the higher social purpose behind their tilling, weeding, and harvesting efforts. One volunteer who was preparing salads—a retired community mobilization professional from the East Coast—radiantly informed me that "this is community development in action." Another, from the senior center, reported that he had moved there from another home specifically in order to enjoy the garden's busy life.

Figure 7.1
Darren Chapman and his community garden crew. Photo by author.

Chapman recalled making a wish, at 13 years old, to live until he was 26—not an uncommon aspiration, he added, among males in his hard-knock neighborhood in South Central Los Angeles. Memories of the garden in his grandfather's backyard, a vibrant meeting place for neighbors and friends, colored his nostalgia for the community-rich 1970s: "It was like living on an Indian reservation; you traded fruits and vegetables for animals that were edible, especially rabbit. People knew who you were and what you were doing most of the time and there wasn't the same kind of suspicion and fragmentation as there is now." There were still jobs in the inner city then, whereas nowadays, as Chapman put it, "low-income means no-income." That is why it was important to him that his "graduates" got a real economic payoff from the self-sufficiency skills and work habits they learned from committing themselves to the gardens.

Chapman's foundation had attracted its share of donations and plaudits, but the working principle of the gardens was "people serving themselves" rather than looking to politicians or professionals for help. Community gardens were sponsored from the top down by municipal agencies in cities like Baltimore, Detroit, and Cleveland, or by nonprofit networks in others. There was no support at this level in Phoenix, and Chapman had a busy sideline as a consultant for churches, school district, and community associations looking to start up gardens in other parts of the Valley. Whatever their motives, he tried to preach that the goal was to empower people and spread the word about nutrition and local food security.

Despite fierce lobbying from Local First champion Kimber Lanning and ASU design activist Nan Ellin, Phoenix mayor Phil Gordon had done nothing to turn over the vacant downtown lots (as many as 60 percent were city-owned) to would-be gardeners. The land was deemed too valuable to risk a fight with community advocates when the city tried to reclaim it for development at some later date. Gordon was a vocal supporter of locally sourced food and farmers markets, but, like most city officials, his interest was framed, if not driven, by the prize of economic development. Dee Logan, a nonprofit organizer who worked with municipalities to start up farmers markets, found this to be a common denominator. Officials saw the markets as "a magnet to bring people downtown," she reported, and they had ways of "dressing it up as a public service," all of which "helped them polish their brand as attractive locations." Such motives, she added, "ran counter to the social justice origins of the farmers market concept," but she played along with them just to get the markets established, often partnering with economic development agencies rather than the Department of Agriculture.

Phoenix's own twice-weekly market, anchored around a semi-permanent indoor store, was the outcome of a rare, successful negotiation over a privately owned downtown lot. Cindy Gentry, its inspirational founder, reminded me that "cities started from markets, and we obliterated ours, so we are working in reverse now." Happy to cater to City Hall by promoting the small restaurants she was helping bring downtown, she herself had a more philosophical cast about the functions of markets: "They are places where you can make visible particular value systems, that's what's important to me, and so it's all about valuing the producers, valuing the social relationships, and valuing what we eat." Gentry and Logan had struggled to bring small producers to the market because the commercial distribution system had a tight lock on the region's farms and had instilled a spirit of competitive distrust among the farmers that was reinforced by the Farm Bureau. "Trash talking," Logan commented, "had to be openly discouraged, and so part of the farmers market compact is that you cannot be derogatory to your neighbor's produce." As with every other part of the food movement, Gentry learned that "you have to make a commitment to be with the people whose behavior you want to change."

Gentry had no compunction about "working within the system," even with the likes of Walmart, and she accepted that the value shift in food consciousness was happening primarily among her more affluent customers. But her abiding motivation was to use this consciousness to address hunger. Community Food Connections, the nonprofit that ran the market, was particularly active in "underserved areas" where residents had limited access to fresh or healthy produce. "I personally have delivered truckloads of food into some low-income neighborhoods," she recalled, "where I was the only person unloading the truck because the people in line to get the free food didn't want to lose their place." No city, she mused, could be sustainable as long as it was stalked by the specter of hunger.

A stone's throw north of the market, on a block anchored by Conspire cafe, the anarchist hangout, the sidewalks bloomed with some fine examples of guerilla farming. This was the third ring of the local food movement. The plants that encroached on city easements were the work of Farmer John Milton, a free green spirit who had been a schoolmate, in Buckeye, of Matthew Moore, "the farmer artist," and whose landscaping adorned some well-known resorts around the Valley. Milton, whom I met early and intermittently throughout my research, seemed to embody the anarchist principle of self-organization as he plied his many self-taught trades all across the Valley: teaching homesteading and craft skills, from welding to jewelry and crochet, or rainwater harvesting; practicing "farm chefing," garden design, and aquaculture; and building green with materials like rammed earth, adobe, or straw bale. A Sufi in his beliefs, a squatter by inclination, and a dedicated practitioner of the gifting economy, there were very few artisanal tasks at which he had not tried his hand, but his long-term passion was for sustainable farming. Imagining his arrest for illegally gardening on the city-owned easement, he grinned, "If I can go to jail for gardening, that will be the apex of my life. 'Local Man Goes to Jail for Feeding the Homeless' would really the best publicity for what I'm doing."

The first time we talked he had just taken a position as a master gardener at a Gilbert real estate venture called Agritopia. A New Urbanist–style subdivision built around a working farm, it was driven by the owner's Christian principles and promoted as an innovative way of preserving the region's rich agricultural legacy. Quickly disillusioned with the agricultural part of the utopia—it was more of a sales gimmick than he had anticipated—Milton moved further out to set up an agro-tourist operation on Superstition Farms with the owners' son, Casey Stechnij. "Farmer with seeds, looking for land" was Milton's Craigslist ad that caught Stechnij's attention. With command over one thousand head of dairy cattle, Milton and Stechnij were soon running tours, open houses, hayrides, horse camps, and farm educational programs; they launched a storefront selling ice cream and

Figure 7.2
Guerilla farming on a downtown Phoenix sidewalk by Farmer John Milton. Photo by author.

Figure 7.3
Fruits of the labor. Photo by author.

cheese in downtown Phoenix; and staged a high-profile, monthly locavore dinner, prepared by celebrated Valley chefs.

Like some other farm brats of his generation, Stechnij subscribed to the new cultural zeal for agriculture. "Growing up," he recalled, "it was not cool to live on a farm, but now I see a real shift." In his mind, some of the appeal was being driven by new fears about resource scarcity. "Food security," he speculated, "is the reason for acquiring an agricultural knowledge base, and people want that food security in times of great stress." He hoped to make his life on the farm, but his father had other ideas. The older generation had sought out land that lay in the path of development as part of their retirement plans. The subdivisions had leapfrogged over Superstition Farm in the last few years, and the father did not want to miss his chance of cashing out. By contrast, the son had a principled disdain for real estate development. It was a generational conflict that was being played out on more than one Valley farm.

For nomad farmers like Milton, looking to throw down with a kindred spirit, the situation at Superstition Farm was a little too precarious. He talked of plans to move on to a new 100-acre farm with Stechnij, but there was nothing he wanted more than the yeoman dream—ten to twenty acres of his own. From this green base, he would plug his other homesteading skills into the burgeoning Valley subcultures that valued self-reliance or local provision. For Anglos like himself who had grown up in farming areas, it was all about reclaiming "knowledge that had skipped a generation," and distilling some of the democratic promise of the irrigation society that had driven Western settlement a century before, filling out the Phoenix Basin with more than 500,000 acres of productive farmland at its peak.

PIMA REDUX

The agrarian hankering of young growers like Milton, Stechnij, Moore, Petersen, and Chapman was in sharp conflict with the Valley mind-set that saw agriculture as simply a holding zone for land until housing came along to realize its highest value. There were places, however, where that mentality did not apply, and one of them lay in the dead center of the Sun Corridor. The 372,000-acre Gila River Indian Community (GRIC) was the largest undeveloped land mass in the United States that was contiguous to a major metropolitan area. The northern boundaries of the reservation presented a stunning contrast in land use. On one side, the brown-roofed subdivisions of Chandler, Gilbert, and Ahwatukee were tightly packed to the curb. Across the road, on the reservation, featureless desert scrub stretched off to the horizon. Gazing at the housing on the Gilbert side of the Hunt Highway, Henrietta Lopez, who gave me several tours of GRIC's new irrigation infrastructure, remarked that "the houses looked nice, but needed too much maintenance" for her liking, and noted that many of the plants and trees were imported. "We only use what we need," she said of the tribal land ethic. "We believe everything in the environment is here for a purpose, all the plants have a function."

Any proposal to turn reservation land into a housing commodity was bitterly contested. At the height of the real estate boom, tribal leaders were under great pressure to lease acreage for housing development, but they held out.[16] At its northern gateway, GRIC's casinos, resorts, and Lone Butte Industrial Park exploited its proximity to Phoenix, but those developments had all been contained within the pockets around the Chandler freeway interchanges, and it seemed likely that the rest of the GRIC reservation would remain a sparsely populated island in a sea of subdivisions. A new kind of pressure, however, was building on the tribal council to lease water to Valley cities from the proceeds of a monumental water rights settlement GRIC negotiated with the federal government in 2004. The agreement,

Figure 7.4
Hunt Highway, Gilbert subdivision housing to the right, undeveloped Indian land to the left. Photo by author.

which awarded the community 653,000 acre-feet of the state's allocation of 2.8 million acre-feet of Colorado River water, was by far the largest Indian water settlement in the nation. For those fixated on the resource balance of the region, the settlement instantly transformed GRIC into a major player in the water brokerage game ("the water OPEC of central Arizona," as one wag inevitably put it). For most of the GRIC members, however, the water was a long-sought-after chance to restore the reservation's agricultural heartland and revive farming practices that had been lost for three or four generations.

The Pima (Akimel O'odham), who shared the reservation with a smaller community of Maricopa (Pee Posh) at its western end, had a hallowed status in U.S. history as the people whose farming bounty helped to provision desert-challenged Anglos in dire need. Federal troops deployed to suppress the Apache, and later, California-bound emigrants on the Gila Trail, both relied heavily on Pima hospitality and the abundance of their fields to ward off starvation. Corn, beans, squash, cactus syrup, fish, pumpkin, melons, and winter wheat were some of the staple products of the Pima's riverine oasis, at a time when the Gila River flow was 300 feet wide in some places. With a well-developed *acequia* irrigation system inherited from the Hohokam, the fields, which produced three harvests a year and had no need for crop rotation, were something of a marvel to passers-by. There is a long record of travelers' tributes to the generosity of the Pima and their ability to carve out a successful economic niche within the emergent Southwest economy.[17] Pima men and women also earned the reputation of "Good Samaritans of the Desert" by scouting for emigrants in distress on the arduous trek between Tucson and the Gila settlements.[18]

Starting in the 1880s, the sustaining Gila flow began to dry up. Overgrazing and mining on the uplands and beaver trapping around the headwaters took their toll on the watershed, and then Mormon settlers simply siphoned off most of the surface water on the Upper Gila with the creation of the Florence Canal in 1886. There was even evidence that the settlers deliberately wasted quantities of water in order to deprive the Pima.[19] Facing destitution and starvation within a decade, the decline of the community was precipitous. The green oasis of their farmlands turned to dust, and their resort to commercial harvesting of mesquite entirely denuded the once-dense bosques along the river banks.[20] The spectacle of the starving Pima stimulated a high-minded debate in Congress about the morality of Indian policies, and their plight was presented as a primary argument for Reclamation, but the only solid outcome was a federal offer to relocate the tribe to Indian territory in Oklahoma.

The first legal complaints about the theft of Pima water were lodged in 1921 (*United States v Gila Valley Irrigation District*), and so it took more than eighty years before a final resolution was reached. Rod Lewis, the GRIC counsel who negotiated the settlement, started working on the case in 1972, though he was quick to note that the legal battle had been more or less continuous since the water dried up. "It was not a direct line," he recalled. "There were a lot of starts and stops with delays in litigation and changing judges, and several attempts to settle which were unsuccessful. The delays were so frustrating that, in the late 1980s, we filed to represent ourselves in court. By that time, we had lawyers representing the community who were familiar with the case. My predecessors, who had been involved since 1950, and I put that case together in the late 1980s and it culminated in the 2004 Act." Lewis had been the first Native American lawyer to win a case before the Supreme Court (over whether the state could levy sales taxes on reservation transactions) and so it was fitting that he presided over one of the most complicated pieces of legislation in modern Indian, not to mention Western, history.[21] Since everyone in the region had a stake in water allocation, the list of interested parties, including several municipalities and water authorities, was considerable. As long as the GRIC claim remained open (and the solidity of its legal standing always guaranteed an eventual resolution), it was a potent threat to the water management plans of the state and its major urban centers. With a wry grin, Lewis concluded, "I think people were relieved finally to get this issue resolved in Central Arizona, and folks in the Phoenix metro area could breathe a little easier."

Tribal members who yearned most to restore the actual river to the reservation had staked a very strong legal claim (in 1974) on the entire annual 2 million acre-feet flow of the Gila, based on the Western water doctrine of prior appropriation. Since the 2004 settlement mostly involved the allocation of CAP water, this meant that the Gila, the sustaining heart of the community (Akimel O'odham means "river people"), would never again flow with any regularity through tribal lands. Without the river itself, the once famous riparian ecosystem would thrive only in history books, though efforts were underway to restore pockets of it along the former river banks—areas that ethnobotanist Amadeo Ray described as fallen into the state of a "disturbed wasteland."[22] So, too, there was widespread skepticism that traditional farming practices could be restored on a significant scale. Until the river ran dry, the Pima had been a *rancheria* people, whose subsistence agriculture centered on small lots of several acres, with plentiful diversity among the crops. In the intervening century, non-Indian outsiders, who were leased sizable acreages by the Bureau of

Indian Affairs, had introduced "clean farming"—"large fields with clean borders maintained by herbicides, monoculture cropping, and concrete ditches from which phreatophytes (water-loving plants like cottonwoods) have been carefully eradicated."[23] The community's own 16,000-acre Gila River Farms, the centerpiece of the 20,000 acres currently farmed on GRIC land, was laid out in the same industrial fashion. Export cash crops (durum wheat for Italian pasta makers, or Pima Gold citrus and Pima Cotton bound for Japan) were the norm on these acreages. None of the produce found its way into reservation stores, and only a handful of tribal members worked noncommercial lots.

Economics and ecology aside, the impact of this drastic historical shift in agricultural practice could be found in the health of tribal members themselves, devastated over time by the rapid deterioration of their traditional riverine culture and diet. Decades of dependence on government food rations—white flour, lard, canned meats, and other sugary processed foods—contributed to an obesity epidemic and the highest rates of adult-onset diabetes in the world.[24] Indeed, fresh produce was not offered through the government program until 1995. The 580-square-mile reservation was itself a food desert, and most residents faced a long round trip to a supermarket in Chandler or Casa Grande if they wanted to buy fresh produce. As with many indigenous peoples whose cultural and economic integrity had been ruined, poverty, alcoholism, and drug abuse were rife. All in all, the community's degraded health was a shocking fate for a people who had once tended the nutrition heartlands of the region's economy. The damming up of the Salt and Gila rivers had brought forth all of the creature comforts of modern Phoenix, but only at the expense of the tribal people's well-being.

The settlement water brought the promise of renewed sovereignty and economic buoyancy, but, just as important, an opportunity to rebuild the community's health and cultural resilience through the revival of farming. As many as 146,000 acres of the GRIC lands were being slotted for agricultural production; traditional farming techniques were now being taught systematically to schoolchildren, community gardens had popped up, and a Tohono O'odham native seed bank was being drawn on for use throughout the community and by other Indian tribes in the region. So, too, members who had moved off the reservation were being tempted by the newfound prospect of restoring the soil on family allotments. Shannon Rivers, one of GRIC's representatives to the UN, was among them. "Can I go home," he mused, "and get my tribal house and do some planting, or else go to where my allotment is and build my house there and do that? At this particular juncture in my life it sounds more and more like a better solution than living out here [in South Phoenix] and trying to struggle. I'm not saying that going back to the rez is not going to be a struggle, but I know people who are going home back to their native community, and saying 'I want to try to live that pride.'" Rivers, who had been off the reservation since he was a child, was well versed in the values of native sustainability from his work at the UN and at other assemblies of the indigenous. His urban life skills, shaped early by a wayward youth and then by varied career experiences, hardly equipped him for any kind of livelihood on the land. Nonetheless, the happenstance of the recession with the rapid progress on GRIC's water distribution plans had turned his head.

The backbone of the endeavor was an ambitious 2,400-mile irrigation system of canals, laterals, and underground pipelines. Some of the canals were built on top of the ancient Hohokam network, while others involved a renovation of the federal San Carlos project, which brought water (but not nearly enough) from the Coolidge Dam in the 1920s. Monies from the 2004 settlement ensured that new canals could be constructed for carrying up to 173,000 acre-feet of the allocation. This meant that the hard-won rights would not exist only in the form of "paper water," to which a tribe has rights but lacks the resources to put to use.[25] For the whole system to be built out as planned, some additional revenue would probably be required. Under the settlement, GRIC could lease as much as 100,000 acre-feet to entities within the state, and with water prices likely to rise sharply in the coming decades, the revenue potential was huge. But for a significant portion of the tribal membership, the prospect of selling water—both a sacred resource and the community lifeblood—was simply inappropriate.

"Do you sell the water," asked Rivers, "as non-Indians have always done with natural resources—land, water, coal, or gold? Do you do the same thing they do, because you see it as an economic resource that could somehow sustain your community a little longer? That is a way to continue your survival, but are you really surviving if you give up something that is so culturally and spiritually tied to your people? Can you sell it, if you are dying culturally?" David DeJong, the irrigation system's project director, acknowledged that "there are a whole series of cultural issues involved. Many people in the community see that they fought for many years to bring the water back and now that they have it, don't want to turn around and 'sell' it, as they might say." "But," as he pointed out, "if they do nothing, then the water stays on the market, and someone else uses it, so the community gets absolutely nothing." DeJong predicted that "with the major shortages predicted for the Upper Colorado by 2050, this community will be the only entity with a major source of water available, and it will be

Figure 7.5
Canal and "clean farm" on Gila River Indian Community lands. Photo by author.

in the driver's seat." Without presuming "that the community would want to give up its agricultural heritage at that time," he pointed out that the opportunity to lease out the water "will certainly be extremely lucrative. In some respects, they will face very difficult decisions about whether to generate an enormous amount of revenue which GRIC can use to develop things we cannot even fathom today."

The federally funded irrigation project, which DeJong headed up, had burst into life with a zeal reminiscent of the Reclamation initiative itself. In its initial phase, at least, hydrologists, engineers, land-use planners, and environmental and cultural resource experts all worked together on a coordinated vision of community restoration. In an era where the Bureau of Reclamation had closed the door on megawater projects, here was one that channeled a romantic intensity almost equivalent to that of the earlier era. Not only that, the Reclamation vision of settling freeholders on semiarid land was being echoed here on the Gila River reservation. The nineteenth-century federal efforts to assimilate Indians into the yeoman farmer mold had culminated in the Dawes Act, which broke apart common land into privately owned lots, and permitted outsiders to lease Indian land. One intent of the legislation was to force Indian communal life to cede to the Jeffersonian ideal of self-reliant growers. Unlike other tribes, for whom sedentary agriculture was quite alien, the *Gileños*, as the Spanish called them, had been farmers for centuries, and their Hohokam forebears were among the most successful agriculturalists and water engineers of pre-Columbian times.

Reclamation's critics had long questioned whether desert farming was worth the effort or warranted the use of scarce water resources. The dismal ecological record of irrigation agriculture in the West added to the skepticism about the Gila River community's plans. But there could be no second guessing the right or the will of the Akimel O'odham and Pee Posh to pursue such an enduring cause. Anglo farmers in the region had not hesitated to sell their birthright to developers because it was an automatic cultural reflex for them to regard land as a commodity. In Indian country, no such permission existed. Nor were there too many alternatives to using the bulk of the GRIC settlement water for farming. Interest in siting solar projects on tribal land was running high (especially because they would not have to undergo costly and time-intensive NEPA reviews), but it was by no means clear that, legally speaking, the water could be allocated to nonirrigable uses.[26] On balance, restoring the farmlands might turn out to be the single best use of the region's water. After all, GRIC's 650,000 acre-feet would otherwise go to servicing hundreds of square miles of new, high-carbon sprawl. Instead, there was a good chance that a large portion would be earmarked for growing local food.

If the reservation lands were to host an agrarian revival, an intra-tribal contest lay ahead, between traditional, multicrop agriculture, which tends to be carbon-absorbing, and industrial monocropping, which is a large source of carbon emissions. Would the future belong to the large-scale export farming currently practiced by the Gila River Farms and other producers of commercial crops like alfalfa? Or would organic, local food provision win out? Gila River Farms planned to double its industrially farmed acreage once the new water came in, and it would take some heroic efforts to establish an alternative model. Tended by a handful of sprightly elders, the Vah-Ki Growers Cooperative had made a good start on a two-acre lot where maize, tepary beans, dates, squash, okra, chiles, melons, and stone fruits flourished in each of two growing seasons. Two of the coop's members, Janet Haskie and Danny Williams, showed me where the expansion of their site would depend on the new irrigation canals, and, just as important, where it would require agreements with the often large number of lottees who would have to approve agricultural use of their allotments.[27] The elders had been selling their produce on the reservation and had promoted their permacultural activities both as a traditional cultural outlet and as a dietary solution to the diabetes crisis. But neither reported much of a return on their efforts. "Diabetes is a struggle for survival for us," Haskie pointed out, "and our people are just not motivated enough." "It can be done," affirmed Williams, "but our people don't know how to do it." He had worked all his life on GRIC's commercial farms, and so he had to consult his grandparents about techniques when he himself started poly-crop gardening.

Haskie's son, David Van Druff, taught agricultural classes at the nearby Ira H. Hayes High School, one of a number of GRIC schools that had established agriculture as part of its curriculum in the years since the water settlement. His students, he reported, "crossed their arms at first," but some developed a passion for gardening, especially since his classes were thick with lessons about the "rich agrarian culture" of their ancestors. He said he had been thwarted in efforts to push traditional agriculture to the tribal government—"it wouldn't do any harm if they threw some of the casino money into it"—and so had reverted to what he called the "backdoor tactic" of training the next generation of farmers in the school. His students, after all, were the ones who would take on the challenge of restoring their heritage as "river people," and, if they prevailed, the result would be a clear-cut victory for regional sustainability. Locally grown food looked to be a large part of the urban future, and the GRIC farmlands, with a secure water supply and no prospects of being turned over to developers, would be the most obvious local source, just as they had been a century and a half before.

The return of the water was a striking example of environmental justice finally being delivered. Anglo settlement, after all, could only have thrived in the Phoenix and Gila Basins if the Akimel O'odham's and Pee Posh's means of subsistence was cut off. Restoring that lifeline took a hundred years of determination and acute sacrifice on the part of a people who, first of all, refused to beg, and then refused to settle for less than their integrity owed them. Each year spent chipping away at the legal obstacles meant another year of suffering for Pima and Maricopa who bore the burden in the decline of their health and livelihood. Remedying the injustice became the vehicle for imagining a more sustainable future, not only for themselves but for the region as a whole. Implementing the blueprint for that future would be a forbidding test for tribal governance. With the means, finally, to live up to long-preserved cultural values, the community would also be prey to outsiders bent on exploiting its newfound water wealth, and to insiders seeking to profit from the enticements on offer.[28] This was the dilemma of the resource curse with which Indian communities in the West were long familiar. The option of sticking with dependency on the government or making a deal with the mining corporations had been a Hobson's choice, but the only alternative was to live lightly on the land and try to eke out a living from nonindustrial crafts. In most cases, this dilemma was played out on tribal lands far removed from urban centers, but GRIC had many cities pressing on its border: Phoenix, Ahwatukee, Gilbert, and Chandler to the north, Casa Blanca and Maricopa to the south, and the future Superstitionville to the east. The Akimel O'odham and their Pee Posh neighbors would be making their choices in a fully metropolitan setting.

CHAPTER 8

Delivering the Good

"The scientists here are in the forefront of being conscious about how unsustainable we are. We have a large number of people working on these problems and trying to lay out the analysis and the trade-offs. So we probably have a leg up."

Sharon Harlan, ASU sociologist

Why did I choose to end this book with the Gila River Indian Community's effort to win back its water? Because it is a parable about how democracy and its courts can not only serve but also be served by the quest for sustainability. The GRIC water settlement brought a long struggle for environmental justice to a triumphant conclusion. Delivering justice meant that a large portion of the region's available resources would be sequestered from the growth machine. Instead of supplying a new generation of low-density tract housing, the water could now be used to produce healthy, local food for the area population, and, if nonindustrial agriculture prevailed, the result would be a double win for carbon reduction. Surely, this is how a green polity ought to act, redressing the claims of those who have been aggrieved, and doing it in a way that extends long-term benefits for all.

If all responses to environmental injustice were able to follow suit, it would be a welcome model for moving forward. Even if the Gila River example is unlikely to be replicated in other places, its guiding spirit is a sound one. What if the key to sustainability lies in innovating healthy pathways out of poverty for populations at risk, rather than marketing green gizmos to those who already have many options to choose from? These are not mutually exclusive options, of course, but the lessons I took away from my research convinced me of the pressing need for clear alternatives to the eco-apartheid syndrome that afflicts Phoenix and so many other cities. Building a low-carbon economy by targeting only the LOHAS demographic (Lifestyles of Health and Sustainability, the upmarket segment of 40 million, or 20 percent of consumers, nationally) will end up doing little more than adding a green gloss to patterns of chronic inequality. Likewise, placing all of our faith in clean-tech fixes will cede too much decision making to a closed circle of experts who, regardless of their technical prowess, will have no power to prevent the uneven application of their solutions.[1]

Another reason for ending with the Gila River is that it is a hopeful story in a field that is filled with foreboding and despair. With each new grim bulletin about ecological decline, public impatience with government inaction and corporate obstruction is giving way to a more chronic morbidity about the future. Even if the political obstacles to carbon policymaking were to rapidly dissolve, many have concluded that it may already be too late to take meaningful steps to avert drastic climate change. Better to accept the foreseeable consequences by trying to anticipate, and adapt to, the worst scenarios. Indeed, any sober reading of the IPCC's last

Figure 8.1
Where the Gila River once flowed. Photo by author.

comprehensive appraisal of the problem (the Fourth Assessment Report in 2007) would support this very conclusion.[2] In the course of researching and writing this book, I confess to being sorely tested by this same mentality. Antonio Gramsci's motto—"pessimism of the intellect, optimism of the will"—was never more relevant than to the uncertain domain of climate politics.

While similar in mood to the end-time psychology that has driven so many millennialist religious creeds, the morbidity that chews on our minds is based on precise scientific calculations, not dogma about supernatural occurrences. Nor is it quite like the omnipresent Cold War fear of being vaporized in a thermonuclear attack—nothing so abrupt is on the cards, only a slowly accelerating decline that has long since normalized what an eco-apocalypse feels like. Yet the source of the fatalism—a rise in global temperature—is so novel, in historical terms, that it overshadows perennial human anxieties about shortages in the supply of basic needs. Concern about rapidly approaching mileposts of resource depletion like peak oil, peak water, and peak food is being trumped by the ultimate catalyst of disaster—the irreversible trigger point that climatologists refer to as DAI (Dangerous Anthropogenic Interference). This is commonly recognized as the 2-degree threshold for global warming, or 450 ppm of atmospheric carbon dioxide, although not a few climate scientists have put the critical threshold around the 400 ppm mark, and some activists have gone even lower, pushing for 350 ppm.[3] With carbon levels already at 390 ppm, and with the vessels of international climate policy still stalled in windless doldrums, many thoughtful people now believe that only a catastrophic ecological event can precipitate the sense of urgency required to fill the sails.

Others, like James Lovelock, progenitor of the Gaia theory, have advised that to properly confront the threat of climate change, "it may be necessary to put democracy on hold for a while."[4] This belief, that civil liberties should be suspended until adequate action can be taken, has its advocates, not least among those who favor top-down geo-engineering schemes to manipulate the global climate balance. In the race to decarbonize, it is often assumed that the quickest form of emissions reduction is the best one and that the means will justify the ends. Such attitudes lend themselves to authoritarian measures of the sort entertained by Lovelock. Any solution is worthy of consideration, one might respond, but not if it subverts democratic pathways. After all, the primary reason for climate inaction has not been a failure of democracy, but rather a failure to throw off the stranglehold of fossil power upon democracy.

A more common response can be heard from those who prize their own civil liberties above those of others. They are more inclined to favor some version of the "lifeboat ethics" popularized by Garrett Hardin in 1974, which held that sharing resources more equitably with the world's poor would capsize any effort at ecological stability.[5] After all, Hardin argued, the lifeboats of rich nations only had so much room, and those already onboard were unlikely to give up their places. The warmed-over social Darwinism preached by Hardin (a cofounder of FAIR) has found new acolytes in the fractious debate about global warming, fueling a backlash against the notion that rich nations owe a carbon debt to poor ones, let alone a humanitarian lifeline to swimmers trying to catch up.

The initial trigger for Hardin's lifeboat ethics was concern, among early environmentalists, about the Malthusian specter of runaway population growth. When global rates of growth began to slow in the 1990s, the more unsettling prospect of unchecked cross-border migration was wheeled in as a replacement ogre. In recent years, and in response, "forting up" has become a staple prop of anti-immigrationist sentiment, and it has sharpened the appetite for walling off borders and securing resources for a long hoard. Pseudo-environmentalist arguments, as I discussed in chapter 6, are now regularly enlisted in support of this outlook. The Hardinites at FAIR and allied organizations acknowledge that the lifestyle of citizens in affluent nations is a groaning burden on the world's carrying capacity. But rather than argue for reforming these high-carbon ways, their proposed solution is to prevent immigrants from adopting them, either through mass deportation or by turning the U.S.–Mexican borderlands into a vast military prison.

The more strident practitioners of this kind of greenwashing lay themselves open to charges of nativism, or advocacy for bastioned national fortresses. But heavily guarded resource islands have also been cropping up *within* national borders, as part of what economist Robert Reich once called the "secession of the successful."[6] The rise of the gated community is most often cited as an example of forting up, or visible proof that the well-off are turning their backs on the rest of society by securing a protected enclave for themselves and their goods.[7] But arguably the most stable evidence of hoarding can be found in the statistics of class polarization, for it is there that we can see the long-term impact of efforts on the part of the affluent to repossess and cache resources. This, at least, is one way of interpreting the response to the seminal *Limits to Growth* report issued in 1972. In the four decades since the Club of Rome sounded its loud alarm about unsustainable growth, we have seen a sharp, upward redistribution of wealth and resources in almost all developed or developing countries, but especially in the fast-growth economies.

Not long after the report was issued, the norms of public provision, which had guaranteed a measure of equity in many industrialized countries, fell under attack. Tax reform, fiscal austerity, deregulation and privatization, structural adjustment, the crumbling of secure work, and the general shredding of social welfare dramatically eroded most of the postwar gains for working people, and pushed them underwater. The only compensation on offer was a lottery ticket in the speculative housing market—sparking a highly volatile round of land development, which ended in the worst global recession since the 1930s. In retrospect, it is fair to conclude that the message of *Limits to Growth* was not ignored. It did get through to the elites for whom it was prepared, and they responded by squirreling away whatever resources they could carry off from the commonwealth. Denial is the term commonly used to describe resistance to evidence of climate change and other ecological threats. Yet the cumulative record of this steady pillage suggests the opposite has been occurring.

Much of the plunder was extracted by wielding the "power of market forces." For those who believe that market forces can be put to better ends, the advent of green capitalism has promised a new economic footing in the form of pollution credit markets, carbon taxes and offsets, green-collar investment, ecoconsumerism, and balanced development. Advocates of green capitalism, like Paul Hawken, Jonathon Porritt, and Amory Lovins argue that natural resources are chronically underpriced because ecologically destructive growth is so highly subsidized. Putting a proper price on these resources, they insist, is the best way of preserving them, or, in the case of fossil fuel, of stopping us from using them, and so it is the most effective recipe for more sustainable forms of capitalist growth.[8] Others argue that environmental protection is best ensured by entrepreneurs in the private sector, and not by government action.[9] Critics of these free marketeering views have retorted that capitalist growth of any sort, has shown itself to be hostile to nature, and that green capitalism is just a ruse to expand the reach of profit taking into every small corner of the natural world. Capitalism, after all, must create, or expand into, new markets, or it will die. They argue that the trend toward turning the natural world into tradable commodities should be viewed as a way for capitalism, and not nature, to survive, and only in the short term, because green capitalism will not be able to avoid destroying the commons.[10]

As for the concept of sustainability itself, its widespread embrace by the world's most destructive corporations as a way of boosting shareholder value shows how easily its name can be lent to greenwashing. Thus, we see the likes of Rio Tinto, Ford, Shell, Alcoa, DuPont, Siemens, and Dow Chemical being hailed as ecological stewards whenever they pay homage to the "triple bottom line" of economic, social, and environmental values.

Certainly, there is profit to be harvested from institutionalizing green values. But none of these corporations have offered to factor the degradation of air, water, and soil into their production costs, nor can they really afford to do so. Indeed, it has become all too apparent that everyone is for sustainability, especially when its meaning is spun to suggest that the ecological crisis can be managed by some technical adjustments to business as usual—by some combination of reforms to our personal conduct and that of capitalist institutions.[11]

Ecological economists, a tiny subset of their field, tend to be more exacting in their definition of sustainability. For those who believe the ecological crisis is a direct outcome of capital's exhaustion of nature's storehouse, any form of economic growth that does not bequeath an equivalent stock of nonrenewable resources to the next generation is unsustainable by definition. These resources are viewed as natural capital (as opposed to human-made capital) and their life-support functions are threatened by the ceaseless expansion demanded by capitalist growth.[12] Economists in this camp often appeal to the concept of "throughput" in analyzing whether the energy and raw materials used by any community is extracted and expended at a rate that allows the ecosystem to regenerate. Holding throughput at a steady or constant rate is considered the mark of a sustainable economy, ensuring that the next generation will inherit that equivalent stock of natural capital.[13]

Yet in an era of busy international trade, the effort to measure throughput for any given community is like collecting sand with a fork. The routine importation of goods and resources from far and wide voids any meaningful ties a large city might have to local carrying capacity, and so every metropolis depends on vast amounts of "ghost acreage" elsewhere to feed, clothe, and house residents. In principle, for a city to minimize its throughput, most of the output it discharges would need to be recycled as an input, resulting in a closed loop. But globalization has compromised any tight connection between inputs and outputs. The average food item in the United States travels 1,500 miles, and even more to cities, like Phoenix, that are geographically isolated. With the exception of locally grown produce that makes it into farmers markets or the supermarket distribution system, Greater Phoenix imports almost everything its residents consume: water, energy, manufactured goods, and perishable products. Any calculation of net resource transfers would reveal a huge debt to poorer regions of the world, whose natural resources, further degraded by monocrop agriculture, industrial pollution, land grabs, and deforestation, are utilized to support the household consumption of the populations of Scottsdale, Mesa, or Cave Creek.

For good reasons, the sustainability rankings that U.S. and European cities use to measure their performance shy clear of such calculations.[14] The point of these ranking indexes is to encourage local improvements in environmental quality and efficiency. For example, the mayor's office in Phoenix will take pride in the city's open space preservation, fledgling light rail system, water management policies, and clean-fueled municipal fleet. On the negative side of the ledger, points will be deducted for its poor air quality, simmering urban heat island, parking fundamentalism, and lingering attachment to single-use Euclidean zoning. The outcomes are technical assessments of the record of urban policymakers, but they are also aimed at reflecting and rewarding citizenly virtue. A steady rise in SustainLane's national rankings would buttress Mayor Phil Gordon's 2009 declared intent to make Phoenix "the greenest city in America." It would also attract green-collar investors, tourists, health-seeking residents, and plaudits, in the history books, for his administration.

Readers will note that I have not dismissed this kind of bookkeeping in the preceding pages. Bettering the balance sheet is an important target for activist-residents, green advocates, and sympathetic policymakers. Insofar as formal indicators of progress tend to boost morale and inspire new goals, they are the incremental DNA of urban improvement. Yet it has to be recognized that these checklists conform to managerial norms of measuring sustainability because they are made up of easily quantifiable items: more solar roofs, less airborne particulates; more transit riders, less water use per capita; more housing density, less golf courses. Greening the world, from this standpoint, suggests that the ecological crisis can be fixed by making slight technical adjustments to people's habits and interactions with their daily environments. When sustainability is defined by a set of metrics, it reflects a purely physical understanding of how societies strive to be ecologically resilient. By contrast, there are no indexes for measuring environmental justice, no indicators for judging equity of access to the green life, and no technical quantum for assessing the social sustainability of a population. The vogue for green governance by the numbers is a recipe for managing, rather than correcting, inequality.

In the course of researching this book, I kept coming across evidence that the key to addressing biophysical damage and eco-depletion lies as much in the drive for equity as in the kinds of technical improvements that show up in the manager's metrics. Confronted with resource limits, can individuals and communities renounce hoarding and practice mutual aid? Can the well-provisioned respond in kind to the environmentalist claims of the poor? Will the risk levels of the most vulnerable populations—the canaries in the mine—be accepted as the baseline for formulating green reforms and policymaking? These are questions of social character, and I found steady proof of their importance in the testimony of my interviewees. In each of the problem areas I chose to investigate, it was apparent that a large part of the regional challenge lay in building cross-town cooperation and ensuring access and inclusion for populations who are habitually ignored by the green marketing of the private sector and by the "green city" campaigning of City Hall. Time after time, Phoenix turned out to be a textbook illustration of the need to adapt the tenets of environmental justice as the lead principle of green conduct.

The most obvious example was the distribution of pollution hazards, which shows a long-standing pattern of burden loaded against low-income neighborhoods dominated by minorities. Communities treated as dumping grounds for waste disposal and hazardous industry are a world apart from those with access to fresh air, open space, and clean water. There is nothing sustainable in the long run about one population living the green American dream while, across town, another is still trapped in poverty and pestilence. Either the green wave has to lift all boats, or else those who can afford a berth in the lifeboat will come to believe that Hardin's dismal scenario is not only logical but also ethical. The case studies of South Phoenix, Maryvale, East Phoenix, and Lone Butte, which I documented in chapter 4, showed that committed individuals and their community-based organizations could make small but significant, dents in the patterns of discrimination, and, in doing so, could raise the bar on pollution prevention for everyone. Similar lessons about rectifying inequities are drawn, in other chapters, from the top priorities on the region's sustainability roster—urban growth management, water conservation, downtown revitalization, renewable energy, economic recovery, and immigration policy.

As residents of the fastest-growing American metropolis in the postwar decades, Phoenicians' concerns about the environmental costs of urban sprawl multiplied. Typically, these anxieties revolved around the toll on nonrenewable water supplies, the impact on air quality of commuting patterns, and encroachment on fragile desert ecosystems. By contrast, the steady transfer of resources, amenities, and wealth away from the center city to the suburbs and satellite cities of Greater Phoenix drew much less attention as environmental concerns. Planning, taxation, and energy policies that favored low-density suburban life were tilted against the needs and aspirations of inner-city residents whose neighborhoods are now "food deserts," far removed from decent employment and amenity centers. Green modifications to master-planned communities on the urban fringe will not remedy the indifference. The construction of higher-density,

New Urbanist-style developments like Verrado, or the yet unbuilt Mesa Proving Grounds and Superstition Vistas will do little to reduce the region's carbon footprint and are likely to enlarge it if they give a new lease of life to the growth machine. By contrast, a concerted program of equity-minded green investment in the myriad vacant lots that dot central urban areas would transform and humanize the character of the metropolis.

For most urban planners and quality-of-life advocates, downtown revitalization is the preferred antidote to sprawl, and it has not bypassed Phoenix. In the battle over downtown that I document in chapter 3, artist communities were able to complicate the role they usually play in other cities as involuntary agents of gentrification. Contending with developers bent on refurbishing downtown for a new money class, artist activists have pushed for municipal policies that favor a "sustainable downtown," with a strong emphasis on income diversity, affordable housing, mixed-use zoning, and fine-grain planning. But their ability to get heard at City Hall is not matched by the low-income residents of downtown areas, many of whom are being chased out of town by the crackdown on immigrants. Unless their needs are adopted as priorities, the resulting destabilization of their neighborhoods will leave residual residents almost as vulnerable as the victims of subprime lending, who are stranded in the foreclosure belts of the inner and outer suburban rings.

Vigilance about water scarcity is inherent to the Western lifestyle, and Central Arizona's growth machine depends on successful efforts to secure supplies from remote sources. With the Upper Colorado River in the twelfth year of a serious drought, and with Phoenix in the dead center of U.S. climate warming, the cost of bringing in the next bucket of water is certain to escalate. If and when water shortages begin to show up, the capacity of the region's communities to share their supplies with each other will be a telling test of resilience and mutual aid. The Hohokam irrigation civilization that subsisted in the Phoenix Basin for a millennium faced a similar test of regional cooperation, and ultimately failed. All prudent estimates suggest that it is not too late to discourage, through taxation and other kinds of pricing, the growth of populations on the urban periphery who will be most vulnerable to water shortages.

Turning Central Arizona into a center for solar production promises to harness the state's most abundant natural resource, while hopes of a recovery for the economy, currently stymied by an overreliance on the homebuilding industry, may hinge on the ability to create green-collar jobs that pay a living wage. Yet the extremist politics of the state legislature and the monopolistic might of the major utility companies stand in the way. Efforts to jump-start the renewable manufacturing sector may not have comprehensive government support at a time when it is most needed. No less fragile is the bold quota requirement for distributed energy generation set by the state's utility commission. Yet the mechanism for attaining that quota is flawed. Independent household production has broad democratic appeal, but local citizen control over clean-energy provision will only come about by dismantling the monopoly of the utilities, along with their funding structure for rooftop generation—currently a form of regressive taxation on renters and poorer homeowners.

The last object of my investigations—immigration policy—is the one that has sparked the most corrosive public sentiment. Arizona's harsh anti-immigration laws and Maricopa County's brutal policing are spurred by the anxiety of Anglos about losing demographic and political dominance. But these inhospitable responses are also shaped by stoked-up fears about population pressure on scarce resources. With the volume of environmental refugees on the rise, it can be concluded that migration to Central Arizona is, in part, already a side effect of the region's hydrocarbon emissions, and that border-crossers should have a legitimate claim on sanctuary as a result. Yet nativists seem hell-bent on turning the state into the kind of exclusion zone that is distinctive of resource hoarding. As for the state's Latinos, with or without papers, the trauma and stigma of criminalization will endure for generations unless a more humanitarian, and genuinely cross-cultural, accord emerges out of the movement for immigrants' rights.

In each of these sectors of green attention outlined above, I found activists, advocates, and practitioners intent on changing the rules and patterns of urban life. Even those who were most preoccupied with their own neighborhoods had an eye on the citywide or regional consequence of their ideas and actions. Most of them took it for granted that their cities were a proving ground of sustainability and were quick to accept that successful or model outcomes in their own backyard might have an impact well beyond the Southwest. Some had even come to share the belief that Metro Phoenix was an exemplar of sorts, if only because the challenges faced by a growth-dependent desert metropolis seemed particularly insurmountable. They were certainly right that cities are on the front line. After all, 35 to 45 percent of the world's carbon emissions come from cooling or heating cities, and 35 percent to 40 percent more from urban industry and transportation.[15] As for Phoenix's model status, the evidence collected in this book may help to clarify whether it deserves that kind of attention.

If so, it will be quite a different status than the one assigned by the authors of the 1979 *Arizona Tomorrow* report commissioned from the Hudson Institute. In that document, based on predictions about the nature of metropolitan life in the year 2012, the growth of Phoenix was seen as a happy "precursor of post-industrial America." Moreover, it was assumed that the luckiest populations in the "advanced capitalist nations worldwide" were going to live the same way. "We are not claiming that the Arizona lifestyle is *the* lifestyle of the future," the authors asserted. "We are saying it is *a* lifestyle of the future, and that it is one of the first manifestations, or precursors, of a national and international trend of a post-industrial marriage between an appealing environment and new technology where lifestyle considerations are the central organizing principle around which society is organized."[16] If Phoenix today is still a precursor of the future, it is for quite different reasons. In the intervening decades, it has been all but concluded that the ecological costs of the Arizona lifestyle are far too high. Any homegrown effort to slice those costs will be a gift to populations all over the globe who strain to supply and service the practitioners of that high-carbon lifestyle, not only in the Sunbelt of the United States but also among the elites of their own countries.

Jonathan Fink, academic leader at ASU's Global Institute of Sustainability, reported that Metro Phoenix has "the largest number of federally funded research programs designed to help us understand how cities can grow sustainably."[17] Indeed, ASU is building its new research identity around the claim that the region is "sustainability's test bed," capable of generating solutions that can be applied elsewhere, and especially to fast-growth, semiarid cities where much of the world's population is increasingly concentrated. If they prove exportable, these applications might be one small way for an American metropolis like Phoenix to repay some of the debt incurred by its disproportionate use of resources and its large share of greenhouse gas emissions—many times greater than its counterparts in poorer countries. Cost-effective remedies for mitigating heat and pollution, conserving water and wildlife, and generating clean energy are all plausible candidates for export.

But truly sustainable solutions are never applied in a social vacuum, nor do they emerge from one. The idea behind technology transfer—that practical applications can be developed in one society and transplanted effectively to another—is a naive one, and the historical record of such transfers shows that they are generally used to benefit elites disproportionately. The Green Revolution of the postwar period, aimed at addressing Third World hunger, is often cited as a striking example. The transfer of high-yield seed technologies to countries like India did, by most measures, boost grain harvests. But the accompanying introduction of industrial agriculture also resulted in the displacement of tens of millions of small farmers, the reduction of crop biodiversity, and the destruction of biosystems through the new technological dependence on pesticides, chemical fertilizers, and controlled irrigation. Without a concomitant change in social distribution, the technology transfers did little to ease the structural causes of hunger, and ended up increasing hydrocarbon emissions. Cut off from the traditions of self-sufficient farming, the poor had less access to land resources, and, in most cases, to purchasing power than they did before.[18] The latest version of this initiative, the African-Led Green Revolution (AGRA), is based on the mass introduction of genetically modified seeds, and many fear it will generate similar results on the African continent as the earlier model did in India.[19]

One can well imagine a similar fate befalling solutions for sustainable urbanism. If these practices are not directed by and toward principles of equity, then they will almost certainly end up reinforcing patterns of eco-apartheid. Private investment, consumer niche marketing, and government policies favored by moneyed voters may well succeed in nurturing showpiece pockets of green living, but these oases will coexist with human and natural sacrifice zones on the other side of the tracks. Policing and zoning will minimize the visual and sensory shock flung up by the disparity between the two, but it will be more and more difficult to hide the mounting damage to life, land, and the atmosphere. Large cities are the first, and possibly the last, places where green action can make an appreciable difference. But they also harbor a staggering range of inequalities and will continue to do so if the greenest innovations are simply additions to the range of buys already available to affluent populations, like the environmental equivalent of new apps for our iPhones. That is why the road ahead for Phoenix, and for cities like it, does not lie simply in acting out of concern for "our children and grandchildren"—as it is so often phrased. To be on the right path we should also take directions from the needs and claims of today's most vulnerable and affected populations.

NOTES

INTRODUCTION

1. Environment Arizona, *Too Much Pollution: State and National Trends in Global Warming Pollution from 1990 to 2007* (Phoenix, November 2009), accessible online at <http://cdn.publicinterestnetwork.org/assets/267985d0d7ad6641a3 c383fd91c49b19/Too-Much-Pollution-AZ.pdf>.
2. Metro Phoenix ranked 11th out of the 25 worst metro areas in the American Lung Association's 2010 study of ozone pollution, but number one in rankings for dust pollution. The Arizona Department of Environmental Quality claimed that the results were skewed by off-the-scale readings from a single agricultural monitor in a dust-beset area of Pinal County. Shaun McKinnon, "Valley Has Worst Dust Pollution in U.S.," *Arizona Republic* (April 28, 2010).
3. Tony Davis, "Expert: AZ in Climate-Change Bull's-Eye," *Arizona Daily Star* (February 18, 2009). For a snapshot of the impact of climate change on the Southwest, see Jonathan Overpeck and Brad Udall, "Dry Times Ahead," *Science* 328 (2010), 1642–1643.
4. See Rick Perlstein, *Before the Storm: Barry Goldwater and the Unmaking of the American Consensus* (New York: Hill & Wang, 2001).
5. Estimates are from the Global Carbon Project, at <http://www.globalcarbonproject.org/>.
6. For a sample document, see The Copenhagen Diagnosis, assembled by a team of international researchers, accessible online at <http://www.copenhagendiagnosis.org/>. The Fourth Assessment of the Intergovernmental Panel on Climate Change (2007) can be found at <http://www.ipcc.ch/publications_and_data/publications_and_data_reports.shtml#1>.
7. The Copenhagen Climate Communiqué, accessible at <http://www.c40cities.org/news/news-20091215.jsp>. See also the work of the Urban Climate Change Research Network (UCCRN), at <http://www.uccrn.org>.
8. Cited in Peter Newman, Timothy Beatley, and Heather Boyer, *Resilient Cities: Responding to Peak Oil and Climate Change* (Washington, D.C.: Island Press, 2009), 4.
9. Warren Susman, *Culture as History: The Transformation of American Society in the Twentieth Century* (New York: Pantheon, 1984), 242–243.

10. M. Christine Boyer, *Dreaming the Rational City: The Myth of American City Planning* (Cambridge, Mass.: MIT Press, 1983).

11. Andres Duany, Elizabeth Plater-Zyberk, and Jeff Speck, *Suburban Nation: The Rise of Sprawl and the Decline of the American Dream* (New York: North Point Press, 2001); James Howard Kunstler, *The Long Emergency: Surviving the Converging Catastrophes of the Twenty-First Century* (New York: Atlantic Monthly Press, 2005); *The Geography of Nowhere: The Rise and Decline of America's Man-Made Landscape* (New York: Simon and Schuster, 1993).

12. "Experts Discuss Phoenix's Heat Island Effect," *ASU News Now* (December 18, 2009), accessible at <http://asunews.asu.edu/20091218_urban_heat>. Anthony Brazel, "Urban Heat Island Affects Phoenix All Year-Round," *Arizona Republic* (September 22, 2007).

13. William Fulton, Rolf Pendall, Mai Nguyen, and Alicia Harrison, *Who Sprawls Most? How Growth Patterns Differ Across the U.S.* (Washington, D.C.: Brookings Institution, Center for Urban and Metropolitan Policy, July 2001).

14. Edward Abbey, *Desert Solitaire: A Season in the Wilderness* (New York: McGraw Hill, 1968), 126.

15. Rebecca Solnit, "Dry Lands," review of James Lawrence Powell, *Dead Pool: Lake Powell, Global Warming and the Future of Water in the West*, *London Review of Books* 31, 23 (December 2009). In his bleak essay, "A Reflection on Cities of the Future," moralist James Kunstler predicted the abandonment of many U.S. cities: "In some it will be a lot worse. Phoenix, Tucson, and Las Vegas will just dry up and blow away, since local agriculture will not be possible, and they will be afflicted with severe water problems on top of all the other problems growing out of energy scarcity and an extreme car-dependent development pattern." See <http://www.kunstler.com/mags_cities_of_the_future.html>. Gary Nabhan, the esteemed Northern Arizona food advocate, calls for a drastic downsizing and re-engineering of the metropolis in "Isn't It Time to Rationally Plan the Dismantling of Metro Phoenix?" accessible at <http://garynabhan.com/i/archives/362>.

16. In a remarkable essay, Mike Davis analyzes the efforts of some writers to imagine the reclamation of devastated cities by wildlife and vegetation. "Dead Cities: A Natural History," in *Dead Cities and Other Tales* (New York: New Press, 2002), 361–400.

17. Max Page, *The City's End: Two Centuries of Fantasies, Fears, and Premonitions of New York's Destruction* (New Haven: Yale University Press, 2008).

18. Testimony of Roger Revelle, U.S. Congress, House 84 H1526-5, Committee on Appropriations, Hearings on Second Supplemental Appropriation Bill (1956), 467.

19. Roger Revelle, "The Role of the Oceans," *Saturday Review* (May 7, 1966), 41.

20. See Jeff Goodell, *How to Cool the Planet: Geoengineering and the Audacious Quest to Fix Earth's Climate* (New York: Houghton Mifflin Harcourt, 2010); and Eli Kintisch, *Hack the Planet: Science's Best Hope—or Worst Nightmare—for Averting Climate Catastrophe* (Hoboken, N.J.: Wiley, 2010); James Rodger Fleming, *Fixing the Sky: The Checkered History of Weather and Climate Control* (New York: Columbia University Press, 2010).

21. The scholarly literature on urban sustainability includes Kent Portney, *Taking Sustainable Cities Seriously: Economic Development, the Environment, and Quality of Life in American Cities* (Cambridge, Mass.: MIT Press, 2003); Peter Newman, Heather Boyer, and Timothy Beatley, *Resilient Cities*; Joan Fitzgerald, *Emerald Cities: Urban Sustainability and Economic Development* (New York: Oxford University Press, 2010); Eugenie Birch and Susan Wachter, eds., *Growing Greener*

Cities: Urban Sustainability in the Twenty-First Century (Philadelphia: University of Pennsylvania Press, 2008); Peter Newman and Isabella Jennings, *Cities as Sustainable Ecosystems: Principles and Practices* (Washington, D.C.: Island Press, 2008); Gwendolyn Hallsmith, *The Key to Sustainable Cities: Meeting Human Needs, Transforming Community Systems* (Philadelphia: New Society, 2003); Douglas Farr, *Sustainable Urbanism: Urban Design with Nature* (Hoboken, N.J.: Wiley, 2008); Scott Kellogg (with Stacy Pettigrew), *Toolbox for Sustainable City Living* (Boston: South End Press, 2008); and Matthew Kahn, *Green Cities: Urban Growth and the Environment* (Washington, D.C.: Brookings Institution Press 2006).

22. Of the many sustainability studies to come out of ASU, two might be noted here. From 1997, Charles Redman and Nancy Grimm, who helped launch ASU's new Global Institute of Sustainability, have been directing a long-term study of changes in the urban ecology of Central Arizona (see <http://caplter.asu.edu>). In 2003, an interdisciplinary team of ASU academics and policy officials compiled a wealth of useful data and analysis in the *Greater Phoenix 2100 Regional Atlas: A Preview of the Region's 50-Year Future* (Tempe: Arizona University Press, 2003).

23. Paul Bracken (with contributions from Herman Kahn), *Arizona Tomorrow: A Precursor of Post-Industrial America* (Croton-on-Hudson, N.Y.: Hudson Institute, May 1979), 4. See Thomas Sheridan's useful analysis of the report in "Arizona: The Political Ecology of a Desert State," *Journal of Political Ecology* 2 (1995), 41–57.

CHAPTER 1

1. Craig Childs, "For Phoenix, as for Hohokams, Rise Is Just Like the Fall," first published in *High Country News* (May 27, 2007).

2. Among the scholarly studies, the foundational work is Joseph Tainter, *The Collapse of Complex Societies* (Cambridge: Cambridge University Press, 1990). Others include Norman Yoffee and George Cowgill, eds., *The Collapse of Ancient States* (Tucson: University of Arizona Press, 1998); Charles Redman, *Human Impact on Ancient Environments* (Tucson: University of Arizona Press, 1999); and Brian Fagan, *Floods, Famines, and Emperors: El Niño and the Fate of Civilizations* (New York: Basic Books, 1999).

   More recent titles, influenced by fears about the impact of climate change, include Martin Rees, *Our Final Hour: A Scientist's Warning* (New York: Basic Books, 2003); James Lovelock, *The Revenge of Gaia* (New York: Basic Books, 2006) and *The Vanishing Face of Gaia: A Final Warning* (New York: Basic Books, 2009); Eugene Linden, *Winds of Change: Climate, Weather and the Destruction of Civilization* (New York: Simon and Schuster, 2006); Ronald Wright, *A Short History of Progress* (New York: Carroll and Graf, 2005); John Leslie, *The End of the World: The Science and Ethics of Human Extinction* (New York: Routledge, 1996); Shierry Weber Nicholsen, *The Love of Nature and the End of the World* (Cambridge, Mass.: MIT Press, 2002); Mayer Hillman, *The Suicidal Planet* (New York: Saint Martin's Press, 2007); Gwynne Dyer, *Climate Wars: The Fight for Survival as the World Overheats* (Oxford: Oneworld, 2010); Heidi Cullen, *The Weather of the Future: Heat Waves, Extreme Storms, and Other Scenes from a Climate-Changed Planet* (New York: HarperCollins, 2010); Peter Ward, *The Flooded Earth: Our Future in a World without Ice Caps* (New York: Basic Books, 2010); Dianne Dumanoski, *The End of the Long Summer: Why We Must Remake Our Civilization to Survive on a Volatile Earth* (New York: Crown, 2009); Mark Lynas, *Six Degrees: Our Future on a Hotter Planet* (Washington, D.C.: National

Geographic, 2008); David Orr, *Down to the Wire: Confronting Climate Collapse* (New York: Oxford University Press, 2009); James Hansen, *Storms of My Grandchildren: The Truth about the Coming Climate Catastrophe and Our Last Chance to Save Humanity* (New York: Bloomsbury, 2009); Mark Hertsgaard, *Hot: Living Through the Next Fifty Years on Earth* (New York: Houghton Mifflin Harcourt, 2011); Fred Pearce, *The Last Generation: How Nature Will Take Revenge for Climate Change* (London: Eden Project Books, 2007) and *With Speed and Violence: Why Scientists Fear Tipping Points in Climate Change* (Boston: Beacon Press, 2007).

3. Jared Diamond, *Collapse: How Societies Choose to Fail or Succeed* (New York: Viking, 2004). Post-apocalyptic films that followed *The Day After Tomorrow* include *Happy Feet* (2006), *Ice Age: The Meltdown* (2006), *Wall-E* (2008), the remake of *The Day the Earth Stood Still* (2008), *9* (2009), *2012* (2009), *The Road* (2009), *Avatar* (2009), and *The Book of Eli* (2010).

4. This term is used by Ronald Bailey in *Ecoscam: The False Prophets of Ecological Apocalypse* (New York: St. Martin's Press, 1993).

5. Rob Nixon, *Slow Violence and the Environmentalism of the Poor* (Cambridge, Mass.: Harvard University Press, 2011).

6. In making this very argument, Frederick Buell points out that we are "living within a time when significant biospheric legacies that have been part of human beings' practical, psychological, and spiritual lives since their beginning as a species are disappearing." *From Apocalypse to Way of Life: Environmental Crisis in the American Century* (New York: Routledge, 2004), 78.

7. Rebecca Solnit, *A Paradise Built in Hell: The Extraordinary Communities That Arise in Disaster* (New York: Viking, 2009), 3. Similar claims for camaraderie have been made about soldiership, and, of course, about acts of political solidarity. For an example of the latter, see David Harvie, Keir Milburn, Ben Trott, and David Watts, eds., *Shut Them Down! The Global G8, Gleneagles 2005 and the Movement of Movements* (New York: Autonomedia, 2006).

8. David Doyel, "Irrigation, Production, and Power in Phoenix Basin Hohokam Society," 85–89; and John Ravesloot, "Changing Views of Snaketown in a Larger Landscape," 91–98, in Suzanne and Paul Fish, eds., *The Hohokam Millennium* (Santa Fe, N. Mex.: School for Advanced Research Press, 2007).

9. Todd Bostwick, *Under the Runways: Archaeology of Sky Harbor International Airport* (Phoenix: Pueblo Grande Museum, 2008).

10. The data from these investigations is analyzed in David Abbott, ed., *Centuries of Decline During the Hohokam Classic Period at Pueblo Grande* (Tucson: University of Arizona Press, 2003).

11. Center for Desert Archaeology, "Immigration and Population Collapse in the Southern Southwest," *Archaeology Southwest* 22, 4 (Fall 2008). For further research of the Coalescent Communities Project, see <http://www.cdarc.org/what-we-do/current-projects/migration-dynamics/coalescence-and-diaspora/project-history-the-coalescent-communities-project/>.

12. See Emil Haury, *The Hohokam, Desert Farmers and Craftsmen: Excavations at Snaketown 1964–1965* (Tucson: University of Arizona Press, 1976). In the postwar years, this interpretation took on Cold War overtones with Julian Hayden's focus on defensive fortifications and military struggle in the region. *Excavations, 1940, at University Indian Ruin* (Tucson: Southwestern Monuments Association, 1957).

13. Charles Redman et al., "Group Report: Millennial Perspectives on the Dynamic Interaction of Climate, People, and Resources," in Robert Costanza, Lisa J. Graumlich, and Will Steffen, eds., *Sustainability or Collapse? An Integrated History and Future of People on Earth* (Cambridge, Mass.: MIT Press, 2007), 115–150.

14. Glenn Schwartz and John Nichols, eds., *After Collapse: The Regeneration of Complex Societies* (Tucson: University of Arizona Press, 2006); Patricia McAnany and Norman Yoffee, eds., *Questioning Collapse: Human Resilience, Ecological Vulnerability, and the Aftermath of Empire* (New York: Cambridge University Press, 2009).

15. For a diverting account of the modern culture of the canals, see the last chapter of Bruce Berger's *There Was a River: Essays on the Southwest* (Tucson: University of Arizona Press, 1994).

16. Richard Hofstadter, *The Age of Reform: From Bryan to F.D.R.* (New York: Knopf, 1955), 54. Also see the classic essay by Paul Wallace Gates, "The Role of the Land Speculator in Western Development," *Pennsylvania Magazine of History and Biography* 66 (July 1942): 314–333.

17. Marc Reisner, *Cadillac Desert: The American West and Its Disappearing Water* (New York: Viking, 1986), 44.

18. Thomas Sheridan, *Landscapes of Fraud: Mission Tumacácori, the Baca Float, and the Betrayal of the O'odham* (Tucson: University of Arizona Press, 2006), 125.

19. Patricia Nelson Limerick suggestively follows out this gambling motif in *Desert Passages: Encounters with the American Deserts* (Albuquerque: University of New Mexico Press, 1985).

20. See the classic account by Wallace Stegner, *Beyond the Hundredth Meridian: John Wesley Powell and the Second Opening of the West* (Boston: Houghton Mifflin, 1954).

21. Grady Gammage, Jr., *Phoenix in Perspective: Reflections on Developing the Desert* (Tempe, Ariz.: Herberger Center for Design, ASU, 1999), 22.

22. Donald Worster, drawing on the theories of Karl Wittfogel, is the primary exponent of the hydraulic West, in *Rivers of Empire: Water, Aridity, and the Growth of the American West* (New York: Pantheon Books, 1985).

23. William Ellsworth Smythe, *Conquest of Arid America* (New York: Harper & Brothers Publishers, 1900).

24. Hofstadter, "The Agrarian Myth and Commercial Realities," in *The Age of Reform*, 23–59.

25. Constance Perin develops this analysis persuasively in *Everything in Its Place: Social Order and Land Use in America* (Princeton: Princeton University Press, 1977). For an updated account of how that mentality fueled the long housing boom in the 1990s and 2000s, see Alyssa Katz, *Our Lot: How Real Estate Came to Own Us* (New York: Bloomsbury, 2009).

26. Rick Perlstein, *Before the Storm: Barry Goldwater and the Unmaking of the American Consensus* (New York: Hill & Wang, 2009), 19.

27. See Janine Schipper, *Disappearing Desert: The Growth of Phoenix and the Culture of Sprawl* (Norman: University of Oklahoma Press, 2008).

28. Charles Redman and Ann Kinzig, "Water Can Flow Uphill," in Charles Redman and David Foster, eds., *Agrarian Landscapes in Transition: Comparisons of Long-Term Ecological and Cultural Change* (New York: Oxford University Press, 2008), 238–271.

29. Bradford Luckingham, *Phoenix: The History of a Southwestern Metropolis* (Tucson: University of Arizona Press, 1989), 74.

30. Richard Seager et al., "Model Projections of an Imminent Transition to a More Arid Climate in Southwestern North America," *Science* 316, 5828 (May 25, 2007): 1181–1184. The Global Change Research Program forecast can be found online at <http://www.globalchange.gov/publications/reports/scientific-assessments/us-impacts/full-report/regional-climate-change-impacts/southwest>.

31. Henry Brean, "Study Gives 50–50 Odds Lake Mead Will Dry Up by 2021," *Las Vegas Review-Journal* (February 13, 2008).

32. Tony Davis, "Tucson's Source of Water Runs Low," *Arizona Daily Star* (March 4, 2010), quoting Tom McAnn, CAP's assistant general manager for operations, planning, and engineering.

33. Juliette Jowit, "Experts Call for Hike in Global Water Price," *The Guardian* (April 27, 2010).

34. According to an April 2010 survey by Circle of Blue, a family of four using approximately 100 gallons of water per day pays about $34 per month in Phoenix, where average daily per capita residential use is 115 gallons per day. The equivalent bill in Seattle is $72.78, and residential use per capita is 52 gallons per day. *The Price of Water: A Comparison of Water Rates, Usage in 30 U.S. Cities*, accessible online at <http://www.circleofblue.org/waternews/2010/world/the-price-of-water-a-comparison-of-water-rates-usage-in-30-u-s-cities/>.

35. The 2000 Report of the World Commission on Dams can be found at <http://www.dams.org/report/>. See also Patrick McCully, *Silenced Rivers: The Ecology and Politics of Large Dams* (London: Zed Books, 2001); Thayer Scudder, *The Future of Large Dams: Dealing with Social, Environmental, Institutional and Political Costs* (London: Earthscan, 2005); Arundhati Roy, *The Cost of Living* (New York: Modern Library, 1999).

36. Lawrence MacDonnell, *From Reclamation to Sustainability: Water, Agriculture, and the Environment in the American West* (Boulder: University of Colorado Press, 1999).

37. Donald Worster, *Under Western Skies: Nature and History in the American West* (Oxford: Oxford University Press, 1992), 56.

38. Thomas Sheridan, "The Big Canal: The Political Ecology of the Central Arizona Project," in John Donahue and Barbara Rose Johnston, eds., *Water, Culture, and Power: Local Struggles in a Global Context* (Washington, D.C.: Island Press, 1998), 167.

39. For an account of the role of water supply in the urban growth of Central Arizona, see Douglas Kupel, *Fuel for Growth: Water and Arizona's Urban Environment* (Tucson: University of Arizona Press, 2003).

40. Reisner, *Cadillac Desert*, 303, 296.

41. Shaun McKinnon, "For Parched State, Wet Winter Means Quenched Thirst," *Arizona Republic* (March 17, 2010); "Lake Mead at 54-Year Low, Stirring Rationing Fear," *Arizona Republic* (August 12, 2010). By the end of 2010, the state was proposing to forego a portion of its 2011 CAP allocation, destined for underground water storage, in order to forestall the further depletion of Lake Mead down to the trigger level for reductions. Shaun McKinnon, "Arizona Drought Prompts Unusual Colorado River Water Proposal," *Arizona Republic* (December 26, 2010). A strong La Niña in the winter months increased the

snowpack in the Upper Basin and sent higher than average flows of water into the Colorado, easing the threat of rationing for the time being. Shaun McKinnon, "Lake Mead Replenished by Snowfall,"*Arizona Republic* (April 19, 2011).

42. Jim Holway, Peter Newell, and Terri Sue Rossi, "Water and Growth: Future Water Supplies for Central Arizona," paper presented at *Water and Growth: Workshop on Future Water Supplies for Central Arizona* (Global Institute of Sustainability, ASU, June 2006).

43. Shaun McKinnon "Tighter, Costlier Water Shifting Focus to Curbing Demand," *Arizona Republic* (December 27, 2009).

44. Paul Hirt, Annie Gustafson, and Kelli Larson, "The Mirage in the Valley of the Sun," *Environmental History* 13, 3 (July 2008): 482–514.

45. Patricia Gober, *Metropolitan Phoenix: Place Making and Community Building in the Desert* (Philadelphia: University of Pennsylvania Press, 2006), 206.

46. See the 2003 Smart Water report of Western Resource Advocates, "A Comparative Study of Urban Water Use Efficiency Across the Southwest," accessible online at <http://www.westernresourceadvocates.org/water/smartwater.php>.

47. Karen Smith, *The Magnificent Experiment: Building the Salt River Reclamation Project, 1890–1917* (Tucson: University of Arizona Press, 1986).

48. Maude Barlow and Tony Clarke, *Blue Gold: The Fight to Stop Corporate Theft of the World's Water* (New York: New Press, 2002). In particular, see Oscar Olivera and Tom Lewis's account of the fight to prevent privatization of the Cochabamba water supply by Aguas del Tunari, a subsidiary of U.S.-based Bechtel in *Cochabamba!: Water War in Bolivia* (Boston: South End Press, 2008).

49. Western states adopted prior appropriation as a way to maximize a scarce resource and encourage settlement, though some have claimed that its origins were antimonopolistic, and intended to thwart would-be speculators from cornering resources. See Sandi Zellmer and Jessica Harder's useful overview, "Water as Property" (The Water Center, University of Nebraska-Lincoln, 2006), accessible online at <http://digitalcommons.unl.edu/watercenterpubs/2>. For a historical survey, see Donald Pisani, *Water, Land, and Law in the West: The Limits of Public Policy, 1850–1920* (Lawrence: University Press of Kansas, 1996).

50. Scholars of water policy issued an influential critique in "America's Waters: A New Era of Sustainability; Report of the Long's Peak Working Group on National Water Policy," *Environmental Law* 24 (1994). See also Sarah F. Bates, David H. Getches, Lawrence MacDonnell, and Charles F. Wilkinson, *Searching Out the Headwaters: Change and Rediscovery in Western Water Policy* (Washington, D.C.: Island Press, 1993); Charles Wilkinson, *Crossing the Next Meridian: Land, Water, and the Future of the West* (Washington, D.C.: Island Press; 1993); Marc Reisner and Sarah Bates, *Overtapped Oasis: Reform or Revolution for Western Water* ((Washington, D.C.: Island Press, 1990); and Robert Glennon, *Unquenchable: America's Water Crisis and What to Do About It* (Washington, D.C.: Island Press, 2009).

51. For its obituary, see Charles Wilkinson, "Prior Appropriation 1848–1991," *Environmental Law* 21 (1991). For its afterlife, see Gregory Hobbs, Jr., "Priority: The Most Misunderstood Stick in the Bundle," *Environmental Law* 37 (2002).

52. Jon Talton, "Water and Arizona's Future," *Rogue Columnist* blog, (July 19, 2010), at <http://roguecolumnist.typepad.com>.

53. James Lawrence Powell, *Dead Pool: Lake Powell, Global Warming, and the Future of Water in the West* (Berkeley: University of California Press, 2009), 239–240.

CHAPTER 2

1. Robert Collins, *More: The Politics of Economic Growth in Postwar America* (New York: Oxford University Press, 2000); Richard Douthwaite, *The Growth Illusion: How Economic Growth Has Enriched the Few, Impoverished the Many and Endangered the Planet* (Dartington, Devon: Resurgence Books, 1992); Clive Hamilton, *Growth Fetish* (Crow's Nest, Australia: Allen & Unwin, 2003).
2. See Alan Brinkley's account of the rise of growth liberalism in *The End of Reform: New Deal Liberalism in Recession and War* (New York: Knopf, 1995).
3. Dennis Meadows, "Evaluating Past Forecasts: Reflections on One Critique of the Limits to Growth," in Robert Costanza, Lisa Graumlich, and Will Steffen, eds., *Sustainability or Collapse? An Integrated History and Future of People on Earth* (Cambridge, Mass.: MIT Press, 2007), 405, 407.
4. Andre Gortz expands on the irrationality of the GDP in *ecologica,* trans. Chris Turner (London: Seagull Books, 2010).
5. Harvey Molotch, "The City as a Growth Machine," *American Journal of Sociology* 82 (1976), 309–332.
6. Rob Melnick, ed., *Urban Growth in Arizona* (Phoenix: Morrison Institute for Public Policy, ASU, 1988). "Most urban planners and elected city officials like to see high-density, multi-use, infill-type developments. Many Arizonans want single-family homes with space for pools, barbecues, and fences. Local master plans need to reconcile this contradiction" (p. xxxii).
7. Pam Stevenson, "Interview with Grady Gammage, Jr." *CAP Oral History Project,* 7, accessible online at <http://www.cap-az.com/includes/docs/oral/Interview%20 with%20Grady%20Gammage%20final.pdf>.
8. Grady Gammage, Jr., *Phoenix in Perspective* (Tempe, Ariz.: Herberger Center for Design, 2003), 148.
9. Ibid., 79.
10. Doug MacEachern, "A Strategy to Grow Jobs," *Arizona Republic* (January 31, 2010). Ruth Simon and James Hagerty, "One in Four Borrowers Is Underwater," *Wall Street Journal* (November 24, 2009).
11. Bob Christie, "Arizona Sets Another Foreclosure Record in 2010," *Arizona Republic* (December 31, 2010).
12. Daniel González, "Questions Mount Over Drop in Illegal Immigrant Population," *Arizona Republic* (February 21, 2010).
13. Jonathan Laing, "Phoenix Descending: Is Boomtown U.S.A. Going Bust?" *Barron's* (December 19, 1988).
14. According to Ken Silverstein, Brewer also considered selling off "most of the state's prisons, including maximum-security units and death row." "Tea Party in the Sonora: For the Future of G.O.P. Governance, Look to Arizona," *Harper's Magazine* (July 2010), 35–42.
15. Peter Wiley and Robert Gottlieb, *Empires in the Sun: The Rise of the New American West* (Tucson: University of Arizona, 1985).
16. Ann Markusen et al., *The Rise of the Gunbelt: The Military Remapping of Industrial America* (New York: Oxford University Press, 1991).

17. Carl Abbott, *The Metropolitan Frontier: Cities in the Modern American West* (Tucson: University of Arizona Press, 1993), 60.

18. Kenneth Jackson, *Crabgrass Frontier: The Suburbanization of the United States* (New York: Oxford University Press, 1985).

19. Bradford Luckingham, *Phoenix: The History of a Southwestern Metropolis* (Tucson: University of Arizona Press, 1995), 107.

20. Larry Sawers and William Tabb, eds., *Sunbelt/Snowbelt: Urban Development and Regional Restructuring* (New York: Oxford University Press, 1984).

21. Carl Abbot, *The New Urban America: Growth and Politics in Sunbelt Cities* (Chapel Hill: University of North Carolina Press, 1981), 6.

22. Rick Heffernon, Nancy Welch, and Rob Melnick, eds., *Sustainability for Arizona: The Issue of Our Age* (Phoenix: Morrison Institute for Public Policy, ASU, 2007), 17.

23. Elizabeth Tandy Shermer, "Creating the Sunbelt: The Political and Economic Transformation of Phoenix, Arizona" (Ph.D. dissertation, University of California, Santa Barbara, 2009).

24. David Harvey takes the New York fiscal crisis as a point of origin for neoliberalism in *A Brief History of Neoliberalism* (Oxford: Oxford University Press, 2005).

25. Philip Vandermeer, *Phoenix Rising: The Making of a Desert Metropolis* (Carlsbad, N. Mex.: Heritage Media Corp, 2002), 47.

26. For example, Proposition 303 (passed in 1998) provided for $20 million of state general revenue annually for the purchase or lease of State Trust Land for open-space preservation. It was drafted by the growth lobby as an explicit rival to Proposition 202, the urban growth initiative. The list of parks and preserves that now ring Great Phoenix include South Mountain, Estrella Mountain, Squaw Peak, San Tan Mountains, Camelback Mountain, North Mountain, McDowell Mountain, White Tank Mountains, Cave Creek, Superstition Wilderness, and the North Sonoran Preserve.

27. Barry Goldwater, *The Conscience of a Majority* (Englewood Cliffs, N.J: Prentice-Hall, 1970), 62.

28. Kent Portney, *Taking Sustainable Cities Seriously* (Cambridge, Mass.: MIT Press 2003).

29. The architectural heritage of "designing with nature" is most obviously traced to the influence of sometime resident Frank Lloyd Wright, and his Taliesin West complex, in the northeast of the city. Vernon Swaback is the Scottsdale-based architect most associated with that legacy. See his *Creating Value: Smart Development and Green Design* (Washington, D.C.: Urban Land Institute, 2007). The Phoenix area has also hosted the design of several green prototype homes, one of which is documented in David Pijawka and Kim Shetter, *The Environment Comes Home: Arizona Public Service's Environmental Showcase Home* (Tempe: Herberger Center for Design Excellence, ASU, 1995).

30. Rob Krueger and David Gibbs, eds., *The Sustainable Development Paradox: Urban Political Economy in the United States and Europe* (New York: Guilford Press, 2007).

31. Van Jones, *The Green Collar Economy: How One Solution Can Fix Our Two Biggest Problems* (New York: Harper, 2008), 59.

32. Ibid., 64.

33. Vandermeer, *Phoenix Rising*, 64.

34. Carol Heim, "Leapfrogging, Urban Sprawl, and Growth Management: Phoenix, 1950–2000," *American Journal of Economics and Sociology* 60 (January 2001), 245–283.

35. Carl Abbott, *How Cities Won the West: Four Centuries of Urban Change in Western North America* (Albuquerque: University of New Mexico Press, 2008), 230.

36. Carl Abbott, "Southwestern Cityscapes," in Robert Fairbanks and Kathleen Underwood, eds., *Essays on Sunbelt Cities and Recent Urban America* (College Station: Texas A & M Press, 1989), 67.

37. Ibid., 77.

38. Robert Lang and Jennifer LeFurgy, *Boomburbs: The Rise of America's Accidental Cities* (Washington, D.C.: Brookings Institution Press, 2007), 150.

39. Gary Nelson, "Mesa Biggest 'Boring' City in U.S.," *Arizona Republic* (January 6, 2009).

40. The concept of "ghost acreage" is taken from Georg Borgstrom, *The Hungry Planet: The Modern World at the Edge of Famine* (New York: Macmillan, 1965).

CHAPTER 3.1

1. See David Owen's argument for Manhattanization, in *Green Metropolis: Why Living Smaller, Living Closer, and Driving Less Are the Keys to Sustainability* (New York: Riverhead, 2009).

2. Jane Jacobs, *The Death and Life of Great American Cities* (New York: Random House and Vintage Books, 1961).

3. Robert Burchell, Anthony Downs, Sahan Mukherji, and Barbara McCann, *Sprawl Costs: Economic Impacts of Unchecked Development* (Washington, D.C.: Island Press, 2005); Peter Gordon and Harry Richardson, "Prove It: The Costs and Benefits of Sprawl," *The Brookings Review* 16, 4 (Fall 1998): 23–26; Real Estate Research Corporation, *The Costs of Sprawl: Environmental and Economic Costs of Alternative Residential Development Patterns at the Urban Fringe*, 3 vols. (Washington, D.C.: U.S. Government Printing Office, 1974); Gregory Squires, *Urban Sprawl: Causes, Consequences and Policy Responses* (New York: Urban Institute Press, 2002); Robert Bruegmann, *Sprawl: A Compact History* (Chicago: University of Chicago Press, 2006); Oliver Gillham, *The Limitless City: A Primer on the Urban Sprawl Debate* (Washington, D.C., Island Press, 2002).

4. Neil Smith, *The New Urban Frontier: Gentrification and the Revanchist City* (New York: Routledge, 1996); Rebecca Solnit, *Hollow City: Gentrification and the Eviction of Urban Culture* (New York: Verso, 2001); Derek Hyra, *The New Urban Renewal: The Economic Transformation of Harlem and Bronzeville* (Chicago: University of Chicago Press, 2008); Lance Freeman, *There Goes the Hood: Views of Gentrification From the Ground Up* (Philadelphia: Temple University Press, 2006).

5. Roger Noll and Andrew Zimbalist, eds., *Sports, Jobs, and Taxes: The Economic Impact of Sports Teams and Stadiums* (Washington, D.C.: Brookings Institution Press, 1997); Mark Rosentraub, *Major League Losers: The Real Cost of Sports and Who's Paying for It* (New York: Basic Books, 1999); Joanna Cagan and Neil deMause, *Field of Schemes: How the Great Stadium Swindle Turns Public Money into Private Profit* (Monroe, Me.: Common Courage Press, 1998); Kevin Delaney and Rick Eckstein, *Public Dollars, Private Stadiums: The Battle over*

Building Sports Stadiums (New Brunswick, N.J.: Rutgers University Press, 2003).

6. See David Perry and Wim Wiewel, eds., *The University as Urban Developer: Case Studies and Analysis* (Armonk, N.Y.: M. E. Sharpe, in cooperation with the Lincoln Institute of Land Policy, 2005).

7. Andrew Ross, *No-Collar. The Humane Workplace and Its Hidden Costs* (New York: Basic Books, 2003); Michael Indergaard, *Silicon Alley: The Rise and Fall of a New Media District* (New York: Routledge, 2004).

8. *The Economist,* "The Geography of Cool" (April 13, 2000).

9. June Manning Thomas and Marsha Ritzdorf, eds.,*Urban Planning and the African-American Community: In the Shadows* (Oakland, Calif.: Sage, 1996); Charles Abrams, *Forbidden Neighbors: A Study of Prejudice in Housing* (New York: Harper, 1955); Douglas Massey and Nancy Denton, *American Apartheid: Segregation and the Making of the Underclass* (Cambridge, Mass.: Harvard University Press, 1993).

10. The average 2005 income of Arizona's top 5% of families was $223,081, and that of the bottom 20% was $15,719. Economic Policy Institute and Center on Budget and Policy Priorities, *Mind the Gap: Income Inequality, State by State* (February 2006).

11. Jon Talton, *Rogue Columnist* blog, accessible at <http://roguecolumnist.typepad .com/rogue_columnist/2009/06/phoenix-101-the-old-city.html>.

12. Jon Talton, *Concrete Desert* (New York: St. Martin's Press, 2001); *Camelback Falls* (New York: St. Martin's Press, 2003); *Dry Heat* (New York: St. Martin's Press, 2004); *Cactus Heart* (Scottsdale, Ariz.: Poisoned Pen Press, 2007); and *South Phoenix Rules* (Scottsdale, Ariz.: Poisoned Pen Press, 2010).

13. Betty Webb, *Desert Noir* (Scottsdale, Ariz.: Poisoned Pen Press, 2001); *Desert Shadows* ((Scottsdale, Ariz.: Poisoned Pen Press, 2006); and *Desert Run* (Scottsdale, Ariz.: Poisoned Pen Press, 2008).

14. All of the state's investigative reporters lived in the shadow of the murder of *Arizona Republic's* Don Bolles, who was investigating the role of organized crime in land swindles when he was blown up by a car bomb in 1976. Reporters from across the nation converged on Phoenix to conduct a study, known as the Arizona Project. The team-produced series of reports was launched on March 13, 1977, in newspapers such as *Newsday, The Miami Herald, The Kansas City Star, The Boston Globe, The Indianapolis Star, The Denver Post,* and *The Arizona Daily Star.* See the description by Investigative Reporters and Editors (IRE) at <http://www.ire.org/history/arizonaproject.html>. For an evocative account of the heyday of Phoenix mob-driven land swindles, see Zachary Lazar's effort to reconstruct the role his accountant father (victim of a gangland murder the year before Bolles) played in the infamous operations of Ned Warren, "The God Father of Land Fraud." *Evening's Empire: The Story of My Father's Murder* (New York: Little, Brown, 2009).

15. Bradford Luckingham, *Phoenix: The History of the Southwestern Metropolis* (Tucson: University of Arizona Press, 1989), 196.

16. Dennis M. Burke, a participant, has written a glowing account of the Forum in "Remembering the Future: The Phoenix Futures Forum," accessible online at <http://goodgovernment.org/phoenixfutureshistory.htm>.

17. The Valley report was the first of several, published by Neil Peirce, in *Citistates: How Urban America Can Prosper in a Competitive World* (Washington, D.C.: Seven Locks Press, 1993).

18. John Findlay, *Magic Lands: Western Cityscapes and American Culture After 1940* (Berkeley: University of California Press, 1992), 265.

19. The homeless (attracted to the city's mild winter climate though they suffered terribly in the summer months) were moved from areas considered eligible to developers to a campus south of the Capitol Mall district. The profile for the average homeless person in Phoenix is a single white male in the age range of 30 to 39 years old, according to Central Arizona Shelter Services.

20. See "Spiked," *Phoenix New Times* (September 4, 2003).

21. Rosalyn Deutsche, *Evictions: Art and Spatial Politics* (Cambridge, Mass.: MIT Press, 1998); David Ley, *The New Middle Class and the Remaking of the Central City* (Oxford: Oxford University Press, 1996); David Harvey, "The Art of Rent: Globalization, Monopoly and Cultural Production," in *Socialist Register* (London: Merlin Press, 2002), 93–110; Richard Lloyd, *Neo-Bohemia: Art and Commerce in the Postindustrial City* (New York: Routledge, 2006).

22. Among the condo loft developments that sprang up in the downtown area were Orpheum Lofts (TASB), Lofts on Central, Artisan Homes, and Artisan Village (Eric Browne), Soho Lofts, Summit at Copper Square (David Wallach), Lofts at Orchidhouse (Brownstone Residential), Monroe Place (Grace Communities), Tapestry on Central (United Properties), Lofts at Filmore (William Mahoney), Palm Lane (Mardian), Campaige Place (Tom Hom Group), Roosevelt 11, Evergreen 9, Portland 38 (JAG), and Portland Place (HabitatMetro).

23. Richard Florida, *The Rise of the Creative Class: And How It's Transforming Work, Leisure, Community, and Everyday Life* (New York: Basic Books, 2002). On Florida's visit to Phoenix, see Michele Laudig, "Speech Therapy: Richard Florida Jump-Starts Downtown Dialogue," *Phoenix New Times* (October 30, 2003). To gauge the newspaper's own interest in cultivating a creative "scene," see Amy Silverman, "The Cool Index," *Phoenix New Times* (December 4, 2003).

24. In its Arizona Policy Choice 2001 report, *Five Shoes Waiting to Drop on Arizona's Future*, the Morrison Institute for Public Policy had put the case for attracting knowledge workers.

25. In the throes of the Great Recession, Florida wrote an epitaph for the "end of easy expansion" in the Sunbelt. There were now very few prospects, he had concluded, for revitalizing fast-growth cities like Phoenix. "Their character and atmosphere," he predicted, "are likely to change rapidly." "How the Crash Will Reshape America," *Atlantic Monthly* (March 2009).

26. The best rebuttal to the Florida bandwagon can be found in Jamie Peck, "Struggling with the Creative Class," *International Journal of Urban and Regional Research* 29, 4 (2005): 740–770. See also Andrew Ross, "The Mercurial Career of Creative Industries Policymaking in the U.K., the E.U., and the U.S.," in *Nice Work If You Can Get It: Life and Labor in Precarious Times* (New York: NYU Press, 2009).

27. Catalyx report (George Borowsky, Project Leader), "Phoenix Downtown: Right Place. Right Time!" (August 15, 2004).

28. Arizona Chain Reaction, Downtown Phoenix Arts Coalition (D-PAC), Phoenix Coalition of Historic Neighborhoods, The Community Housing Partnership, Local Initiatives Support Corporation (LISC), *Downtown Voices: Creating a Sustainable Downtown* (Phoenix, August 2004).

29. For a convenient graphic summary, see Sophia Meger, "Revealing Phoenix," *Shade* magazine (October 2004): 60.

30. *Phoenix General Plan Update: Transitioning to a Sustainable Future*, public hearing draft (December 2010), at <http://phoenix.gov/webcms/groups/internet/@inter/@citygov/@future/@planphx/documents/web_content/052978.pdf>.

31. Arthesia, *Metro Phoenix DNA: A Strategy Book* (Phoenix: MPAC, 2008), 22.

32. Ibid., 11, 14.

33. Reports by MPAC or its embryo, the Maricopa Regional Arts and Culture Task Force, include *A Place for Arts and Culture: A Maricopa County Overview* (2003); *Vibrant Culture–Thriving Economy: Arts, Culture, and Prosperity in Arizona's Valley of the Sun* (2004); *Creative Connections: Arts, Ideas & Economic Progress in Greater Phoenix* (2006); MPAC and Greater Phoenix Economic Council, *Perceptions Matter: Attracting and Retaining Talented Workers to the Greater Phoenix Region* (2007); MPAC and Behavior Research Center, *Arts, Culture and the Latino Audience* (2008); and a report commissioned from the Shugoll Research group, *Cultural Participation Study for Maricopa County: Community-Wide Survey of Attitudes and Trends* (2007).

34. See Ann Markusen's essays on arts-based development, including "The Artistic Dividend: Urban Artistic Specialization and Economic Development Implications" (with Gregory Schrock), *Urban Studies* 43, 10 (2006), 1661–1686; "Urban Development and the Politics of a Creative Class: Evidence from the Study of Artists," *Environment and Planning* 38, 10 (2006), 1921–1940; "An Arts-Based State Rural Development Policy," *Journal of Regional Analysis and Policy* 37, 1 (2007), 7–9.

35. Nan Ellin "Introduction" in Nan Ellin and Edward Booth-Clibborn, eds., *Phoenix: 21st Century City* (Phoenix: Booth-Clibborn Editions, 2006), 1. Also see the dossier edited by Ellin, of ASU student and faculty proposals, "For Phoenix to Flourish," in *Shade* (October–November, 2004), 52–96.

36. The Creative Capital organization was commissioned by the Arizona Commission for the Arts and other groups to study the potential for developing the regional arts economy. Its report concluded that the state of the arts was at a "tipping point" and that the right kind of support would foster the transition from a DIY culture to a more permanent and mainstream establishment. See Creative Capital, *State Research Project: Findings for Arizona and Maine* (New York: Creative Capital, September 2007). For a broader social analysis, see Hans Abbing, *Why Are Artists Poor? The Exceptional Economy of the Arts* (Amsterdam: Amsterdam University Press, 2002).

37. Ellin, in *Phoenix: 21st Century City*, 2.

38. Benjamin Leatherman, "T.G.I.F: Is the Party Over?" *Phoenix New Times* (September 1, 2005).

39. Steve Weiss, comments in a speech to commemorate six years of DVC activity, at the Matador restaurant, Phoenix, March 2010.

40. David Hess, *Localist Movements in a Global Economy* (Cambridge, Mass.: MIT Press, 2009).

41. The use of artists as a revitalization tool was directly echoed in the first of the goals articulated for the Artist Storefront Program, initiated in 2004: "Eliminate slum and blight, and promote redevelopment and neighborhood revitalization."

42. The most ultra member of the original Phoenix artists coalition, Michael 23, carried the expressive spirit of the downtown arts scene out of town when his Firehouse community established an outpost in the old mining town of Miami, 70 miles east of Phoenix in 2009. The cluster of arts spaces there was soon

large enough to mount its own artwalk and their fire performances were welcomed by the authorities. "They are a little bored out there," he reported, and more than tolerant of our "little bit of cultural latitude," especially if it brought energy and attention to a town in decline.

43. Chesney was fired, and many of his projects, including the arts district, were sidelined, when a new mayor took office in January 2011. See Monica Alonzo, "Will El Mirage Ever Be Able to Emerge from the Shadow of Luke Air Force Base?" *Phoenix New Times* (February 24, 2011).

CHAPTER 3.2

1. The right to housing was one of original nine rights proposed by FDR in his 1944 bill of rights, and indeed the 1948 Housing Act promised a "decent home in a suitable living environment for every American." In 1996, in response to the cumulative pressure of numerous international human rights documents, the State Department asserted that it "must make clear for the record that the U.S. does not recognize the international right to housing," and that it preferred a weaker recognition that decent housing was simply an ideal to be pursued. Stanley Moses, "The Struggle for Decent Affordable Housing: Debates, Plans, and Policies," in *Affordable Housing in New York City: Definitions/Options* (New York: Steven Newman Real Estate Institute, Baruch College, 2005).

2. Robert Bruegmann, *Sprawl: A Compact History* (Chicago: University of Chicago Press, 2005). Joel Kotkin and Wendell Cox are the most consistent advocates of this view. See their respective blogs, at <http://www.joelkotkin.com> and <http://www.newgeography.com/>.

3. Terry Goddard, "Housing Affordability: Arizona's Quiet Crisis," in Ray Quay, ed., *Greater Phoenix Regional Atlas: A Preview of the Region's 50-Year Future* (Tempe: Arizona State University , 2003), 55.

4. Robert Bullard, ed., *Growing Smarter: Achieving Livable Communities, Environmental Justice, and Regional Equity* (Cambridge, Mass.: MIT Press, 2007), 36.

5. Elizabeth Kneebone, *Job Sprawl Revisited: The Changing Geography of Metropolitan Employment* (Washington, D.C.: Brookings Institution, 2009); Michael Stoll, *Job Sprawl and the Spatial Mismatch Between Blacks and Jobs* (Washington, D.C.: Brookings Institution, 2005); Edward L. Glaeser, Matthew Kahn, and Chenghuan Chu, *Job Sprawl: Employment Location in U.S. Metropolitan Areas* (Washington, D.C.: Brookings Institution, 2001).

6. Patricia Gober, *Metropolitan Phoenix: Place Making and Community Building in the Desert* (Philadelphia: University of Pennsylvania Press, 2005), 157.

7. The argument is set forth in Bullard, ed., *Growing Smarter*. Also see Robert Bullard, Glenn Johnson, and Angel Torres, *Sprawl City: Race, Politics, and Planning in Atlanta* (Washington, D.C.: Island Press, 2000).

8. Downtown Voices Coalition, *Downtown Voices: Creating a Sustainable Downtown 2010 and Beyond: A Six-Year Progress Report* (2011), 6.

9. Michael Pyatok, "Elegant, Empathetic, Affordable Housing," interview in *Whole Earth Magazine* (Summer 1999).

10. Andrew Ross, "Housing, Immigration, and Fairness," *Harvard Design Magazine* (Fall, 2007).

11. See Mike Davis, *Magical Urbanism: Latinos Reinvent the US City* (New York: Verso, 2000).

12. Bradford Luckingham, *Phoenix: The History of a Southwestern Metropolis* (Tucson: University of Arizona Press, 1989), 22, 19.

13. David Diaz, *Barrio Urbanism: Chicano, Planning and American Cities* (New York: Routledge, 2005); and Michael Mendez, "Latino Lifestyle and the New Urbanism: Synergy Against Sprawl" (MA thesis, MIT, 2003); and "Latino New Urbanism: Building on Cultural Preferences," *Opolis* 1, 1 (2005).

14. MARS put Phoenix on the national cultural map at a time when the city's museums and mainstream galleries considered Chicano art to be "folk art." For an account of the impact of the movement, see Lucy R. Lippard,*Mixed Blessings: New Art in a Multicultural America* (New York: Pantheon Books, 1990).

15. Craig Anderson, "Phoenix-area Real-estate Market May Face New Reality," *Arizona Republic* (January 30, 2011).

CHAPTER 4

1. After a dam on the Tempe Town Lake collapsed in July 2010, conservationists questioned whether a billion gallons of water should be used to refill it, at a time of serious drought. See Dianna M. Náñez, "Tempe Town Lake Can be Refilled with Stored Water," *Arizona Republic* (August 20, 2010).

2. A summary of the Army Corps of Engineers' Feasibility Report on Rio Salado can be found at <http://phoenix.gov/planning/btbfeasibility.pdf>.

3. Jahna Berry, "Residents Seeking Closure of S. Phoenix Asphalt Plant," *Arizona Republic* (July 28, 2009).

4. According to a 2006 ASU report by Sara Grineski, "metropolitan Phoenix ranks in the top five US cities for asthma-related deaths. Approximately 8 percent of the Phoenix population has asthma, and research conducted in a low-income Latino neighborhood found that 16 percent of children under 19 years old had been diagnosed by a doctor as having asthma; this is twice the national average." "Social Vulnerability, Environmental Inequality, and Childhood Asthma in Phoenix, Arizona: A Report to the Community" (unpublished, but accessible online at <http://caplter.asu.edu/research/research-projects/research-home/research-highlight-5/>).

5. Bob Bolin, Sara Grineski, and Timothy Collins, "The Geography of Despair: Environmental Racism and the Making of South Phoenix, Arizona," *Human Ecology Review* 12, 2 (2005).

6. Emmett McLoughlin, *People's Padre: An Autobiography* (Boston: Beacon Press, 1954), 40.

7. Andrew Kopkind, "Modern Times in Phoenix: A City at the Mercy of Its Myths," *New Republic* (November 6, 1965), 15.

8. Geoffrey Padraic Mawn, "Phoenix, Arizona: Central City of the Southwest, 1870–1920" (Ph.D. dissertation, ASU, 1979), cited in Bolin, Grineski, and Collins.

9. Summarizing research by ASU's Sharon Harlan and Darren Ruddell, Shaun McKinnon reported that "for every $10,000 an area's income rises, the average outside temperature drops one-half degree Fahrenheit," "Wealth Buys Rescue from Urban Heat Island," *Arizona Republic* (September 20, 2009).

10. For an account of the barrio displacement, see Peter Dimas, *Progress and a Mexican American Community's Struggle for Existence: Phoenix's Golden Gate Barrio* (New York: Peter Lang Publishing, 1999).

11. In one of my first interviews in Phoenix, geographer Kristin Koptiuch observed that "when you go from North Scottsdale to South Phoenix, you go over a socioeconomic and political edge into a bottomless pit." She vividly referred to this experience as "urban vertigo."

12. Robert Nelson, "Fire," *Phoenix New Times* (December 5, 2002).

13. Robert Bullard, *Dumping in Dixie: Race, Class, and Environmental Quality* (Boulder, Colo.: Westview, 1990); and *Unequal Protection: Environmental Justice and Communities of Color* (New York: Random House, 1994); Luke Cole and Sheila Foster, *From the Ground Up: Environmental Racism and the Rise of the Environmental Justice Movement* (New York: NYU Press, 2001); Laura Pulido, *Environmentalism and Economic Justice: Two Chicano Struggles in the Southwest* (Tucson: University of Arizona Press, 1996); Julie Sze, *Noxious New York: The Racial Politics of Urban Health and Environmental Justice* (Cambridge, Mass.: MIT Press, 2006); Winona LaDuke, *All Our Relations: Native Struggles for Land and Life* (Boston: South End Press, 2008); David Naguib Pellow, *Garbage Wars: The Struggle for Environmental Justice in Chicago* (Cambridge, Mass.: MIT Press, 2002).

14. Nelson, "Fire."

15. Originally, Don't Waste Arizona was the name for the coalition that fought against the ENSCO incinerator in the late 1980s. Formally incorporated by Brittle in the aftermath of that campaign, it is now run by himself and his partner as a membership service organization.

16. Martha Reinke, "Nonprofit Cashing in on Lawsuits," *Phoenix Business Journal* (June 23, 1996) at <http://www.bizjournals.com/search/results.html?Ntt=%22Martha%20Reinke%22&Ntk=All&Ntx=mode%20matchallpartial>.

17. For an account of the Hayden campaign, see Diane Sicotte, "Power, Profit and Pollution: The Persistence of Environmental Injustice in a Company Town," *Human Ecology Review* 16, 2 (2009).

18. Matthew Whitaker, *Race Work: The Rise of Civil Rights in the Urban West* (Lincoln: University of Nebraska Press, 2005), 200.

19. The South Phoenix Industry Challenge Good Neighbor Partnership 2005–2008: Final Project Report (July 2008) accessible online at <http://www.phoenixindustrychallenge.com/Final_Report.htm>.

20. Terry Greene (Sterling), "Tales from the Dark West Side," *Phoenix New Times* (June 27, 1990).

21. A good deal of my summaries rely on Terry Greene (Sterling)'s *Phoenix New Times* articles on the topic, especially "Piecing Together the West-Side Cancer Cluster (February 22, 1989); "Tales from the Dark West Side" (June 27, 1990); "Raiding the Maryvale Cancer Budget" (January 30, 1991); "The Pain of Maryvale" (October 24, 1996); and "Bottomless Well" (February 3, 2000).

22. Ted Smith, David A. Sonnenfeld, and David Naguib Pellow, eds., *Challenging the Chip: Labor Rights and Environmental Justice in the Global Electronics Industry* (Philadelphia: Temple University Press, 2006); David Naguib Pellow and Lisa Sun-Hee Park, *The Silicon Valley of Dreams: Environmental Injustice, Immigrant Workers, and the High-Tech Global Economy* (New York: NYU Press, 2002).

23. The wells were first tested after TCE was discovered in a plume of contaminated groundwater that originated under the Hughes Aircraft plant in Tucson in 1981. Tucsonans for a Clean Environment formed, and initiated a lawsuit on behalf of 2,000 residents, charging that the TCE pollution had made them ill. The company settled in 1990 for $85 million.
24. Chris Farnsworth, "Down the Drain: Judge Flushes Allegations That Water Was Tainted by Motorola," *Phoenix New Times* (June 18, 1998).
25. Terry Greene (Sterling), "The Cost of Toxic Spills: Here's How You'll Pay for Motorola's Contamination," *Phoenix New Times* (August 19, 1992).
26. Diana Balazs, "EPA Investigating Water Plant's Woes," *Arizona Republic* (January 24, 2008).
27. Terry Greene (Sterling), "Disaster Response," *Phoenix New Times* (July 1, 1992).
28. Terry Greene (Sterling), "Motorola: The Story So Far," *Phoenix New Times* (December 30, 1992).
29. Cited in Electronic Industry Good Neighbor Campaign, *Sacred Waters: The Life-Blood of Mother Earth; Four Case-Studies of High-Tech Water Resource Exploitation and Corporate Welfare in the Southwest* (Albuquerque: Southwest Network for Environmental and Economic Justice and the Campaign for Responsible Technology, 1997), 47.
30. Terry Greene (Sterling), "Unanswered Prayers and Questions," *Phoenix New Times* (October 7, 1992).
31. Terry Greene (Sterling), "A Year Inside the Motorola Mess; Sinners and Victims, Warriors and Regulators," *Phoenix New Times* (December 30, 1992).
32. Lenny Siegel, "A Tale of Two Semiconductor Cities: Why It Took So Long to Investigate Vapor Intrusion in Phoenix," Center for Public Environmental Oversight (March, 2010), accessible at <http://cpeo.org/pubs/PhoenixVI.pdf>.
33. Kathleen Stanton, "Finally, a Crackdown on Polluters," *Phoenix New Times* (September 20, 1989).
34. Electronic Industry Good Neighbor Campaign, *Sacred Waters*, 6.
35. Ibid., 44.
36. John Herbert, *Phoenix: Economic Capital of the Great Southwest Sun Country!* (Phoenix, 1958). Quoted in Todd Andrew Needham, "Power Lines: Urban Space, Energy Development and the Making of the Modern Southwest" (Ph.D. dissertation, University of Michigan, 2006), 53.
37. Shaun McKinnon, "CO_2 Pollution Soars in Arizona," *Arizona Republic* (November 13, 2009). Environment Arizona reports on the topic can be found at <http://www.environmentarizona.org/reports>.
38. Quoted in Dennis Wagner, "Tribe's Environmental Fight," *Arizona Republic* (November 2, 2009). After the 2005 closure of the Mohave Generating Station, the Just Transition Coalition was created to address the economic impact on the affected Navajo and Hopi tribal communities. The coalition includes the Indigenous Environmental Network, Honor the Earth Foundation, Apollo Alliance, Black Mesa Water Coalition, To'Nizhoni Ani, Grand Canyon Trust, and the Sierra Club.
39. Needham, *Power Lines*, especially chs. 3, 6, and 8.
40. Quoted in Mark Dowie, *Losing Ground: American Environmentalism at the Close of the Twentieth Century* (Cambridge, Mass.: MIT Press, 1995), 152.
41. The Salt River Pima-Maricopa Indian Community, GRIC's cousin to the north, houses The Pavilions, a 140-acre retail mall that is one of the largest commercial developments ever built on Indian land.

42. "American Indian/Alaska Native Program and Project Inventory" Centers for Disease Control and Prevention (2006), accessible at <http://www.cdc.gov/omhd/populations/AIAN/PDFs/FY06CDCAIANPrograms407.pdf>.

43. See the health consultation report on the site by Agency for Toxic Substances and Disease Registry, at <http://www.atsdr.cdc.gov/HAC/pha/GilaRiver022305-AZ/GilaRiverIndian022305-AZ-pt1.pdf>.

44. Gary Nabhan, "Rooting Out the Cause of Disease: Why Diabetes Is So Common Among Desert Dwellers," in Carole Counihan and Penny Van Esterik, eds., *Food and Culture: A Reader* (New York: Routledge, 2008); Cynthia Smith, "Food Habit and Cultural Changes among the Pima Indians," in Jenny Joe and Robert Young, eds., *Diabetes as a Disease of Civilization: The Impact of Culture Change on Indigenous Peoples* (New York: Mouton de Gruyter, 1994).

45. In 1979, the U.S. Air Force commissioned the landmark "Ranch Hand" study to assess the possible health effects of military personnel's exposure to Agent Orange and other chemical defoliants sprayed during the Vietnam War. The results, published in 1998, found a 166 percent increase in diabetes (requiring insulin control) in sample studies of soldiers exposed to the toxins in the course of their deployment.

46. Rob Nixon, *Slow Violence and the Environmentalism of the Poor* (Cambridge, Mass.: Harvard University Press, 2011).

47. Ward Churchill and Winona LaDuke, "The Political Economy of Radioactive Colonialism," in M. Annette Jaimes, ed., *The State of Native America: Genocide, Colonization, and Resistance* (Boston: South End Press, 1999).

CHAPTER 5

1. Interstate Renewable Energy Council, *U.S. Solar Market Trends 2009* (Latham, N.Y., July 2010), 10. Accessible online at <http://irecusa.org/wp-content/uploads/2010/07/IREC-Solar-Market-Trends-Report-2010_7-27-10_web.pdf>.

2. Curtis Moore and Alan Miller, *Green Gold: Japan, Germany, the United States and the Race for Environmental Technology* (Boston: Beacon Press, 1994).

3. Eric Janszen, "The Next Bubble: Priming the Markets for Tomorrow's Big Crash," *Harper's* (February 2008).

4. Henry Brean, "Heidi Fleiss Gives Up on Plan for Brothel for Women," *Las Vegas Review-Journal* (February 10, 2009).

5. Koch Industries is ranked No. 10 among top corporate polluters and has been fingered as the number one funder of libertarian campaigns against Obama policies. Jane Mayer, "Covert Operations: The Billionaire Brothers Who Are Waging a War Against Obama," *The New Yorker* (August 30, 2010).

6. In a 2010 article in *Rolling Stone*, Jeff Goodell reported, "By last year, according to the Center for Public Integrity, the number of lobbyists devoted to climate change had soared by more than fivefold since 2003, to a total of 2,810—or five lobbyists for every lawmaker in Washington. 'I had no idea this many lobbyists even existed in Washington,' says former senator Tim Wirth, now head of the United Nations Foundation. Only 138 of the lobbyists were pushing for alternative energy—the rest were heavily weighted toward the old fossil-fuel mafia, most of whom oppose tough carbon caps." "As the World Burns," *Rolling Stone* (January 6, 2010).

7. Sean Sweeney summarizes the varied contributions of labor unions in "More Than Green Jobs: Time for a New Climate Policy for Labor," *New Labor Forum* (Fall, 2009). A portion of this chapter also appeared in *New Labor Forum*, 19, 3 (Fall, 2010) as "The Greening of America Revisited: Can the U.S. Create High-Skill Green Jobs?"

8. Barbara Rose Johnston, Susan Dawson, and Gary Madsen, "Uranium Mining and Milling: Navajo Experiences in the American Southwest," in Barbara Rose Johnston, eds., *Half-Lives & Half-Truths: Confronting the Radioactive Legacies of the Cold War* (Santa Fe, N.Mex.: School for Advanced Research Press, 2007).

9. In 1955, the Association for Applied Solar Energy organized an epochal conference that had 900 registrants from all over the world. See *Proceedings of the World Symposium on Applied Solar Energy*, Phoenix, Arizona, November 1–5, 1955 (Menlo Park, Calif.: Stanford Research Institute, 1956).

10. Victor Dricks, "The Sun Sets on Solar," a six-part series, *Phoenix Gazette* (November 22–29, 1992).

11. Quoted in Thomas Friedman, *Hot, Flat, and Crowded*, 2d ed. (New York: Farrar, Straus & Giroux, 2009), 449–452. For Friedman, First Solar is a prime example of the U.S. neglect of renewable technologies.

12. Robert Glennon, "Is Solar Power Dead in the Water?" *Washington Post* (June 7, 2009).

13. In a useful and up-to-date survey on the prospects and barriers to developing solar energy as a practical alternative in the Southwest, Robert Glennon and Andrew Reeves outline the reliance of utility-scale solar farming on vast water supplies. "Solar Energy's Cloudy Future," *Arizona Journal of Environmental Law and Policy* 1, 1 (2010): 91–137.

14. Todd Woody, "Desert Vistas vs. Solar Power," *New York Times* (December 21, 2009).

15. Mayes's other big accomplishment at the ACC was to push through an energy-efficiency standard (in July 2010) that required utilities to achieve 20 percent annual energy savings by 2020.

16. Ralph Nader, preface to Daniel Berman and John O'Connor, *Who Owns the Sun? People, Politics, and the Struggle for a Solar Economy* (White River Junction, Vt.: Chelsea Green, 1996).

17. On the history behind electricity deregulation in the 1990s, see Sharon Beder, *Power Play: The Fight to Control the World's Electricity* (New York: New Press, 2003); Timothy Brennan et al., *A Shock to the System: Restructuring America's Electricity Industry* (Washington, D.C.: Resources for the Future, 1996); Ed Smeloff and Peter Asmus, *Reinventing Electric Utilities: Competition, Citizen Action and Clean Power* (Washington, D.C.: Island Press, 1997).

18. Richard Rudolph and Scott Ridley, *Power Struggle: The Hundred-Year War Over Electricity* (New York: Harper & Row, 1986).

19. Solar Lobby, *Blueprint for a Solar America* (Washington, D.C., 1979).

20. Peter Fox-Penner, *Smart Power: Climate Change, the Smart Grid, and the Future of Electric Utilities* (Washington, D.C.: Island Press, 2010).

21. SRP's efforts to maintain its profile as a public utility have long been dogged by campaigns to erode that status on account of its alleged "socialist" basis. See Andrew Needham, "The End of Public Power: The Politics of Taxation in the Postwar Electric Utility Industry," in Kimberly Phillips-Fein and Julian Zelizer, eds., *What's Good for Business: Business and Politics Since 1945* (New York: Oxford University Press, 2012).

22. In exchange for the permit, the company had to set aside a $5 million fund for renewable-energy projects in northern Arizona, and promised to clean up some of its dirtier plants. Ryan Randazzo, "Arizona's Last New Coal Plant?" *Arizona Republic* (March 18, 2010).

23. Andrew Ross, *Fast Boat to China: Corporate Flight and the Consequences of Free Trade* (New York: Pantheon, 2006).

24. Friends of the Earth, "Climate Policies and Action: A Comparison between the United States and China," accessible at <http://www.foe.co.uk/resource/evidence/china_us_comparison.pdf>.

25. Todd Woody, "Silicon Valley's Solar Innovators Retool to Catch Up to China," *New York Times* (October 12, 2010); Matthew Wald and Tom Zeller, "Cost of Green Power Makes Projects Tougher Sell," *New York Times* (November 8, 2010).

26. From the Chinese perspective, the project offered valuable know-how on building large-scale solar plants. According to Ahearn, "we will bring people over in order to transfer our knowledge related to the design and engineering of the plant. It's an IP transfer in that regard. By the time we step back, they will be using designs and methodologies and components that are consistent with well designed solar plants." Ucilia Wang, "First Solar's Gift to China: How to Build a Solar Farm," *GreenTech Solar* (September 10, 2009). Accessible online at <http://www.greentechmedia.com/articles/read/first-solars-gift-to-china-how-to-build-a-solar-farm/>.

27 Ryan Randazzo, "Arizona Paid Steep Price to Lure First Solar Plant," *Arizona Republic* (April 9, 2011).

28. Erin Ailworth, "Evergreen Solar to Shift Some Operations to China," *Boston Globe* (November 4, 2009); Keith Bradsher, "Solar Panel Maker Moves Work to China," *New York Times* (January 14, 2011).

29. Apollo Alliance and Good Jobs First, *Winning the Race: How America Can Lead the Global Clean Energy Economy* (March 2010), accessible online at <http://www.goodjobsfirst.org/pdf/winningtherace.pdf>.

30. Richard Kazis and Richard Grossman, *Fear at Work: Job Blackmail, Labor and the Environment* (Philadelphia: Library Company of Philadelphia, 1990).

31. See George Monbiot's assessment of U.K. plans for a feed-in tariff, "Are We Really Going to Let Ourselves Be Duped into This Solar Panel Rip-Off?" *The Guardian* (March 1, 2010), and the resulting dialogue with Jeremy Leggett, that begins with Leggett's response, "Solar Panels Are Not Fashion Accessories," *The Guardian* (March 3, 2010). An interesting Arizonan take on the pricing of solar energy can be found on Paul Symanski's *Rate Crimes* blog, at <http://ratecrimes.blogspot.com/>.

32. Norman Myers and Jennifer Kent, *Perverse Subsidies: How Tax Dollars Can Undercut the Environment and the Economy* (Washington, D.C.: Island Press, 2001).

33. Michael T. Klare, *Blood and Oil: The Dangers and Consequences of America's Growing Dependency on Imported Petroleum* (New York: Metropolitan Books, 2004); and *Resource Wars: The New Landscape of Global Conflict* (New York: Metropolitan/Owl Books, 2001).

34. James Hoggan, *Climate Cover-Up: The Crusade to Deny Global Warming* (Vancouver: Greystone, 2009); Naomi Oreskes and Erik Conway, *Merchants of Doubt: How a Handful of Scientists Obscured the Truth on Issues from Tobacco Smoke to Global Warming* (New York: Bloomsbury, 2010); Eric Pooley, *The*

Climate War: True Believers, Power Brokers, and the Fight to Save the Earth (New York: Hyperion, 2010); Clive Hamilton, *Requiem for a Species: Why We Resist the Truth About Climate Change* (London: Earthscan, 2010).

35. See Iain Murray, "Green-Jobs Fantasy," *National Review* (March 8, 2010). The German study is from a think tank, Rheinisch-Westfälisches Institut für Wirtschaftsforschung (RWI), and is titled "Economic Impacts from the Promotion of Renewable Energies: The German Experience," The Spanish study was conducted by researchers at King Juan Carlos University and is titled "Study of the Effects on Employment of Public Aid to Renewable Energy Sources." A rebuttal of the latter by Tracey de Morsella, "Debunking the Spanish Study on The Dire Result of Green Jobs Creation," can be found at <http://greeneconomypost.com/debunk-spanish-study-green-jobs-1582.htm>.

36. The campaign got a boost in January 2011, when Gary Pierce, a nuclear advocate, cemented the GOP's 3–2 ACC majority by replacing the term-limited Mayes, as chair of the commission.

37. Matthew Benson, "Governor Wants More Nuclear Plants in Arizona," *Arizona Republic* (January 6, 2010).

38. Jones, *The Green Collar Economy*, 15.

39. In the 1980s, the developer John F. Long built Solar One, the world's first solar subdivision. The 24-home community in Glendale had its own solar array, with the capacity to sell energy to SRP. The utility ended up charging community residents 9.5 cents per watt watt while buying energy from the array at 2.4 cents. *Who Owns the Sun*, 185.

40. See Berman and O'Connor, *Who Owns the Sun*.

41. Stephen Lyons, ed., *Sun: A Handbook for the Solar Decade* (San Francisco: Friends of the Earth, 1978). The handbook, which collects the views of major advocates of libertarian energy technologies, such as Murray Bookchin, Ivan Illich, Paul Goodman, Amory Lovins, and Lewis Mumford, was published to influence the energy choice of the time—between the "radioactive" and "the sunlit path," as David Brower's preface put it. Its publication coincided with the staging of Solar Day, designed to embarrass the Carter administration for its dismal energy policies.

   In *The Sun Betrayed: A Report on the Corporate Seizure of U.S. Solar Energy Development* (Boston: South End Press, 1979), Ray Reece tells the story of how the large utilities coopted the energy and vision of the 1970s solar movement. David Morris, *Self-Reliant Cities: Energy and the Transformation of Cities*, first published in 1982 and reissued in 2008 (Minneapolis: New Rules Project), provides a specifically urban slant on this movement.

42. Ryan Randazzo, "SRP Out of Money for Solar-Power Rebates," *Arizona Republic* (October 4, 2010).

43. Timothy Luke, *Ecocritique: Contesting the Politics of Nature, Economy, and Culture* (Minneapolis: University of Minnesota Press, 1997), 104.

44. Ibid., 113.

45. Shermer, "Creating a Proper Educational Climate," in *Creating the Sunbelt*, 443–457.

46. John Sperling, "SolarCAT: A Practical Path to Energy Independence," at the Sierra Club's symposium on Climate Recovery in Washington, D.C. (May 13, 2009). Accessible online at <http://www.reapinfo.org/reap3/about/eti.html>.

CHAPTER 6

1. Quoted in Matthew Whitaker, *Race Work: The Rise of Civil Rights in the Urban West* (Lincoln: University of Nebraska Press, 2005), 77.

2. Audrey Singer, Susan Hardwick, and Caroline Brettell, eds., *Twenty-First-Century Gateways: Immigrant Incorporation in Suburban America* (Washington, D.C.: Brookings Institution, 2008), 26.

3. The 150-million figure was first estimated by Norman Myers and Jennifer Kent, "Environmental Exodus: An Emergent Crisis in the Global Arena" (Washington, D.C.: Climate Institute, 1995); and Norman Myers, "Environmental Refugees: Our Latest Understanding," *Philosophical Transactions of the Royal Society* 356 (2001): 16.1–16.5. *The Stern Review: The Economics of Climate Change*, commissioned from economist Nicholas Stern by the U.K. government in 2006, put the figure at 200 million. See also Environmental Justice Foundation, *No Place Like Home: Where Next for Climate Refugees?* (London: Environmental Justice Foundation, 2009). The term "environmental refugees" was first introduced in Essam El-Hinnawi, "Environmental Refugees," U.N. Environmental Program (1985).

4. International Federation of Red Cross and Red Crescent Societies, *World Disasters Report* (2001).

5. Michael Oppenheimer, Shuaizhang Feng, Alan Krueger, "Linkages Among Climate Change, Crop Yields and Mexico–US Cross-Border Migration," *Proceedings of the National Academy of Science* (July 2010), accessible online at: <http://www.pnas.org/content/early/2010/07/16/1002632107.full.pdf>

6. Michelle Leighton Schwartz and Jessica Notini, *Desertification and Migration: Mexico and the United States* (Washington, D.C.: U.S. Commission on Immigration Reform, 1994).

7. U.S. Department of Defense, *Quadrennial Defense Review* (2010), accessible online at <http://www.defense.gov/qdr>.

8. Peter Schwartz and Doug Randall, *An Abrupt Climate Change Scenario and Its Implications for United States National Security?* (Emeryville, Calif.: Global Business Lab, 2003).

9. The CIA reports, "A Study of Climatological Research as It Pertains to Intelligence Problems" and "Potential Implications of Trends in the World's Population, Food Production, and Climate", are reprinted in Impact Team, *The Weather Conspiracy: The Coming of the New Ice Age* (New York: Ballantine, 1977).

10. Aside from the Ehrlichs' book, a good deal of the public consciousness about overpopulation was influenced by Garrett Hardin's essay, "The Tragedy of the Commons," *Science* 162 (1968): 1243–1248, and by William Ophuls, *Ecology and the Politics of Scarcity: Prologue to a Political Theory of the Steady State* (San Francisco: W. H. Freeman and Co., 1977) . The concept of overshoot was most fully developed in William Catton, *Overshoot: The Ecological Basis of Revolutionary Change* (Urbana: University of Illinois Press, 1980).

11. Matthew Connelly, *Fatal Misconception: The Struggle to Control World Population* (Cambridge, Mass.: Harvard University Press, 2008).

12. See Heidi Beirich (edited by Mark Potok), *Greenwashing: Nativists, Environmentalism, and the Hypocrisy of Hate* (Montgomery, Ala.: Southern Poverty Law Center, July 2010).

13. Betsy Hartmann, "Conserving Racism: The Greening of Hate at Home and Abroad," *Znet* (December 11, 2003).

14. Rationalizing the principles behind the Sierra Club takeover attempt by an anti-immigrant faction in 2004, Bill McKibben mused, "If you're worried about shredding the global environment, the prospect of twice as many world-champion super-consumer Americans has got to worry you." "Does It Make Sense for Environmentalists to Want to Limit Immigration?" *Grist: A Beacon in the Smog* (March 1, 2004). Accessible online at <http://www.grist.org/article/mckibben-immigration>.

15. The legislative record began in 1996, when Russell Pearce, then director of the state motor vehicle division, drafted a bill requiring proof of citizenship of applicants for a driving license. Bilingual education was banned in 2000, and Proposition 200, passed in 2004, denied public benefits to the undocumented. In 2006 voters endorsed ballot measures that required out-of-state college tuition from Arizona residents with no proof of citizenship, denied bail to undocumented charged with a crime, and adopted English as the state's official language.

16. Tanton's racialized apocalypse is well reflected in Jean Raspail's *The Camp of the Saints*, a cult novel among nativists, which depicts how starving Third World refugees invade Europe at some time in the near future.

17. Federation for American Immigration Reform, "Illegal Immigration Costs Arizonans $2.7 Billion," accessible at <http://www.fairus.org/site/PageNavigator/issues/arizona_immigration_costs>. Nationally, FAIR estimates that the public cost of the undocumented runs to $113 billion annually. Jack Martin and Eric Ruark, "The Fiscal Burden of Illegal Immigration on United States Taxpayers" at <http://www.fairus.org/site/DocServer/USCostStudy_2010.pdf?docID=4921>.

18. A Thunderbird School of International Management study showed a new benefit to the state of $318 million per year. "The Economic Impact of Arizona–Mexico Relationship" (2003). In "The Effect of Immigration on Productivity: Evidence from US States," Giovanni Peri concluded that "an increase in employment in a US state of 1% due to immigrants produced an increase in income per worker of 0.5% in that state." National Bureau of Economic Research, Working Paper No. 15507 (November 2009), accessible at <http://www.nber.org/papers/w15507>. Also, see Terry Greene Sterling's demolition of FAIR's estimates in "FAIR-y Tales," *Village Voice* (December 1, 2010).

19. Heidi Beirich, *Greenwashing*, 8.

20. Janice Kephart and Bryan Griffin, "Hidden Cameras on the Arizona Border: Coyotes, Bears, and Trails" (Center for Immigration Studies, July 2009), accessible online at <http://www.cis.org/Videos/HiddenCameras-IllegalImmigration>.

21. Defenders of Wildlife, "On the Line: The Impacts of Immigration Policy on Wildlife and Habitat in the Arizona Borderlands." Accessible online at <http://www.defenders.org/programs_and_policy/habitat_conservation/federal_lands/border_policy/index.php>. Also, see the Sierra Club video "Wild Versus Wall," accessible at <http://www.sierraclub.org/borderlands>.

22. Border Action Network, Border Solutions, Borderlinks, and *Alianza Indigena Sin Fronteras*/Indigenous Alliance Without Borders are among other immigrant rights groups active in Tucson.

23. Stephen Lemons, "Blood's Thicker Than Water: As Thousands Die in the Arizona Desert as a Result of U.S. Border Policy, an Army of Activists Intervenes," *Phoenix New Times* (February 25, 2010).

24. Cited from the No More Deaths volunteer handbook in Lemons, "Blood Thicker Than Water."

25. The death of Josseline Quinteros, a 14-year-old border-crosser, became a mobilizing cause for many of the samaritans. See Margaret Regan's account in *The Death of Josseline: Immigration Stories from the Arizona–Mexico Borderlands* (Boston: Beacon Press, 2010).

26. Two books by Michael Logan offer insights into the Phoenix/Tucson contrast from an environmental perspective. *Fighting Sprawl and City Hall: Resistance to Urban Growth in the Southwest* (Tucson: University of Arizona Press, 1995); *Desert Cities: The Environmental History of Phoenix and Tucson* (Pittsburgh: University of Pittsburgh Press, 2006).

27. Locally, the most critical coverage of Arpaio can be found in the pages of *Phoenix New Times*, from owner Michael Lacey and columnist Stephen Lemons. Indeed, Lacey and cofounder Jim Larkin were arrested by Sheriff Joe's deputies in 2007 after they published a story revealing details of a grand jury subpoena against the newspaper: "Breathtaking Abuse of the Constitution," *Phoenix New Times* (October 18, 2007). The view from the metropolitan East Coast is neatly captured in William Finnegan, "Sheriff Joe," *The New Yorker* (July 20, 2009). For an early agitprop memoir, see Joe Arpaio and Len Sherman, *America's Toughest Sheriff: How We Can Win the War Against Crime* (Irving, Tex.: Summit Publishing Group, 1996).

28. Kris Kobach, "Attrition Through Enforcement: A Rational Approach to Illegal Immigration," *Tulsa Journal of Comparative & International Law* 15 (2008).

29. Quoted in Alia Beard Rau and Mary Jo Pitzl, "Momentum Built Up over Years Led to New Immigration Law," *Arizona Republic* (May 9, 2010).

30. Tom Rex et al., "Greater Phoenix: Demographic and Socioeconomic Characteristics," in *Greater Phoenix Forward: Sustaining and Enhancing the Human-Services Infrastructure* (Tempe, Ariz.: Morrison Institute, 2008), 11–12.

31. Greg Palast, "Behind the Arizona Immigration Law: GOP Game to Swipe the November Election," *Truthout* (April 26, 2010), accessible online at <http://www.truthout.org/behind-the-arizona-immigration-law-gop-game-to-swipe-the-november-election58877>.

32. Among the many examples of Abbey's racism was this comment, in a letter to the *New York Review of Books* (December 17, 1981): "The tendency of mass immigration from Mexico is to degrade and cheapen American life downward to the Hispanic standard. Anyone who has made a recent visit to Mexico, or even to Miami, Florida, knows what I mean."

33. Ian Angus and Simon Butler, "Should Climate Activists Support Limits on Immigration?" *Monthly Review* Zine (January 25, 2010).

34. Oscar Olivera and Tom Lewis, *¡Cochabamba! Water War in Bolivia* (Boston: South End Press, 2004).

35. The Cochabamba summit ended with a call for international recognition of the rights of climate migrants. See "The People's Agreement of Cochabamba," at <http://pwccc.wordpress.com/2010/04/24/peoples-agreement/>. Yet the risk of pursuing this path is that official identification may create yet another class of immigrant to be held in the limbo of refugee camps and detention centers, or lost in the maze of temporary visa categories. Besides, how easy is it to distinguish between border-crossers displaced by neoliberal trade policies, and those set in motion by climate change? As long as the former are treated like invaders and felons, is it likely (or even just) that the latter would earn a special status?

36. The Bali Principles of Climate Justice, adopted by the International Climate Justice Network in August 2002, set the framework for global-scale action on the topic. They were modeled on the 1991 Principles of Environmental Justice, adopted at the First National People of Color Environmental Leadership Summit held in Washington, D.C., in October 1991.

37. The Perryman Group, *An Essential Resource: An Analysis of the Economic Impact of Undocumented Workers on Business Activity in the US with Estimated Effects by State and by Industry* (April 2008), at <http://americansforimmigrationreform. com/files/Impact_of_the_Undocumented_Workforce.pdf>.

38. Valeria Fernández, "Pregnant Latina Says She Was Forced to Give Birth in Shackles After One of Arpaio's Deputies Racially Profiled Her," *Phoenix New Times* (October 22, 2009).

39. The lives of Central Arizona's undocumented immigrants are adroitly documented in reporter Terry Greene Sterling's book, *Illegal: Life and Death in Arizona's Immigration War Zone* (Guilford, Conn.: Lyons Press, 2010). For a harrowing account of the narco wars in the U.S.–Mexican borderlands, see Ed Vulliamy, *Amexica: War Along the Borderline* (New York: Farrar, Straus & Giroux, 2010).

CHAPTER 7

1. Carole Gallagher, *American Ground Zero: The Secret Nuclear War* (Cambridge, Mass.: MIT Press, 1993); Valerie Kuletz, *The Tainted Desert: Environmental and Social Ruin in the American West* (New York: Routledge, 1998); Richard Misrach and Myriam Weisang Misrach, *Bravo 20: The Bombing of the American West* (Baltimore: Johns Hopkins Press, 1990); Mike Davis, "Dead West: Ecocide in Marlboro Country," in *Dead Cities: And Other Tales* (New York: New Press, 2002); Rebecca Solnit, *Savage Dreams: A Journey into the Landscape Wars of the American West* (Berkeley: University of California Press, 2000); Ward Churchill and Winona LaDuke, "Native North America: The Political Economy of Radioactive Colonialism," in Annette Jaimes, ed., *The State of Native America: Genocide, Colonization, and Resistance* (Boston: South End Press, 1999).

2. Carl Abbott, *The Metropolitan Frontier: Cities in the Modern American West* (Tucson: University of Arizona Press, 1993), 60.

3. Phoenix was one of the sites for a New Deal program that created thirty-four resettlement communities nationwide geared to part-time subsistence farming. The Phoenix Homesteads, which today enjoy historic district status and which still function as a distinct community, were built on semi-rural tracts east of Camelback in 1936 and 1937. Strongly supported by FDR, they were clearly driven by the Jeffersonian ideal of rural virtue and were designated for those knocked off their feet by the Depression. Robert M. Carriker, *Urban Farming in the West: A New Deal Experiment in Subsistence Homesteads* (Tucson: University of Arizona Press, 2010).

4. Gary Nabhan, "Dismantling Metro Phoenix" (December 3, 2006), accessible at <http://garynabhan.com/i/archives/362>.

5. These estimates are from the Morrison Institute for Public Policy's study *Megapolitan: Arizona's Sun Corridor* (Tempe: Arizona State University , May 2008). The Tucson-based Sonoran Institute produced its own economic report in 2010, *Tucson's New Prosperity: Capitalizing on the Sun Corridor,* accessible online at <http://www.sonoraninstitute.org/index. php?option=com_docman&task=cat_view&gid=133&Itemid=177>.

6. Edward Abbey, "The BLOB Comes to Arizona" (1976), in *The Journey Home: Some Words in Defense of the American West* (New York: Dutton, 1977), 146–157.

7. Morrison Institute for Public Policy, *Megapolitan*, 41.

8. Grady Gammage, Jr., et al., *The Treasure of the Superstitions: Scenarios for the Future of Superstition Vistas* (Tempe, Ariz.: Morrison Institute for Public Policy, 2006), 8.

9. *Superstition Vistas Scenario Report* (East Valley Partnership/Pinal Partnership/ Arizona Land Department, September 2009), 22–23. A more recent project brochure called *Superstition Vistas: Unlocking its Potential—A Vision for 21st Century Opportunities* (July 20, 2010) can be found at <http://www.frego.com/ beta/wp-content/uploads/SV-brochure-final-small.pdf>.

10. Advisory Services Panel, ULI, *Williams Gateway Area, Mesa, Arizona: Strategies for an Urban Gateway* (Washington, D.C.: Urban Land Institute, 2007), 15, 22.

11. Editorial, "A Look at Where We Are Headed in the Next Decade," *Arizona Republic* (December 31, 2009).

12. Carol Heim, "Leapfrogging, Urban Sprawl, and Growth Management: Phoenix, 1950–2000," *American Journal of Economics and Sociology* 60, 1 (2001), 245–283.

13. According to a 2000 Brookings Institution study, the city of Phoenix reported 43 percent of its area as vacant land. Michael Pagano and Ann Bowman, *Vacant Land in Cities: An Urban Resource* (Washington, D.C.: Center on Urban and Metropolitan Policy, 2000). In 1995, the city of Phoenix initiated an infill program, whereby tax credits, incentives, and waivers were offered to those willing to build in central-city areas. Yet the program was aimed exclusively at owner-occupied, single-family homes and included no mixed-use provisions. In addition, the program put no caps on the price of qualifying homes, so many of the recipients of the subsidies turned out to be well-heeled. Amy Silverman, "Outing Infill," *Phoenix New Times* (September 21, 1995).

14. Peterson produced his own published guides, the Simple Sustainability Series, including *My Ordinary Extraordinary Yard* (Phoenix: Urban Farm Press, 2009).

15. Brad Lancaster, *Rainwater Harvesting for Drylands: Guiding Principles to Welcome Rain into Your Life and Landscape*, Vols. 1 and 2 (Tucson: Rainsource Press, 2006, 2007).

16. By contrast, the Salt River Pima-Maricopa Indian Community, which lies to the east of Scottsdale, has leased much of its western border to developers and non-Indian farmers.

17. David DeJong argues that the Pima were well on their way to sustaining this central niche when the water was cut off. *Stealing the Gila: The Pima Agricultural Economy and Water Deprivation, 1848–1921* (Tucson: University of Arizona Press, 2009).

18. Ibid., 23. By contrast, the Tohono O'odham authorities have been sharply criticized in recent years, for not offering the same kind of humanitarian services to immigrants who cross the reservation lands south of Tucson. See Stephen Lemons, "Blood's Thicker Than Water," *Phoenix New Times* (February 25, 2010).

19. DeJong, *Stealing the Gila*, 70.

20. George Webb's memoir is a poignant historical source. *A Pima Remembers* (Tucson: University of Arizona Press, 1959).

21. Rodney Lewis and John Hestand, "Federal Reserved Water Rights: Gila River Indian Community Settlement," *Journal of Contemporary Water Research & Education* 133 (May 2006), 34–42.

22. Amadeo Rea, *At the Desert's Green Edge: An Ethnobotany of the Gila River Pima* (Tucson: University of Arizona Press, 1997), 56.

23. Ibid., 65.

24. Carolyn Smith-Morris, *Diabetes Among the Pima: Stories of Survival* (Tucson: University of Arizona Press, 2006); Jovana Brown, "When Our Water Returns: Gila River Indian Community and Diabetes," *Enduring Legacies Native Cases* (Evergreen State College, 2009) at <http://www.evergreen.edu/tribal/cases/collection/health.htm>.

25. Daniel Kraker, "The New Water Czars," *High Country News* (March 15, 2004).

26. Honor the Earth, an organization founded by Winona LaDuke in 1993, has become a prominent force for indigenous sustainability. See the report on "Sustainable Tribal Economies" and also the petition "Energy Justice in Native America: A Policy Paper for Consideration by the Obama Administration and the 111th Congress," accessible at <http://www.honorearth.org/>.

27. The legacy of the Dawes allotment system presented a formidable obstacle. A lot with fractionated ownership now had as many as 500 shareholders. To build a house required 100 percent consent from all the owners. A decision to start farming required 51 percent consent.

28. In early 2010, there was an abrupt reversal of tribal policy on plans for a new freeway that would skirt the northern edge of the community lands. This last section of the 202 loop had long been fought by environmental justice activists in South Phoenix—its scheduled route took it through city blocks that already hosted the worst air quality in the metropolis. As the route snaked around South Mountain (a sacred Indian site), transportation planners had the choice of running the freeway along the northern GRIC boundary and facing down fierce resistance from upscale Ahwatukee homeowners, or requesting a right of way across tribal lands. After years of downplaying the request, tribal leaders abruptly announced their willingness to negotiate the proposal. The turnaround was a rude shock to GRIC's youth and environmental activists who had made a cause out of opposing the freeway. Why would GRIC authorities volunteer to host the last piece of freeway in the metro Phoenix sprawl puzzle? Was it being seen as a relatively cheap piece of good neighborly insurance? Or had the appetite for economic gain won out? In February 2012, a No Build referendum option for the Loop 202 expansion route won a plurality of GRIC membership votes, yet the Tribal Council, under pressure from pro-freeway developers, continued to weigh the options.

CHAPTER 8

1. For an optimistic view that technological innovation will enable cities to become resilient in the fact of climate change, see Matthew Kahn, *Climatopolis: How Our Cities Will Thrive in the Hotter Future* (New York: Basic Books, 2010).

2. Fourth Assessment Report of the Intergovernmental Panel on Climate Change, approved in detail at the IPCC Plenary XXVII (Valencia, Spain, November 12–17, 2007), accessible at <http://www.ipcc.ch/publications_and_data/ar4/syr/en/contents.html>.

3. The 42-member Alliance of Small Island States (most immediately threatened by rising sea levels) adopted the mantra of "1.5 to stay alive" as a negotiating platform for the Copenhagen climate summit.

4. Leo Hickman, "Interview with James Lovelock: 'Fudging Data Is a Sin Against Science,'" *The Guardian* (March 29, 2010), accessible online at <http://www.guardian.co.uk/environment/2010/mar/29/james-lovelock>.

5. Garrett Hardin, "Lifeboat Ethics: The Case Against Helping the Poor," *Psychology Today* (September 1974): 38–43.

6. Robert Reich, "Secession of the Successful," *New York Times Magazine* (January 20, 1991).

7. Edward J. Blakely and Mary Gail Snyder, *Fortress America: Gated Communities in the United States* (Washington, D.C.: Brookings Institution Press, 1999). Setha Low, *Behind the Gates: Life, Security, and the Pursuit of Happiness in Fortress America* (New York: Routledge, 2003).

8. Paul Hawken, Amory Lovins, and Hunter Lovins, *Natural Capitalism: Creating the Next Industrial Revolution* (New York: Little, Brown, 1999); Paul Hawken, *The Ecology of Commerce: A Declaration of Sustainability* (New York: HarperCollins, 1993); Jonathon Porritt, *Capitalism As If the World Matters* (London: Earthscan, 2005).

9. Terry Lee Anderson and Donald R. Leal, *Enviro-Capitalists: Doing Good While Doing Well* (Lanham, Md.: Rowman & Littlefield, 1997); *Free Market Environmentalism* (New York: Palgrave Macmillan, 1991). For a business perspective, see Gregory Unruh, *Earth, Inc.: Using Nature's Rules to Build Sustainable Profits* (Cambridge, Mass.: Harvard Business Press, 2010); and Daniel Esty and Andrew Winston, *Green to Gold: How Smart Companies Use Environmental Strategy to Innovate, Create Value, and Build Competitive Advantage* (New Haven: Yale University Press, 2006).

10. Joel Kovel, *The Enemy of Nature: The End of Capitalism or the End of the World?* (London: Zed Books, 2002); Martin O'Connor, ed., *Is Capitalism Sustainable? Political Economy and the Politics of Ecology* (New York: Guilford Press, 1994); John Bellamy Foster, *The Ecological Revolution: Making Peace with the Planet* (New York: Monthly Review Press, 2009); James Gustave Speth, *The Bridge at the End of the World: Capitalism, the Environment and Crossing from Crisis to Sustainability* (New Haven: Yale University Press, 2008).

11. Rob Kruger and David Gibbs, eds., *The Sustainable Development Paradox: Urban Political Economy in the United States and Europe* (New York: Guilford Press, 2007).

12. Robert Costanza, ed., *Ecological Economics: The Science and Management of Sustainability* (New York: Columbia University Press, 1991); Herman Daly and Joshua Farley, eds., *Ecological Economics: Principles and Applications* (Washington, D.C.: Island Press, 2003); Ann Marie Jansson et al., eds., *Investing in Natural Capital: The Ecological Economics Approach to Sustainability* (Washington, D.C.: Island Press, 1994).

13. Other urbanists have made a case for studying the "metabolism" of a city. The analogy is with the metabolic processes of organisms, and it is in the lineage of Robert Park, Ernest Burgess, and the Chicago School. Herbert Girardet is a prominent exponent of this approach in *Creating Sustainable Cities* (New York: Chelsea Green, 1999).

14. A short list of these ranking indicators includes SustainLane's *U.S. Sustainability Indicators,* San Diego's *Sustainability Competitiveness Index,* New Jersey's *Living with the Future in Mind,* the Resource Renewal Institute's *Green Plan Capacity Index* and its *State of the State* scorecard, and the *Oregon Benchmarks.*

15. Mike Davis, "Who Will Build the Ark?" *New Left Review* 61 (January/February 2010): 41.

16. Paul Bracken (with contributions from Herman Kahn), *Arizona Tomorrow: A Precursor of Post-Industrial America*, 1.

17. Jonathan Fink, "Arizona Can Be Sustainability's Test Bed," in Rick Heffernon, Nancy Welch, and Rob Melnick, eds., *Sustainability for Arizona: The Issue of Our Age* (Phoenix: Morrison Institute for Public Policy, November 2007), 49.

18. Vandana Shiva, *The Violence of Green Revolution: Third World Agriculture, Ecology and Politics* (London: Zed Books, 1991); Amartya Sen, *Poverty and Famines: An Essay on Entitlement and Deprivation* (New York: Oxford University Press, 1981); Kenneth Dahlberg, *Beyond the Green Revolution: The Ecology and Politics of Global Agricultural Development* (New York: Plenum Press, 1979).

19. Anuradha Mittal with Melissa Moore, eds., *Voices from Africa: African Farmers and Environmentalists Speak Out Against a New Green Revolution in Africa* (Oakland, Calif.: The Oakland Institute, 2009); Elenita Daño, *Unmasking the New Green Revolution in Africa: Motives, Players and Dynamics* (Penang, Malaysia, Bonn, Germany, and Richmond, South Africa: Third World Network, Church Development Service, and African Centre for Biosafety, 2007); Noah Zerbe, *Agricultural Biotechnology Reconsidered: Western Narratives and African Alternatives* (Trenton, NJ: Africa World Press, 2005); Raj Patel, *Stuffed and Starved: The Hidden Battle for the World Food System* (New York: Melville House, 2008).

INDEX

Page numbers in **bold** indicate illustrations.

anti-immigrant bill (*continued*)
  Dupnick and, 196
  Gutierrez on, 198–99
  immigration regulation and, 203
  Kobach on, 197
  Latinos and, 112, 197–98
  lawsuits and, 195
  Maricopa County and, 196
  Mother's March against, **210**
  Palest on, 201
  protests following, 209, **210**
  Republicans and, 6
  signing, 190–91
  Stewart on, 200
  surveillance and, 197
anti-immigrant sentiment, 26, 186,
    199–202, 203
anti-takings movement, 213
antiunion laws, 207
Apache Junction, 72, 216
Apollo Alliance, 151, 163, 165
Apollo Group, 184
Apollo Project, 183–84
APS (utility), 159, 174
Arcadia Bioscience, 181
Arendt, Hannah, 198
Arizona
  boycott of, 123, 186, 195, 206
  budget cuts, 137
  climate change in, 5
  conservative movement, 5–6
  federal funding, 63–65
  fiscal shortfall, 62
  foreclosures, 57–58
  fossil-fuel pollutants and, 5
  housing values (2009), 57
  income gap, 261n10
  Latino population, 113–14, 185,
    200–201
  lifestyle ecological costs, 249
  mass assembly builders in, 57
  political leadership in, 62
  population, 58, 185
  pro-nuclear campaign, 168
  PV per capita, 148
  RES and, 157
  retiree communities, 47
  solar power and, 148–49
  tribal authorities, 22
  undocumented population, 58

  unemployment, 57
  voter propositions in, 62
  water in, 38, 41–42, 43, 47
Arizona Biltmore Hotel, 3, 4
Arizona Cardinals, 84
Arizona Chain Reaction, 89
Arizona Corporation Commission
    (ACC), 155, 168
Arizona Department of Environmental
    Quality (ADEQ), 124–25, 130, 134,
    136, 137, 139
Arizona Diamondbacks, 81
Arizona Highways (magazine), 67
Arizona Project, 261n14
Arizona Republic (newspaper), 19, 82,
    191, 222
Arizona Research Institute for Solar
    Energy, 174
Arizona State University. *See* ASU
    (Arizona State University)
Arizona Strategic Planning for Economic
    Development, 58
Arizona Tomorrow (study), 19, 249
Arizona Town Hall, 18
Arizona Vision Weavers, 69
Arpaio, Joe, 26–27, 190, 196–98,
    205–6, 274n27
ARRA (American Reinvestment &
    Recovery Act), 9
arsenic, 118, 124, 164
Arthesia, 92, 93
arthritis, 143
Artisan Village lofts, 87
Artist Storefront Program, 96,
    263n41
Artists Relocation Program, 102
Artlink, 95
arts and artists
  art studios, 85
  artist communities, 81–82, 84–89,
    100–101, 247, 263n42
  Chicano arts, 114, 265n14
  in El Mirage, 102–3
  land art, 34
  as model citizens, 101
  in Phoenix, 92–96, 263n36
  as revitalization tool, 263n41
Arup (firm), 222
Ashcroft, John, 190
asphalt, 118–20

"For Phoenix, as for Hohokams, Rise is Just Like the Fall" (Childs), 22
formaldehyde, 118
fossil-fuels, 5, 53, 167
Four Corners Power Plant, 140
Fox, Ed, 159
FreedomWorks, 6
freeways, 122, 277n28. *See also* highways
Fregonese, John, 218
Friedman, Thomas, 163
Friend, Rebecca, 165–66
fuel enrichment, 153
Fukushima Daiichi power plant, 168
Futures Forum, 82–83, 92

gambling, 31
Gammage, Grady, Jr., 31, 55–57, 217
Garcia, Carlos, 206–7
Garcia, Isabel, 195–96
Garden City movement, 76
Garden of Tomorrow, 224
gardens and gardening, 12, 57, 222–26, 233
gasoline products, 128
gated communities, 242
Gateway Airport, 220
GDP, growth in, 51, 53
Geddes, Patrick, 17
Gentry, Cindy, 226–27
George Washington Carver Museum and Cultural Center, 114
Germany, PV per capita, 148
Gibbs, Lois, 130
Giffords, Gabby, 195
Gila River, 5, 25, 29, 231–33, **240**
Gila River Alliance for a Clean Environment (GRACE), 143, 145
Gila River Environment for Youth, 145
Gila River Farms, 233, 236
Gila River Indian Reservation (GRIC)
  agricultural production, 233
  boundaries, 229–30
  canals, **235**
  clean farming on, **235**
  freeways and, 277n28
  Gila River Farms and, 233
  hazardous waste and, 145
  locally grown food and, 237
  Lone Butte Industrial Park and, 142

United States v Gila Valley Irrigation District and, 232
  water and, 230–31, 233–35, 239
Gilbert, 72, 229, **230**
Glendale, 102, 271n39
Glennon, Robert, 156
Global Carbon Project, 7
Global Institute for Sustainability (ASU), 10, 19, 175–76, 253n22
global warming, 7, 23–24, 60, 167, 190, 241. *See also* climate change
Global Warming Solutions Act (2006), 68
GMA (Groundwater Management Act), 43
Gober, Patricia, 39–40, 45
Goddard, Terry, 81–83, 92
Gold Canyon, 218
gold prospectors, 31
Golden Gate barrio, 122
Goldman Sachs, 156
Goldwater, Barry, 3, 5, 33, 42, 62–63, 66
Goldwater Institute, 65, 168
golf balls, decomposition of, 14
Good Bubble, 4, 150–54
Good Jobs First, 165
Goodall, Jane, 190
Goodell, Jeff, 268n6
Goodyear, 72
Gordon, Phil, 9–10, 68, 77–78, 104, 245
GPEC (Greater Phoenix Economic Council), 161, 165
GRACE (Gila River Alliance for a Clean Environment), 143, 145
Graham, John, 59
Gramsci, Antonio, 241
Gray, Chuck, 61
graywater, 223
GRD (Groundwater Replenishment District), 44
great houses, 25
Great Recession, 9, **54**, 55
Great Sonoran, 69
Greater Phoenix Economic Council (GPEC), 161, 165
green building, 69–70
Green Building Program, 69
green capitalism, 243
green cities, 8–9

North American Free Trade Agreement (NAFTA), 186–87
North Indian Bend Wash aquifer, 133
North Phoenix, 67
Norton, Gale, 39
nuclear energy, 153–54, 167, 168, 169
nuclear weapons testing, 146

Obama, Barack, 64, 151, 153, 162, 168, 183–84
Official English legislation, 191
oil drilling, 170
Optimum Population Trust, 190
Osborne, Amanda, 170
Osuna, Ruth, 114
outsourcing, 163
Overpeck, Jonathan, 5
overpopulation, 188
Owens Valley Aqueduct, 31
ozone pollution, 5, 251n2

Palast, Greg, 201
Palin, Sarah, 6
Palo Verde (nuclear plant), 45
Paradise Valley, 112, 133
Pasqualetti, Mike, 172, 173
The Pavilions (mall), 267n41
PCA (Phoenix Community Alliance), 83, 87, 91, 96
Peace and Dignity spiritual journeys, 208
Pearce, Russell, 190–91, 203, 205, 273n15
Pee Posh tribe, 142, 231
Peirce, Neal, 19, 82, 261n17
People's Republic of China (PRC), 66, 132, 161–66, 270n26
People's World Conference on Climate Change and the Rights of Mother Earth, 203–4, 274n35
Peri, Giovanni, 273n18
Perkins, Tammy, 105
pesticides, 143, 146
Peterson, Greg, 223–24
Phoenix
    air quality, 5
    arts and artists in, 92–96, 263n36
    biomedical campus, 99, 174
    branding, 89–93

as carbon-neutral city, 9–10
civil rights in, 127
density of, 11, 71–72
downtown (see downtown Phoenix)
dust pollution, 5, 251n2
economy, 29
federal funding, 63, 64–65, 81
foreign-born residents, 186
government of, 10
government regulation and, 63
Great Recession and, 9
green city aspirations of, 9–10
Green City program, 104–6
green gap, 79
green homes in, 259n29
greenhouse gas emissions, 249
growth of, 29, 54–55, 71, 210–11, 249
homeless in, 110, 262n19
imports, 98–99, 244
income disparity in, 79
infill program in, 276n13
jobs in, 107
labor in, 63
land development in, 33
Latino population, 113–14, 185
local procurement policy, 99
major firms in, 63
map of Greater, **2**
median income, 108
noncooperation in, 46–50
origin myth, 185
original names, 30
ozone pollution, 5, 251n2
parks and preserves, 259n26
population, 13, 22, 55, 71, 121, 185
public transportation in, 11
school desegregation, 123
solar sources, 5
suburban housing, 56–57
sunshine in, 148
supersuburbs of, 72
temperature issues, 10, 122, 265n9
urban village model, 83
vacant land in, 226, 276n13
warehouse district, 84, 99
water and, 12, 39, 42, 256n34
zoning ordinances (1960s), 97–98
See also East Phoenix; North Phoenix; South Phoenix

Smith, John Y. T., 28
Smythe, William Ellsworth, 32
Snaketown, 25
Snell, Frank, 63
soil pollution, 143
Solana, 156
Solar Day, 271n41
Solar Lobby, 158
Solar One, 271n39
solar power
  Arizona and, 148–49
  ASU and, 176
  China and, 161–66, 270n26
  Pasqualetti on, 172, 173
  rooftop, 172–73
  solar boom and, 154–60
  solar cells, 161
  solar coops, 160
  solar farms, 157, 160
  solar panels, 147, 161–63
  solar subsidies and, 154
  sources, 5
  tax credits, 161
  University of Arizona in Tucson
    and, 174
SolarCAT, 181, **183**
Solnit, Rebecca, 13–14, 24
sorghum, 34, **35**, 181
South Mountain, 277n28
South Phoenix
  asphalt plants and, 118–19
  fires, 124
  groundwater contamination in, 132
  hazardous waste and, 5, 122, 125–26
  living conditions, 121–28
  mixed land use in, 116
  pollution prevention in, 246
  toxic emissions in, 127–28
  vacant land in, 224
  water supply in, 45
  See also CRSP (Concerned Residents of
    South Phoenix)
South Phoenix Multi-Media Toxics
  Reduction Project, 127
Southern Poverty Law Center, 189
Southwest Network for Environmental
  and Economic Justice, 137
Southwest Solar Technologies
  (SST), 181–82
Sperling, John, 180–81, 183, 184

sports stadiums, 76, 85, 94
Sprague, Tim, 109
sprawl, 11, 57, 71, 76, 106, 220. *See also*
  suburbs
SRP. *See* Salt River Project (SRP)
SST (Southwest Solar
  Technologies), 181–82
stadiums, sports, 76, 85, 94
Stardust Center, 111–12
Stark, Louisa, 108
Stechnij, Casey, 227, 229
Stericycle, 142, 143–44
Sterling Energy, 166
Stewart, Jon, 200
Stewart, Warren, Sr., 208
stimulus package, 65, 151, 157, 171
Stinkweeds, 98
storage, energy, 180–83
Strategic Plan (PCA), 91
Strategic Vision (DPP), 91
street names, 113
subdivisions, **37**, 44, 214, 215–16
subsistence farming, 275n3
suburban housing, 56–57
suburbanization, 8
suburbs, 55, 72, 76. *See also* sprawl
sugoi (plant), 143
Sumco, 139
Sumimoto, 139
Summers, Larry, 52–53
Sun Corridor, 149, 215, 216, 229
Sun Valley Parkway, 222
Sunbelt, 4, 47, 64, 214
SunBelt Holdings, 59
Suns, Phoenix, 81
Suntech, 161, 169, 176
Superfund sites, 129, 132–33, 138
Superstition Farms, 227, 229
Superstition Mountains, 216–17
Superstition Vistas (SV), 217–20, 247
Superstitionville, 218
Support Our Law Enforcement and Safe
  Neighborhoods Act (2005), 186
Surprise, 72, 102
sustainability
  corporate embrace of, 243–44
  in desert, 28
  ecological economists on, 244
  local food and, 215
  localist movements and, 98

urban planning, 78
urban renewal projects, 75
urban village model, 83
urbanization, 20, 73

vacant land, 222, 224, 226, 247, 276n13
Vah-Ki Growers Cooperative, 236
"Valley Destiny" (Peirce), 82, 261n17
Valley Forward, 117
Valley National Bank, 63, 64
Valley of the Sun, 4–5, 68, 148, 149
Van Druff, David, 237
Vandermeer, Philip, 66
Verde River, 25
Verrado (community), 222, 247
Via Campesina, La, 202
volatile organic compounds (VOCs), 132
voter propositions, 62

wall, border, 192–94, **198**, 242
Walmart, 179–80
Walton, Rob, 180
Waltz, Jacob, 217
Warehouse District, 84, 99
Warren, Ned, 33
wartime production programs, 63
water
    agriculture and, 38
    allocation, 41–43, 47
    in Arizona, 38, 41–42, 43, 47
    collective provision for, 46
    conservation on demand side, 44–45
    drinking water, 124, 129, 133, 134, 137, 138
    graywater, 223
    GRIC and, 230–31, 233–35, 239
    groundwater (see groundwater)
    housing developments and, 43–44
    Indian allocation, 42–43
    land development and, 31–32
    management and supply privatization, 38, 47
    megawater projects, 235
    Phoenix and, 12, 39, 42, 256n34
    prices, 43
    rainwater, 223
    rationing, 42
    restrictions, 12
    rights, 47, 214
    Scottsdale consumption, 45

    -sharing system, 48
    in South Phoenix, 45
    supply distribution, 45
    See also irrigation agriculture;
        irrigation farming; wells
Water Quality Assurance Revolving Fund
    (WQARF), 129
Water Resources, Department of, 139
Watson, Paul, 190
weatherization, 171–72
Webb, Betty, 80
Weiss, Steve, 96, 97
wells, 43, 129, 133, 134, 138, 267n23
West, Cyd, 92–93
West Valley, 134
West Van Buren plume, 134
Western Climate Initiative, 6
wheat, 34, **35**
Whitaker, Matthew, 127
Wilcox, Mary Rose, 199
wilderness preservation, 214
wildlife refuges, 192
Williams, Danny, 236–37
Williams, Jack, 207
Williams Air Force Base, 220
Williams Gateway project, 220–21
Williamson, Jeff, 13
Wittfogel, Karl, 255n22
Women's Ecopreneur Project, 102
workforce housing, 108
World People's Conference on Climate
    Change, 15
World Scientist Warning to
    Humanity, 52
Worster, Donald, 41, 255n22
WQARF (Water Quality Assurance
    Revolving Fund), 129
Wright, Frank Lloyd, 259n29

xeriscaping, 12, 57

Yaqui reservation, 111
Yingli, 163
Youth United for Community
    Action, 145

Zahn, Tony, 84, 100
zoning, 78, 97–98, 116, 212
zoos, 13
Zurich, 93